Investment Management in Boston

Investment Management in Boston

A HISTORY

David Grayson Allen

University of Massachusetts Press
Amherst and Boston

IN ASSOCIATION WITH
Massachusetts Historical Society
Boston

Copyright © 2015 by University of Massachusetts Press
All rights reserved
Printed in the United States of America

ISBN 978-1-62534-103-7 (paper); 102-0 (hardcover)

Designed by Sally Nichols
Set in Minion Pro
Printed and bound by Sheridan Books, Inc.

Library of Congress Cataloging-in-Publication Data

Allen, David Grayson, 1943–
Investment management in Boston : a history / David Grayson Allen.
    pages cm
"In association with Massachusetts Historical Society, Boston."
Includes bibliographical references and index.
ISBN 978-1-62534-103-7 (pbk. : alk. paper) — ISBN 978-1-62534-102-0 (hardcover :
alk. paper) 1. Finance—Massachusetts—Boston—History. 2. Financial services
industry—Massachusetts—Boston—History. 3. Investments—Massachusetts—
Boston—History. 4. Investment advisors—Massachusetts—Boston—History. I. Title.
HG184.B67A45 2014
332.609744'61—dc23
                        2014027582

British Library Cataloguing-in-Publication Data
A catalogue record for this book is available from the British Library.

Published with the support of the Massachusetts Historical Society

For Grayson, who led the way.

CONTENTS

Supplemental materials are available online at http://scholarworks.umass.edu/umpress
as cited in the notes.

ACKNOWLEDGMENTS

This book began over a decade ago as a project of the Massachusetts Historical Society when William M. Fowler Jr. was the society's director. Early on, Carl Brauer conducted a number of interviews for the project. Under Fowler's successor, Dennis A. Fiori, the project went into high gear. Conrad Edick Wright, Worthington C. Ford Editor and Director of Research, managed the project and formed a peer review group to read my chapters as they were completed. Although some members of that group have left or died, two of the stalwarts were Michael Yogg, former managing director, Putnam Investments, and Thomas Doerflinger, former executive director, U.S. Equity Strategy at UBS in New York. Fittingly, both had earlier earned Ph.D.s in U.S. history and could evaluate my work from two professional perspectives. Others, such as W. Nicholas Thorndike, also served when specialized expertise was useful for the project. Financial support for the book came from both the Fidelity Foundation and the Putnam Foundation, as well as several anonymous donors.

There are many others to thank, particularly the many active and retired investment managers I came to interview. Not only did they provide me with the information I sought, but they also introduced me to others I talked to later on. Their names appear in the notes. Libraries and other repositories were particularly important as this volume tapped into many seldom used printed and manuscript sources. These included the Massachusetts Historical Society, Boston Athenaeum, Baker Library Historical Collections at Harvard Business School (Laura Linard), MIT Libraries, Harvard Law School Special Collections, Manuscripts and Archives at the Yale University Library, Concord (Massachusetts) Free Public Library, Boston Redevelopment Authority (Gregory W. Perkins), the Fidelity Investments Corporate Archives (Susan Keats and Senior Archivist Elena Demetriades), and the Massachusetts State Library. Among others helpful at certain stages were Nancy Baker, Nicole Leonard, Lionel Spiro, and Mike Curran, who, along with Laura Linard and me, tried to save the historical records of the Boston Stock Exchange from oblivion.

More recently, I have been grateful for the roles that Bruce Wilcox, director of University of Massachusetts Press, and Brian Halley, my editor, have played in moving the manuscript to publication, as well as Margaret A. Hogan for her strong and valuable copyediting skills, and others at the press. Lastly, I wish to thank Julyann for her support and advice, long before, during, and hopefully long after the writing of this book, as well as my son, Grayson, who might well have been on his way to a career as a historian until he decided to go into venture capital and to teach others about the subject, including his father.

Investment Management in Boston

Introduction

The last time someone wrote a book on the financial history of Boston, or one that bore such a title, was in 1916, almost a century ago. At that time, Charles Phillips Huse published his *The Financial History of Boston,* which covered the period from 1822, when Boston became a city, to 1909. It had nothing, however, to do with private investment management, an important but neglected subcategory of financial history, even in Huse's day. Rather, he wrote a history describing the municipal finances of Boston in relation to the major urban improvements the city undertook in the nineteenth and early twentieth centuries. The volume covered important municipal developments, including the winning of the city charter, the establishment of a permanent debt and growth of expenditures, the building of the city's waterworks as well as land and street improvements, the annexation of nearby towns, the development of the park system, the beginnings of Boston's subway system, and the growth of metropolitan districts. Clearly, public projects and their financing were predominant issues during this era of Progressive municipal improvements, and had been for some time. The book provided a fitting background for that group's interest in cities, the coming of the "city beautiful" movement, and the growth and expansion of municipal betterment projects, both then at their height.[1]

By 1916, however, Boston had also become a leading U.S. center for private investment management, even though that aspect of the city's financial history might not have been obvious to Huse or many of his contemporaries. For almost three centuries, individuals, institutions, and businesses in New England, and especially the area around Boston, had managed a growing accumulation of financial assets. This practice first began for local and regional clients, but by the nineteenth and twentieth centuries, had spread across the nation and is now part of an increasingly expanding world economy. In the process, and particularly in the last five or six decades, Boston has become by many measures one of the most important global investment centers.

This book has been written to weave that story together through a rich group of historical resources. They include many seldom-used manuscript collections and printed materials, including older documents from largely untapped sources, new kinds of information and institutional records, and even contemporary interviews to help better understand the revolution that has taken place in Boston's financial service industry since the end of World War II. The first part of this book explores the area's early history of financial management in an agrarian and then industrial context between the seventeenth and nineteen centuries. The story begins with a discussion of the background of fiduciary responsibility for charitable institutions that New Englanders inherited from their medieval and early modern English past, and continues with a description of endowment management at some of the region's colleges, schools, and churches during the colonial and early national periods. None of this heritage was necessarily unique to New Englanders, as other colonists received this tradition as well. In time, however, the region, particularly its center in Boston, began to develop important approaches to investment that would distinguish it from places to the South and West.

English settlers to Massachusetts brought with them in the 1630s varying amounts of wealth, although few were rich. Nevertheless, over the next several generations, New Englanders started accumulating assets—from agrarian, craft, and artisan pursuits—and, importantly, created an investible surplus beyond the basic cost of necessities. Despite these efforts, New England was regarded as the poorest region—compared with the South and Middle Atlantic colonies—on the eve of the American Revolution.[2] But by the late eighteenth and early nineteenth centuries, as the region became wealthier through overseas trade, domestic manufacturing, and investments in other parts of the country, respected men in Boston and surrounding communities came to provide fiduciary services for wealthy families, often because family heads were away, sometimes half way around the world, or because their services included taking care of family wealth for later generations.

By the 1830s, these men, often known as "Boston trustees," were given unique and broad discretionary judgment over how they invested assets under their charge by the Massachusetts Supreme Judicial Court in its formulation of the "prudent man rule." That rule, and the broad growth of trusts and trust law in Massachusetts, set the commonwealth apart from other states and served as the basis for a series of unique developments in how assets were managed in Boston and environs over the next two centuries. These included a variety of new services and products, such as investment counsel, family offices, and the mutual fund. Other aspects of Boston's financial and investment history—its unique stock exchange, the growth of commercial banking and trust companies, the role of the Massachusetts business trust, and the development of "alternative investments" in venture capital, private equity, and hedge fund businesses—are all covered in this volume. While Boston cannot claim to be the most significant player in the United States in all of these modern asset classes, it consistently ranks high, making it, in combination with the city's relatively small size, the most important overall center of asset management in the United States today.

And so while Boston was on its way to distinguishing itself as an investment center by the turn of the twentieth century, it still had a ways to go to become a driving force in the city's and region's economy. Despite early positive signs, there was nothing inevitable about Boston's future role as an asset manager. From an early twentieth-century perspective, for instance, asset management could become more important only if the role and position of other occupations declined. As the century progressed, Boston was forced to change its economic base considerably, and in doing so, provided a more favorable environment for the financial services industry. Earlier, the city had been a center of manufacturing for many small industries before and after the revolution. Large-scale manufacturing of woolen and cotton cloth, shoes, and other goods followed throughout the nineteenth and into the twentieth centuries. The city continued to be a manufacturing and transportation center well into the 1920s and 1930s, until the local economy broke down and a new one developed slowly in the decades following World War II.

Compared with the present and to paraphrase Leslie Poles Hartley, the Boston of the 1930s was like "a foreign country" in which "they do things differently there." At that time, Boston had become an important city for publishing, even more so than when it was better-known as a literary center a century earlier. It had the country's largest dry dock and the world's largest fish-freezing and storage plant facility. The paper, wool, textbook, and cotton manufacturing industries were centered there, while its port had the second largest volume of ocean-borne traffic in the United States. The city's leather district and surrounding area handled much of the country's hides used for leather and the manufacture of shoes. Boston was the principal market for wool in the entire Western Hemisphere, and one-third of all rubber shoes in the country were manufactured there. The city was also the entrepôt for various raw products including jute, burlap, goatskins, fleeces, bales of cotton, fruit, sugar, and coffee, all passing through on their way to other destinations.

Boston was a chemical and pharmaceutical center, with companies producing sulfuric, nitric, hydrochloric, and acetic acids, and alum, ammonia, salts, and other chemicals that were made for use in the production of paper, textiles, and leather products. It produced shoe polishes for distribution around the world. Other chemicals were used in making steam hoses, bowling balls, and rubber soles. The technique of quick freezing of food was invented in Boston at that time, while the city also manufactured cod liver oil and disinfectants, and had one of the world's largest manufacturing facilities for soap production.[3]

Less and less of this world of Boston enterprise survived World War II, and the city's broad economic diversity was also on its way to decline. According to the Boston Redevelopment Authority, by 1950 only 20 percent of the city's gross product of $5.7 billion was due to manufacturing; this sank to 12 percent by 1970 even though the city's gross product had risen to $9.4 billion. By 1960 "many people believed Boston was a hopeless failure, a hopeless business back-water." Even Mayor John F. Collins believed that in the late 1950s, "people had given up on Boston." At the same time, financial services in Boston rose from 22 to 33 percent of the gross product, and 60,000 new white-collar jobs were created in Boston from 1960 to the mid-1970s, with a good number of them in financial services. To some degree, investment management and financial services generally were becoming increasingly prominent as more traditional forms of employment, like manufacturing, were declining. "Dirty Old Boston" was on its way to becoming a gentrified city.[4]

Even before the 1970s, when Boston's financial district was starting to go through significant reconstitution and growth, the Hub was beginning to be touted as a financial capital.[5] In 1950, for instance, a *Boston Globe* article noted that the Boston Advertising Club "found to be true what every industrialist in the country already knows: One end of the financial axis of the United States is in Boston; the other in New York. Of $2,000,000,000 invested throughout the country, for example, Boston has furnished more than half the money. The rest has been furnished by New York and the rest of the country combined. Boston supplies the financial power, New York and Boston alternately determine direction." The article goes on to state that "Boston is actually the country's financial capital," citing its centuries-old reputation for conservative investing and its role as the traditional supplier of "most of the venture capital for the country," as well as the work done by Boston trustees.[6]

Boston was also frequently featured in articles about investing and investment. One 1959 *Business Week* article summed it all up when it noted

> The management of large sums of money—their own and that of others—is the chief characteristic of Boston's financial community. Its banks and trust companies handle about $4-billion in their port-folios. Mutual funds got their start in Boston, and Boston's mutual

funds have a market value of more than $4.6-billion. Private trustees and investment counselors handle well over $5-billion. The portfolios of Boston's cultural and educational institutions—including Harvard—amount to more than $1-billion. Taken together, Boston's money managers are responsible for some $15-billion in investments.

New York's financial community handles a much bigger amount—but Wall Street, money market to the nation and the world, is as much a banker and broker as it is an investor. Boston is pre-eminently an investment center, and its State Street community claims more experienced investment men per capita than any other city in the country. Moreover, Boston is confident that in the exacting job of investing funds for either income or appreciation, it bows to no one.[7]

As those words were being written, Boston was becoming a new and revitalized city. To a large extent, the growth of the city's asset management industry continued to parallel this transition into the twenty-first century. Under Boston mayors John B. Hynes and John F. Collins in the 1950s and 1960s, the Back Bay rail yard was transformed into the Prudential Center with shops and apartments, while Boston's West End was razed and a new city government center was created. Hynes's and Collins's successor, Mayor Kevin White, presided over the renewal of Faneuil Hall and the Quincy Market complex, further urban renewal in the area between Copley Plaza and the South End, reclamation of the Charlestown Navy Yard, and improvements along Boston's waterfront from the North End to Rowes Wharf. By the 1970s, when the financial community was beginning a period of rapid growth, Boston was emerging from a period as a stagnant pocket of American industry and declining economic fortunes, which had compelled many Bostonians to leave the city for the suburbs and the jobs they found there. The city was gradually being transformed into the "New Boston."[8]

By 1980, Boston had turned the corner with a lower unemployment rate and personal income that was rising faster than the nation as a whole.[9] And what emerged by the twenty-first century was a prominent financial services industry, with many new and different kinds of assets to manage, and new or expanded industries, such as Boston's and the region's large stake in education, high technology, and science and healthcare. Boston's investment community played an important role in that transformation and, in turn, that transformation ineluctably changed Boston's importance in the global investment world. As this book documents, Boston is usually ranked first, second, or third in nearly every modern category of investment products and services, which, when combined, makes it the most important investment center in the United States.

While this book looks at investment from both a Boston and national perspective, one of its most important revelations from either is the profound impact of the decade of the 1970s on the investment and, more broadly, financial industry. Although most historians focus on the 1920s and especially the 1930s as a period of fundamental change in the investment community, more profound change occurred decades later. Beginning with steep inflation at the end of the 1960s, a decline in the stock market, the erosion of the mutual fund industry, the end of fixed brokerage commissions in 1975, the galloping rise of prices, the introduction of Employee Retirement Income Security Act (ERISA), and other important events and developments, the U.S. investment community was changed forever, and this development simultaneously enhanced Boston's role in it.

I

FROM SETTLEMENT TO INDUSTRIALIZATION

CHAPTER 1

Investment Management in Early New England

Boston's position as a center of asset management started early and affected a broad range of institutions and organizations. In 1638, within a couple of years of the school's founding, the "Colledge at Cambridge" received its first major gift, one that would remain its most prominent donation for half a century. That gift, given to support the new college's endowment, consisted of £779 17s 2d in cash and a personal library, and it came as a bequest from Rev. John Harvard, for whom the college was soon named. Like many of the colleges at Oxford and Cambridge in England stretching back into the medieval period, Harvard was one of a long list of educational institutions named after its most important early patron.

While the term has evolved over time, an *endowment* is a fund set up by a benefactor or benefactors to help maintain an institution, charity, or school. These funds are established for more permanent, long-term uses such as providing the income to pay for a minister's salary, finance the construction of a building, or support student scholarships or professorships. Endowments are, in effect, capital gifts, not just casual doles for immediate use. And in order to achieve long-range objectives, that money or other sources of wealth at the time had to be "lett out" or invested by the institution's trustees or fiduciaries to make more wealth in the form of income so that the institution can finance its long-term goals. One of the central questions concerning early New England endowments was whether monies coming from tuition or other regular sources could cover current operating expenses or was the institution compelled to use the interest and principal from the endowment to pay for them. The size of the institution and its field of donors, how it managed current expenses, and the state and stage of the economy were all factors in determining whether an institution's endowment would flourish or wither.

From a seventeenth-century perspective, the concept of charitable bequests was a relatively new notion following the decline of weak medieval institutions. As W. K. Jordan has noted, "The mediaeval system of alms, administered principally by the monastic foundations, was at once casual and ineffective in its incidence, never seeking to do more than relieve conspicuous and abject suffering." Decades before Henry VIII dissolved the monasteries in England, benefactions to monastic foundations had already declined precipitously, and a new secular orientation toward charity began to take hold. Poverty was dealt with by late Elizabethan and Jacobean legislation that gave responsibility for the poor to local parishes and created "massive endowments" from private sources "designed to eradicate its causes by a great variety of undertakings, among which the extension of educational opportunities was not the least." Indeed, "the whole realm stirred as men began to discover that they could create institutions of social change and reformation with their own wealth and charity." This philanthropic revolution ended during the first half of the seventeenth century—just after the "Great Migration" to New England had taken place—and was connected to the more dramatic shifts taking place in English religion and politics.[1]

In this new age, the benefactors or donors to charities, a rising mercantile aristocracy in London and other urban areas and the new gentry of the Tudor and Stuart countryside, took on much of the social responsibility. The secularization of charity was institutionalized in 1601 when Parliament passed the first English charity act, whose preamble listed what were regarded as charitable purposes. They included "the relief of aged, impotent, and poor people; the maintenance of sick and maimed soldiers and mariners; schools of learning; free schools and scholars in universities; the repair of bridges, ports, havens, causeways, churches, sea banks, and highways; the education and preferment of orphans; the relief, stock, or maintenance of houses of correction; marriages of poor maids; support, aid, and help of young tradesmen, handicraftsmen and persons decayed; the relief or redemption or prisoners or captives; and the aid or ease of any poor inhabitants covering payments of fifteens, setting out of soldiers, and other taxes." Any institution that claimed to be a charity had to have a purpose that fell within the spirit and intent of the preamble, had to exist for the benefit of the public, and had to be exclusively charitable.[2]

Based on this list of purposes, Jordan found through probate research that donors contributed to charities under five major headings and twenty-four subheadings. These included the poor (household relief or outright relief, general charity, the aged); social rehabilitation (relief of prisoners, loan funds, workhouses and stocks for the poor, apprenticeship schemes, hospitals and care of the sick, marriage subsidies); municipal betterments (general municipal uses, companies for the public benefit, public parks and recreation, roads and bridges); education (colleges and universities, schools, scholarships and fellowships, libraries); and religion (church general, prayers, church repairs, maintenance of the clergy, lectureships, church building). While only a few of these purposes were duplicated in colonial Massachusetts, the tradition of endowing charitable uses for education and, to a lesser extent, religion found a congenial home in the Bay Colony and, as settlement extended, throughout early New England.[3]

The law of charitable trusts or endowments grew in tandem with the growth in charitable uses and, in its early stages, without much legal definition. A product of equity and its courts, trusts provided a mechanism for the donor to distribute private property to beneficiaries but without the necessity of having to secure charters of incorporation from the Crown or Parliament.[4] This unique combination of features would also be significant in nineteenth-century Massachusetts with the birth and development of what became known as the Massachusetts business trust, even though the Commonwealth had no courts of equity, also known as courts of chancery. In England, where "the law courts recognized . . . they would not enforce uses, . . . Chancery came rapidly to undertake responsibility not only for the enforcement of duties upon the legal owner but for the protection of the beneficiary in his interests in the trusteed property." Chancery operated on a broad and a narrower scale. Through chancery, large estates held together by the strict rules of law and feudal tenure became devisable. Not only were charitable trusts used in the process of creative destruction of a dying feudal system, they also became the instruments of social betterment in a more secularized society. The number and size of charitable trusts or endowments throughout England during this period grew at a prodigious rate.[5]

Selective Migration of the Charitable Trust to New England

Early New England was a far simpler society, so few of the charitable uses found in contemporary England came over with the Puritan settlers. Furthermore, the process of asset management was much more informal, at least for much of the colonial period, and in many instances we do not know exactly who managed these resources. Sometimes they are identified but often not, with only the record books surviving. In the case of churches, they probably were managed by lay officers and local merchants, and in the case of other institutions, there were usually treasurers and others who handled the financial concerns of the organization and who likely performed this function.

Early on, most colonial assets were in land and cash, but by the postrevolutionary world, they started coming from a variety of other sources, which required
more distinctive managerial identity, skill, and expertise.

Another important problem for study of the colonial period is distinguishing assets collected for current needs from those gathered for long-term purposes. For instance, there is some evidence that early New England churches
received gifts from parishioners, but it is not clear whether these were meant
for the current use of the needy or something more permanent. In an examination of early Middlesex County probate records, David D. Hall found evidence
of significant contributions of money and livestock to Thomas Shepard and
his congregation in Cambridge, given in part to the church's elders for the
poor and, in the case of Shepard, for "the supply of the wants of the Church of
Christ." Whether the gifts and bequests for this latter use ever amounted to a
capital gift or endowment is not certain. Town land used permanently as an
endowment to help pay a minister's salary lasted perhaps as long as a single
generation before it became an item of negotiation with ministerial candidates, who wanted ownership of the land, not just the income provided from
its rental. This "contractualism" during the second generation of New England
ministers led to formal, written relationships in which the successful candidate
often received land, a house lot, a house, and a fixed salary, though frequently
the land and house would revert back to the town should the minister leave.
Despite this latter feature in many town arrangements—ultimate town control
over these property assets—they were not managed like an endowment since
they were occupied or used by successive ministers, and, consequently, no
income was collected from them.[6]

Church Endowments

Wealthy Puritans in both Old and New England shunned buying
stained-glass windows or other forms of decoration, or of erecting memorials
in their churches. In their place, churchgoers chose buildings with simpler
interior designs, although they frequently commissioned silversmiths to create
church silver. Much of this was done not to endow a church with a useful and
valuable asset but rather to enhance the reputation of the donors. Only in more
recent times, when churches have sold their silver at auction to provide funds
for ongoing programs and building restorations, has church silver come to
serve as a form of endowment.[7]

While rural New England churches have left little evidence of permanent
charitable uses and even less of their management, the same was not true for

wealthier congregations in such principal towns as Boston. And unlike other money that might have been spent after current overhead expenses were met, these funds were set up to provide for specific uses. In 1763, for instance, the heirs of the Thomas Greene family established what soon became known as the Greene Foundation to support an assistant minister at Trinity Church. The heirs provided a fund of £500 from Greene's estate, which was matched with another £500 sum collected from "funeral Subscribers." The fund's objective was to raise £50 in interest for his salary, by letting out the money—in sums of £100, £200, or even £600—to "Gentlemen" who paid interest "on their several Bonds or Obligations."[8]

Other Boston churches, including those with Puritan origins, set up relatively involved financial systems for managing their charitable activities. The Old South Society, founded in 1669 and known today as the Old South Meeting House, created a number of funds for various purposes. Besides setting them up to pay for the sacraments, the poor, ministers, and widows, and creating numerous ways to generate money for these funds through capital subscriptions, pew seat fees, and collections for feasts and thanksgivings, the church set up a "Pious and Charitable Fund" in the late 1730s for "an evangelical treasury" that would pay for Bibles and "books of piety." While none of these funds were commingled until about 1800, they all had a common investment policy: "The principal moneys shall be either constantly 'let out' to interest, or laid out in some real estate bringing in some income, or building on or improving the real estate which shall belong to said church." Like other institutions at the time, neither borrowers nor sureties could be members of the congregation.

By the last half of the eighteenth century, if not earlier, church funds were invested in a variety of securities and various mediums of exchange (currency and paper money), depending on the economic climate. For many years, the funds were invested in province, that is, Massachusetts, notes. When that currency declined in value, however, the church moved to buy more valuable Spanish dollars "at a great discount" (i.e., losing in the transaction) and then moved on, in time, to old tenor (inflated) province notes, then lawful money (based on the value of silver), and then again province notes. During the revolution, the money was placed in bonds and "mortgages of good real estate," both of which required some time before they provided interest. After nationhood, the church moved to United States and Massachusetts "State stocks," that is, state bonds, followed by profitable 9 percent investments in stock of the Massachusetts Bank.[9] As a result, the church "stock" or poor fund rose more than tenfold from £513 in 1761 to $16,000 by 1800.[10]

Other Boston church records detail rather complex, if not somewhat chaotic, accounts of income and expenses for their charitable activities. The Second

Church (also known as the New Brick Church), for instance, set up several funded accounts, again called "stock," for the poor, the sacraments, the ministry, and so forth. By 1733, it became apparent that the money was not being managed well, and the money for the poor, "arising from several Donations," was placed in "a distinct account," and that the income of this money, whether "invested in the Church's House in *Ship-street,*" used to improve the church, or set "out at Interest, be henceforth wholly applied to the reliefe of the Poor, and to no other use whatsoever." As of 1773, the church had again apparently returned to the previous, haphazard practice of money management, as the "Communion Stock" was also being used for widows of the church and to support the minister's salary, as well as to repair a sacramental cup.[11]

School Endowments

Perhaps the only permanent endowments created in colonial New England whose assets could be managed to create income for the institution were at some schools and the region's few colleges. Roxbury Latin School, founded in 1645 as the oldest private school in the country, was essentially set up to educate the sons of donors to the school.[12] Indeed, it was a "free school" only in the sense that there were no tuition fees. The sixty-four original donors, who signed the school's Agreement of 1645, pledged that they and their heirs would make annual donations to the school in perpetuity to provide for its maintenance. The donors also had the right to select the school's trustees, who were for some time called *feoffees,* a common name for trustees of various local English institutions.

Over time, the seven feoffees, a self-perpetuating body that managed the school and its finances, sought to bring in a few boys who came from outside of Roxbury or whose fathers paid no donation. Gradually, second-generation descendants of the original donors, who had little direct connection with the school, began to raise concerns about paying in perpetuity for services they did not want or need, especially as more and more boys were able to receive an education without their families' having to make donations. The increasing expense of the school, the uncertainty about the future contributions of donors, and the desire to remain private without support from town taxes eventually led the school to look for more permanent sources of income.[13]

During its earliest years, donations to Roxbury Latin had gone to pay for immediate expenses, not to create a capital account or endowment. To remedy this situation, John Eliot, the Puritan missionary to the Indians and a founder of the school, was able to interest Thomas Bell, a strong supporter of

Eliot's charitable causes, to provide the beginnings of an endowment fund. An early Roxbury inhabitant, Bell had returned to England in the 1650s where he became a successful merchant. In his will of 1671, he made a bequest to the school of some 151 acres he owned in Roxbury. But rather than giving the property to the school, he set up a group of three trustees who were to use the income from the land to benefit the school. The bequest did nothing for the complaining school donors until the feoffees pared their annual contributions in half. As a result, the bequest only marginally improved the financial condition of the school.

The feoffees made other mistakes in the years that followed, one of which was almost catastrophic. In 1687, they persuaded the Bell trustees to lease their lands on a long-term basis (500 years) for £18 per year. There were a few short-term gains from this scheme, but with rising inflation in the early eighteenth century, the relative fee the trust received from renting its land declined, and the school could pay less and less for its schoolmaster. As a result, Roxbury Latin endured a series of new, nonpermanent schoolmasters, which took its toll on the school. By 1715, the feoffees had also found a long-forgotten pledge of the General Court to provide Roxbury with 500 acres of land to help "toward the Maintenance of the ffree Schoole" there. After a few years of effort, the town received the land for the benefit of the school, but by 1770, it had sold that property and used the proceeds to help a section of the town, and thereby deprived the school of another means of support. In the meantime, the feoffees in 1717 had decided to take legal action against the long leases, and after a grueling battle up the court system and considerable legal fees, the Superior Court forbade the leases as being contrary to English law. With the shorter leases and the flexibility to adjust rents, the school was able to hire a more capable schoolmaster with the income of the Bell bequest, which accounted for £45 of the school's annual income of £72 in 1731.[14]

With rising inflation, the need for another schoolhouse, and other expenses, the financial condition of the school remained in jeopardy during the remainder of the colonial period. Indeed, in 1761, Bell's trustees petitioned the General Court for permission to sell a piece of Bell's land, acknowledging by their action that "only by depleting the assets of Bell's bequest was the School surviving." During the 1780s, the school's troubles continued. It sought and received permission from the legislature to sell its "Great Lots" to provide for additional income, and there was a rupture between the school's feoffees and the Bell trustees, which led to the school's temporary closing.

While Roxbury Latin was eventually able to work through this ordeal following the establishment of a new school charter (the Charter of 1789), by means of establishing subscriptions and charging the families of students directly, the broader problem with precollegiate private New England schools was that their endowments were simply too small to generate sufficient income to be used for any purpose other than the school's general (and often immediate) needs. In addition, the school's trustees (feoffees) were usually too inexperienced to operate effectively, with limited ways to make investments. The Roxbury Latin example, replicated elsewhere, suggests that, except for collegiate institutions, colonial New England endowments would remain small until substantial changes in the economy provided new routes for investment and schools received larger bequests more frequently.[15]

Other private schools founded in the colonial or early national period also had small or nonexistent endowments, with the exception of those provided by the benefactors whose money or bequests helped to create the schools. New England's earliest boy's boarding school, Dummer Academy (1763), was created as a bequest in the 1761 will of Lieutenant Governor William Dummer.[16] Dummer's farm, house, and real estate in Newbury were set aside for "this special use and trust, viz. that the whole of Ye rents, issues and profits thereof shall in the first place be appropriated, laid out, and expended in erecting, building and furnishing a Grammar school house . . . and . . . toward the maintenance of the Grammar school Master in said school." In 1762, the will's trustees built the schoolhouse of the "Dumr Charity School" with income derived from rental of Dummer's house and farm. Once chosen by the trustees, the schoolmaster could remain in his position for life "unless because of sickness, age, ineptitude, or profligacy he were to be disqualified by the Board of Overseers of Harvard College." Furthermore, after the completion of the schoolhouse, the "annual rents, issues and profits" of the estate were put into the schoolmaster's hands for the benefit of the school. The first schoolmaster had Dummer's house turned into a boardinghouse for his students, and used the farm to supply the needs of the school.

This arrangement was restructured when the school was incorporated in 1782. Under its new charter, a board of trustees ran the school, selected the schoolmaster, and handled the fiduciary duties. During the 1790s and early 1800s, the trustees improved the school's physical plant by repairing the Dummer house, provided the schoolmaster with his own dwelling, and erected a new barn to replace outworn structures. Nevertheless, the school remained small with fewer than a dozen students, and enrollment seemed to be on the decline.

While the farm brought in an income of about £93 per year, and the students paid tuition, the school needed to find additional support. In 1793, it, like other private schools in Massachusetts, applied to the state for a grant of land similar to the kind of compensation revolutionary soldiers received. In 1797 after the legislation was passed, the school received one-half of a township in Maine. The grant came with stipulations; the school had to establish the location of the land and improve it, and then the school had to have a number of families settle on the land within a specific period of time. Fortunately, the school found a buyer for its Maine lands before it had to make improvements and incur those expenses, selling it for 3 shillings 3 pence an acre. The school's audit of 1806 showed that its holdings, not including its own lands and buildings, were valued at $13,871.33. The Governor Dummer Academy seemed to have had a very different fate from the Roxbury Latin School. While Dummer's financial struggles were not over, the school was established later, founded under a moderately sufficient bequest, never got too large in its early years, and was able to profit from the growing importance and value of land in the early nineteenth century.[17]

Schools established later than Governor Dummer received even more resources early on and got off to stronger starts. The trustees of Phillips Academy Andover, established in 1778, received from the well-to-do Phillips family (especially Samuel and John of Exeter, New Hampshire) some 140 acres on Andover Hill and 200 acres in the town of Jaffrey, New Hampshire. In addition, the two grantors gave the trustees a total of £1,614, with "the money put to interest on good security," and the land to be "let out on proper terms" for the benefit of the "public FREE SCHOOL or ACADEMY in the south parish of the town of Andover." Throughout their lifetimes, the Phillips family gave numerous gifts, including about £7,000 to help "poor children of genius," stock in the Andover Bridge Company also to help charity scholars, and one third of John Phillips's estate after he died.[18] Substantial endowments at private schools had, at last, come of age.

College Endowments

New England colleges often presented more complex pictures when it came to their endowments. During Harvard College's earliest years, from 1636 to 1712, income came from four different sources. The first included gifts and bequests in the form of money or commodities that could be easily converted into cash for immediate use. As noted earlier, the first and most prominent donation came as a bequest from Rev. John Harvard but was soon followed in 1641 by a successful fundraising campaign in England for the colony and college by Hugh Peter and Rev. Thomas Weld, which netted about £875 for the Cambridge school. The century produced a number of English benefactors, especially those with Puritan backgrounds, but by the end of the period, particularly after the colony lost its charter, these endowment sources all but dried up.[19]

Another resource for the college came from annual fundraising from alumni, but unlike most contemporary annual fundraising drives, these gifts were often paid in perpetuity, or the nearest thing to it. For instance, in an elaborate document written in 1650, Boston merchant John Newgate pledged to pay the college £5 per annum "forever," with that amount coming out of revenue from various owners of his farm at Rumney Marsh after his death. Other perpetual annuities came from the income of Boston "Housing and Tanpitts" or a farm in Norfolk, England. Substantially more income was derived from a third source, the lands and buildings given to the college, but not all of it was rent-producing because some was used by the college while other assets remained unimproved or unclaimed. Land donated to the college by benefactors at this time ranged from 100 to 800 acres in several Massachusetts towns, and up to 1,000 acres in what later became Maine. The final category consisted of gifts of books, building materials, and equipment. Over 40 percent of the college's library in the 1720s comprised books given as gifts.[20]

Taking all into account, donations made by individuals to Harvard from 1636 to 1715 amounted to a little over £10,090.[21] Of that sum, money collected amounted to £5,299, a little more than half of the donations. New Englanders contributed £431 as gifts and £2,278 as legacies, whereas English donations were mostly legacies (£1,642) with the remainder (£823) as gifts. Many of these individuals were merchants or from merchant families, but most of it did not come from college graduates. Average yearly income from the assets rose from £18 in the 1648 to 1652 period to £156 from 1693 to 1712, and subsidized about 40 percent of the college's per student cost. Money "lett out" on personal bonds or mortgages, which was usually secured debt, was set at a rate of 8 percent until 1693 when it dropped to 6 percent.[22]

Over the course of this period, the composition of Harvard College's assets changed significantly. In 1669, Harvard's cash and securities—cash; bills, bonds, mortgages; grain and livestock due or on hand; old bills and bonds; and interest and rent due or overdue—accounted for 35 percent of total endowment assets. By 1712, these sources amounted to 59 percent. Capitalized rents from college-owned lands and from the annuities given by individuals had been as high as 42 percent of the endowment in 1669 but declined to just 18 percent in 1712. Harvard's capitalized ferry, which ran between Cambridge and Boston, totaled 63 percent of assets in 1652 but declined precipitously to 23 percent in 1712. The century-long decline of rents, annuities, and Harvard's exclusive ferry revenue, and the rise of cash and securities, all took place as Harvard's endowment increased more than sevenfold over sixty years, from £793 in 1652 to £3,678 in 1682 and £5,265 in 1712.[23]

The Harvard treasurers employed the college's cash in a number of ways.

For instance, money from the Mowlson-Bridges Scholarship Fund (1643), the college's first permanent endowment, was borrowed by the colony government between 1685 and 1713. At 6 percent interest, this created £263 14s for the college on £162 16s 4d of principal. When Treasurer John Richards received money from the estate of English merchant Sir Matthew Holworthy in the late 1670s, he immediately let it out on twenty-one bonds in amounts varying from £10 to £270 at a rate of 8 percent. In contrast with these opportunities, the college received little in rents from land it owned because land was not a scarce commodity at the time. Furthermore, ventures in mining, fishing, shipbuilding, trading, or lumbering were all deemed too risky for the college to take on by itself. As a result, much of its investment activity was as a small money lender, similar to the local charitable endowments in England. Normally, the borrower signed a document binding him for twice the amount of the loan, or else it was constituted as a mortgage deed to his property, should he not repay the loan in a timely manner. Throughout the century, the college treasurer invested and reinvested the college funds, and also made sure that delinquent debtors paid back their loans.[24]

With money let out almost as soon as it came back in, Harvard College fared much better financially at the end of the seventeenth century than it had only a few decades earlier. While eighteenth-century New England had its own unusual financial challenges, including the effect of depreciating paper currency in the middle decades and a consequential write down on investments, Harvard's assets increased steadily. During the years from 1711 to 1805, total donations from individuals rose from $45,535 (for 1636–1710) to $133,384, government support increased from $17,503 to $103,554, and the permanent endowment expanded from $5,377 to $86,096. During this period, Thomas Hollis and his family gave the college £5,850 to endow two professorships and scholarships for twelve students. Between 1712 and 1740, bequests to the college averaged £200 a year, with half going to scholarships and a quarter each to professorships and unrestricted uses. After the fire at Harvard in 1764, the college received £3,475, with £1,496 of it coming from England and £1,204 from Boston.[25]

In 1715, the college's personal estate was nearly £3,800 while its real estate yielded rents of about £280 a year. On the eve of the revolution, when John Hancock became Harvard's treasurer in 1773, he was entrusted with bonds and notes worth almost £15,450. As during the previous century, most of the college's portfolio was in bonds or loans to private individuals. These had amounted to about 45 percent of all endowment assets in 1712, but the figure rose in later years to 59 and then 75 percent of the total. Ferry income dwindled down to one-third of its former position by 1777, and by early in the nineteenth

century, it had become valueless because of the construction of the Charles
River Bridge, in which Harvard also had an interest, between Cambridge and
Boston. Real estate became a more substantial item in the endowment, primarily because it had taken on increased value with population growth. By
1807, stocks appeared among Harvard's holdings for the first time, with bank
issues comprising 71 percent of that asset category. By 1809, that proportion
was substantially reduced to about half of the total, and during the 1810s, the
college acquired shares of the Middlesex Canal and the Charles River Bridge
companies, two important local transportation concerns.

Another important shift in the late 1700s was from private individual
loans to investments in government bonds. This change took place during
the Revolutionary War when the college acquired "Continental loan-office
certificates" and "Massachusetts treasury notes," whose values declined precipitously during the conflict. Following the war, the value of these securities
steadily rose, and in a single year alone, between 1790 and 1791, increased from
£28,000 to £43,000. By 1807, public securities constituted about 80 percent
of Harvard's endowment assets, whereas in 1777, private bonds or loans had
represented some 81 percent of the total.[26] A significant change in investment
policy and practice had taken place when Harvard moved from small loans
to stockholdings and government securities over a quarter of a century, and it
was one that would endure.

Although Harvard's stock holdings dropped from $149,000 to $88,000
between 1810 and 1827, much of that change was related to large outlays spent
for capital purposes, including construction of several buildings. Ironically,
this building splurge came as a result of a Massachusetts law passed in 1814 that
gave the college a $10,000 annual grant derived from a tax on banks. Over the
next decade, the college provided better salaries and other benefits, and began
an ambitious building program, only to realize that the program was far more
costly than the award made by the legislature.[27]

With so few colleges founded in the colonial era, it is important to look at
some other New England academic institutions beyond the Boston area to
understand how endowments were both generated and used. New England's
second oldest college, Yale, was founded in 1701. A consideration of Dartmouth
College, founded at the end of the colonial period in 1769, adds geographical variation to examinations of these institutions into the early nineteen
century.[28]

Compared with Harvard, Yale's early endowment presented a very different
story. The school's earliest major benefactor, Elihu Yale, gave the "Collegiate
School," as it was then known, a large box of books, a portrait of King George
I, and East India goods that were sold on arrival in Boston for a little over

£560. For these gifts, the school decided to name in his honor a new building in New Haven, Connecticut, where the college had moved in 1718, but because of a printing error, the college itself was named Yale.[29] Aside from this gift, Yale had been dependent from its earliest days upon numerous small contributions that tended to pay for immediate expenses rather than help to create a permanent endowment.[30] As a result, Yale's endowment by 1747 had little to show for itself except the college lands, which consisted of a number of small parcels in and around New Haven, including the "College Yard" and lot of the president's house, as well as divisions of land given to others in New Haven, a 628-acre farm in Salisbury, and 300-acre lots given by the General Assembly in 1741 to the college in the towns of Canaan, Norfolk, Goshen, Cornwall, and Kent (all in Litchfield County in the northwestern corner of the state), plus a 95-acre farm in Rhode Island given by Rev. George Berkeley, who became Bishop of Cloyne.[31]

For significant support during the eighteenth century, Yale had no major benefactors like Harvard did and instead relied increasingly on the colony of Connecticut for land grants to support its endowment and major capital expenses such as buildings.[32] These requests to the colony had begun when the college was founded with a £80 grant every year until 1755, and included a pledge of £500 for the construction of a building when the college moved to New Haven; income on the sale of land by the state and an impost on rum in 1716 and 1722 for £480; the Litchfield County lands, approved in 1732; £35 in compensation to the parish in Windham, Connecticut, when its minister Thomas Clap left to become president of Yale in 1740; and Yale's first broad tax exemption in 1745. During the next twenty-five years, Connecticut's General Assembly paid for assorted costs of Yale buildings—repairs of the president's house, the construction of new buildings, and expenses to finish the chapel totaling £1,524. Sources for some of these later funds included proceeds from a captured French frigate and the first state college lottery.[33]

While Yale received by one estimate $145,000 in gifts and grants between 1701 and 1830, the sum was far behind Harvard at the time of the revolution.[34] In 1774, Harvard assets included about £15,000 in bonds, which yielded £900 in interest a year, £100 in income from its Charlestown ferry, £100 in rents from land and other miscellaneous income, plus £450 it received at the time as an annual grant from the Massachusetts legislature. Thus Harvard's annual income from these nontuition sources amounted to about £1,550 "Lawful Money," or about six times what Yale earned.[35]

Ezra Stiles, who kept these comparative figures, became Yale's president in 1777. At that time, the college's annual income consisted of student tuition and fees of about £500 and income from the endowment of £236. Some £160 of the latter came from the rent of college lands, while £76 was interest from £1,230 it loaned to individuals. That year, Yale decided to use this part of the endowment to provide a loan to the fledgling U.S. government, a risky proposition at the time but one that paid off well in the following decade. By 1791, it had made £770 on certificates of the U.S. Loan Office. Still, the college endowment was little changed at about £1,175 in 1791, and the state still provided funding for campus buildings and endowed a new professorship, while some private sources helped to purchase equipment.[36]

The college's finances were chronically weak and continued so into the nineteen century. By the 1820s, Yale had become involved with investing in Eagle Bank, sponsored by the college's treasurer, James Hillhouse, and his friends who included the inventor Eli Whitney. Considered a smart investment move, the college actually pushed for special legislation that would allow it to invest more than $5,000, the statutory limit, in a single bank. It then acquired stock and even borrowed to acquire more. Making loans without sufficient collateral and equal to the capital of the bank, the bubble burst in September 1825, with the college ending up with a debt of $21,000 and the loss of endowment for the Dwight Professorship of Didactic Theology. In the end, the college's endowment income, not including library funds, declined to only $1,800 annually, while its debts amounted to $19,000. The school again turned to the General Assembly, but in that instance, the legislature turned its back on the college and declined to help.[37]

Despite the loss due to the failure of Eagle Bank, the experience ultimately provided Yale with the resolve to find new sources of funding to give its endowment a more permanent footing. The failure lowered college income to a point where it was scarcely sufficient to handle the costs of college maintenance and repairs, while tuition fluctuated and was insufficient to support endowed professorships or even college officers adequately. The college records noted in 1823 that "to raise and sustain a College, therefore, of an elevated character, it is not enough simply to create the establishment; something must also be done in one form or another, to defray a part of the expense of instruction." Although it still took some time to organize, the college printed its first financial statement in 1830, and then in 1831–1832, it instituted what later became known as its Centum Milia Fund, the school's first alumni endowment drive. Near the end of 1832, the goal to raise more than $100,000 had been reached, and within a couple of years, the fund drive had created enough income to erase the college deficit and actually achieve a small surplus. While the great fund drive did not put an end to the college's growing needs for buildings, professorships, and other resources, it helped the school to turn the corner financially, and provided for a more enduring endowment in the institution's future.[38]

Other early college endowments broadly followed similar patterns, although each was tied often to its specific location and when the institution was established. At nearly the opposite end of the colonial period chronologically from Harvard, Dartmouth College was founded in 1769. Reverend Eleazer Wheelock had started "Moor's Charity School" in 1754 in Lebanon, Connecticut, at his own expense, but after a successful fundraising trip to England, monies he received probably went to Dartmouth College as well as the other school, which he relocated to Hanover, New Hampshire. There, the two were considered by many as "different branches of the same institution," even though the property of the school was not merged with the college until the late nineteenth century. Both institutions received their first permanent endowments from the state of Vermont in 1785, when the school was given land in Wheelock, Vermont, from which it derived income from sales and rentals of the land of about $150 a year. It was the college, however, that gained substantially from Vermont's largess, as it held most of the 23,000 acres of the township that was not given to Moor's Charity School or for the support of the town ministry and schools.

Later that decade, the college received other large tracts of land from John Phillips (the benefactor of Phillips Exeter Academy and Phillips Academy Andover), who contributed several hundred acres of land in Warren and Sandwich, New Hampshire, to support a divinity professor from the land's leases and rents, and 285 bushels of wheat to buy a wood lot for the professor. The last major land endowment came in 1807 from New Hampshire, which granted the college a tract of land "amounting to six miles square" in the northern part of the state. Although the lands failed to attract long-term leases and rents, by the twentieth century they were yielding large timber harvests and impressive income.

By the 1820s, endowments that Dartmouth received, with the exception of one large alumni's legacy of lands in Illinois, Wisconsin, and Michigan, arrived in the form of cash or stock. The $10,000 Charity Fund established in 1823, for instance, was subscribed to in cash and "interest-bearing obligations were taken for the larger part of the remainder." The Charity Fund represented a change of the college's objectives, which were then focused on creating professorships and scholarships, erecting buildings, and realizing other specific and tangible goals. Although wealthy men created endowment funds, subscriptions like the Charity Fund often included whole classes or contributors of more modest means. In addition to specific uses and a broader range of benefactors, Dartmouth was receiving new asset sources. For instance, by the 1830s, a legacy was received by the college for scholarships that included bank stock. A decade or two later, Samuel Appleton, the wealthy Boston merchant with childhood ties to New Hampshire, endowed the college largely for a professorship with a combination of money and "legacy stocks," including "manufacturing stocks," worth over $50,000. Another Dartmouth benefactor, who established the college's astronomy observatory in 1852, simply left the money "on deposit in the Atlas Bank" in Boston for Dartmouth to use. By the Civil War, the transition from agrarian to commercial and industrial wealth—from land to cash, stocks, and other securities—was largely complete for endowment gifts received by the college.[39]

The story of endowments at these schools and colleges—except for misfortunes due to poor investing or the stage of the economy when the institution was founded—followed a fairly predictable pattern. By and large, endowments were small in the seventeenth to mid-eighteenth centuries because donors' money likely went to the institution's immediate needs, and much of what was truly an endowment was in land, which fetched little in rents or sales price. During this era, the small amounts of money in endowments were put "out to Interest," but treasurers and other officials had to supervise repayment from these borrowers, who often had little collateral. Change started coming when endowment assets shifted from land to cash or its equivalent, and came in large amounts by individuals who had amassed fortunes in trade and later manufacturing. The Phillipses, the Hollis family, and manufacturers like Samuel Appleton helped these institutions create sizeable and sustainable endowments, which could support large capital projects like buildings yet would grow over time through new investment in government securities, bonds, and stocks, the vehicles of the nineteenth century.

Mutual Benefit and Philanthropic Institutions

Investment management in colonial New England was not restricted to educational or religious institutions; a variety of mutual benefit and philanthropic institutions, many of them supporting various specifically named recipients or working groups, also participated.[40] For instance, funds of the Boston Episcopal Charitable Society, founded in 1724, were set up to "be distributed to the proper objects of charity belonging to the Episcopal Church; and no other persons shall at any time hereafter be considered as intituled to relief from this institution." Members of the society paid their subscriptions at quarterly meetings to create "the principal Stock," which was to "be punctually put to interest." Like many similar institutions of the time, "every borrower of the Society's money shall find two sufficient Surities; and in the case of any money be loaned to any person or persons not of this town of Boston, his or their sureties shall be of the inhabitants of this town; and if the interest of any of the Society's bond be unpaid two months after it shall become due, and upon the treasurers demanding same, sufficient satisfaction be not given, the said Bond or Bond[s?] shall be put in suit."[41]

As an added safeguard, no member of the society could either borrow or act as a surety, unless he was acting in "a public capacity" as a warden, vestryman, or committee of a church or of a church that was to be built. The president and trustees of the society were given power to retain more of the interest to enlarge the fund's principal, and as a result, it grew quickly. In its extant account books, stock and interest of the society increased threefold from £1,900 in 1786 to $24,000 in 1835. By the early nineteenth century, many of the subscriptions were paid in various stocks and bonds, ranging from Massachusetts 3-, 5-, and 8-percent "stock" (i.e., bonds); U.S. 3-, 4-, 6-, or 7-percent stock; 6-percent U.S. Navy "stock"; to shares in the U.S. Bank, Middlesex Canal Company, Boston Bank, Union Bank, or Massachusetts Hospital Life Insurance Company, with interest in the form of dividends coming from these sources. Managers of the society's stock do not seem to have orchestrated the shift to newer forms of assets, but those assets that came in simply reflected the larger changes going on in the economy.[42]

Other groups, like the Charitable Irish Society, founded in 1737, were set up the same way. Intended "for the Releif of Poor, aged, and infirm Persons, and such as have been reduced by sickness, shiprack, and other accidental Misfortunes," members contributed on a regular basis until the collection reached £50. At that point, it could be "put to Interest," and after £12 of interest was collected (nothing was to be taken from the principal), it could be distributed, with "no one to receive more than 40 shillings" until the collected funds and interest increased. The society's officers let out the funds "at Interest to substantial Persons, taking Bond with two Surities for every sum." If borrowers did not repay principal and interest when due, they were given three months before they were sued. In addition, to "keep up a good Harmony in said Society, no Member is to be admitted as a Borrower or Surety."[43]

Another charitable organization, founded a few years later in 1742, was limited to persons who commanded ships or had commanded them in the past. During the monthly meetings, members of the Boston Marine Society placed 6 pence sterling in "the Box" to support the relief of members and their families. Fines of another 6 shillings were imposed on members who failed to attend the meetings or the funerals of brother members. The widows and orphans of members received what the member had paid in and "whatever else the Box could afford," or "the ability of the Box," while old and infirmed members received annual relief payments if they had paid their dues for seven years. Although few of the earliest records exist, by 1754, the society's practices were codified into "laws," including one "that no moneys belonging to this Society shall be let at Interest but upon Bond and Collateral Security of Land under a Good Title, and without any Incumbrances of it at Least the Value of double the Sum Let and Lying in this Province in or near the town of Boston as may be."[44] Like other early Massachusetts charitable institutions, the Boston Marine Society had a consistent source of revenue through its membership, similar provisions on lending money, no set rules (except for eligibility) on what they could give away, and no ambition to make a "profit," although a strong desire and rules to avoid using the organization's principal.[45]

While all of these charities sought to increase the size of both their contributions and interest to support larger relief efforts, a number of benevolent or charity organizations founded after the revolution came to take on more modern or secular characteristics that we associate with the concept of insurance—organizations that sought to limit the kinds of loss or liability they would cover and focus instead on creating a surplus or profit for its subscribers. Shortly after its founding in 1786, for instance, the Massachusetts Congregational Charitable Society set up a fifteen-year annuity program primarily to "support the widows and children of deceased ministers." While the society started out opening a subscription "to those persons who may be disposed to support the benevolent purposes of the institution of this Society," it was quickly transformed into a wider program in which subscribers paid a contribution to create an annuity.

Based on actuarial calculations, male subscribers paid a basic charge of £5.5 each year at the time of admission, which was increased by 10s 6d for each half year of age he was in excess of his wife's age, up to ten years. If the subscriber was more than ten years older than his wife, it would cost him an additional 21 shillings for every half year. Provided that the payments were made, the subscriber's wife received an £8 "Annuity for Life" if her husband lived a year and made two annual payments, £9 a year if he lived for two years and made three annual payments, and £10 if he lived for three years and made four annual payments. The annuity would increase £1 for every year that the annuitant lived beyond the third year. The society was different from other charitable societies of the past. The subscriber gained not only a direct benefit for his beneficiary, but the return was also more precisely calculated and predetermined, and paid each year rather than in a lump sum whose value was determined by size of the organization's funds or assets and what it customarily gave to beneficiaries. Subscribers had to pass something akin to a medical examination, as no "fraudulent Intrusions into the Society of persons who may be dying by concealed Destempers" were allowed, and it needed fifty subscribers in order for the annuity plan to work. The society's annuity plan abruptly ended in 1801 for unexplained reasons, and returned to the familiar charitable model that provided relief to the wife and family of the clergyman regardless of the husband's participation in annual subscriptions.[46]

A more successful example of the transition from charitable to noncharitable uses of mutual societies had taken place only a few years earlier in 1798, when the Massachusetts Mutual Fire Insurance Company was founded. After reaching subscriptions of $2 million, the corporation was authorized to issue insurance policies for "any Mansion House or other Building within the Commonwealth, against damage arising to the same by Fire, originating in any cause except that of design in the insured and to any amount not exceeding four fifths of the value of any Building." There were some other restrictions or limitations, such as the rate of hazard originally agreed upon for the structure, and additional assessments on subscribers should a fire's cost surpass the assets of the company. Policies had a seven-year life. The president and directors vested subscribers' monies within sixty days in either U.S. or Massachusetts bonds, or in bank stock. Interest from these funds would be used to pay for claims and to establish a $10,000 reserve fund. This company, however, provided one distinct difference from other mutual societies, under which "each of the insured shall, at the expiration of his Policy or Policies, have a right to demand and receive from the Corporation his share of the remaining funds, in proportion to the sum or sums by him actually paid."[47]

While financial records for the first several years of the company are virtually nonexistent, by June 2, 1807, the trustees reported that, "in their opinion it is proper, that the dividends for policies which expire on the first day of July next, should be made and declared on the following principles and estimates Vizt. Real Estate 33,000 Dollars: Furniture & Stationary $333.33; Eight pCent Stocks at par: Six pCent Stocks and Deferred-debt at 96pCent: together with the money that may be on hand: from which are to be deducted the several sums in dispute with costs; dividends on Policies voted to be null & void; and the Reserved Capital." Dividend payments probably began a year or two earlier when the oldest of the seven-year policies became null and void.[48]

The shift of mutual benefit and philanthropic institutions from strictly charitable to profit-making organizations was on its way by the first decade of the nineteenth century and culminated, for this period of time, in 1818 with the founding of the Massachusetts Hospital Insurance Company, which started out essentially as an insurance company but was soon transformed into a trust or investment company.[49]

Colonial and postrevolutionary New England had witnessed not only the growth of asset management in various kinds of institutions—schools, colleges, churches, and benevolent and mutual benefit societies—but also a sharp transition in the kinds of assets managed from land and natural resources to stocks and bonds, as well as direct investment in financial institutions and industrial enterprise.[50] A new phase in New England investment management took place with the rise and growth of stocks and bonds for investing, the development of insurance companies and brokerage firms, and, at the same time, the emergence of a new and unique fiduciary, the Boston trustee, which are all the subjects of the chapters that follow.

CHAPTER 2

The Creation of Wealth in Boston's Nineteenth-Century Commercial and Industrial Economy

The changing investment management options for New England institutions from the seventeenth through the early nineteenth centuries—from rents on land to the accumulation of stocks and bonds—was itself part of the transition that the region had experienced by the period of the American Civil War. By the time of that conflict, the New England economy had passed through several major transformations in which investment played an important role. In rural areas, agriculture had gone from a relatively self-sufficient practice to a more specialized, regionalized, and dependent farming culture, while in urban areas, where wealth in the region was being created at a faster pace, many inhabitants became part of an expanding and lucrative world commerce epitomized in the so-called China trade, far surpassing that created by colonial merchants and one in which many local fortunes were made. These ventures not only created surpluses for later investment purposes; they were investments in their own right, as merchants sought to acquire potentially profitable goods while finding ways to minimize their risk.

Following two other events, the passage of the Embargo Act (1808) and the War of 1812, which led to a decline in trade, Boston and nearby towns also became part of another economic transformation, in which the fortunes of a group of local merchants were used to invest in the local textile mills and to profit from the mills' growth. By the 1850s, however, after a rise then fall again in overseas commerce and a decline in the mills, "Boston money" shifted once again to investment opportunities in the American West, particularly in the development of railroads and mining.

The new economic worlds that Bostonians experienced led to the growth and development of many investment institutions, including insurance companies and commercial banks, which are the topic of a subsequent chapter. Many of those institutions were profit-making ones, which created an expanding number of local Boston stockholders in the process.[1] Furthermore, not only did Bostonians invest their capital in existing companies; they also helped to finance the development of new enterprises. As stock and bond opportunities grew from "government stock" (bonds), and insurance and bank stocks shifted to stocks and bonds in mills, railroads, and other enterprises, there was a need to channel these transactions as well as to create a venue to sell and underwrite new issues. The new financial institution that resulted, the stock exchange, also helped to popularize stock and bond investing to a larger number of potential investors.

Boston established its own stock exchange in 1834, only a few years after the effective start of those founded in Philadelphia and New York. Much of the growth in stock and bond trading came from the expertise offered by emerging brokerage firms, which also served as investment banks for the underwriting and distribution of stock issues. These companies, such as Paine Webber and Kidder, Peabody—which would become household words nationwide in the century that followed—not only underwrote Boston mills and western railroads, but by the end of the nineteenth century, were acting as investment bankers for major companies like General Electric and the Bell Telephone Company, both headquartered in Boston.

Perhaps more important than brokerages and investment banks was the fact that much of the stock in these enterprises was owned by Bostonians. The Calumet & Hecla Mining Company, a post–Civil War copper mining enterprise in upper Michigan started and underwritten by Bostonians, soon accounted for half of all U.S. copper production, and its value quickly outstripped the accumulated wealth made in Boston's China trade, textile mills, and western railroads. Its shares, tightly held by about eight hundred mostly Boston stockholders, rose in value from roughly $30 a share in 1868 to $530 by 1898, and during that thirty-year span, paid out over $131,000 in dividends on a relatively modest $3,000 investment. The wealth created by this one stock alone helped to support many Boston families (and the fees of many "Boston trustees") well into the twentieth century.[2]

From an Agrarian to an Industrial Society

Although New England industrialism took place within an urban context, it would not have been possible without the development of a broader regional capital market that included Boston's agrarian hinterlands. During much of the seventeenth century, eastern Massachusetts towns practiced agriculture much like they had in England, including the raising of the same crops and animals as well as engaging in familiar household manufacturing. By the late decades of the seventeenth century and through the middle of the eighteenth, however, farmers adapted to regional markets, producing goods and using land more efficiently to develop interregional and specialized products, a process that would only accelerate in the nineteenth century. Farmers went from a relatively self-sufficient state of agriculture to a more market-oriented one, and by doing so, helped to create the active capital market necessary for industrial expansion in the early nineteenth century.[3]

Exactly when that transition from a barter to a market or "capitalist" economy took place has been the subject of countless articles by historians and an attendant controversy for more than three decades. What these debates show is that the economic cultures of merchants and manufacturers as well as farmers were remarkably similar—both employed precapitalistic and capitalistic practices, though perhaps for different reasons—and that a broader regional capital market (including Boston and nearby agrarian towns) emerged in the early 1780s and developed into the early nineteenth century.[4]

The transformation of the regional capital market involved the movement of farm capital from almost exclusively physical assets, such as implements and livestock, to more liquid assets, such as stock holdings in canal companies and mills in infrastructure and manufacturing sectors, which produced higher returns. By the 1780s, such holdings appear for the first time in inventories of decedents in Middlesex County, Massachusetts, to the north and west of Boston, including shares of stock in bridges, turnpikes, banks, insurance companies, and companies, as well as state and federal government notes. By the 1830s, this transition had become more widespread and uniform, as estates in both urban and rural areas of the county held roughly equal amounts of securities. As economic historian Winifred Rothenberg has noted, if the findings of other historians show that substantial holdings of securities were common in eastern cities by the late 1840s, then "it is clear that they *had begun* to be important in the Massachusetts countryside sixty years earlier." Borrowing an agricultural term, individuals came to see interest as the *improvement* of money, and viewed the lending of money no longer as a mutual aid among men but more as the productive use of that resource. Again, this change could be seen beginning in the 1780s, when, for instance, local Massachusetts probate courts began charging interest when a party caused delays involving the administration and disbursement of estates as well as similar court costs. Interest was seen more and more as the "money value of time." During the postrevolutionary period and into the nineteenth century, credit networks among decedents thickened (with more credit partners than in previous generations) and widened (going beyond the decedent's town or adjacent towns to more distant communities). As a result, lending became less personal and more likely based on the best lending rates, which, in turn, enabled Massachusetts to become the earliest focus of industrialization in the United States by the beginning of the nineteenth century.[5]

To the Far Corners of the Globe

Besides an expanding local capital market, another development that followed the American Revolution was the resurgence of mercantile activity in Boston, which soon created a new wealthy group of Bostonians and a magnitude of wealth that the town had not seen before. While colonial Boston merchants had accumulated substantial wealth, becoming the colony's major benefactors and the town's social and political leaders, their area of trade was largely circumscribed by the British to European countries and the West Indies, and occasionally to destinations as far away as West Africa and Madagascar. While the revolution offered political liberation for many Americans, it gave its merchants—now largely a new group with divergent backgrounds, who enriched themselves through privateering during the war—a wider, though much less protected, territory in which to trade. Independence created other new opportunities after the war. Before the conflict, goods from China had come from British merchants, but in 1785, Elias Hasket Derby of Salem decided to send his *Grand Turk* on the first New England voyage to India and China. This was followed in 1790 when the first Boston ship, the *Columbia,* returned from China to its home port (fig. 1).

While the *Grand Turk* had been preceded to China by a New York ship, the *Empress of China,* about a year earlier, the trade to that destination was soon dominated by Boston merchants. Unlike the Europeans, Americans traded not with specie but relied on natural resource products, such as ginseng, furs (primarily sea otter skins), and lumber, which they obtained in their own country or harvested from a then-disputed area now covering the northwest coastal area of the United States. In Canton, the only Chinese port opened to foreigners, these Boston traders exchanged their goods for Chinese porcelains, silks, tea, and other exotic goods. So familiar did these merchants become on the northwest coast that Native Americans, who sold them fur skins, called all Americans they encountered simply "Boston men."[6]

Bostonians also maintained a long-term presence in China. Thomas Handasyd Perkins, who would become Boston's mercantile leader in the

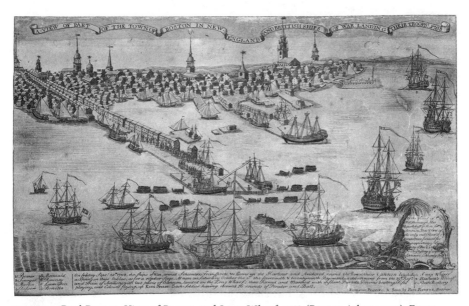

FIGURE 1. Paul Revere, *View of Boston and Long Wharf,* 1768 (Boston Athenaeum). From commerce to investment: much of what became the Boston financial district "State Street" in the nineteenth century was on filled-in land on either side of Long Wharf, Boston's mercantile center of the seventeenth and eighteenth centuries.

early nineteenth century, as well as Ephraim Bumstead, William Sturgis, and Thomas T. Forbes and his brother John Murray Forbes, all ended up in Canton, some for extended stays.[7] Some, like John P. Cushing, remained there for decades, acting as agent for Boston merchants' interests and managing their factories, while others, like Robert Bennet Forbes, sailed ships in and out of China to locations all over the world for most of his active life. The boom time for this trade lasted from about 1785 until the Embargo Act of 1808, and then it resumed again after the War of 1812. Between 1810 and 1840, the Boston firm of Bryant & Sturgis carried on about half of the U.S. trade between North America and China in the Pacific. Boston's China trade ended in the early 1840s when a combination of factors—the decline of sea otter pelts, changing fashions, civil unrest in China, disease affecting the Native American population, and, most importantly, more international competition in China, which produced a decline in profits—took their toll. In addition, the Massachusetts legislature imposed a prohibitive tax on goods sold at auction, which compelled Boston ships from China to dock in New York.[8]

During this period, Boston extended its trade to Russia and India. Innovator Frederic Tudor exported ice cut from New England ponds to Calcutta and other tropical destinations. He made a large fortune and became known as the "Ice

King of Boston." Another example of impressive overseas adventuring was a series of trade activities in India that Fisher Ames, a Federalist congressman from Dedham, made over a decade from 1794 to 1804. Initially through William Gray, a Salem ship owner and merchant, Ames invested 1,500 Spanish milled dollars to buy cotton and cloth goods in Calcutta in his first deal, which cleared a 17.5 percent return. In his other eleven ventures, each growing larger in scale, Ames generally did much better, in some cases amassing returns of well over 100 percent. Ames's success was largely due to several factors he learned from experience: spreading his risk over several vessels, always being concerned about the cost of insurance, and operating on the notion that goods are dearest during wartime when their delivery to Boston was at much greater risk.[9]

The taxable valuation of goods brought to Boston jumped from $15 million in 1800 to almost $277 million by 1860. By about 1857, however, much of Boston's trade with India and China, as well as in manufactured dry goods to other parts of the United States, had begun to decline due to the growing position of New York and its branch commission houses, the development of railroads, and other factors.[10]

"From Wharf to Waterfall"

While the China trade epitomized Boston's changing fortunes after the revolution, more subtle developments were taking place closer to home. The town of Boston soon attracted a burgeoning urban population, and at the same time saw the expansion of small-scale manufacturing. While Boston had been the largest town in British North America in the seventeenth century, by the 1730s it had declined in size due to a variety of factors, including wars, epidemics, fire, and the local economy, and left the community more insular and provincial than it had been previously. As a result, it was surpassed in size by New York and especially Philadelphia. Boston was never to regain that former lead, and while its growth rate was lower than its two rivals, it did begin to rebound in the 1780s, rising from about 10,000 inhabitants (down from about 15,000 a decade earlier) to 18,000 in 1790, and then to 25,000 in 1800.[11]

As a result (and cause) of this postwar growth, Boston's maritime trade was revitalized, and the construction trades expanded with a building surge in both the public and private sectors. Boston also experienced more in-migration from the countryside, and a larger proportion of heads of household paying property taxes, but it also witnessed the beginnings of more economically stratified neighborhoods. During the 1790s and the beginning years of the next century, the same years as the boom in commerce, Boston merchants used their money to improve the town by buying and restoring wharves and docks and constructing piers; tearing down Beacon Hill to create a residential area; erecting bridges to Cambridge, Charlestown, and South Boston; and building the causeway or "Mill-Dam" in the Charles River estuary to provide water power for mills. Yet most of this early expansion was curtailed following the embargo with Great Britain and subsequent War of 1812, as commerce dropped and local real estate lost value.[12]

Boston's boom after the revolution also brought about a resurgence of manufacturing activity. From its inception and long before the rise of nineteenth-century industrialism, Boston had been a manufacturing center. Shipbuilding had been a recognized activity in Boston from before 1650, as had the manufacture of textiles, boots, shoes, and leather as well as printing, iron working, and glass- and brickmaking. Following the revolution, the legislature encouraged certain industries, often providing bounties, while Massachusetts's needs, as part of a new independent nation, encouraged the production of others. Rope and cordage, cotton duck, sail cloth, woolens, paper, clocks, and mathematical instruments were all produced locally. There was a growth in distilleries, sugar refining, the manufacture of soap and candles, textile printing, and rope walks for the production of twine and lines. All of these activities took place within the boundaries of Boston and virtually coterminous Suffolk County, while in the nearby vicinity, workers made tools (axes, hoes, and shovels), cotton and linen sheeting, thread, gloves and mittens, shoes, powder, and large quantities of brick and other building materials, all before the turn of the nineteenth century. As a result of the troubles with Britain, from about 1808 to 1814 there was also an intensified movement to develop domestic industries and factories. Between 1810 and 1815 alone, more than seventy factories were built in neighboring Rhode Island. Boston and surrounding towns would soon follow, with much larger and more dominant industrial complexes. There was about to be, as Samuel Eliot Morison once remarked, a shift "from wharf to waterfall," as well as Boston's first major exposure to venture capital activity.[13]

For the most part, investors in fledgling New England mills were a different group of businessmen than those who participated in worldwide trade. China merchants did not redirect their investments to mills after the embargo and War of 1812, but usually continued on with trade in China into the early 1840s. On the other hand, many of the early investors in the mills did have mercantile backgrounds, but they were often merchants and retailers in European goods, like Francis Cabot Lowell and Nathan Appleton, or were interested in redirecting their investments from trade to mills, such as young Patrick Tracy Jackson, who came to realize that his brother-in-law's textile mill offered better returns. Others, like Amos and Abbott Lawrence, were too young to enter the

China trade when the former arrived in Boston in 1807 and soon became merchant shopkeepers. But within a few years, their firm, which handled mostly
cotton goods from England, had grown prosperous enough for them to invest
in the New England textile industry, just then taking off. A few men from the
China trade—Thomas Handasyd Perkins, William Sturgis, and John Perkins
Cushing—made some modest investments in the Lowell mills, but they were
largely the exception.

Like Sturgis, Cushing was a transitional figure, as he changed his investments from foreign trade to domestic industry from the 1830s through the
1850s. The son of a sea captain, Cushing became an orphan at a young age and
was sent to the care of his uncle Thomas Handasyd Perkins in Boston. The
boy was schooled in Perkins's trading house, and as a young man was sent to
Canton in 1805 where illness of his superior at Perkins & Company forced him
to take over his uncle's Chinese business, which he successfully ran for over
twenty years. In this capacity, Cushing was involved in many businesses. He
was a wholesale buyer and seller of goods and a commission merchant, but he
also bought and sold ships, stored goods, was a banker, dealt in insurance, kept
customer accounts, and worked in bills of exchange, credit, and specie—all
tasks required of international merchants of the day.

Cushing returned to Boston in 1828 worth over $600,000. He still partici-
pated in China ventures, buying shares of interest in various ships and cargos
going to or from the Far East, but after a few years, he began to find opportunities closer to home. By 1832, for instance, Cushing had invested $454,500
in foreign trade and $356,149 in domestic investments. Ten years later in 1842,
however, he was completely out of foreign investments, putting his $1,117,692
in U.S. concerns. Cushing's investments, overseen by his bankers, Bryant &
Sturgis, through much of his investing life and receiving an annual commission of 2.5 percent on income, were consistently managed with an interest in
obtaining earnings rather than speculative profits and an effort in keeping
them widely diversified. The record of his investments also shows change over
time as new opportunities developed, but he shunned highly speculative securities in canals, western state and municipal bonds, and western lands. Over
time, he placed his investments in cash; notes and personal loans; government
and railroad bonds; insurance, bank, manufacturing, and railroad stocks;
and some real estate. By the time of his death in 1862, Cushing's holdings of
$2,299,941 had again been reordered with notes and personal loans rising to
29.1 percent, railroad bonds growing from 2 to almost 15 percent, manufacturing stocks declining from over 27 to just 13 percent, and railroad stocks moving
down from nearly a quarter to only about 18 percent of his investment assets.[14]

Other men from the China trade, particularly younger men like John

Murray Forbes, came back from their foreign sojourns and leapfrogged their investing to western railroads and other internal improvements, bypassing opportunities closer to home. A close-knit group, the younger China traders were, as one study of western railroads has noted, "accustomed to managing far-flung enterprises" and reappeared back in the United States just "when the West offered great opportunities to capital and entrepreneurial talent." Indeed, perhaps the most relevant connection between the mills and the China trade was that country's growing share of U.S. exports of cotton cloth, rising from about a third of all exports to nearly 60 percent by the end of the 1850s, was all transported on U.S. ships. By and large, investment in the textile mills was made by others and was due to factors largely unrelated (but possibly in reaction) to the China trade.[15]

Three developments helped to shape the growth of textile mills. One was the completion of the Middlesex Canal in 1803, which connected the Merrimack River near Lowell with Charlestown on the Charles River, and would later provide the system of transportation linking raw cotton from boats in Boston to future mills along the Merrimack and then cotton cloth back to the harbor for shipment. A second was the impact of the embargo and war with England, which by interfering with commerce, helped to increase the price of imported goods and expand production in certain industries like the manufacture of wool and cotton cloth. Finally, there was the invention, or rather the reinvention and improvement, of cotton and woolen machinery by Francis Cabot Lowell, who brought together the elements necessary to create what became the New England industrial mill. Lowell, who had made his money in shipping, land speculation, and wharf real estate in Boston, and had an interest in cotton, both raw and finished cloth, went to Britain in 1810 to study English cloth manufacturing. He visited a number of mills and was able to recreate from memory, following his return to the United States, the Cartwright power loom, whose export was forbidden by British law.

A mill using the power loom was far more technologically advanced than Samuel Slater's 1790 water-powered spinning mill. While the spinning was done at Slater's mill, outworkers had to make the cloth at home. After 1813, Lowell's power loom made cloth in the factory at one centralized location, ended the use of outworkers, and brought about the beginnings of what became an increasingly efficient manufacturing process—the factory system. It was "the first in any country to apply all the processes of the manufacturer of textiles—from the raw material to the finished piece—in one factory, as the scientific embodiment of all such processes in complete and harmonious operation." It also brought thousands of New Englanders from farms to factories and a new life in an industrializing economy.[16]

Lowell's Boston Mill in Waltham on the Charles River became the precursor of the cotton mills set up in Lowell in 1822 and later in Lawrence, Massachusetts, but similar mills were established along rivers throughout New England. While all of these mills were outside of Boston's territorial limits, the city remained a manufacturing center and conduit throughout the nineteenth century, with goods produced worth $4 million in 1780 and rising to about $150 million by 1880. Of more consequence than its manufacturing importance, however, was the dependence of textile manufacturers on "Boston capital," which was estimated to run about $300 million a year. The impact of the mills and factory system on Boston and New England soon became a transformational experience. Daniel Webster, who as late as 1820 opposed any tariff or special legislative treatment for the mills, believed that if such favors were granted, "the whole face of New England society" would change within two generations. Its impact was actually felt much earlier, and to a far greater degree, than Webster could have imagined.[17]

The Boston Associates

Lowell's Boston Manufacturing Company in Waltham only started to produce goods in 1815 and struggled for a few years after, due to the postwar economic decline and the dumping of British goods on the American market. Steadily, however, more goods were manufactured until, by the early 1820s, demand for cloth outstripped supply. In the meantime, the mill started paying larger and larger dividends, and in fewer than ten years (by 1822), had returned to investors more than their initial investments. Between 1817 and 1826, dividends averaged about 19 percent annually. Once reluctant to invest, now many clambered for the opportunity to build new and even larger mills.

The next move was to locate mills and an industrial community on the fall line of the Merrimack River in East Chelmsford (renamed Lowell in 1824). This was undertaken by Lowell and Patrick Tracy Jackson, who had been deeply involved in the Boston Mill in Waltham, and increasingly by merchant Nathan Appleton. The first of the new mills, the Merrimack Manufacturing Company, was capitalized at $600,000 with shares initially costing $1,000 each. Twenty-seven individuals became subscribers, or more than twice the number of the Boston Manufacturing Company. The mill began operation in 1823, and two years later it increased its authorized capital twofold to $1.2 million so that it could build three more mills. A separate enterprise, the Locks and Canals Company, was formed in 1824 and owned by the Merrimack Company shareholders. The company transferred land and leased waterpower rights to new mills as they came on line. These included the Hamilton, Appleton, and Lowell Mills, to which were added the Suffolk, Tremont, and Lawrence Mills by 1830.

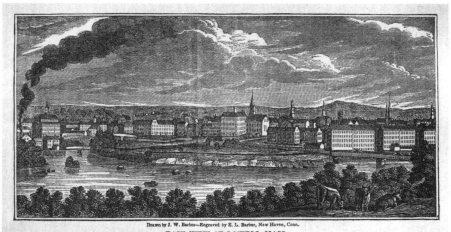

Drawn by J. W. Barber—Engraved by E. L. Barber, New Haven, Conn.

EAST VIEW OF LOWELL, MASS.

The above is an eastern view of the central part of Lowell as seen from the elevated ground on the Dracut or northern side of Merrimac river. The entrance of Concord river into the Merrimac is seen on the left.

FIGURE 2. John Warner Barber, *View of Lowell*, 1839 (Boston Athenaeum)

Two other mills followed—the Boott in 1835 and the Massachusetts in 1839 (fig. 2). The cloth produced by each Lowell mill was highly specialized, ranging from fancy calicoes to flannels, underwear and stockings, and cassimeres. The Lawrence Manufacturing Company was capitalized at over $1.3 million principally by the Lawrence brothers, who no longer imported textiles but instead had become the leading house for selling U.S. manufactured cloth. They expanded their operation in 1845 when they formed the Essex Manufacturing Company in Lawrence, a few miles downstream from Lowell, and then two other mills in that town in the late 1840s and early 1850s.[18]

Like Waltham, the Lowell and Lawrence mills did well for their stockholders. Annual dividends fluctuated considerably, from 0 to over 15 percent. At the Merrimack Mill, dividends were 10 percent in 1825, the first year they were paid, while over the next decade, according to Nathan Appleton's records, they averaged 10.25 percent before climbing to 14.9 percent from 1836 to 1845. Dividends were similar at other mills, though probably a little less. Economic factors, such as the Panic of 1837, affected both profits and dividends—profits in eleven textile mills fluctuated between 2.3 and 19.1 percent of net worth, while dividends ranged from 0 to 22.32 percent of paid-in capital—during the years between 1836 and 1845. What was striking about these dividends was that over a longer period, from the late 1830s to the beginning of the 1860s, they nearly matched every dollar of earnings. All of this was taking place at a time that cotton textile production was expanding at almost geometric proportions.

Between 1805 and 1830 alone, New England textile mills increased production from a mere 46,000 to almost 142 million yards of cloth per year.

The number of stockholders in these enterprises was small in the beginning, but over time those numbers expanded. The Boston Mill, for instance, started out with only 12 shareholders, with a majority of stock held by only 4 of them. By 1828, the number of stockholders had grown to 74, with the largest holding at 50 shares, and then in 1836, the number increased to 110, with 25 shares being the largest holding. At the Lowell mills, ownership was dispersed in a similar manner. There were only 5 stockholders in the Merrimack Company when it was founded, but twenty years later in 1842, the number had climbed to 390. The expansion of ownership was not the result of a broad dispersion of shares, since many of the subsequent owners were actually members of a few families who received shares as gifts or inheritance. At one mill, there were eventually some fourteen Appletons who owned stock.[19]

Still, the overall trend was the dispersion of ownership through the sale of stock, a substantial portion of which was apparently sold by early owners to finance shares in newer mills, even if control of the mills remained in the hands of a small, concentrated group of owners. By the late 1850s, women and trustees (of estates, the so-called Boston trustees) owned one-quarter of the shares in the cotton textile mills of the region, although it appears that most of these women were related to previous or original stockholders. Nevertheless, stockholding was becoming more widespread and was not just limited to textile merchants, as it had been in the 1830s. Also, unlike other industries, there were few foreign or non–New England stockholders. This insured that the dispersion of wealth in mill stocks over time was almost purely local.[20]

While not all early mill owners made fortunes off of their investments, many did, and by 1845, some eighty men, often referred to as the "Boston Associates," had interests in thirty-one textile companies, which controlled a fifth of the total capacity of the U.S. textile industry. From this nexus of textile manufacturing, the group spread its influence throughout Boston financial institutions over the next several decades. As one account further elaborates,

> Seventeen of them would serve as directors of seven Boston banks commanding over 40 percent of the city's authorized banking capital, twenty would be directors of six insurance companies carrying 41 percent of the state's marine insurance and 77 percent of its fire insurance, and eleven members would serve on the boards of five railroads operating in New England. Nathan Appleton alone served as president or director of 22 companies in the textile industry, was director of the Boston Bank and the Suffolk Bank, and was at one time or another the president, director, and finance com-

missioner of the Massachusetts Hospital Life Insurance Company, "the largest financial institution in New England." As if their overlapping business interests were not enough to knit them together, the Appletons, Lawrences, Cabots, Lowells, Jacksons, Brookses, Amorys, Thorndikes, Gorhams, and Duttons were all linked by marriage and cousinhood as well.[21]

Although the *Boston Associates* was and is an historian's term to describe this group, contemporaries recognized that a wealthy class of Bostonians (including these men and others) was rising, and that they were the product of Boston's growth and investment opportunities. Boston's population in the early nineteenth century expanded rapidly, growing from about 18,000 inhabitants in 1790 to 93,000 in 1840 and then to almost 137,000 in 1850. While Boston's ranking as a port had slipped from first to second before the revolution, it remained the country's second ranking seaport during the antebellum years and beyond, reflecting its strong role in commerce. Between commerce, mills, and the beginning of investment expansion to the West with the railroads, this expanded group of Bostonians was known by 1846 as simply the "Boston aristocracy."[22]

In that year, an anonymous local writer penned *"Our First Men": A Calendar of the Wealth, Fashion and Gentility,* an account of the rising Boston aristocracy, a phrase that was "constantly repeated in newspapers and political speeches, as well as in conversation" of that day. The author noted that while the city's population had doubled between the mid-1820s and mid-1840s, its wealth had quadrupled. The publication's four hundred men worth $100,000 or more, many of whom had made their fortunes during that interval, seemed to confirm that fact. Likewise, the sixteen men worth over $1 million—Samuel, Nathaniel, and William Appleton; Peter C. Brooks; John Bryant; Ebenezer Francis; Amos, Abbot, and William Lawrence; Thomas Handasyd Perkins; Jonathan Phillips, David Sears; Robert G. Shaw; William Sturgis; Thomas Wigglesworth; John D. Williams—represented possibly half of the country's millionaires and certainly competed in number with New York City's millionaires of the period.[23]

The wealth created in commerce and manufacturing, as well as railroads, mining, and many other opportunities later in the century, would provide the basis for family trusts, managed by a unique Boston institution, the "Boston trustee," throughout the remainder of the nineteenth and well into the twentieth century. Boston money in the future would also nurture other financial institutions, such as brokerages and investment banking, and create widespread ownership of stocks, bonds, and other unique developments, such as the Massachusetts business trust and investment counsel.

Investment Expansion to the West

Bostonians were early to see the value of internal improvements. In 1793, the Massachusetts legislature incorporated the twenty-seven-mile Middlesex Canal, an undertaking that would take ten years to complete and become the first considerable project of its kind in the United States. Yet implementation of such improvements set Massachusetts apart from other states. It was first with both canals and railroads but not as immediately successful with those improvements compared to other states.[24] And while other states relied to a larger degree on public funding of improvements, such as the building of New York's Erie Canal, Massachusetts's projects usually sought private financing through stockholders, such as the construction of the Charles River Bridge.

The Middlesex Canal was an only mildly successful enterprise, aiding the transport of raw materials and finished goods between Boston and the Merrimack River mills, but revenues began to fall in the 1830s, with the building of a railroad between those two points. Other canal proposals, except for one connecting Worcester with Providence, Rhode Island, were planned but never materialized because of highly optimistic cost estimates and a growing realization that railroads were a more efficient means of transport. One proposed project was to connect Boston to the Hudson River, but even its calculated cost seemed too small to take into account the effort needed to overcome the hilly and mountainous terrain. Instead, interest in Boston turned to the possibility of a railroad even before the first commercially successful attempt at one took place in England, where George Stephenson ran with his locomotive, "Rocket," in 1830. That early Boston railway—a four-mile tramway with cars pulled by horses—was set up in 1826 by Gridley Bryant, with the financing of Thomas Handasyd Perkins. Called the Granite Railway, the cars transported granite from the Quincy quarry to the site of the Bunker Hill Monument, then being constructed by Bryant.

The Granite Railway proved to be the death knell for any scheme to build a Massachusetts canal that extended through the state, and gave support to the idea of a railroad running east-west, a project that was soon presented to the legislature by Perkins and others. While the Granite Railway served as the original U.S. railroad line, other railroads, powered by steam locomotives, were being created in Massachusetts and elsewhere. Charters for the Providence and Lowell Railroads were granted in 1830, while work on the first three lines, the Boston & Lowell, the Boston & Providence, and the Boston & Worcester, were completed by 1835 (fig. 3). Nevertheless, other cities—New York, Philadelphia, and Baltimore—and the state of South Carolina moved

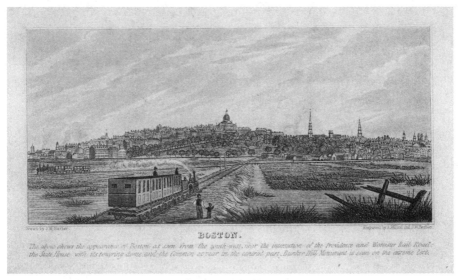

FIGURE 3. Asaph Willard, *Trains Crossing the Back Bay,* 1839 (Boston Athenaeum)

ahead of Boston, despite Boston's early lead in 1826. The railroad from Boston to Albany, acting as an extension of the Boston & Worcester, was chartered as the Western Railroad Corporation in 1833. By the following year, the road had so interested New York investors that they tried to subscribe the entire stock, "but it was declined on the ground that its acceptance 'might throw the whole enterprise into the vortex of the stock-gambling operations of Wall Street.'" Boston interests wanted to retain control, and they were also worried that if it came into the hands of New Yorkers, their influence might affect both construction and completion of the line.[26]

Although mills, insurance companies, and banks had little difficulty in securing backers, finding subscribers to the Boston & Worcester stock proved formidable. Josiah Quincy Jr., later mayor of Boston, pored over the ward voting list to identify those who had not subscribed to the railroad stock and then approached them "to learn whether he is willing to help on with this great undertaking." Quincy largely failed in finding prospective subscribers, likely due in part to the then-current concern about legislative charters in light of the recent U.S. Supreme Court decision involving the Charles River Bridge, a rival public bridge built in 1828 from Cambridge to Boston, which destroyed the value of stock in the private Warren Bridge, which spanned the same river nearby. In that case, stockholders lost all of their exclusive revenue from tolls when the commonwealth allowed the building of a rival public bridge. With little private support, the Western Railroad was financed largely by the commonwealth ($5 of 7 million), and the railroad was completed in the early 1840s.

The whole experience of internal improvements in Massachusetts was mixed, if not downright discouraging. They had helped to link major population centers within the state but failed to provide a stimulus to transform the local economy (like the mills had done), as was the case in New York and states to the West where canals and (eventually) railroads raised the overall growth potential of those regions. Also, there seemed to be a lack of popular interest in investing in such schemes, as well as reluctance by Boston capitalists to invest in enterprises that had state-imposed constraints. Above all, it became clear that "individual enterprise and [the] private capital of Boston" would have to go elsewhere—to the Midwest in particular—to expand the antebellum economy and find an environment in which to make money.[26]

Boston's China traders, likely recognizing an end to their kind of business in the years ahead, began to invest in out-of-state railroads as early as about 1839, when John Perkins Cushing, through his investment advisers John Bryant and William Sturgis of Bryant & Sturgis, began buying stock in New York and Pennsylvania railroads. Other veterans of the China trade, such as the brothers Robert Bennet and John Murray Forbes, made their first investments in railroads in 1843, speculating in one in western New York. Bostonians soon became the "advance guard" of railroad development. It was estimated that by 1845, $30 million of the estimated $130 million invested in railroads by that date had come from Boston. As one correspondent to a Pennsylvania railroad president wrote, "the Boston people are certainly the only Community who understand Rail Roads. At the present time they have more money than they know what to do with."[27]

Boston investors had their first major opportunity with the financing of the Michigan Central, a railroad running from Detroit to Kalamazoo whose final destination was to be Chicago.[28] John W. Brooks, formerly from Massachusetts and with railroad experience in New York State, tried to find backers for the railroad, which, when completed, would help to link the East Coast to Chicago. Eventually, on a trip to Boston in 1846, he was able to attract the interest of John Murray Forbes and John E. Thayer, a stockbroker and investment banker whose company would eventually become the well-known firm Kidder, Peabody & Company (Kidder, Peabody). As railroad financier Charles Francis Adams Jr. noted about thirty-five years later, "it was the first considerable venture of the kind which eastern men had made at the West, and, feeling a natural doubt as to its outcome, they went into it slowly and with great hesitation." A Boston syndicate, which included the Forbes brothers, Thomas Handasyd Perkins, William Sturgis, and John Bryant, bought the railroad from the state of Michigan for $2 million, despite the protests of some in the legislature that they were surrendering the state's sovereignty to "a company of Yankee speculators." The investors then transferred the company's headquarters to Boston (the first of many to follow), where John Murray Forbes became its president. The railroad, which needed both refurbishment and expansion, eventually was connected to Chicago in 1852 after a (torturous) series of negotiations and agreements with various parties in Indiana and Illinois.[29]

The railroad having reached Chicago, John Murray Forbes's next plan was to link it with the Mississippi River. He raised capital for the Chicago & Aurora, the first leg in his plan, to join up with the north-south-running Illinois Central, which was financed by Augustine Heard and other former Boston China traders and some New York interests. At Mendota, Illinois, where those railroads met, Forbes then built a railroad to the west and south to Galesburg. This was followed by two separate lines, one to Burlington and the other to Quincy, Illinois, both on the Mississippi, and a third line heading southeast to Peoria on the Illinois River. With the link completed in 1856, Forbes then combined the three roads, renaming it the Chicago, Burlington & Quincy Railroad. All of these developments had been planned strategically, beginning with meetings in Boston with the local Illinois railroad interests and followed by Forbes's now familiar role as "capital-mobilizer," and with secrecy, so that rivals might not gain some financial advantage or sabotage the plan. By 1854, Forbes and several other Boston capitalists financed the struggling Hannibal & St. Joseph Railroad (from east to west Missouri), which, when completed in 1859, extended his railroad system from Detroit to the Missouri River and Kansas border. By now Forbes was committed to an east-west railroad system. A year earlier, he and his brother had helped to promote another railroad, this one through Iowa. Although delayed by the Civil War, the Burlington & Missouri River Railroad, eventually linking western Illinois to Omaha, Nebraska, was completed in 1870, and integrated into the Chicago, Burlington & Quincy Railroad two years later. In all of these endeavors, Forbes had been successful in disposing of railroad stocks and bonds to other capitalists, many from Boston, through Boston brokerages like John E. Thayer's. As seen with mill securities a few years earlier, the securities eventually ended up in the hands of individuals, institutions, and trustees, many also from Boston.[30]

Railroad expansion beyond the Missouri River to the West Coast began with the congressional charter for the Union Pacific Railroad in 1862, giving investors a $60 million loan of government bonds and significant land grants along the future course of the railroad. A new Pacific Railroad Act was signed two years later, which provided for some additional incentives to private investors, but the size, scope, and liabilities for such a project proved difficult for those who wished to undertake it. To reduce the risk, a separate corporation, the Credit Mobilier, was set up at the time of the first construction contract to act as contractor for the enterprise. The new entity and its stockholders would receive the profits made between the contracted and actual costs of the railroad construction, leaving much less for Union Pacific shareholders.

Brothers Oaks and Oliver Ames, the wealthy sons of a shovel- and toolmaker in North Easton, Massachusetts, as well as some other Boston backers, soon invested heavily in the railroad and Credit Mobilier. Under their leadership, the project moved along quickly, particularly after a contract was completed with the Central Pacific Railroad to build their railroad east from California. The two roads completed work in May 1869, when they reached Promontory Point, Utah. In spite of the stunning success in completing this portion of the transcontinental railroad with such speed, the Credit Mobilier contract soon came under scrutiny, produced a national scandal, sullied the Ames's reputation, and eventually led the Union Pacific to fall into the hands of a railroad speculator, the infamous Jay Gould. Nevertheless, Bostonian capitalists had played a significant role in building the railroad, and New Englanders still held one-third of its stock in 1884.[31]

In the meantime, other Boston investors decided to move their railroad interests to the South and West, to a line that became the Atchison, Topeka & Santa Fe. This new railroad was even more closely associated with Boston capital than either the Chicago, Burlington & Quincy or the Union Pacific. Indeed, over 96 percent of the road's 569,100 shares were owned by Bostonians in 1883, while ten years later, a book about the Boston Stock Exchange noted that the Atchison "has never been other than a Boston property, and it has represented the chief interest of Boston and New England in Kansas and the growing West for nearly twenty years. It has been the distinguishing feature of the Boston Stock Exchange because its securities were for many years listed in no other market." Originally incorporated in 1859, it had expanded to over 7,000 miles of track from Kansas City southwest through Kansas, Colorado, New Mexico, and Arizona to southern California by the end of 1887, after which it spread into Mexico.[32]

The first stages of the road, from Kansas City to Topeka, and then to the western border of Kansas, had been the idea of local interests, but by the early 1870s, the project had attracted the attention of a new kind of Boston investor, a brokerage and underwriting company known as Kidder, Peabody. The firm was the successor of John E. Thayer & Brother, which had been intimately involved in the earlier western railroads of Forbes and other Boston investors, selling railroad stocks and bonds. The new business was founded in 1865 by Henry P. Kidder, and Francis H. and Oliver W. Peabody. From 1870 to 1873, it sold over $15 million in stocks and bonds to finance the road to the Kansas-Colorado border, with the first train reaching that destination at the end of 1872. In the meantime, the railroad had expanded north from Kansas City to Atchison, Kansas, on the Missouri River, where it secured access to the Hannibal & St. Joseph Railroad and the Chicago, Burlington & Quincy for connections and transport of corn, wheat, and cattle to the eastern markets.

The Atchison lacked a clear transcontinental direction until 1878, when it obtained a charter from a New Mexico railroad to complete the track to southwest New Mexico, where it joined up with the Southern Pacific, which ran from Arizona to Los Angeles and San Francisco. The relationship between the two companies proved difficult, and the Boston Atchison interests chartered another company to build along the Arizona-Mexico border. This eventually gave the Atchison full direct access from the Missouri River to the Pacific by 1882. In the meantime, it also organized in 1880 the Mexican Central Railway Company "under Massachusetts laws" to build a railroad from Mexico City northward, eventually expanding it to El Paso on the New Mexico border; the road was later extended to the Gulf of Mexico and the Pacific Ocean. As one account noted later, the first Mexican Central securities were "subscription blocks . . . appearing upon the Boston market, under which $5,397,500 was raised." Although forced to make a financial and managerial reorganization in 1889–1890 due in large part to economic reasons (competition, crop failures, falling rates, and "other calamities"), by the early 1890s, the Atchison made an annual return of $50 million, or, as the same source noted, "it may be viewed as an industrial army of 35,000 men spread half across the continent and handling a commercial business that in its collections and disbursements foots up $200,000,000 per annum." By 1892, net earnings were over $2 million a year.[33]

The Atchison, Topeka & Santa Fe was the culmination of Boston railroad building, and according to a *Boston Herald* writer in 1880, it was "the splendid child of Boston energy and enterprise." Boston had been "the nation's principal market for railroad capital" between 1840 and 1855, and railroad financing to 1880 had "given Boston a financial standing which is directly comparable with that of New York, and is inferior to that of no other city on the continent."[34]

While railroad investing had been largely a success for its Boston investors, still other Bostonians made money from investments not related to internal improvements. Probably the most important was that of Quincy Adams Shaw when he created the Calumet Mining Company to exploit the copper riches of Michigan's northern peninsula. Shaw, the son of another Boston merchant and real estate owner, and a distant relative of Samuel Shaw, who was supercargo on the first U.S. ship to China, had little interest in business himself. Rather, he enjoyed travel and adventure, living in Paris, where he developed an interest in art, and visiting the American West with his friend and Harvard classmate historian Francis Parkman. Edwin J. Hulbert, a surveyor who knew northern Michigan well, came to Shaw to ask Shaw to help finance Hulbert's copper company after locating a rich load of the metal. Shaw and other Bostonians bought a controlling interest in Hulbert's company and reorganized it into the Calumet Mining Company. They then gave Hulbert the funding to buy additional land.

In 1866, Alexander Agassiz, the son of the famous Harvard naturalist and Shaw's brother-in-law, visited the site of the copper mining interest, which was located on the Keweenaw Peninsula in northern Michigan. Agassiz brought back a positive report about the prospects for the company but also strongly recommended that the Boston backers buy land to the south of the Calumet interests, which was quickly organized as the Hecla Mining Company. The Boston capitalists soon fired Hulbert and his brother for deceiving the investors and running a lax mining operation, and put Agassiz in charge of it. The young Bostonian had no faith in the Hulberts but a strong conviction in the mines, whose wealth he believed was "beyond the wildest dreams of copper men." Setting up the mines proved difficult for Agassiz, but by 1869, the Hecla was paying a dividend of $5 per share on shares that had cost that much only three years earlier. Shortly thereafter, the Calumet was paying a $5 dividend on shares that were worth only $1 in 1866. Before long, the two mining companies, which had merged, accounted for half of all U.S. copper production.

The copper mines had a far-reaching impact on Boston, where most of the shares were owned. Indeed, nearly all of the Calumet & Hecla's eighty thousand shares were owned by about eight hundred stockholders, predominantly from Boston. A $3,000 investment in the mines in 1868, when shares could be purchased for $30 each, paid out dividends of $131,250 over the next three decades, and during that interval, share prices jumped to $530. "Coppers" had been a gold mine for Bostonians, clearly eclipsing the wealth created from China, the textile mills, and even the railroads combined. Once again, those Bostonians willing to take risks on little-known investments received substantial rewards.[35]

The Boston Stock Exchange

Commerce, mills, and railroads were not the only ways Bostonians made money in the nineteenth century; they were just the most well-known and best-documented examples. Bostonians made fortunes elsewhere—in western gold mines, Cuban sugar plantations, South American markets, and western land companies. For example, the Boston and Western Land

Company acquired holdings in Illinois, Missouri, and Wisconsin, while the American Land Company, also controlled by Bostonians, with timberlands in Wisconsin, was owned by Daniel Webster, Ralph Waldo Emerson, and many other noted New Englanders. The opportunities seemed endless, and many Bostonians, however cautious, seemed to be in the middle of all of this activity, usually through the purchase of stocks and bonds.

To create the kind of securities market New Englanders would have known in 1890—or 1860, for that matter—required an *actively* traded and *large* group of securities, or more than the securities of the two banks and two insurance companies, the few outstanding loans of the federal government, and the "5 per cents" of the Commonwealth of Massachusetts that had existed in 1798. Such an active market also needed a place to conduct business (a stock exchange, not just the proverbial coffee house) that would provide capital and create a broader market for existing securities, a professional class of brokers and dealers, an investing public interested in buying and selling securities, and a growing number of security options. In addition, that market needed a way to underwrite those new securities in the form of investment banking services. While the state and federal governments, insurance companies, and banks, whose bonds or stocks represented the securities market of the postrevolutionary world, could all handle their securities by themselves, by the time of the Civil War, that market had been significantly expanded by the stocks and bonds of private companies in manufacturing, mining, and the railroad industries, which required specialized underwriting and distribution services performed by brokers and investment bankers.[36]

Long before Boston created a formal stock exchange in 1834, regular quotations were printed in local publications, and the town had securities brokers, often merchants who dealt with the rising flow of state and continental debt obligations from the Revolutionary War as well as those of unpaid soldiers in that war. The earliest quotations in Boston probably appeared in the *Massachusetts Centinel* in July 1786, and were followed three years later by the regular reporting of monthly quotations for the Boston market in the *Massachusetts Magazine*, beginning in March 1789. References to brokers occurred a little earlier, such as an advertisement of Bostonian Joshua Eaton, a merchant of commodities like wine, sugar, rum, cheese, and candles, who advertised in the July 14, 1784, issue of the *Massachusetts Centinel* for "Public Securities of every denomination Negotiated: Business on Commission, transacted with attention and punctuality, and every favor gratefully acknowledged." This was followed two weeks later in the same publication with another advertisement: "Wanted, A sum of New Hampshire State-Notes: Enquire at the Land-Office.—At this office all kinds of Publick Securities, New-Emission Money, Orders on Collectors, &c are negotiated."

By the 1790s and the decades that followed, this type of market, in Boston, New York, and Philadelphia, became more specialized and differentiated, though not rigidly so. They included dealers, who purchased securities for themselves or others; stock-jobbers, who acquired and held on to securities for themselves; and brokers, who bought and sold only for customers on commission (rather than make a favorable deal for themselves before selling to their customer), while the sales of securities were conducted by auctioneers.[37]

Although Boston's stock exchange was not the oldest in the United States, its two competitors—in New York and Philadelphia—were little more than embryonic in form from the 1790s through the 1830s. While some New York dealers came together in a coffee shop and set up a series of fourteen rules in 1791, the agreement had little time to function before the market crashed in the spring of 1792. In May 1792, twenty-four brokers signed another accord, the so-called Buttonwood Agreement, a single sentence in length, pledging not to "buy or sell from this day for any person whatsoever, any kind of Public Stock, at a less rate than one quarter per cent Commission." Historians consider this agreement just as unsuccessful as the first. It was not until 1817, following the expansion of federal debt securities during the War of 1812, that New York brokers organized again, this time successfully as the New York Stock and Exchange Board, whose name was simplified in 1863 to the New York Stock Exchange. Philadelphia's exchange was founded in 1790, but its earliest activities and organization still remain sketchy because of the scarcity of records that have survived. Early state turnpike and bank stocks, including the First Bank of the United States, were traded there in the early 1790s, but like New York, it was not until during and after the War of 1812, when Congress authorized the borrowing of about $80 million, and in the era that followed, when new banks were chartered, canals were built, and manufacturing was begun, that both exchanges began to prosper. The Boston exchange came on the scene only a short time later.[38]

By the 1830s, Philadelphia's exchange was in decline, due in part to the demise of the Second Bank of the United States, while the fortunes of the New York and Boston exchanges were on the rise. By that decade, Philadelphia's share volume was only 14 percent of the New York exchange. As one historian has commented, "Philadelphia's stock exchange was a fairly insignificant institution until the 1830s and not terribly important thereafter." During this period and throughout the rest of the century, New York's and Boston's growth followed the rising expansion of securities trading. By 1835, for instance, only a year after it was founded, the Boston Stock Exchange had 55 stocks listed compared to 80 at the New York exchange, and from 1837 through 1840, Boston traded an average of 22.2 issues daily compared with 18.3 for New York (Philadelphia averaged only 5.2 issues). In addition, before the Civil War, the New York Stock Exchange never achieved dominant control over even a majority of issues traded in its region, and by some estimates, "in the 1820s and 1830s the trading volume outside the board was approximately three times the volume traded within."[39]

By 1860, however, the New York Stock Exchange was the largest securities exchange in the country, and by about 1890 dominant enough that many Boston brokers were obliged to set up offices in New York or correspondence relationships with New York firms. By that time, however, the basic characteristics of the two exchanges had been forged. Boston's exchange, like Philadelphia's earlier, focused on its local clientele, but it was also more interested in buying and holding (i.e., investing rather than speculating) in local companies or New England enterprises outside of the region. On the other hand, New York saw itself as a growing stock trading center, which, with the help of "call loans" to finance that trading and the explosive growth of stocks and bonds of railroad companies in the late nineteenth century, propelled it into becoming the country's most important exchange by volume traded and securities listed. New York achieved that dominance between about 1890 and 1905 with the passage of one other milestone, when the exchange went from listing only a few industrial concerns to "the nation's most important market for industrial securities." Previously, the Boston exchange had listed more "industrial" securities than its rival.[40]

Boston's exchange began on October 13, 1834, when thirteen Boston brokers met to organize the local securities market with the creation of the Boston Brokers' Board, or Boston Stock and Exchange Board, which later became known simply as the Boston Stock Exchange. Two weeks later, the *Boston Advertiser & Patriot* reported that "the greater number of stock and exchange brokers in this city have organized themselves in a board which will meet daily for the transaction of general business relating to matters of exchange, to be called the Boston Stock and Exchange Board. The system, which they will adopt, will be similar to the one adopted by the Board in New York, and from which the mercantile part of the community has received so much benefit." Before its creation as the nation's third oldest stock exchange, Boston brokers had no common meeting place or regular meetings to handle transactions and exchange market information. Few of the brokers had offices, and in order for them to execute orders, clients had to deposit their orders in boxes placed in one of the city's "mercantile" buildings. Contemporary stockbroker Joseph Martin described investors at the Boston Stock Exchange as "a large class, comprising not only *capitalists* so termed, but a host of persons of smaller means, who seek out some one of the various securities as an investment for their surplus means."[41]

Martin noted that the first nonbank, nongovernment securities in Boston were the mill stocks, which became available by at least 1826 and had become numerous within the next three years. Martin listed some twenty-three largely New England manufacturing stocks by 1844 and forty-one by 1855, which included Boston Gas Light, Lawrence Machine Shop, Lowell Machine Shop, Manchester Print Works, New England Glass, Sandwich Glass, and New England Worsted. Between 1835 and 1845, fourteen railroad stocks became available, and by 1855, that number grew to forty, primarily in New England but some in Pennsylvania, New York, and other states. These were all regarded as "New England Railroad Stocks" because they were principally traded on the Boston exchange. There were also various "miscellaneous companies," which included from about 1835 onward certain western land companies, Boston wharves, the Boston Exchange Company, Boston Water Power Company, and others, while the number of mining companies and their stocks grew rapidly from about 1850 onward. At the time of the exchange's founding, there were about thirty-seven bank stocks and eighteen insurance stocks as part of the exchange's "active list." Customers could also purchase and sell state bank notes and certain public securities, or exchange currency. Early on, the exchange helped to encourage trading activity. In 1835, for instance, stocks for three New England railroads—the Boston & Worcester, Boston & Providence, and Boston & Lowell—were so active that prices rose as much as 135 percent, even though the lines had been in operation for less than a year.[42]

Within a decade, the original thirteen stock exchange members had grown to thirty-six, and within another ten years, there were seventy-five members. The original headquarters for the exchange was on State Street, on the upper story of a building used by the Washington Bank. In 1844, the exchange moved to the fourth floor of the new Merchants Exchange Building (see fig. 5). Periodically, it moved into other buildings at 40 State Street (the Union Building) in 1853, the Howe Building at 13 Exchange Street in 1863, and in 1885 to more adequate quarters in the old Merchants Exchange Building, all in the general vicinity of State and Congress Streets. In the beginning, each member had a seat—a particular chair and desk on the exchange floor from which he conducted his trading business with other brokers during two trading sessions per day. With their more spacious quarters after 1885, the exchange maintained continuous daily sessions from 10 a.m. to 3 p.m. Before 1885, however, business was conducted in a precise and orchestrated way:

> The President of the Exchange opened each session and, taking up each stock in which trading was permitted, "called" each stock in turn. Upon the call of the stock, all members having orders in it would state their position and endeavor to effect transactions. When all had been accomplished, the President would then proceed to call

the next stock, and so on through the entire list. At stated intervals, all business would be halted until the Secretary of the Exchange, who kept a record of them, would read over the list of completed trans- actions up to that time for verification. In the event of any dispute, business was again suspended until the President, upon a vote of the members present, could decide upon the rights of the matter.

Until 1844, all transactions were considered private. Thereafter, price quota- tions were given to the press.[43]

Business at the exchange grew as more and more securities were listed, and by the 1890s, it was noted repeatedly that volume on the Boston Stock Exchange was "second only to that of the New York Stock Exchange." Textile mills and railroads were prominent in the early years, with the latter securities maintaining their importance over a longer period of time. The mills of Lowell and Lawrence; Manchester, New Hampshire; and Lewiston, Maine, were all dependent on Boston capital. The exchange was important for transactions involving four industries—western railroads, copper mining (in the Michigan Upper Peninsula), the early telephone industry, and the electrical industry.[44]

Besides the important railroads mentioned previously—the Michigan Central; the Union Pacific; the Chicago, Burlington & Quincy; the Atchison, Topeka & Santa Fe; and the Mexican Central—the exchange had a substantial interest in the Northern Pacific and its constituent lines. Through the exchange, Boston investors developed copper mining ("Coppers" as they were called) not only through the Calumet & Hecla Company but also with the Copper Range, Quincy, and Mohawk developments on Michigan's Upper Peninsula and later others in Montana. They were also involved in gold mining in the far West. Local companies participating in the exchange included the United Shoe Machinery Corporation, the United Fruit Company, and the American Woolen Company. In 1888, the exchange listed 180 stocks and 170 issues of bonds. By 1930, there were bonds from 265 different corporations, representing 363 sepa- rate issues with a face value of $3.075 billion. Some 313 corporations were listed, including 55 mining companies, 24 railroads, 60 manufacturing plants, and 172 other enterprises, ranging from public utilities to investment corporations.[45]

The Emergence of Brokerage Firms and Investment Banking

The growth of investing in stocks and bonds and the founding of the Boston Stock Exchange soon led to the rise of a group of prominent antebel- lum Boston stockbrokers—Samuel Gilbert Jr.; Ralph Huntington; Hamilton

Willis; Ossian D. Ashley; James P. Brewer; and Aaron W. Spencer to mention a few—yet none created a brokerage firm that lived on beyond its founder's active years in the business. Despite this lack on continuity, one Boston brokerage firm, Richardson, Hill & Company, was able to boast in 1893 that "our Boston banking houses are among the largest in the world, and their combined capital is much greater than that of any other department of trade in the country."[46]

Business in Boston brokerage houses took off following the Civil War. Most of the successful post–Civil War brokerages had been forged by apprentices from earlier firms or, in some cases, by a generation entirely new to the business. Many of these Boston stock brokerages, previously called "stock and exchange" brokers, were now referred to as "bankers and brokers," meaning usually a general banking and stock commission business, though occasionally there was in some brokerages a small-scale (compared to today) investment banking function as well. In the end, the shift in words describing the business was less important than the evolving nature of the business, a diversified operation combining banking and investments, which, in turn, was dependent on expertise and opportunities.

One of the earliest permanent Boston brokerages was Kidder, Peabody, founded in 1865. Henry P. Kidder had served as a junior partner in the banking house of John E. Thayer & Brother, a longtime investment partner of John Murray Forbes and others, for twenty-eight years. The company had a large commission stock business, made substantial transactions in foreign exchange, and issued letters of credit for travelers and merchants on Baring Brothers & Company of London. Kidder, Peabody saw itself as representing "those enduring principles of equity which form the substantial basis of Boston's financial supremacy in the United States." Over the course of the next century, Kidder, Peabody, as underwriter and distributor of corporate and government securities, would be "among the half-dozen most prominent and influential investment firms in the country," and would be "intimately associated with so many of the nation's major business and financial developments."[47]

Besides Kidder, Peabody, one of the most successful Boston brokerages was Paine & Webber (later called Paine Webber & Company and then PaineWebber), which was founded by William Alfred Paine and Wallace G. Webber in October 1880. Both men had previously worked as clerks at the Blackstone National Bank in Boston. With a seat on the Boston Stock Exchange, the pair took a small office on the third floor of 48 Congress Street in May 1881, "just large enough for themselves and the two employees who composed their staff." Paine, who ran the company until his death a few weeks before the 1929 stock market crash, believed that the growth of the company was due to "remembering certain fundamentals" about the business:

> In a very real and legal sense, your broker is your agent and trustee. Not only are you entitled to receive from him the best of mechanical service in the execution of your orders, but as your agent, as trustee of the property which you place in his hands, he is obliged to exert himself to the utmost of your interest.
>
> You are entitled to all his information and to the benefit of his reasoned and considered opinion about the properties which you own or consider owning.
>
> For it must never be forgotten that the "scraps of paper" called bonds and stock certificates are not the colored counters in a game. The bonds are evidence of debts to you; the stock certificates, of ownership in enterprises which should be sound, vital and profitable.
>
> With complete and detailed information, it is not too difficult to determine the real value of any business, and on no other basis can intelligent investing be possible.[48]

Interestingly, Paine reflected two important Boston investing principles, which had been and continued to be important: Boston brokers considered their clients as having a trustee relationship, not just making a financial transaction, and clients relied on the broker's knowledge of the properties he or she owned or considered owning. Furthermore, Paine saw Bostonians as a buying rather than a trading or selling society, by focusing on the value of securities and how "sound, vital and profitable" those securities (and the businesses they represented) were.

In 1881, the two partners brought in a third, Charles H. Paine, and the firm became known as Paine, Webber & Company. By 1890, Charles had secured a seat on the New York Stock Exchange (for $36,300) to help facilitate their business. In an 1893 advertisement, Paine, Webber & Company referred to itself as "prominent among the enterprising banking and brokerage houses, which have contributed largely to the financial supremacy of the Boston Stock Exchange." Webber and Charles Paine retired in 1894 and 1906, leaving William with the opportunity to expand his business beyond Boston and turn it into one that reflected his business ideals and philosophy.

William briefly attended Charlestown High School before he "felt it necessary to find employment." A job at the Blackstone National Bank gave him the opportunity to learn about the banking business. The writer of the firm's history noted that "by running errands, by taking the places of other clerks and tellers during noon hours and vacations, and by studying intensively the needs of the bank's customers, he crowded into eight years an experience and a training which proved invaluable when he became a banker on his own account." Lifelong learning, extensive reading, and an appreciation for customer service all helped him to develop his business. As he noted, "the first man who comes into the office may be interested in Polish bonds, the next man in water power in the Southwest. In order to be of real service to these people a banker must know a great deal about a great many subjects. And if he can't be of real service, he's lost."[49]

For thirty years beginning in 1899, Paine, Webber & Company expanded geographically, largely to midwestern industrial cities and scattered locations in the Northeast, and reflected the growth of securities sales by the general public. This expansion began with an office in Houghton, Michigan (1899), near the copper mining district of northern Michigan, "where the firm has been identified with the copper industry since the early days." Paine, Webber had twenty-five offices "and private wire connections" by the time of the 1929 stock market crash.[50]

By the turn of the twentieth century, Boston brokerages had developed at least two strikingly different models of development, one focused more and more on investment banking and the other on the retail brokerage business. Boston had also developed many other successful investment banking and brokerage firms, whose prominence in Boston and elsewhere would continue throughout most of the twentieth century. Included among them were Lee, Higginson, & Company (1848), H. C. Wainwright & Company (1860), R. L. Day & Company (1862), F. S. Moseley & Company (1878), Jackson & Curtis (1879), Hornblower & Weeks (1888), Tucker, Anthony & Company (1889), and Moors & Cabot (1890).

Boston at the End of the Nineteenth Century

Nineteenth-century Boston had witnessed a growth of industry and business as well as personal investment. By 1880, the city had become well known not only for its cotton and woolen mills but also for the manufacture of boots and shoes, making more than half of the U.S. production of these products. Boston was the largest wool market in the country and the headquarters of the nation's fish business, and it was still a national leader in dry-goods trade. As one historical study from the 1880s noted, "It is second only to New York in the ownership of Western and Southern railroad stocks and other securities. The Boston Exchange has the lead of all Exchanges in the country, except that of New York, in the extent and variety of the list of securities dealt in, and in the amount of business done." Furthermore, the city's imports from abroad were valued at more than any other port, except for New York, while its exports of general merchandise were second only to New Orleans. As a result, the same study declared, "the enterprise with which Boston capitalists seek new investments of a promising character [has become] proverbial."[51]

Boston had become a leader in the securities market. By 1834, Peter P. F. Degrand, a Boston auctioneer and "Stock, Exchange, and Money Broker," advertised that he offered stock in thirty-seven banks and twenty-six insurance companies. And because of its role in the development of mills and other manufacturing concerns (as well as railroad securities), the Boston Stock Exchange, which Degrand helped to create, became the principal U.S. market for industrial securities before 1900. "Not surprisingly," one leading historian of investment banking has noted, "the two leading investment banking firms of that city—Kidder, Peabody, and Lee, Higginson—were among the first private banking houses of established national reputation distributing such issues." Investment banking found good places to conduct business in cities like Boston, where wealth was concentrated and stock exchanges were well-established institutions.[52]

Besides being a center for the investment business, personal investment through Boston trustees, trust companies, brokerages, and other financial institutions had also become a way of life in Boston. An active investment culture had come early and was well-entrenched before the Civil War. Even as late as 1933, Boston writer John Marquand noted that "Boston is one of the richest securities markets in the world: a well-known investment house with offices in Boston and Chicago reports that it sells more securities in Boston in a month than in Chicago in a year."[53]

Bostonians were also "buy and hold" investors. They and other New Englanders, by themselves or through financial advisers, generally bought in units of fewer than one hundred shares, or "odd lots" as they were called. This practice became so widespread by "an unusually large investment public" that before 1930, the Boston Stock Exchange had "expanded its facilities to serve such a demand." Still, small but accumulating purchases had a pronounced effect. According to a 1959 report, "there are more stock owners per capita in New England than in any other section and Massachusetts and New Hampshire have more than any other state—five times as many as Texas. New Englanders represent only about six per cent of the country's population, but they constitute more than 17 per cent of the nation's stockholders." New England had become "a great reservoir of investment funds. Here, probably more than any other part of the country, its people are inclined to buy and pay for their securities, and put them away as long-term investments."[54]

II

FROM THE NINETEENTH THROUGH THE MID-TWENTIETH CENTURY

CHAPTER 3

The Practice and Legacy of the Boston Trustee

Not all investment in the early nineteenth century was being managed by the heads of private institutions or their treasurers. In John McLean's will, approved and allowed in Boston in November 1823, the testator had provided a house, personal property, and $35,000 for the benefit of his wife, Ann Amory McLean. He also named Jonathan and Francis Amory, the brother and cousin of his wife, as executors and as trustees for a $50,000 trust he created for his wife's benefit. According to the will, the trust would be divided between Harvard College and Massachusetts General Hospital after her death. The two organizations quickly disapproved of the Amorys' investment policy, believing that the purchase of shares in manufacturing and insurance companies was not "a safe and discreet investment." Furthermore, they sought to have the trust handed over to them, stating that they would provide what the testator McLean had wanted to achieve from that instrument, namely an annuity of $3,000 a year for his widow.

The executors politely disagreed, arguing that they had been named trustees by McLean and that their investment strategy offered Ann McLean, who was their trust client, the potential of larger dividends during her lifetime even though such actions might potentially diminish capital from the estate—that is, the funds the college and the hospital would ultimately receive. They knew to whom they owed their duty.

The controversy ultimately became a legal case, and in March 1830, Judge Samuel Putnam for Massachusetts Supreme Judicial Court decided in favor of the surviving trustee, Francis Amory (fig. 4). The judge noted the confidence that John McLean had placed in the two trustees because he did not require them to provide security, except for their own bond, and that each was

FIGURE 4. Chester Harding, *Judge Samuel Putnam,* ca. 1826–1830
(George Putnam Jr.)

accountable "simply for his own acts, doings and defaults" as a trustee. McLean
himself had been a wealthy man and sophisticated investor—76 percent of
his own estate of $228,120 was invested in manufacturing, insurance, and
bank stocks. Furthermore, McLean had not limited them to investments that
yielded simple interest because he wrote about investments that yielded dividends and profits that would produce an annuity of $3,000 a year. Putnam
also noted that all investments had their problems, and that bank shares, the
preferred type of investment of the college and hospital, were no safer than
those of manufacturing and insurance companies, and therefore did not present a lesser investment hazard.[1]

Even though he recognized that trustees were always liable for "gross neglect
and willful management," Putnam had a much broader view of their investment policy: "All that can be required of a trustee to invest, is, that he shall conduct himself faithfully and exercise a sound discretion. He is to observe how
men of prudence, discretion and intelligence manage their own affairs, not in

regard to speculation but in regard to the permanent disposition of their funds, considering the probable income, as well as the probable safety of the capital to be invested." Putnam concluded by noting that trustees held a special place and required some special protection for the service they provided: "Trustees are justly and uniformly considered favorably, and it is of great importance to bereaved families and orphans, that they should not be held to make good, losses in the depreciation of stocks or the failure of the capital itself, which they held in trust, provided they conduct themselves honestly and discreetly and carefully, according to the existing circumstances, in the discharge of their trusts." At the end, he stated that if trustees were held accountable for such losses, "no prudent man would run the hazard of losses which might happen without any neglect or breach of good faith."[2]

The Rise of "Men of Prudence": A Context for Change

Like most legal cases, the so-called *Amory* case and its "prudent man rule," which allowed a trustee wide latitude in making investment decisions for beneficiaries, reflected, rather than caused, broad social and legal changes taking place at the time. The testamentary trustee, or trust under a will, as described in the case and involving both fiduciary and stewardship components, was a relatively new concept in Massachusetts law.[3] Before this time, equity law had been virtually nonexistent in Massachusetts, and its legal foundation was based squarely on common law. As a consequence, courts barred attempts to create trusts under wills because they lacked an equitable remedy in cases of trusts. In 1804, for instance, the Supreme Judicial Court stated that, "if the conveyance was in trust the court could not have compelled the execution of it; and until the legislature shall give us further powers we can do nothing upon subjects of *that* nature." Nine years later, Judge Charles Jackson reaffirmed this position when he complained in *Bridgen* v. *Cheever* that "this is one of the numerous cases in which suitors are exposed to loss and inconvenience for want of a court with general chancery powers. But it is not for us to remedy the inconvenience." In other words, trusts, either testamentary or charitable, required equity jurisdiction as the basis for their legal authority.[4]

In England, issues involving testamentary or charitable trusts had been handled by a system of jurisprudence called equity law, a remedial justice at the time associated with the chancellor's office (hence, courts of chancery), which grew alongside the country's better known common law system. Equity developed to resolve issues that common law could not. Lack of chancery jurisdiction or equity powers in Massachusetts law went back to the very founding of the colony and to the original 1629 charter itself, which, like others of the period, was actually to be used to set up a business, not an overseas government. As such, there was no place for a chancery jurisdiction, although by the end of the charter period, the colony's General Court (primarily a legislative body that also served as a judicial court of appeals) had exercised some equity jurisdiction in cases ranging from the cancellation and re-execution of a deed to the intent of a benefactor of a charitable trust. As these random cases grew in number, they eventually led in 1685 to the passage of an act to create formally an equity jurisdiction because, hitherto, "there hath been no way provided for relief against the rigour of the common law but by application to the General Court."[5]

All of this, however, was to no avail because the colony's charter had been revoked a year earlier, and once the new charter arrived in 1692, royal authority refused to give to the General Court the power to create a court of chancery. While no separate court of equity was created during the rest of the colonial period, as before, some equity issues crept in because justices of the inferior and superior courts had power over relief on mortgages, bonds, and other penalties in deeds, and in cases brought by individuals who continued to petition the General Court on equity issues as under the colony's original charter.[6]

With the passage of a state constitution in 1780, the legislature was given the authority to establish a separate chancery jurisdiction, but it chose not to do so. It did pass a statute in 1798 to provide equitable authority in cases of foreclosure or redemption of mortgages. In its 1808 report, a legislative committee discussed the lack of equitable remedies for testamentary trustees, among others, because there was no equity court in the commonwealth, and by 1810, there was a bill put forward to establish one. In the end, the legislature decided to infuse its common law courts with equity powers, granting the Supreme Judicial Court equity powers—specifically, jurisdiction over trusts—in 1818. In "An Act for Giving Further Remedies in Equity," that court was given "power and authority to hear and determine in equity, all cases of trust arising under deeds, wills, or in the settlement of estates; and all cases of contract in writing, where a party claims the specific be a plain, adequate, and complete remedy at law."[7]

Over the next few decades, badgered by judges in their written decisions, the General Court followed this step with grants to the courts of other equity powers, including the determination of the rights of partners, joint tenants, and tenants in common in property; the recovery of property that could not be replevied; the right to make discovery on such property and to make all orders and injunctions where there was no plain, adequate, and complete remedy at law (1823); and equitable relief in cases of waste and nuisance (1827), fraud

(1855), and accident and mistake (1856). The following year, the court was given "full equity jurisdiction according to the usage and practice of chancery in all cases where there is not a plain, adequate and complete remedy at law."[8]

Court jurisdiction over trusts in 1818 was followed in succeeding decades by court decisions that made trustees immune or protected them from claims made against the estate by third parties, the monetary demands of beneficiaries, or, as in the *Amory* case, the preservation of independent investment judgment. The result, here and in the years ahead, was that wealthy New England trading, manufacturing, and investing families would be able to keep their fortunes relatively intact through family trusts managed by Boston trustees, while succeeding generations could live off the income from those trusts. So seamless and successful was this transition that even before the Civil War, Oliver Wendell Holmes Sr. admonished his readers to "put not your trust in money, but put your money in trust."[9]

Also, the growth and development of trust law involving individuals had a parallel development with "voluntary," often unincorporated business associations, or what soon became known as Massachusetts business trusts. The story of the Massachusetts business trust is long and complex, and serves a significant role in the Massachusetts business culture of the late nineteenth and early twentieth centuries. It would later become the model for the "Boston-type" open end trust that we now call the mutual fund, which began in 1924 with the creation of the Massachusetts Investors Trust. While the road leading to the mutual fund is discussed in a later chapter, suffice it to say here that the Massachusetts business trust originated at about the same time in the early nineteenth century and involved a trust arrangement in which the trustees managed and controlled the property of the business and had a fiduciary duty to its beneficiaries, just like that described in the *Amory* case.[10]

Trustees took charge of trusts once wills were probated and the court appointed (or a will named) one or more trustees. While Boston trustees had wide discretion on investments, their appointment was limited, as in most states, to the lives of persons named in the trust plus an additional twenty-one years, which could extend the life of the trust to perhaps eighty or ninety years under some circumstances. The trust itself made the trustee the *legal owner* of the property put into the trust by the benefactor, with a right to buy, sell, rent, or loan the property as if it were his, while the beneficiary became the *equitable owner,* or one who had claims on the trust property.

A trust essentially breaks the unity of title to an asset between legally owning it and having beneficial enjoyment of it. In this process, the trustee becomes the fiduciary, the person who manages and controls the capital of the trust and is responsible for it, but is also "under instructions laid down by the owner" of that trust. Donald Holbrook, a Boston trustee of the 1930s, also noted that a trustee's duties went beyond just that of a fiduciary. "Besides the actual management of property, it is understood that the trustee's counsel is available on a great variety of matters which are of concern to trustee beneficiaries, who are accustomed to turn to the trustee as the logical person to act as their confidential and judicial adviser." Holbrook recognized that earlier Boston trustees had been lawyers but that the profession had become "increasingly more specialized and the trust practice became the dominant concern of some offices over time." In addition, it was a career and tradition that often passed from father to son, requiring that "adequate experience and essential training were provided before the responsibility of trusteeship was dropped on younger shoulders."[11]

The Boston trustee developed in other ways to create a unique institution to manage and protect wealth. Culminating in a Massachusetts legal case in 1882, the commonwealth upheld the notion of the spendthrift trust, whereby trustees were given ultimate power over estates. The decision limited heirs who could not sell or give away their interest in the estate, and made the estate immune from creditors. By contrast, other states rejected such practices, limiting trusts to years not generations (through the so-called rule against perpetuities), and never provided the kinds of immunities to trustees that Massachusetts did. Indeed, on the issue of independent investment judgment, New York courts forbade trustees from investing in railroad, bank, manufacturing, or insurance company stocks for investments, allowing only "real estate, bonds of individuals secured by first mortgages of real estate, first mortgage bonds of corporations, and municipal securities." New York and others states specifically formulated a "legal list" of investments that limited what trustees could acquire. If these investment limitations were breached, the trustee might be subject to a lawsuit.[12]

Growth and Development of the Boston Trustee Practice

It is probably impossible to assign a date to when the first "Boston trustee" emerged. These men, often lawyers, seem to have originated from two distinct sources—individuals who handled testamentary trusts and others who acted to safeguard the wealth of living individuals. The former likely existed as far back as colonial times, when lawyers would be assigned to handle testamentary trusts by Massachusetts county probate courts, which expected those "trustees" to have the trust principal safely and well invested in the years that followed. That certainly was the practice by the end of the eighteenth century when George Richards Minot, the first of at least four generations of Minots, started his law career in 1782 at 39 Court Street in Boston. Minot was the grandson of Colonel Stephen Minot, owner of "Minot's T" with Andrew Faneuil at the end of Long Wharf, and son of another Stephen, a Boston merchant, "whose estate had been much reduced by events of [the Revolutionary] war." George graduated from Harvard College in 1778, then read law with Fisher Ames in the law office of William Tudor and was admitted to the bar in 1781.

While there is evidence in Minot's extant papers that he acted as a trustee for individual estates (and at least one educational institution), it did not occupy much of his time as a practicing lawyer. In fact, most of his relatively brief professional life was in appointed or elective offices, such as clerk of the Massachusetts House of Representatives and vice president of the Massachusetts convention that ratified the U.S. Constitution in 1788. He also served as judge of probate in Suffolk County, then Boston Municipal Court, and finally the Court of Common Pleas. His other great interest was as a historian, writing works on provincial Massachusetts and Shays's Rebellion. "A lifelong invalid, his work interrupted often by sickness," his eulogist noted, Minot died in 1802 at the age of forty-one. Not surprisingly, his trustee practice was not recognized in his obituaries or remembrances.[13]

The Minot law office was closed until 1805, when George's son William (1783–1873), reopened it after completing his legal education. Early on, William was trustee for the Boston Franklin trust fund, created in 1789 from a codicil of Benjamin Franklin's will, when Boston and Philadelphia were each given equal sums to invest. During William Minot's sixty-four years of service as trustee for the bequest, the Boston Franklin fund grew from $4,400 to $125,000, and by 1972, the Boston fund stood at $1.7 million compared with Philadelphia's $326,000. Still, trustee work was more the exception than the rule. The shift from general legal to trust work was gradual for the Minots. William, for instance, had a general practice well into the 1840s, but by the latter part of that decade, he became increasingly more involved with estate work, and his son William Jr. (1817–1894), who joined his father in 1841, was doing it almost exclusively two decades later.[14]

William Minot III (1849–1910), of the next generation of Minots, came to the office in the 1870s, and his siblings Laurence and Robert soon joined. Together they were responsible for helping to repeal the law that allowed double taxation on mortgages, as well as for developing building laws in Boston, both key interests of Boston trustees, who sought to appreciate the value of the estate property they managed. In addition, the brothers helped to establish the Boston Real Estate Trust, one of the earliest real estate trusts for investment of trust funds, and were instrumental in creating the Boston Personal Property Trust in 1893, which later became instrumental in the development of the mutual fund. Laurence and Robert soon formed their own firms at 18 Tremont Street. William III's son William IV worked in his father's office and became head of the three Minot offices when they merged in 1921.

While the Minots were developing the trustee management business, others focused on the business of property management. Later, the two would join forces, moving the Minot firm closer to the management of real property rather than securities. One of these property management businesses was started in the early nineteenth century by Moses Williams, who invested in Boston real estate profits he had made in a food and wine company that he had established with his brother. He soon became a large Boston real estate owner and was the first of several Moses Williams to be president of the Central Wharf Corporation. His grandson, also Moses Williams, was trained as a lawyer but focused on the management of estates, and was president of various organizations, including State Street Trust Company, and director of American Telephone and Telegraph Company and the Boston & Maine Railroad Company. In 1894, a third Moses Williams was admitted to the bar and joined his father's practice. In 1907, the younger Williams merged his practice with Francis R. Bangs, a Harvard classmate, calling it Williams & Bangs. It took over the business of another firm, Bangs & Wells, which largely managed property as trustees under testamentary trusts.[15]

By 1935, all of these offices—Minot, Williams, and Williams & Bangs— then located at 18 Tremont Street, were consolidated into Minot, Williams & Bangs, and continued the same business in the management of trusts and property that they had done individually for well over a century. In 1949, Minot, Williams & Bangs was merged with DeBlois & Maddison, becoming Minot, DeBlois & Maddison. DeBlois & Maddison had its origins in 1820, when David Sears, a Boston merchant, formed a group to build a public market. After the Boston City Council objected to his plan, Sears amended his charter, renaming his group the "Fifty Associates" with permission to buy, sell, and manage real estate. The group became an advocate for long-term ground-rent leases. In 1920, the company was renamed for its principal owners, George L. DeBlois and Arthur N. Maddison, who had come to the firm thirty years earlier. In 1985, Minot, DeBlois & Maddison, by then referred to as "the nation's oldest real estate consulting firm," was sold to Leggat, McCall Companies to strengthen its real estate services capabilities in providing advice to clients and appraisal services on a fee basis. Later, the trustee management portion of Minot, DeBlois & Maddison helped to form the basis of a new firm, Rice, Heard & Bigelow, which deals as a private, not corporate, trustee for individuals and estates.[16]

Trusteeship as practiced in Boston had other origins as well. In addition to the asset management of estates of deceased individuals, trustees worked directly with merchant families who entered into an investment-trustee arrangement because they were far away from home or too busy with business affairs to take on an active investment role. This type of trust relationship probably did not develop until the early nineteenth century with the creation of new wealth in the region. Indeed, it was not until about 1820, following the expansion of trade after the War of 1812, that there was a sufficient rise in wealth to create this relationship, which has since come to dominate the popular notion of a "Boston trustee."[17] As with those who worked with testamentary trusts, trustees' relationships with sea captains, merchants, and other wealthy individuals are largely undocumented. Information about the work and clients of these trustees can only be gleaned from the smattering of remains in widely scattered document collections.[18]

While the Minots might be regarded as among the earliest documented testamentary trustees, certainly the earliest and best known acting trustee of living individuals was Nathaniel Bowditch of Salem. Bowditch is usually identified as a mathematician, astronomer, and navigational chart maker, whose most celebrated work was as author of the *New American Practical Navigator* (1802). After studying algebra, calculus, Latin, and French as a young boy, he spent his adolescent years as a ship's clerk on four voyages to India and the Far East, and regularly gave to Captain Henry Prince and his uncle, Jonathan Ingersoll, the money he had made to invest for him. On his fifth and last voyage, he was master and part owner of the ship. After returning to Salem in 1803, he carried on with his mathematical studies but also continued to invest in far-flung mercantile ventures. Combining those studies with his firsthand experience at sea, Bowditch soon went into the insurance business, becoming the first insurance actuary and the president of the Essex Fire & Marine Insurance Company in Salem in 1804. In 1823, he was named actuary and director for the Massachusetts Hospital Life Insurance Company and moved to Boston, where he also developed an investment management career for individuals who had largely created their wealth, as he had, from the China trade.

While Bowditch may have been generally recognized by his successor trustees as "the *first* individual trustee in Boston" because of his broader public exposure and work with the Massachusetts Hospital Life Insurance Company, he had previously done some trustee investment work in Salem. In 1817, he helped three siblings to set up the Orne Fund, in memory of a deceased brother, to support ministers at the First Church in Salem. The fund was managed by three trustees, including Bowditch. Such arrangements, formal or otherwise, probably existed earlier and may have been set up by others, but Bowditch added some structure to the fund that likely differed from earlier trusts. He kept the trust's funds separate and "rigidly *independent*" from his own. This act marked "a beginning of *professional* trusteeship," according to one of his successors. "Up until the time the Orne Fund was set up, men who held money in trust merely added it to their own funds, but maintained separate records. Bowditch felt that [such commingling of funds] was not a proper way to handle trusts because if they went bankrupt, then all the trust funds shared in the financial disaster and were lost to those entitled to them." Bowditch was also a trustee in Salem for Catherine Andrew, the wife of merchant John Andrew, and for Dudley L. Pickman and Leverett Saltonstall. In 1818, Bowditch was made trustee of a Salem merchant's estate valued at nearly half a million dollars. He, in effect, managed investments for both the living and the heirs of the deceased.[19]

Bowditch's connection with the Massachusetts Hospital Life Insurance Company was an important aspect in the development of the Boston trustee. The insurance company was authorized by the Massachusetts General Court in 1814 to grant annuities on lives of individuals. A later proviso in its charter required it to give to the Massachusetts General Hospital one-third of the profits from those annuity policies. As the result of another legislative act passed in 1824, the hospital was further entitled to one-third of all of the earnings of the insurance company, over and above 6 percent. The insurance company had capital of $500,000, and the most important aspect of its business became the "management of property deposited with it in trust," with a commission charge of .5 percent. For several years, the insurance company paid out 9 percent—8 percent to stockholders and 1 percent, or $5,000 a year, to the hospital—as well as three dividends in the period, which produced a total of $150,687.[20]

Loring, Wolcott & Coolidge

Bowditch's service as a trustee was carried on through his descendants, who worked both separately and together, and by the early twentieth century, through the Loring family with whom the Bowditches intermarried, ultimately leading to the current firm of Loring, Walcott & Coolidge. Jonathan Ingersoll Bowditch, Nathaniel's son, had a long business career in Boston, where he served as president of the American Insurance Company until 1864 and as a Boston trustee. The next generation of Bowditches—Charles P. and Alfred—continued to develop a large, though for the most part separate, trust business; Charles expanded his from his father's clients, "to which he added enormously," while Alfred created a "large trust business" on his own. A glimpse of that growing business and his business practices can be seen in some of Alfred's extant correspondence over a few years in the early twentieth century. In those letters, he talks about finding ways to provide more money for trust beneficiaries, an interest in becoming a company board member because his trusts own substantial amounts of company stock in them, and a desire to find opportunities to visit companies to learn more about their businesses for investment purposes. Bowditch also received numerous inquiries requesting that he become a trust's trustee.[21]

In 1918, Alfred's son-in-law Augustus Peabody Loring Jr. ("Gus"), who had worked for Alfred since 1912 in positions ranging from office boy to clerk, took over the business.[22] Loring was the great-great grandson of Joseph Peabody, who had gone to sea as a young boy and become the richest merchant in Salem by the time of his death in 1844, while Gus's Loring antecedents had founded and headed the Plymouth Cordage Company since 1824. Loring noted later that, when he took over the business, "two-thirds of [it] went out of the office at the time to other co-trustees, as I was considered inexperienced and was rather a young man." Nevertheless, he constantly increased his own business in spite of the fact that he never received a law degree. He "always remained an independent trustee," noted a friend, the historian Samuel Eliot Morison.[23]

Like the previous generation of Bowditches, Loring continued to share an office, this time with the brother of his father-in-law, Charles P. Bowditch, and later with Charles's son Ingersoll Bowditch, who took over his father's business in 1921. Lack of space for an expanding business led Ingersoll in 1927 to set up a new office without Loring, who then moved into his father's law offices, Loring & Coolidge (eventually called Loring, Coolidge, Nobel & Boyd), at 40 State Street. There Loring's trust business was separated from the law firm (and its trust business) as the Loring, Coolidge Service Corporation, offering trust accounting, bookkeeping, and tax services for individual trustees. From that point, the current firm began its corporate history.

Deaths of trustees and the migration of their clients led to further changes. While much of the Coolidge trust business moved on to other trustees following the death of Harold J. Coolidge in the 1930s, Loring's father's trust business was merged into the law firm of Gaston, Snow, Saltonstall, Hunt & Rice, where Loring set up a trust department, which he headed. As a result, the Loring, Coolidge office had its own clients, but it also acted as an accounting cooperative for about twenty different lawyers in the Gaston, Snow office, each of whom "had their own investment philosophy." In the meantime, Loring also took over the substantial business of Ingersoll Bowditch, who had died, making Loring, more or less, "*the continuation* of the Bowditch Office."[24]

The firm that was becoming Loring, Wolcott & Coolidge gradually emerged following World War II. In the 1950s, the office merged with another and changed its name to Loring, Wolcott & Coolidge. It ended its connection with law firms and sought new investment advisors, including Thorndike, Doran, Paine & Lewis, and then David L. Babson. As a result, the firm became an independent and fully consolidated organization. By the 1980s, it also began to hire professionals with a financial rather than a legal background, as most other Boston offices were doing, and began the shift from working with almost exclusively Boston families to servicing a national clientele. It grew from about $291 million to $5 billion in assets under management (AUM) between 1978 and 2008.[25]

Welch & Forbes

While Boston trustees were largely lawyers and handled trust work as a part-time activity in the early nineteenth century, the practice soon developed into a full-time profession. Another early association of trustees, which later developed into a prominent Boston firm, is Welch & Forbes. Unlike Loring, Wolcott & Coolidge, Welch & Forbes was for many years fundamentally a law office that focused on trustee work. Founded in 1838, the firm was established by Edward D. Sohier, better known for his defense in the notorious Parkman-Webster murder case, and Charles Alfred Welch, who was admitted to the bar in 1837. From 1838 to 1888, the year of Sohier's death, the office maintained a general legal practice with some trust work, but after Welch's son Francis Clarke Welch joined the firm, it shifted to one that specialized in managing trusts and settling estates. Francis was considered the leading Boston professional trustee of his day, and was the city's largest taxpayer by about 1900 because, as trustee, he was the registered owner of significant Boston building properties, including many on the waterfront. He was also president of Long, Lewis, and Commercial Wharves. Welch "built several of the wharves and improved and expanded others, in the belief that prosperity of New England depended upon an active Boston Harbor."[26]

In 1910, Edward's son E. Sohier Welch joined the firm. It was at about this time that the firm's investment policy shifted from real estate holdings to investing in bonds and eventually preferred and common stocks as those investment vehicles became more common and safer. Perhaps no other Boston trustee was as successful at the height of the profession in the 1930s as the younger Welch. At that time and into the late 1940s when he died, E. Sohier Welch personally controlled estates worth more than $100 million, regarded by most contemporaries as the largest holding of any Boston trustee.[27]

That trust, however, required a level of responsibility for his clients that went far beyond normal professional business relationships. In a published article, he gave an account of his activities, noting that,

> In addition to all the manifold duties now performed by a fiduciary as a matter of course, we, for our modest six per cent commission on the income collected, may have to arrange for divorces, marriages, funerals, schooling, travel—including a complete itinerary to any part of the world with advice on hotels, money, steamers and luggage—psycho-analysis, renting, buying and selling real estate, running farms, hiring and firing employees and domestic servants, buying and selling motor cars, adjusting claims for motor accidents, arranging balls and debutante parties, buying flowers, wine, underwear, watches, and anything else in the gamut of commerce, and last but not least, drawing wills and trust deeds as frequently as the testamentary desires of a varied clientele seek expression.

Despite the workload, Welch did not always take the largest and most profitable estates because "they are not in our line." He observed that "people come to us for advice on the most intimate and confidential matters. . . . Now and again we have to talk like Dutch uncles—never a pleasure but none the less a necessity. Under these circumstances the older families naturally wish to deal with someone whom they know who moves in the same social environment and has a similarity of tastes and traditions."[28]

Welch had begun his trustee work in 1912, when he was handed his first trust by a retiring trustee and "felt that I was really launched in my chosen profession." As was apparently customary, Welch's own father "was scrupulously careful never to recommend me" except from his introductions to clients; Edward Welch "seemed without interest in the acquirement of business for me, undoubtedly a wise attitude both for me and that of the clients towards me." Soon, however, things picked up. Sohier Welch served as executor of his first estate administration a year later with Philip Dexter, one of Boston's important trustees of the era, who became a friend and close confidant. Welch added tax law to his practice when the Massachusetts income tax was enacted in 1916.

In 1919 when his father died, Welch spent the next two years "of the hardest work I have ever known, entailing an immense amount of detail." In the end, he and a colleague were able to hold on to more than 85 percent of his father's business acquired over the previous fifty years, and only suffered a small loss that was more than made up with new clients. Because of the mores of his day, however, his 1926 divorce had a potentially devastating effect on his business and social world, and threatened his "complete business ruin."

Through the efforts of a colleague and "an appreciation by most of our clients that our services were of a high standard not easily replaced and not affected by my personal affairs [that] we found, when the smoke cleared away, that we had lost only three large accounts and a few small ones." Still, divorce was considered a serious problem for men who held trust relationships in Boston society, and Welch felt compelled to withdraw from the boards of the Boston Symphony Orchestra, the Chicago Opera Association, and others because of their dependence on public support and the fear "that my association with them would be harmful to their interests."[29]

As far as investment policy, E. Sohier Welch deviated from that of his father's generation by investing in stocks. He was a "stock-minded man," one of his young contemporaries noted, never investing more than 50 percent in them (even in the 1930s) but investing in local "blue chip" stocks like United Fruit, Gillette, and United Shoe Machinery Company.[30]

The deaths of prominent Boston trustees in the 1930s and 1940s provided local newspapers, especially the *Boston Herald* and *Boston Traveler,* with the occasion to recount the lives of the trustees and the Boston trustee tradition. The review of Welch's life in 1948 spoke volumes about the legacy of the Boston trustee by the mid-twentieth century. Referred to as a "trustee in the Boston tradition," the newspaper quoted Welch's fiftieth Harvard class report of 1939, which stated that "my chief ambition is to maintain the integrity of my clients accounts unimpaired during these difficult times, and to pass on to my son, Francis, the great responsibility inherited from his father, grandfather and great grandfather" as a Boston trustee.[31]

Following E. Sohier Welch's death in 1948, Welch's son, Francis, and F. Murray Forbes Jr., who had joined the firm in 1932, formed Welch & Forbes. In a 1959 interview, Forbes described the type of office he hoped to maintain: "I hope this office never gets so big that our top brass stops knowing each and every client. Some of our clients like to keep at a distance and transact nothing but business. Others like to feel they are intimate. Some even call us up on weekends, just because they're lonely." But change was in the air as nonlawyers were added to handle the increase in clients and assets the firm was then managing. In 1974, the firm was incorporated and became a registered investment adviser, and in 2001, a Boston-area asset manager, Affiliated Managers Group, acquired an equity investment in the company.[32]

Boston Law Firms

As many early Boston trustees were lawyers, it was not uncommon for Boston law firms, some of the earliest of which were established around the 1860s, to develop trustee practices for individuals and families. And except for a few examples in Philadelphia and New York, this was unique to Boston. Ropes & Gray, which was founded the year the Civil War ended in 1865, treated "services rendered as Trustee, Executor, Administrator, etc.," as something of an extracurricular pursuit until 1877, "perhaps due to the fact that the care of property and estates began at an early day, in somewhat disproportionate volume." John C. Ropes, one of the two original partners, handled much of this work. At a time when "trusts had nothing like their vogue of today," wrote the firm's chronicler in 1942, "Mr. Ropes carried the responsibility of more than a hundred trusts, many of them very substantial in amount." Ropes's co-founding partner was John Chipman Gray, who also taught at Harvard Law School, where he authored some major legal treatises, including *The Rule against Perpetuities* in 1886. "He was given the management of large estates; wills and trusts drafted by him were borne to the safe-deposit box in comfortable assurance; troubled executors, trustees, cotton mills, colleges, charitable foundations, millionaires and poor widows, all came to Mr. Gray; all received kindly courtesy, wise and sane advise."[33]

Probably most Boston law firms from the solo or small practices of the nineteenth century to larger ones in the twentieth were engaged to some degree with trust and trustee work.[34] Writing in the 1970s, Guido R. Perera, a lawyer and noted public figure around Boston, described his earliest days as a lawyer in Hutchins & Wheeler (founded in 1844) in the years just before the stock market crash in 1929. Noting that the principal activity of the firm involved trusts, Perera was able to observe closely the investment practices of a "representative" group of Boston trustees. In such a conservative atmosphere, he believed that most accounts were "unimaginative and contained a high proportion of fixed-income securities," which held them in good stead during the Great Depression. The firm trustees, however, also invested in equities, including General Electric stock, "the star performer" at the time, and E. I. DuPont, as well as "selected railroad stocks, textiles, utilities and banks, the emphasis being on income rather than appreciation of capital." To a lesser degree, accounts also held auto and steel stocks. "To their credit," Perera concluded, "the partners of Hutchins & Wheeler avoided the temptation to seek quick gains or to purchase speculative favorites and thus their trust accounts, although they declined sharply in market value, survived the depression years in relatively good shape."[35]

Following his services in World War II, Perera practiced law at Hemenway & Barnes, a Boston firm widely recognized for its trustee work. That law office had been established in 1863 and is now, though relatively small, Boston's oldest surviving law firm. Founded by Stillman Boyd Allen and John Davis Long, both originally from Maine and with, respectively, earlier careers as a sailor and schoolmaster, the firm, like many of that era, was best known for its litigation practice. Allen was described by one Boston newspaper in the 1880s as "doubtless the most successful verdict getter in accident cases against corporations. Tears are not wanting if it becomes necessary to weep over the sufferings of his clients, and he also exhibits a ready wit and a good deal of strength of advocacy in other than the pathetic parts." Long, who worked outside the courtroom limelight, still managed to cultivate a public image through playwriting, poetry, and, above all, politics, eventually serving as lieutenant governor and then governor of Massachusetts in the late 1870s and early 1880s before returning to the partnership. With the firm's notoriety and success thus secured, it was the second generation of lawyers, beginning with Charles B. Barnes Sr., who moved this law office in a new direction, practicing business law for large local companies and serving as trustees or fiduciaries for the families that owned them.

Soon after joining the firm in 1893, for instance, Barnes came to represent Edward J. Mitton, who had taken over ownership of the Boston department store Jordan Marsh, established by Eben Jordan and Benjamin L. Marsh in 1841. Within a short time, Arthur G. Mitton, Edward's son, joined Hemenway & Barnes, and both he and Barnes handled the legal work for Jordan Marsh and the Mitton family. Another important Barnes client was John T. Spaulding, grandson of an important Boston ship merchant, who with his brother would later donate significant oriental and French Impressionist art collections to Boston's Museum of Fine Arts. Barnes managed this large and important estate and its associated Spaulding family trusts; later, Barnes's son Charles B. Barnes Jr. would carry on this active firm trust and business practice for many other Boston families.

After World War II, Perera was joined at Hemenway & Barnes by another experienced lawyer, Lawrence M. Lombard, who had spent his earlier career at Bingham, Dana & Gould. Lombard soon attracted other new trust clients, including the heirs of Clarence Barron, and family trusts that held controlling ownership in Barron's most important enterprise, the Dow Jones Company. Lombard helped to put the company, owned and managed as a trust, on a financially sound footing and arranged for professional management, which helped to advance the ownership interests of the Bancroft family, Barron's heirs. Within about a half century, Hemenway & Barnes had moved it legal focus from a general practice of law to a more specialized trust and fiduciary practice in the 1950s and 1960s. During that era, the business thrived because the firm also invested in new "growth" stocks, which soon helped to grow client portfolios and attracted new clients. While Hemenway & Barnes would soon redress the imbalance by rebuilding its general line of legal services, it remains one of Boston's most important trustee practices.[36]

By 2000, it was estimated that the top eight Boston law firms handled trust funds worth $15 billion. As a newspaper account that year noted, "The trustee oversees any cash, securities, or property put into the trust, and typi-cally handles everything from taxes to charitable giving to bill-paying, at the owner's direction." Today, investment advice usually comes from the outside. Wellington Management provides it for Ropes & Gray. In other situations it comes from a nonlegal inside group, such as Choate Investment Advisors for Choate, Hall & Steward. Similarly, Bingham Legg Advisors, Mintz Levin Financial Advisors, and Silver Bridge Advisors serve a comparable role for three other Boston law firms.[37]

Ending an Era

While the concept of the Boston trustee remains alive and has actually transformed itself in the post–World War II era, the golden age of this institution was probably from the 1860s through the 1930s. In that capacity, the trustee administered estates, made investments, and gave wide-ranging counsel, and was usually of the same economic and social background as his clients. Old wealth from shipping and cotton and woolen mills was replaced by newer wealth from railroads and the extraction of natural resources, like copper ore, which by the end of the nineteenth century probably accounted for more Boston family wealth than all previous sources. Behind it all was the hand of the private trustee. By 1898, the profession reached an important level of recognition with the publication of Augustus Peabody Loring's *A Trustee's Handbook,* which was expanded several times during the Boston lawyer's life and continues to be a basic source for the profession to this day. Taking into account expanding statute and case law, the book discusses the office of trustee and what one does, the nature of trust property and a trustee's relationship to it, general trustee powers, a trustee's duties, management of funds, and a trustee's liability.[38]

The work of the Boston trustees often brought them into the public spotlight for the worthwhile work they did in the community and, indirectly, for their clients. Resolutions passed by the Boston Bar Association just after the beginning of the twentieth century noted the accomplishments of William Minot: "The repeal of the odious law which worked double taxation of mortgages, the establishment of the Boston real estate trust, having the largest capital of any combination, for the solid investment of trust funds, the sale of the Philadelphia, Wilmington & Baltimore railroad, the preparation of the law for the limitation of debt for the city of Boston, and the enactment of the present building laws of the city of Boston, were all largely brought about and carried to a successful issue by Mr Minot's energy, hard labor and sound judgment." Minot's work on the city's building laws, which undoubtedly had some impact on the assets he held in trust, had started out with "a special journey to Paris in 1892, [where he] studied the problems of the building laws of that city."[39]

In a tribute to Phillip Dexter following his death in 1934, the *Boston Transcript* ran a story about his life but more broadly about the Boston trustee tradition. It noted that Dexter came from "an old family" whose father had been a Boston trustee, serving well-known New England institutions and families for thirty years. A friend had noted of the younger Dexter that he was part of a "fiduciary dynasty" handed down by his father. The article picked this thread of exclusivity up, noting that "the Boston Trustee is a distinct type. The term 'private trustee' only begins to outline him. He is a particular kind of private trustee, the product of that unique social and economic environment which gave shape and character to nineteenth century Boston. . . . Two trustees, practicing in Boston, may administer similar estates, make similar investments and give similar counsel. Yet one will be called a 'Boston Trustee' and the other not." To be a Boston trustee, therefore, a private trustee must be of "established Boston ancestry, serving a clientele kindred in ancestry and tradition."[40]

By the 1930s, the plain, austere life of the Boston trustee, as well as life in general for the Boston "Brahmin," was portrayed in both novels and journalistic accounts in newspapers and magazines. In John P. Marquand's *The Late George Apley,* the protagonist's family achieved great wealth through trade, then manufacturing, after which it moved into trustee work. By George Apley's generation, his law firm handled trust work almost exclusively. Similarly, in George Santayana's *The Last Puritan,* Nathaniel Alden and his nephew Oliver Alden were both recipients of trust funds that had originally come through family mercantile activities, although the younger man became a more Europeanized version of the Boston Brahmin.[41]

Trustees and their clients were also discussed in the press. One reporter, who came with a letter of introduction to a third-generation Boston trustee, remarked, "the office was old, plainly furnished and had a sort of faded charm about it. The walls were decorated with photographs and maps of a bygone Boston. There was no air of opulence, much less of extravagance, but everything was neat and well kept." Once invited into the trustee's office, the reporter noted that it was as "austerely bare of embellishment as the anteroom. Its unvarnished floor shone with the cleanliness of soap and water scrubbing. Yet for all the absence of ornament there was an atmosphere of genuine hospitality and repose." The furniture had been in the office since the trustee's grandfather's day and "will probably remain here as long as they hold together." Furthermore, the trustee remarked, his clients "seem to like this old furniture. It's a part of the tradition that keeps this business going." Modest as well as austere, one trustee quipped, "We're not smart men, but we are prudent. If you want smart fellows, you'd better go to New York. And ask them how they did during the crash."[42]

By the 1930s, a piece in *Fortune* magazine had noted the singular importance of Boston trustees, suggesting that some, like Robert H. Gardiner, E. Sohier Welch, and Philip Dexter, "control sums which are said to approximate $100,000,000 apiece." By that time, investment in new enterprise, which shaped the fortunes of earlier Boston generations, seems not to have been so important a vehicle as before. Instead, trustee investments had become more inwardly directed to "the enormous real-estate holdings of family trusts in downtown Boston." One trustee observed that his father, another trustee, "never invested in anything he could not see from his office window," while a third trustee in 1932 had so much real estate in the city that he contributed $2 million of the entire $67 million Boston tax levy.[43]

While the Boston trustees helped to foster a sophisticated approach to investment, their conservative character also shaped Boston's physical landscape. "The very look of Boston is, in a sense, referable to the family trusts," the *Fortune* article went on to say: "The shabby-genteel, down-at-heel appearance of State Street may not be due altogether to the fact that a large number of State Street buildings are owned by family trusts and managed by family trustees," but it was likely enough to put the family trustee stamp on the street's conservatism, and the same thing could be said about then-contemporary Boston society.[44]

Boston's life and Boston living had become simple and unadorned, and for at least a while, the city had withdrawn from creative enterprise. Critics noted that "Boston is an investor's city" but cautioned that trusteed wealth was "incapable of the risks which productive industry demands." Following the war, however, trusts would again become an important key to Boston's and the region's future and new prosperity, with the rise of venture capital and other investment platforms.[45]

In the meantime, many of the Boston trustees believed that their profession was in decline and that the trust company, begun by the early 1870s, was about to take its place. "Now the private Boston trustee is on his way out," reported *Nation's Business* in 1949. "Despite the skill and discretion with which he managed estates, he is finding it rough going in the complex financial world of today. He is yielding to the banks with their trust departments and expert economists, to the huge investment trusts with their trained staffs." As a result, the sons of trustees were not following in their father's footsteps but joining trust companies and other institutions. Even Boston trustee Donald Holbrook bluntly noted, "We're making our last stand. . . . Eventually the corporate trusts will take us over. After all, banks don't die." There was also the concern that only larger organizations had the capacity to handle more complicated and extensive research and statistical needs as well as changing tax regulations.[46]

While these fears of corporate trustees and trust companies may have appeared real to the Boston trustees of the 1930s and 1940s, they never came to pass. Throughout the middle decades of the twentieth century, Old Colony Trust Company, State Street Trust Company, and most of the other recognized Boston trust institutions were merged into commercial banks, but they soon became the stepchildren of the companies that came to run them. As the banks focused on commercial lending, the trust company division was sapped of any creativity and, instead, produced plain vanilla trust products, losing clients to other asset managers or to death.

While trust companies came to offer little competition, other fiduciaries grew or developed anew. In the postwar world, investment counsel in Boston became larger, family offices and law firm fiduciaries flourished, multiple family offices merged, and investment counsel/mutual fund companies often acquired family assets for their funds. The larger trustee offices, which became corporate trustees—like Welch & Forbes; Loring, Walcott & Coolidge; and Fiduciary Trust—began to hire far fewer lawyers, instead recruiting fiduciaries who had MBAs and investment experience, while law firms received investment advice from outside investment organizations. In the postwar world, the larger trustee offices also attracted a national rather than local clientele. It was a wholly different set of institutions and circumstances that shaped the world of the Boston trustee in the latter half of the twentieth century. As the economy of the postwar world began to take off, a newer group of Boston trustees emerged, taking on as clients families of new wealth for whom they provided new investment alternatives to traditional stocks and bonds.[47]

CHAPTER 4

Financial Intermediaries in Boston through the Early Twentieth Century

In addition to the rise of Boston trustees and the introduction of stocks and bonds as forms of investment, Bostonians were also exposed by the mid-nineteenth century to numerous financial intermediaries, particularly private insurance companies and a growing and expanding banking system, which included not just commercial banks but also savings banks and trust companies. In most cases, these businesses served a dual role—not only did they offer an opportunity to buy stock (except for mutual insurance companies), but they also provided dividends or interest to customers or clients from the investments they made. Shares in banks and insurance companies quickly became the most widespread form of investment in nongovernment securities in the years following the Revolutionary War. By the end of the late 1920s and beginning of the depression, however, Boston had witnessed the decline and then end of its major investment banks. They had been significant institutions throughout the mid- to late nineteenth century, but their demise would confirm a shift by Boston asset managers from a "sell" to a "buy" investment culture, as well as turn those managers to new directions for investment products and services during the twentieth century.[1]

The Development of Boston Insurance Companies and the Expansion of Their Business

The earliest of Boston's financial intermediaries was the insurance underwriter. Insurance as a concept and enterprise grew rapidly between the revolution and Civil War to include three major types of businesses—marine, fire, and life insurance. The first of these, marine insurance, dated back to antiquity and was used to protect ship owners from losses to their ships or cargo due to accidents at sea, sinking, or confiscation during war. Because marine insurance sought to spread risk among a number of ships, the business was largely confined to active ports, and throughout the seventeenth century, colonial ship owners probably used London underwriters.

The first known colonial marine insurance announcement in the British colonies appeared in 1721 in the Philadelphia *American Weekly Merchant,* in which broker John Copson noted that he had made arrangements with several wealthy Philadelphia merchants, who would serve as underwriters. But beyond this and one other notice that year, there are no further details about his business, while other contemporary information suggests that attempts in Philadelphia to set up insurance offices before 1746 "prov'd abortive."[2]

Boston's first underwriter appears to have been Joseph Marion, who started his marine insurance business in 1724. Like the then-contemporary practice in London, Marion probably drafted a policy similar to those developed by London's Lloyd's Association, which described the ship, voyage, premium amount, and conditions of the contract between the ship owner and the policy subscribers. Those subscribers, in turn, acquired a share of the risk (to the vessel and cargo) by the amount they assumed for what became described by the nineteenth century as the "ordinary perils" encountered in a sea voyage. In effect, underwriters customarily received a portion of the cargo for their share of the risk.

Marion's business was apparently successful enough that by 1728, he had proposed to set up the "Sun Fire Office in Boston," which would insure houses and household goods from loss or damage by fire. Nothing seems to have come about from this second enterprise (it would take another seventy-five years before Bostonians actually began to buy fire insurance coverage), but the business of marine insurance contracts continued on through the colonial period. In 1745, there appeared a notice in the *Boston Evening Post:* "The Publick is hereby advertised that the Insurance Office first opened in Boston, Anno Dom. 1724 by Joseph Marion, Notary Publick is still held and kept by him on the North side of the Court house, near the head of King Street, where Money upon the bottom of ships and vessels may also be obtained for a reasonable premium." Marion was not the only Boston businessman engaged in underwriting. Some individual Boston merchants provided the same service through their counting houses, and still others through informal or temporary partnerships to underwrite these risks. Between 1724 and 1801, at least nineteen different individuals ran advertisements in Boston newspapers offering marine insurance services. They included Peter Chardon Brooks, who made his fortune in marine insurance during the 1790s, with the great expansion of trade during that decade, and left at his death in 1849 one of the country's largest estates, estimated at about $2 to 3 million.[3]

Marine insurance went through an important transformation near the end of the American Revolution. Prior to that time, men like Marion had to find underwriters for their policies, but by the early 1780s, insurers such as John Hurd retained a standing "company" of underwriters for his policies, with each underwriter agreeing to underwrite a certain amount for any policy Hurd decided to take on. Besides formalizing the underwriting process by creating a stable of regular underwriters, this shift had another consequence: it put large sums of money into the hands of Hurd and other insurers, which had to be invested to keep their enterprise safe and profitable. In 1784, the Massachusetts General Court incorporated the Massachusetts Bank, which through the acquisition of its shares, created such an investment opportunity. Massachusetts bank stocks would become the largest and most common form of investment by Boston insurance companies over the next century.

By the 1790s, this notion of a capitalized insurance business was carried one step further by means of incorporation, a form of organization first set up in Philadelphia in 1792. Three years later, the Massachusetts legislature incorporated its first insurance company, the Massachusetts Fire Insurance Company, which was capitalized at $300,000 with 3,000 shares. In 1798, the legislature chartered the Massachusetts Mutual Fire Insurance Company with $2 million in capital, and the following year, the Boston Marine Insurance Company received its charter and a capital fund with a minimum of $500,000 and a maximum of $820,000, with shares at $100 apiece. The Boston Marine Insurance Company's investment policy was strictly limited by its charter. The company was to invest almost exclusively in bank stocks, and it did so by acquiring a large number of shares in the Bank of the United States and lesser amounts in several Boston banks, such as the Massachusetts and Union Banks. Its only other investment was $20,000 in real estate.[4]

While Marion's attempt to create a fire insurance business in the 1720s did not work out, the idea eventually caught on, first in Charleston, South Carolina, with the establishment of the Friendly Society in 1735. This organization, however, went bankrupt following a disastrous fire that destroyed two-thirds of the city. Philadelphia provided a more permanent home for fire insurance when the Philadelphia Contributorship for the Insurance of Houses from Loss by Fire was founded in 1752. The contributorship adopted the mutual structure used in some London insurance companies, whereby ownership is vested in policy- rather than shareholders. It was akin to the organization of mutual benefit societies discussed in chapter 1 and to savings banks. Fire insurance faced two major obstacles at the time. Unlike marine insurance, the risk of fire lasted more than a few months, with coverage carrying on for years or decades. Such long-term risk meant an absence of profit for stock or profit-seeking insurance companies, and difficulty in attracting policy/shareholders to mutual companies. Furthermore, people were reluctant to pay premiums because of a common practice in colonial urban areas: victims of fires often received voluntary relief donations from their neighbors and fellow townspeople minimizing the need for fire insurance.

Although three fire insurance companies were established in the 1790s, they remained a hard sell, and by 1799, the Massachusetts Fire Insurance Company was renamed the Massachusetts Fire and Marine Insurance Company, indicating how important (and profitable) the marine insurance business was. By 1803, the insurance capital of these two "stock" insurance companies reached almost $2 million, in addition to money indirectly invested by individual underwriters.

Despite the setbacks associated with the business, fire insurance began to make some headway after the founding of the Massachusetts Mutual Fire Insurance Company. Established by a number of prominent Bostonians, including Paul Revere, George R. Minot, and Elisha Ticknor, the company was not allowed to operate until it insured $2 million worth of property. Since the company could assume only four-fifths of the value of the risk, the incorporators had to find enough policyholders to extend the amount of property insured to $2.5 million. After getting the business under way with offices on State Street, Massachusetts Mutual determined that policies had to be issued for a term of no fewer than seven years. It also spent considerable time determining and settling on rates for insurance premiums, basing them on the type of structure—wood, brick, stone, tile, or other materials—and other tangible considerations. Fewer than three years after the company was formed, one of its policyholders lost his property in a fire. Despite the loss, the trustees of Massachusetts Mutual refused to pay because the property had been changed since the policy was issued to the extent that it had taken on increased risk. As a result, the disagreement led to the first fire insurance lawsuit in the country and a verdict for the policyholder.[5]

Although some progress had been made, fire underwriting in Boston continued to be a challenging experience during the early nineteenth century, and apparently differed from other eastern urban areas where it was more popular. Perhaps noting New England frugality, one 1823 anonymously written Boston insurance tract on fire insurance noted that "He who loses his all at sea by not insuring, instead of sympathy meets with reproach for his temerity. He who suffers by fire, although equally charitable with rashness and imprudence, not only claims exemption from reproach, but appeals with confidence, and often with success, to public sympathy and public donations." For the most part, policyholders were also stockholders in the few companies that offered it. Other companies entered the Boston insurance market in the early nineteenth century, including the New England, Suffolk, and Union Companies, but they and most others confined themselves largely to marine insurance. Merchants might insure their stores or goods, which they obtained on credit or mortgages, but Bostonian homeowners did not insure against the threat of fire.[6]

This attitude changed by the second quarter of the nineteenth century, when interest in fire insurance increased, actually surpassing the marine insurance business, and the number of Boston insurance companies grew. Between 1825 and 1835, for instance, ten new insurance companies were founded. In 1831, the Firemen's Insurance Company was set up strictly for the fire business. By 1836, there were twenty-five Boston insurance companies with about $7 million in capital. These companies invested about half of their funds in bank stocks until the Panic of 1837, when these assets depreciated in value and dividends ceased, creating a loss of capital and income for the insurance companies. Over the course of the next six to eight years, eight insurance companies failed, and Boston insurance capital was reduced by more than 30 percent. This setback also came at a time of heavy fire and marine losses, during a period when the market value of property declined significantly. Between 1838 and 1844, for instance, Boston insurers of marine ventures reduced their risk from $50 to $33 million, while the overall risk from fire losses went from $52 to $42 million.[7]

As these figures suggest, fire insurance had actually surpassed the marine insurance business in size by the late 1830s. Marine insurance did well from 1844 to 1854, with the discovery of gold in California, and insurers were able to secure more favorable contracts thanks to the increase in tonnage shipped. Around 1854, however, substantial ship and cargo losses began to occur at sea, causing stock prices to decline and many companies to stop paying dividends. On the other hand, fire insurance continued to grow, although not enough to bring new entrants into the market. During the Civil War, investments made by Boston insurance companies in U.S. bonds and the stocks of the newly created national banks paid off very well.

By the time of the Civil War, most Boston insurance companies took both marine and fire risks, but they were starting to face competition from companies outside of the state. In 1860, Boston companies received about $1.3 million in fire premiums, roughly $800,000 of which came from Boston companies or individuals. That same year, there were some fifty-one non-Massachusetts insurance companies doing business in Boston, and they did approximately $250,000 in business. But the number of out-of-state insurance companies continued to rise: in 1866, there were seventy such fire and marine companies doing business in Boston and thirty-seven life insurance companies; in 1870, there were ninety-one out-of-state fire and marine companies. Except for some life insurance companies, few Boston companies expanded beyond a local client base, as "the system of scattering risks over a vast area was not popular with our underwriters." Only one did an "agency" business over a broader geographic area, but even this proved to be only experimental. For a time this local client strategy seemed to work. From 1860 to 1871, Boston-based companies paid their stockholders dividends that exceeded 15 percent a year and still were able to retain large surpluses, which were due to the fire business, since marine volume was declining.

Of the four companies that ventured outside of Boston to Chicago, three of them went bankrupt following the Chicago fire of 1871, which seemed to confirm the view of Boston insurance companies that they should take only local risks. The fire in Chicago was followed a year later by a devastating one in Boston, which destroyed a large area in what is now the financial district and downtown, and completely destroyed the logic of selling policies strictly to local businesses and individuals. Business gradually shifted. In 1860, two-thirds of all risks were protected by policies from Boston insurance offices. By 1870, the risks Boston offices undertook were almost evenly divided between Boston and non-Boston locations. By 1880, the 130 non-Massachusetts companies doing business in Boston handled more than three-quarters of the local business. By necessity and experience, Boston's property insurance had become nationalized by the last quarter of the nineteenth century, and local insurance companies no longer played a key investment role, except in the life insurance area, as they had a half century earlier.[8]

In the field of life insurance, Philadelphia started earlier than Boston in developing a variation of this enterprise. In 1759, Presbyterian synods in New York and Pennsylvania set up the Corporation for Relief of Poor and Distressed Widows and Children of Presbyterian Ministers, and a decade later in 1769, clergymen of the Episcopal Church of Pennsylvania formed a mutual association to pay small annuities to the families of the their ministers. These organizations were both insurance and charitable institutions; they may have been structured like insurance companies, but they had a very specialized clientele and were usually supported by gift contributions. They were also similar to beneficial societies in Massachusetts. More modern and generic forms of life insurance were issued by the Insurance Company of North America, a Philadelphia capital stock company, which offered a variety of insurance products, including a handful of life insurance policies, as of the early 1790s, and by the Pennsylvania Company for Insurances on Lives and Granting Annuities, which was incorporated in 1812. Two years later in 1814, the Massachusetts legislature gave to the trustees of Massachusetts General Hospital the right to grant annuities on lives. In 1818, the trustees petitioned the legislature to expand their business beyond annuities and to include life insurance. That year the legislature incorporated the Massachusetts Hospital Life Insurance Company, the country's second oldest life insurance company, for that purpose.[9]

With a capital stock of $500,000 (5,000 shares at $100 par), the charter provided that one-third of the annual net profits of the enterprise should be paid to the trustees of the hospital. In the charter, the legislature also provided that it would not approve of other life insurance companies unless they gave part of their profit to charitable uses. The allocations were changed in 1823, so that stockholders received 6 percent per annum on their investments as well as two-thirds of the profit the company made over that percentage. The first policy was issued in 1823 to John Minot for two years. Short-term policies were typical in early years, as they were used to secure money loaned to the insured rather than provide a financial asset for the policyholder's estate.[10]

Over its early years, Massachusetts Hospital Life attracted business and financial leaders, often Boston trustees themselves, to become trustees, incorporators, and members of its committee of finance. Individuals who served in these positions included Peter C. Brooks, Ebenezer Francis, William Prescott, Josiah Quincy, John Lowell, and William Sturgis, many of whom had made their fortunes in China, the New England mills, or Boston banks. And so, as the trustees looked for someone to head the company on a permanent basis in 1823, they turned to an individual who would eventually transform the organization from one focused on annuities and life insurance to an investment or trust company that derived its capital principally from money held in trust.

The company's selection committee chose Nathaniel Bowditch, then president of the Essex Fire & Marine Insurance Company of Salem, to fill the position, and he agreed. Bowditch believed that neither the annuities nor life insurance business provided a sufficient income basis for the company. Therefore, he advocated that it seek another extension to its charter that would allow it to accept monies in trust. That summer, the Massachusetts legislature approved an amendment to the company's statute of incorporation that allowed the company to invest monies from the sale of annuities or held "*in trust* for and during the lives of any person or persons in notes secured by Mortgages of Real Estate, or by collateral assignment of any of the species of stocks mentioned." That Bowditch would suggest this change was not unusual; while in Salem, he had served as trustee for a fund that supported the minister of the First Church as well as an estate of a Salem merchant that supported charitable work. Both duties provided him with experience in and knowledge about the potential financial rewards this kind of investment opportunity might offer to the company.[11]

While the Massachusetts Hospital Life Insurance Company was established to insure lives, its primary purpose soon became, following the passage of the 1823 amendment, the investment of those deposits it held in trust. By 1826, Bowditch had concluded that "the business of Life Insurance and Life Annuities is at present very small and the whole force of the institution tends toward the trust establishment." At the time, the life and annuities businesses amounted to less than one-tenth of the deposits in trust. By 1830, the Massachusetts Hospital Life Insurance Company had become New England's largest financial institution, with trust accounts of over $4.8 million of its total resources of $5.4 million. It made significant investments in New England manufacturing, becoming "probably the most important single source of intermediate term credit for the Massachusetts textile industry during the nineteenth century," and, soon, railroad companies. As a leading source of capital in New England throughout the nineteenth century, it became the pioneering example of trust and investment companies that would soon develop in the Boston area. As of 1900, the Massachusetts Hospital Life Insurance Company was still among Boston's five largest financial institutions.[12]

The company offered five different types of trust contracts. The most popular was the five-year renewable deposit contract, while two other variants of this contract allowed women in one case and men in the other to make deposits during their lifetimes and no withdrawals, with the money payable to their estates or specified parties after their deaths. Two others—an endowment and deferred annuity, both in trust—were for children, with payments to those beneficiaries at the time men turned twenty-one or women were married. The trust business attracted the funds of "society's dependents"—single women, widows, orphans, children, and the aged—although Bowditch was concerned that the company not take on these deposits because they were the least likely to "be able to accept the risks of management." Massachusetts Hospital Life was also viewed by company officials as a regional business, and Bowditch discouraged deposits from outside of New England. The period of substantial growth in deposits ended in 1830, by which time over two-thirds of the company's assets were held in five-year renewable deposit contracts, with widows and single women making up 40 percent of this category. A broad range of Boston's civic, educational, charitable, and religious organizations—from the Boston Athenaeum and Harvard College to Massachusetts General Hospital and the Provident Institution for Savings—maintained institutional accounts.[13]

The major object of the company was to "always [have] in view the safety of the Capital, rather than the greatness of the income," and to this end, Bowditch and his finance committee sought to make investments as "near riskless as possible" in mortgages, collateral loans, and securities. The company's charter and amendment restricted these types of investments to include only mortgages of property in Massachusetts, U.S. and Massachusetts bonds, and stock from the Bank of the United States or banks chartered in Massachusetts. During its early years, the company's funds were largely invested in mortgages, loaned on collateral, or deposited in Boston banks, with the greater part invested in mortgages. But proportions would change, depending on then-current interest rates. Over time, many of the loans were granted to businesses, financial institutions, and, until prohibited, commercial banks instead of individuals.

One of the principal outlets for the company's growing accumulation of investment funds in the 1820s was in mortgages, particularly those in western Massachusetts. When the region came in for hard times late in that decade, Massachusetts Hospital Life became a source of wrath for farmers there, sparking "political protest [against it] as [a] bastion . . . of privilege spawning inequality and dependence." Bowditch soon found better opportunities locally, shifting the company's investments in mortgages to the quieter environment of Boston and its immediate vicinity. Bowditch's investment policy fared well, even following the Panic of 1837. Mortgage loans had a consistent yield of almost 6 percent, while its collateral loans, bank deposits, and security investments produced yields only slightly less, and dividends from company shares averaged between $7 and $8 until after the Civil War, approaching that of the most profitable banks in Boston at that time. As a result of the growth of the trust business, little remained of Massachusetts Hospital Life's life insurance business by the mid-1840s. It dwindled to insignificance as the new mutual life insurance companies of that era took it over. The company's most important contribution was as a trust company, which some have described "as the 'first' trust company to operate in the United States and, in fact, in the world" (fig. 5).[14]

More typical of the role of Boston life insurance companies was the history of New England Mutual Life Insurance Company. Although chartered in 1835, it was not organized until 1843 and did not issue its first policy until 1844, a year after the first mutual insurance company, Mutual of New York, started business. Regarded as the oldest general life insurance company, New England Mutual was organized—along with five others (including Worcester rival State Mutual) between 1844 and 1847—as a mutual company, in which its policyholders (rather than stockholders) received, in effect, a reduction of premiums in the form of dividends. This feature was patterned after fire insurance and English life insurance companies. Other major Massachusetts insurance companies were founded shortly after this period, with Massachusetts Mutual in Springfield in 1851, and John Hancock in Boston in 1862.

View of the Merchants Exchange, State Street and Adjacent Buildings, 1842.
Etched by Sidney L. Smith from a Lithographic Drawing by Theodore Von Robert.
Published by Charles E. Goodspeed and Company, Boston, 1915

FIGURE 5. Merchants Exchange Building, 1842 (Boston Athenaeum). This building on State Street became the center of Boston business activity from 1842 to 1890, housing the Boston Stock Exchange, numerous insurance companies and brokers' offices, and even a library and other conveniences for merchants. It also helped to permanently associate the name State Street with Boston's rising investment community.

New England Mutual's founder was Willard Phillips, who grew up in western Massachusetts before attending Harvard where he became a scholar and later a tutor. He was admitted to the bar in 1818. His practice soon involved him with questions about insurance law and he produced a *Treatise on Insurance* (1823), which became a staple at the fledgling Harvard Law School. Over the course of the next decade or two, Phillips studied English political economists and wrote a *Manual of Political Economy*. Other publications included two books on "general average," the law involved in maritime claims among more than two parties.[15] As an economist, lawyer, businessman, and scholar, Phillips embraced as many aspects of the antebellum economy in Massachusetts as anyone.

Among these many activities, Phillips also arranged to obtain a charter for New England Mutual, but failing to raise the $50,000 from subscribers needed for the guaranty capital fund, he followed other pursuits, including an appointment as a probate judge, a position he did not give up until 1847, several years after his life insurance company began business. While Phillips knew wealthy men, his own business failure and the provision in his charter that one-third of his company's "profits" would go to Massachusetts General Hospital, acted as deterrents. By the early 1840s, however, Phillips had received support from Charles Pelham Curtis, a lawyer, and James Savage, treasurer of the Provident Institution for Savings; they, in turn, contacted several dozen other prominent Bostonians, ranging from mill owner Abbott Lawrence to China trader and investor John Murray Forbes, to contribute to the fund.

New England Mutual collected $23,500 in premiums in its first year in business. Policy limits were soon raised from $5,000 to $10,000, and restrictions were placed on coverage depending on the insured's travel plans. For instance, the company would not cover the policyholder for travel to the South between May and October in the event of death. (Policyholders in the South and West usually paid higher premiums on the theory that they covered a greater risk of residence, that is, they lived in regions with increased risk of death.) Nearly all sales were placed directly by an applicant to the company, but lawyers, bankers, and agents of other insurance companies also sold policies.[16]

The company employed Elizur Wright, a mathematician, to make reserve calculations. Wright later became known for his pioneering work in the development of actuarial tables used to calculate insurance premiums, and was called the "father of life insurance regulation" because he advocated for laws that required companies to keep adequate reserves and provide cash surrender values (nonforfeiture benefits). Wright also served as Massachusetts Commissioner of Insurance from 1858 to 1866.

Although New England Mutual was not a stock company, with shares used for investment purposes, like other mutual insurance companies it invested monies from premiums. The company's initial investments were made in July 1844 and consisted of $30,000 in Massachusetts state bonds, 100 shares each in two local banks—Eagle and State—that were not represented on the company's board of directors. A few months later, the first mortgage loan was made to an Asa Stearns for $5,000 "on bond and mortgage and $2,000 when house mortgaged shall be finished." At the end of its first year, the company had invested all of its subscribers' capital and net premiums, a sum of $72,000. During the early years, nearly all investments were local. One large exception was in 1851 when the New York state controller required the company to deposit two New York City mortgages worth $100,000 in its care as a necessary requirement to doing business in the state.

While the company invested conservatively, it also diversified and shifted its investments in line with changes in the economy. During its first year of operation, it held 33.9 percent of its assets in U.S. government bonds, a record high that was never reached again. On the other hand, state and municipal bonds were seen as the preferred investments, varying from about 19 to 38 percent from the Civil War until 1879. Railroad stocks were in the company's first portfolio, and its first railroad bonds were purchased a few years later. Both began to grow rapidly in the 1870s and 1880s, reaching their high in 1911, when over 44 percent of the company's assets were in railroad bonds (and about 4 percent in railroad stocks). During the nineteenth century, common and preferred stocks, with higher yields but also corresponding risks, accounted for only about 6 to 8 percent of the portfolio. In that same period, there were also a small number of loans on personal securities, but much of this business gradually moved to commercial banks. Premium notes and policy loans constituted a small percentage of the portfolio, even though the company never regarded them as investments. Between 1860 and 1905, New England Mutual's mortgage investments averaged a 5.2 percent return while its stocks and bonds were about 5.45 percent, below the average of many other insurance companies, but still regarded as responsible, conservative investments.[17]

On a broader scale, Boston created numerous insurance companies throughout the nineteenth century, some of them mutual companies but many others owned by stockholders. By January 1828, for instance, there were seventeen stockholder-owned companies with capital of $4,925,000; eleven of them had been formed since 1823. The numbers fluctuated over time: there were twenty-eight active stockholder-owned companies between 1823 and 1835, twenty-five between 1835 and 1844, nineteen between 1845 and 1855, and twenty-three between 1856 and 1870. Despite success, there was turnover because of "the Ups and Downs of Insurance." Many of these companies failed or closed during times of economic turndown or due to an unexpected rise in claims. "A large number of companies were consequently closed between 1837 and 1845," wrote one observer, "some of them successfully, while others made but small dividends." By the early 1870s, there were approximately thirty different insurance companies.[18]

As far as their investment policy, surviving records for these insurance companies provide only scattered information over brief periods to show how they invested their assets. Generally, Massachusetts required insurance companies to invest about a third of their capital in the stock of Massachusetts state banks and the remainder in real estate mortgages and personal loans secured by bank stock. Beginning in the latter decades of the antebellum period, however, the ratios and composition of these investments changed, as recorded in the annual reports of fire and marine insurance companies sent to the Massachusetts secretary of the commonwealth.[19]

During this period, most insurance companies invested in mortgages and other loans with long maturities, various state and federal public securities, and, to a lesser extent, stocks, particularly in commercial banks. In compiling these figures for his early reports, the secretary of the commonwealth divided Massachusetts between Boston insurance companies and those outside of Boston. There were some significant differences between the two. For instance, in 1839, companies outside of Boston tended to invest more in state bonds (68 to 50 percent), less in real estate (2 to 9 percent), less in real estate secured by mortgages (5 to 13 percent), and less on loans on collateral and personal security (6 to 12 percent). By 1845, the secretary's returns segment out for the first time mutual marine and mutual fire and marine companies, whose investments varied considerably. For example, New England Mutual Marine had over $43,000 in state bank stock and about $5,500 in railroad stock as its major investments, while Equitable Safety had about $74,000 in notes secured by real estate mortgages, over $43,000 in U.S. bonds, one bottomry bond (enabling a shipowner to borrow money to equip or repair a ship) of $3,500, and over $93,000 in state bank stock in its portfolio.

Nevertheless, the overall investment pattern of stock or nonmutual Boston insurance companies before the Civil War was remarkably unchanged throughout the period. There was, of course, an increase in railroad investment (from 1 to 9 percent) and loans on personal security (from 1 to 7 percent), and declines in loans secured by ships and cargos (from 5 to less than 1 percent)—all reflecting economic changes but little else. A shift was seen in the mid-1860s as a result of the Civil War and the financial resources required by the federal government. By January 1865, insurance stock companies had 18 percent of their investment in U.S. bonds and treasury notes, 11 percent in railroad stocks, and another 2 percent in railroad bonds. Still, 48 percent of all investment funds were held in bank stocks. Mutual fire, mutual marine, and mutual fire and marine insurance companies invested somewhat differently, more in U.S. bonds (27 percent) and less in bank stocks (35 percent), but mortgages and real estate holdings amounted to roughly the same as in stock insurance company portfolios (11 to 15 percent, respectively).[20]

There were some modest changes in investment as the century progressed and as new opportunities and less state regulation took hold. Life insurance companies, which became more important after the war, had little in the way of bank stocks, or railroad stocks or bonds in 1866 (about 7 percent in all), although roughly 22 percent of their investments were in real estate mortgages and another 51 percent in "other investments," primarily state and federal bonds. By 1880, the five state mutual life insurance companies then in operation held about 58 percent of their assets in "real estate, stocks, bonds, etc." and another 29 percent in loans on "Mortgages and Collaterals." By 1900, by which time there were seven mutual life insurance companies domiciled in the state (Atlantic, Berkshire, Boston, John Hancock, Massachusetts, New England, and State), the companies had about $93.5 million in assets. As a group, their investments included real estate (8 percent), U.S. bonds (2 percent), other bonds and stocks (45 percent), mortgage loans (31 percent), collateral loans (9 percent), premium loans (1 percent), and cash and other assets (4 percent). As we have seen with New England Mutual, investment policies of these life insurance companies varied widely. As a whole, however, insurance company investment was probably the most conservative of all financial intermediaries of that era, only slowly moving from one asset class to another over time, while bank investments during much of the nineteen century were, by comparison, the most dynamic.[21]

Commercial and Savings Banks, and Trust Companies

Before looking at the history of commercial banks in Boston, it is important to understand how very differently they operated from those of today. Under the laws of Massachusetts, as elsewhere, it was relatively easy to start a bank, and many were.[22] Their purpose was not to provide financial services for the general population but instead to provide services for the bank sponsors themselves or for local businessmen who would bring IOUs or notes to the bank where they were discounted. In discounting the note, the bank would take a percentage out of the note's value and advance to the borrower the rest on condition that the recipient paid off the entire note by the date of maturity. Notes usually could be renewed for an additional percentage fee and had to be endorsed by one or more parties, who would guarantee it if the borrower went into default.

In the early nineteenth century, there were essentially two types of notes. One was commercial paper, which was generated as part of a commercial transaction: a merchant might pay for the products he acquired from a manufacturer with a note (IOU), which he pledged to redeem after selling the goods. Having acquired the note from the manufacturer, the bank would collect payment from the merchant at maturity. The second type of note was an accommodation loan. In this case, the borrower drew up the note and acquired endorsements so that he could obtain credit from a bank to make improvements to plant or equipment, or for some other economic purpose. These notes were discounted by the bank, too, but unlike notes based on commercial paper, they were often renewed. In order to facilitate these transactions, banks created their own bank notes (non–interest bearing IOUs), which, in turn, became the principal form of a circulating medium at the time. Bank notes also got many banks into trouble during the periodic "panics" that plagued the U.S. economy in the nineteenth century. This situation happened less frequently in Boston, where bank notes were generally backed by a higher level of capitalization than in other cities or regions. Furthermore, Massachusetts required that its banks have half of their authorized capital in specie, and for the specie to remain in the bank, where it primarily served as a reserve against the banknotes issued by the bank.

During this period, local banks multiplied, and a substantial part of bank funds ended up in the hands of bank directors, who used them to finance their own personal investments. According to a nineteenth-century proverb, "Banks never originate with those who have money to lend, but with those who wish to borrow money." This insider lending practice was not then controversial and was widely practiced, so much so that one historian has referred to early banks in New England as "controlled directly by entrepreneurs" and functioning "more like investment clubs." Moreover, when investors bought bank stock, one of the principal equities of that period, they were "actually investing in the diversified enterprises of that institution's directors." Banks were at that time largely "vehicles for accumulating capital." All of this would, of course, change as the century progressed—especially as credit became more widely available, banks became strictly commercial institutions, customer deposits became more important in bank operations, and especially as the earnings from banks began to fall in the post–Civil War era due to poorer investment opportunities. As a result of these changes, Boston banks consolidated into larger entities to improve their fortunes and branch banking became more widespread.[23]

Commercial Banks

Like many of the financial institutions already noted, commercial banks were not a part of the Boston scene until after the Revolutionary War.[24] The Massachusetts General Court did not incorporate for another two years the first local bank, which was called the Massachusetts Bank, with authority to hold "£50,000 and no more, in lands, rents and tenements, and £500,000 and no more, in money, goods, chattels and effects [which] it was permitted to sell, grant and devise, alien or dispose of." Furthermore, the Massachusetts Bank could carry on any form of banking or mercantile business it might find desirable. The beginning of banking in Boston came at a critical time because, as one account has suggested, in 1790, about one-fourth of the U.S. population was "directly dependent upon Boston as their financial and commercial capital," and a part of the financial strength and stability of the region was due to the banking system, which would continue to develop throughout the nineteenth century.[25]

Further amendments to the Massachusetts Bank's charter included protection of bank stockholders from the malfeasance of its officers and employees, and a prohibition on the bank's making loans at rates in excess of 6 percent. The bank restricted loans to $3,000 for an individual. No one was allowed to owe the bank more than $5,000 at any one time or be liable as a promiser or endorser of more than $7,500. Notes could not be renewed, and those who failed to meet the bank's deadline were obligated to sell them immediately and then denied the ability to have any notes discounted for a period of time, unless allowed to do so by a unanimous vote of the directors.[26]

Despite such restrictions, the Massachusetts Bank quickly became "unduly profitable." By 1791, the bank's stock was returning 16 percent on its par value. Such results soon encouraged competition and the establishment of a rival, Union Bank, which was incorporated in 1792 with fixed capital of $1.2 million, or almost five times the amount of capital required when the Massachusetts Bank was incorporated. Between 1792 and 1815, as Boston changed from a shipping to a commercial economy, four other Boston banks were so chartered, including Boston Bank (later called "Old Boston"; 1803), State Bank (1812), New England Bank (1813), and Manufacturers and Mechanics Bank (later Tremont Bank; 1814), with combined authorized capital in the six banks of $8,550,000. During the same time frame, seven banks (plus the Bank of North America) were set up in Philadelphia, with a capitalization of $7,743,000; seven banks in New York City, with a total capitalization of $11,840,000; and eight banks in Baltimore, with a capitalization of $6,750,000. Boston was second only to New York City in capitalization for its banks, and rivaled the other Atlantic seaport communities in the number of its banks.[27]

During the antebellum years, Boston banks also began to develop a reputation as conservative and stable institutions that maintained their bank notes at parity with specie.[28] As one Boston bank president noted, "circulation based upon specie, and loans upon strictly mercantile paper, were two of the cardinal principles in the directors' system of banking." The U.S. Constitution had made it illegal for states to print their own money, but privately owned state banks could issue bank notes that were convertible to specie. While the four Boston banks in 1813 had a substantial specie reserve—$4.5 million in specie to $1.5 million in circulating bank notes—it became apparent by the 1810s that the rising number of local banks in other parts of the country, even distant places in New England, were of questionable solvency, particularly in times of economic downturn or depression. By 1824, all Boston banks except one had banded together to form the "Suffolk System" under which they paid the Suffolk

Bank a proportion of $300,000, based on their level of capitalization, to act as their agent for redeeming bills from outside banks by returning them to their place of origination for specie. The Suffolk System was the first of several private regulatory bodies that not only improved the efficiency of Boston banking but, importantly, also helped to instill a sense of public confidence in them.

Soon the system was expanded to include drafts and notes from banks outside of Boston. Like foreign exchange markets, these outside participating banks were each required to deposit $2,000 in specie at the Suffolk Bank and sufficient additional specie to redeem that bank's notes at par any that ended up in Boston. In both cases, participating banks received quick and reliable redemption of its notes, creating a higher level of stability, while Suffolk Bank paid no interest on those deposits, which it could lend to itself at no cost. By 1858, another organization, the Bank of Mutual Redemption, was created to serve as agent for the redemption of bills from all New England banks. Two years earlier, an additional improvement to make the exchange of banks' bills and checks more efficient was developed with the establishment of the Boston Clearing House, which began operations on March 29, 1858. Previously, banks had made daily settlements with each bank separately. Under the new arrangement, all settlements were made through the clearing house. The new facility established a one-day record of exchanges amounting to $31,321,877, which "were settled within an hour and the balances within a short time afterwards." Boston had the second oldest clearing house after New York's, and Boston's soon expanded from servicing twenty-nine to fifty-five Boston banks, and to forty-two Boston area banks by the early 1890s. By 1893, only one bank associated with the clearing house had failed.[29]

Nineteenth-century banks, including those in Boston, were exposed to periodic depressions, often due to overextensions by banks, land speculation, and other factors. By 1837, Boston had thirty-four banks, while the number in Massachusetts outside of Boston numbered ninety-five. Boston banks had $21,350,000 in capital, deposits of $6,560,000, and circulation of $4,386,414, compared with $16,930,000, $1,907,000, and $5,886,704, respectively, for out-of-Boston or "country" banks. During that year, the start of the longest and most serious depression in the nineteenth century, specie payments were suspended by Boston banks. At the same time, those banks created an ad hoc organization, the Associated Banks of Boston, to help maintain public confidence in the banking system. Conditions at most Boston banks were serious but not life-threatening. At the Shawmut Bank, for instance, assets declined by 25 percent to $660,000 during the first four months of the panic, barely allowing the institution enough to cover its operating expenses and pay a small dividend. While many carried on their business, over a dozen

Boston banks failed or had their charters revoked, many of them having been created in better times only a few years before the panic. One of the reforms of the period was increased regulation by the commonwealth, which created a Board of Bank Commissioners to help examine bank records and prevent bad bank practices while protecting depositors and holders of the banks' notes. By the Panic of 1857, banks performed much better; specie was suspended for only two months, and no Boston bank failed. Under the National Bank Law, enacted during the Civil War in 1863, every bank in Boston was encouraged to become (upon pain of a new tax on state bank notes) a national bank, with "national" in its name, by 1865 (fig. 6).[30]

Boston banks continued to do well during the Panic of 1873, difficulties in the mid-1880s, the depression of the early 1890s, and even the Panic of 1907, "which carried down numerous large New York banking institutions." During the 1884 panic, "Boston banks were in such a strong position when the storm broke that they passed through the crisis without recourse to clearing house certificates, whereas the New York banks were forced to issue them," Frederic H. Curtiss, Boston bank official and later chairman of the Boston Federal Reserve Bank, recalled. "In fact, the Boston banks were little affected, their general business being transacted on a more conservative basis and careful preparation having been made in anticipation of financial trouble, which had for months appeared inevitable." During the 1890s, the effects of the economic decline were relatively minimal in Boston. There were brief suspensions of specie but little more. Nevertheless, Boston banks did have by the 1890s one somewhat hidden difficulty, which had originated almost two decades earlier—a growing inability to invest their money locally and an increasing need to find more speculative loans elsewhere. As bank dividend and stock prices declined, it became more and more obvious by the end of the 1890s that Boston banks would need to be consolidated, a process that continued during the first three decades of the twentieth century.[31]

Savings Banks

Boston's first savings bank, sometimes called a mutual savings bank, was the Provident Institution for Savings in the Town of Boston. It was chartered by the Massachusetts legislature in December 1816 and opened its doors in February 1817. Although it was the first incorporated savings bank in the United States, the Philadelphia Savings Fund Association actually began business in November 1816. Other major nineteenth-century Boston savings banks included the Institution for Savings in Roxbury (1825), Warren Institution for Savings (1829), Suffolk Savings Bank for Seamen and Others (formerly the Saving Bank for Seamen in Boston, 1833), East Boston Savings Bank (1848),

STATE STREET IN 1855.

FIGURE 6. Samuel Rowse, *State Street in 1855* (Boston Athenaeum)

Boston Five Cents Savings Bank (1854), Charlestown Five Cents Savings Bank (1854), Franklin Savings Bank (1861), Brighton Five Cents Savings Bank (1861), South Boston Savings Bank (1863), Eliot Five Cents Savings Bank (1864), Boston Penny Savings Bank (1864), Home Savings Bank (1869), North End Savings Bank (1870), and the Wildey Savings Bank (1892), many of them surviving until relatively recent times.

The idea of savings banks became so popular that by 1892, there were 184 savings banks and institutions for savings in the commonwealth, with combined assets of $416 million, and 16 such banks in Boston, with combined assets of over $125 million at that time. Like these and other early savings banks, the Provident was set up to help the less fortunate members of Boston society, the "frugal poor," to save their money rather than wastefully spend it. In addition, and unlike Boston commercial banks, customers received regular dividends on their accounts. In many ways, this type of banking was an outgrowth of mutual benefit societies, part of a movement that transformed New England charity from the 1780s through the 1820s.[32]

While inspired by charitable impulses to become "the Interest Bankers for the poor," and with its first advertising broadside focused on "seamen bound on a voyage" as the kind of customers it sought, the founders nevertheless opened the Provident to all Bostonians on the theory that such a policy would help to provide the confidence needed to build the institution. This open door led to almost immediate success among all classes of Boston society, but soon forced the founders to impose various limitations on wealthier depositors to dampen their interest in the bank. Among other restrictions was a weekly limit on the size of deposits that customers could make, while another cut off the payment of dividends to balances of more than $500. The latter reservation was meant to encourage wealthier depositors to find other alternatives—to place their savings in the Massachusetts Hospital Life Insurance Company or "The Big Savings Bank," as it was sometimes called. The Provident originally paid dividends of 5 percent, which was soon reduced to 4 percent, on money in the depositor's account, an amount it believed it could maintain even in a challenging economic climate, while the remainder of the bank's earnings was parceled out to depositors whose accounts were over a year old in a distribution made every five years. While the extra dividend fluctuated with the times, it averaged about 6 percent. Those earnings increased rapidly from the early 1840s, when the Provident shifted its investment portfolio from short-term commercial bank loans with low earnings to highly profitable long-term loans to industry, which were given to individuals backed by personal security.[33]

This shift in investment policy was the product of the bank's more professional approach to investments and change in investment vehicles. By 1820, the bank had established a subcommittee, a "board of investment," which implemented the broader investment objectives of the bank's board of trustees. The investment subcommittee consisted of three trustees, a vice president, the president, and secretary, and was enlarged in the mid-1830s with three more trustees. By the 1840s, the Provident's officers, especially the president and treasurer, placed increasing reliance on the investment board for leadership in investment decisions. An early shift in the evolution at the Provident from benevolent institution to one run by professional management was an end to the restriction on the size of deposits. Led by the bank's officers, the board of trustees raised limits on deposits to $200,000 and then to $400,000, before removing all such size restrictions. As a result, the bank was opened to a larger group of potential wealthy depositors, who, in turn, provided the bank with more funds to use for investments.

As a small bank, the Provident could rely on Boston commercial banks to hold and invest its funds, but as the bank assets rose and investment alternatives grew, it sought new ways to invest its money. Focused on safe investments, it acquired bank stock and government bonds, and also made private loans. During the antebellum period, the Provident invested about a quarter to a third of its funds in local commercial bank stocks, known for their "reputation of conservatism and stability." Boston bank stocks did well, losing much less of their value in times of depression than bank stocks in other cities. The Suffolk Bank, for instance, had an average annual dividend of 11.5 percent from the late 1810s, when it was established, through the Civil War, while its dividend declined somewhat to 8.3 percent in the decade following the conflict. It also invested about one-fifth to one-quarter (and occasionally more) of its assets in federal government bonds, and by the 1830s, bonds of both Boston and Massachusetts. The third area of investment was in private loans, which fluctuated between about one-half to two-thirds of all assets in a given year. At the Provident (and many other Boston intermediaries), these were almost always long-term loans, some made to commercial banks with no security, others made to businesses on the signatures of officers and guarantors, and increasingly to manufacturing companies on commercial paper.

Significantly, outside of Boston the practice of granting such personal loans was regarded as "extremely risky," and such loans were not made, again showing how Boston's heritage of shipping and industry shaped investment decisions in the city. During the 1840s, manufacturing loans to textile mills grew, becoming about one-quarter of the Provident's assets by the 1850s. By 1858, mortgage loans, which had constituted little of the investment total twenty years earlier, accounted for about 35 percent of the bank's assets, while bank stocks and government bonds declined proportionately. Interestingly, even after restrictions on savings banks' owning shares of railroads or public utility companies were withdrawn, the Provident found it more secure and profitable to provide those companies with loans rather than buy their stocks.

Some thirty years later in the early 1890s, the Provident's investment portfolio changed again, reflecting primarily sedate and presumably more secure local investments. Of its $35.6 million in assets, $7.3 million was invested in city and town bonds, $1.3 million in bank stock, $3.8 million in railroad bonds, $10.6 million in mortgage loans, $10.6 million in collateralized private loans, and $2 million in miscellaneous items. Banks like the Provident were prohibited from charging more than 6 percent on loans as well as certain types of investment throughout most of the antebellum period, and were often limited to only investments in Massachusetts or New England—all restrictions that affected the postwar era as well. But combining a more specialized investment process and diversified investment portfolio, the Provident provides a good illustration of how a Boston intermediary made profitable investments in the nineteenth century.[34]

Trust Companies

While savings banks began in the early nineteenth century and expanded during the Civil War era, trust companies were largely a product of the late nineteenth century, though both institutions provided the long-term loans needed for investment purposes. Although the Massachusetts Hospital Life Insurance Company (1818) has been regarded by some as the first Boston trust company, the more routine development of trust companies began in 1869 with the establishment of the New England Trust Company. Six years later, the Boston Safe Deposit Company, which had been incorporated in 1867, to receive "on deposit for safekeeping" money securities, jewelry, plate, and other valuables, was given broader trust powers "to act as administrator, executor, and in other fiduciary relations" by the Massachusetts General Court, and was authorized to increase its capital stock to $1 million. Other trust companies were founded in Boston during this era, including the Massachusetts Loan and Trust Company (1870), International Trust Company (1879), Bay State Trust Company (1887), American Loan and Trust Company (1881), Old Colony Trust Company (1890), State Street Safe Deposit and Trust Company (1891), and Mattapan Deposit and Trust Company (1891).

Trust banks, acting as corporate fiduciaries, combined a trust business for a rising middle and upper class of customers with a banking department, which provided typical banking functions like checking accounts and loans. They served as savings banks for wealthier individuals, paying dividends on deposits on sums of $500 or more, as well as conducting trust functions, including receipt of money and property in trust from administrators, assignees, guardians, other trusts, corporations, and individuals. These banks also had the power to purchase securities for their customers, a business that started to grow after the turn of the twentieth century. In effect, they acted like a full-scale Boston trustee.

By the early 1890s, Boston trust companies had $62.6 million in deposits and $6.4 million in trust funds, the latter activity only a small portion of assets handled at that time by Boston trustees. Trust companies, however, would become important Boston financial institutions by the early twentieth century, until a number of the most significant ones became affiliated with Boston commercial banks from the late 1920s into the 1950s. The two most dominant Boston trust companies became Old Colony Trust, whose deposits quickly overshadowed its nearest rival, Boston Safe Deposit and Trust Company, by sevenfold. In more recent decades, some Boston trust companies have transformed themselves into commercial banks and then custodial banks (State Street Bank & Trust) or become broad financial services firms (Boston Safe

Deposit and Trust Company, which became the Boston Company in 1970, currently a wholly owned subsidiary of the Mellon Financial Corporation).[35]

The Boston Bank Merger Movement

By the late nineteenth century, Boston had achieved broad success as a stable and conservative home of investment, as demonstrated in the growth of its banking community for over a hundred years. In 1894, the sixty Boston national banks had $53,850,000 million in capital, $170,449,000 in deposits, and a surplus of $19,719,000 with combined resources of $258,848,000. In addition, the city's sixteen savings banks had deposits of $133,137,000 and a surplus of $7,160,000 with combined resources of $140,390,000. The city's eleven trust companies had $7,050,000 in capital, $53,205,000 in deposits, and $5,456,000 in surplus with a total of $74,260,000 in resources. The aggregate of resources for all of these institutions was close to half a billion dollars.[36]

Boston banks had done well as a whole in attracting assets for investment, but by the 1870s, they had begun to find it difficult to invest their money locally and had to rely on more speculative investments elsewhere. In short, there was too much capital for the commercial needs of Boston, which, in turn, made loans cheap and created a limited return on investment. As a result, bank profits plummeted, declining 50 percent between 1871–1875 and 1896–1900. Besides too much money, there were also too many banks, which created too much competition for good loans in Boston for a city its size. With a population of 450,000, Boston had 62 banks with capital of $76 million, whereas New York had 1.5 million people but only 40 banks and $48.35 million in capital. At the same time, Boston trust companies continued to grow in number, and because of their broader charter rights, they became competitors to the national banks. Over the same three decades, bank stock prices and dividends began to fall, and by the 1890s, the principal holders of those stocks, the Massachusetts savings banks, were seeking ways to help improve their value.[37]

While it was unclear that a reduction in the number of banks through consolidation would necessarily improve stock prices and dividends, Massachusetts savings banks, which owned $20 of $50 million of the capital in Boston's commercial banks, sought to merge a number of them. The savings banks, working through a committee they created, signed a formal agreement with Kidder, Peabody to organize an underwriting syndicate that would liquidate the banks' shares in nine of the Boston banks, and reorganize them into an enlarged and reorganized Shawmut National Bank. By the standards of the day, these banks had demonstrated poor financial performance, paying out, with a couple of exceptions, no more than 6 percent in dividends during the previous five years. The new bank, which was reborn as the National Shawmut Bank, was to have between $3 and $5 million in capital compared with its predecessors, which had a total of $8,550,000. Other well-known Boston investment banking firms involved with the underwriting included Lee, Higginson & Company, F. S. Moseley & Company, and R. L. Day & Company. Even though the plan ran into difficulties with some of the targeted banks, and a public that saw the move as both arbitrary and a "gigantic speculation," the merger ultimately proved successful (though the consolidation process was not fully completed until 1907). The new National Shawmut rivaled Merchants Bank, the largest bank in Boston during much of the nineteenth century, eventually surpassing it by 1899. Soon it was "twice as large as the next in size." By way of contrast, Shawmut National was in 1865 only twenty-fourth in assets among the city's forty-two banks.[38]

The consolidation set out to curb the "excess in competition," or, more directly, the "excess in banking capital." The process continued on and strengthened so that by 1910, the number of operating commercial banks had declined to twenty-three compared with sixty in 1895, while the number of trust companies rose from fifteen to twenty-three over the same period. Moreover, average assets in Boston banks and trust companies nearly tripled from $4.3 to $11.7 million between 1895 and 1910, while the ratio of deposits to capital was in excess of 1,000 percent. Earnings, the catalyst for the consolidation movement, improved dramatically as they increased some 63 percent between 1891–1900 and 1901–1910 in Boston national banks (including Shawmut). The rate of return at Shawmut, in particular, rose to 9.3 percent in 1901–1910. compared with 5.7 percent during the period 1886–1895.[39]

This era of consolidation led to fewer competing banks, greater economies of scale, and larger banks, which allowed the remaining institutions greater opportunities to get into more lucrative sectors of the credit market. As these banks grew, they also sought more professionalized boards of directors and presidents, including such individuals as Daniel G. Wing, who became president of the merged Massachusetts National and First National Bank of Boston in 1903. Wing, an outsider from Nebraska, was a member of a prominent Midwest banking family, and had also served as a national bank examiner and as the receiver of two failed Boston banks before he was elected to head the new First National, generally known as "The First." Yet despite the positive developments of the merger era, the consolidation and growth of larger banks in Boston also led to increasing conservatism in lending. Banks increasingly ignored new industries, concentrating on loans to old and proven but declining businesses. That situation would not turn around until the depression and World War II, when a few of the larger banks—The First, Merchants, and

National Shawmut—began to offer capital in the form of business loans, which soon grew and became a nascent form of venture capital.[40]

Throughout the first three decades of the twentieth century, some Boston banks failed while many others merged into larger institutions. From this process, at least four major banks emerged to help define the city's banking community until the closing decades of the twentieth century. During the first decade of the twentieth century, a few other Boston banks failed, while in 1903, the Massachusetts National Bank, Boston's oldest bank, acquired First National Bank, an old conservative bank that had recently been under the control of a speculative traction promoter, and took its name. After 1900, trust companies rose in numbers and entered commercial banking. The Old Colony Trust Company surpassed its rivals in size and expanded from its fiduciary and personal account business to commercial activities, as did Boston Safe Deposit and Trust and the New England Trust Company, which in turn led to more consolidations among national banks. During the 1910s and 1920s, these trends continued with consolidation among banks, especially the trust companies; increased competition; and growth in deposits (see table 1). At the same time, national banks, under the Federal Reserve Act of 1913, were allowed to serve as trustees, executors, and administrators of trust funds, duties from which they had previous been excluded. By April 1915, National Shawmut received permission from the Federal Reserve to set up a separate trust department. Many other Boston national commercial banks soon followed suit.

As the number of banks decreased, some of them became more important while others declined in prominence. Merchants Bank, which had been the largest commercial bank through the latter half of the nineteenth century, remained an important institution but declined in size. By the beginning of the last century, that spot had been taken by National Shawmut, which by 1910 had capital of about $19 million and deposits of $74 million. By 1920, however, under the leadership of Wing, First National, with capital of $36.6 million and deposits of $165,115,000, surpassed it in size. By the end of the 1920s, First National had become the fifth largest national bank in the country, and by 1932 the tenth largest U.S. bank in terms of deposits. Meanwhile, the Boston Five Cents Saving Bank, with deposits of $60.3 million and a surplus fund of $4.3 million, was the largest mutual savings bank.[41]

As banks grew larger, they also became more associated with their clients or the types of businesses they serviced. By 1907, for instance, First National was identified with the United Fruit Company and the United Shoe Machinery Company, two of the city's leading businesses. Banks also started looking to find new fields of business to help set them apart. As the United States shifted from a debtor to a creditor nation at the time of World War I, First National,

TABLE 1. Growth of Boston Banking, 1880–1930
(\$ in millions)

YEAR	NATIONAL BANKS			TRUST COMPANIES			MUTUAL SAVINGS BANKS			TOTAL FOR ALL BANKS		
	NO.	CAPITAL FUNDS	DEPOSITS	NO.	CAPITAL FUNDS	DEPOSITS	NO.	CAPITAL FUNDS	DEPOSITS	NO.	CAPITAL FUNDS	DEPOSITS
1880	54	\$36	\$107	3	\$1	\$9	15	\$2	\$68	72	\$66	\$184
1890	56	\$71	\$144	9	\$9	\$32	14	\$5	\$111	79	\$85	\$287
1900	38	\$58	\$206	16	\$19	\$85	17	\$9	\$166	71	\$86	\$467
1910	20	\$52	\$249	23	\$40	\$181	19	\$16	\$238	62	\$108	\$668
1920	13	\$87	\$439	28	\$69	\$449	22	\$24	\$354	63	\$180	\$1,242
1930	9	\$164	\$996	18	\$50	\$215	22	\$47	\$598	49	\$261	\$1,809

Source: Frederick H. Curtiss, "Fifty Years of Boston Finance, 1880–1930," in *Fifty Years of Boston: A Memorial Volume Issued in Commemoration of the Tercentenary of 1930,* ed. Elisabeth M. Herlihy (Boston: Subcommittee on Memorial History of the Boston Tercentenary Committee, 1932), 246.

for instance, opened its first foreign branch in Buenos Aires, Argentina, in 1917. This was followed in 1923 with a second branch in Cuba, and agencies in London, Paris, and Berlin. By 1927, it claimed to have "foreign correspondents [at] more than 21,000 foreign banks and bankers and is today one of the leading international banks in the world." By contrast, while National Shawmut also set up its own "Foreign Department," it established the Shawmut Corporation of Boston for international banking, and invested in international businesses like the Caribbean Sugar Company after World War I. At the same time, it continued its long-term interest in textile, shoe, leather, wool, cotton, and railroad industries, which remained important, though declining, until the 1930s. Shawmut also found new ones in the underwriting of, among others, telephone and utility company securities, which came largely through its close relationship with Kidder, Peabody. With little demand for commercial loans, other Boston banks set up affiliated corporations to underwrite and distribute securities, including those of the First National Bank (1919), Atlantic Corporation (1924), Old Colony Corporation (1926), and others. These institutions were separated from commercial banks during the depression. Following the McFadden Act of 1927, some Boston commercial banks and trust companies affiliated through the joint ownership of stock, with the commercial bank taking over the commercial business of the trust company, and the trust company taking over the fiduciary business of the commercial bank. One example of this occurred in 1929 when the First National Bank acquired the Old Colony Trust Company.[42]

Besides broader horizons, Boston banks during the early twentieth century became Boston's financial leaders and "a close-knit group and relatively few in number." As a result, there was "a high level of effectiveness when they decided to work together, and it led to a vast number of 'interlocks,'" which largely remained in place until several decades into the post–World War II era.[43]

The Decline of Investment Banking in Boston

During the nineteenth and early twentieth centuries, there were few investment banking houses in the United States better known than Boston's Lee, Higginson & Company, and Kidder, Peabody. John C. Lee, from the prominent Salem shipping family, and George Higginson, his cousin by marriage, founded the former in May 1848 to "offer their services in the purchase and sale of stocks, notes, and exchange," and took a "room recently occupied by the Eagle Bank, No. 47 State Street." Over the next quarter century, the firm grew as a stock brokerage house. In the meantime, it established an interest in foreign exchange, which soon brought it into a growing relationship with London's Baring Brothers. By 1907, Lee, Higginson had its own London office. It was also responsible for building the first safety deposit vaults in Boston, becoming "the principal depository of all securities in the city and a model for other vaults throughout the United States."[44]

After the Civil War, Lee, Higginson, like other Bostonian brokerage/investment bankers, found opportunities in the Midwest in railroads, minerals, and oil, and through the issuance of government bonds. By 1868, the firm included Henry Lee Higginson, George's son, also known as the "Major," who later founded the Boston Symphony Orchestra, and whose brothers-in-law Quincy Adams Shaw and Alexander Agassiz were developing the rich Calumet and Hecla copper mines in northern Michigan. "Our office was a sort of headquarters for the property," the Major later wrote, "and our friends bought a great many shares." By the early 1870s, the firm had turned to financing western railroads, and it remained virtually unscathed in the Panic of 1873 because of its solid investments, its close ties "to a select group of Boston investors, including the officers and directors of various New England financial institutions," and money it could raise in London. During the last forty years of the nineteen century, Lee, Higginson, along with Kidder, Peabody and a small number of New York firms, "occupied a commanding position in American investment banking."[45]

During the late nineteen and early twentieth centuries, Lee, Higginson made public offerings of American Bell Telephone Company, organized in 1880, which became the American Telephone & Telegraph Company, with over half of its shares sold to Boston investors.[46] Lee, Higginson also formed syndicates and distributed bonds for some thirty public service or utility companies then being established throughout the United States. In 1892, it helped to merge the Thomson-Houston Electric Company, a client of many years, and the Edison Electric Company, a J. P. Morgan client, into the holding company known as the General Electric Company. After the turn of the century, Lee, Higginson expanded to Chicago and New York, and developed a trained sales force (no longer just "counter men") to deal with a rising group of smaller investors. This raising large sums of money for new ventures was a departure from the previous fifty years. The sales force was under the direction of James J. Storrow, a Bostonian with Lee and Higginson family connections, who would become a leader of the next generation of the company. Storrow also became involved in developing a syndicate to finance William Durant's General Motors Company, a collection of over twenty companies including the Buick Motor Car Company, which Durant formed in 1908. Storrow served for several years as chairman of the trustees that took over the ailing General Motors and raised the $15 million (then $9 million more) needed to help reorganize it and develop its distribution system.[47]

While still retaining its Boston offices, by the 1920s, Lee, Higginson and Kidder, Peabody had shifted their investment banking operations to New York. In its new location, Lee, Higginson became known for underwriting industrial companies, such as United Fruit, Goodyear Tire and Rubber, Shell Union Oil, Victor Talking Machines, International Paper Company, United Drug, National Leather, and Phillips Petroleum. During the 1920s, Lee, Higginson also financed and distributed shares of Ivar Kreuger's International Match Corporation, which, founded by the international financier Kreuger, the so-called Swedish Match King, sought to create a worldwide match monopoly. Lee, Higginson sold millions of dollars of these securities to investors, trust companies, and banks. In 1932, however, as his holding company fell apart, Kreuger committed suicide, and a month later examination of his companies' records showed he had risen through embezzlement, forgery, and swindling. The consequences were particularly serious in Europe, where banks in Germany and Austria failed, the price of silver collapsed, and gold was shifted from one country to another—all contributing to further instability in a worsening depression. Closer to home, the news quickly affected his principal U.S. bank, Lee, Higginson, which went bankrupt shortly thereafter. It was soon revealed that Lee, Higginson had neither conducted an independent audit of Kreuger's main company, Kreuger & Toll, nor examined the value and quality of Kreuger's pledged capital, including what he substituted for the capital he had originally pledged. In effect, Lee, Higginson failed to look after its own interests or that of its clients when it came to the Kreuger securities.

Although Lee, Higginson was soon reorganized, and restricted its work to the issuing and distribution of securities, it was never the investment banking powerhouse it had once been. Its reputation was the foundation of its business, and having lost that reputation, it could never regain it. Perhaps the most telling aspect of the firm's change of fortune was the decision to locate the main headquarters of the reorganized company in New York, while Boston became only a branch office.[48] Almost twenty years later, Boston social critic and newspaper man Louis Lyons looked back and described the impact of Lee, Higginson's demise on the Boston financial community: "The once tight financial hegemony of State Street has been sorely defeated. Lee, Higginson Company fell apart over Kruger and Toll, the Swedish match monopoly that crashed with the cosmic swindle and subsequent suicide of Kruger, ruining half the doctors on Marlborough Street. When the squat, pillared edifice of Lee, Higginson was torn down to make a parking space, an era of State Street ended. No two names were more potent in the financial world than Lee and Higginson."[49]

The situation for Kidder, Peabody, another Boston investment bank, was also dire following the stock market crash, but it had a much better out-come—with a Boston twist. Successor to the brokerage firm of J. E. Thayer & Brother, which was founded in 1824, Kidder, Peabody had established an international reputation during the late nineteenth century as Boston's leading banking house. During its heyday, it expanded its foreign exchange and trade credit businesses, financed western railroads and technology companies like General Electric and American Telephone & Telegraph. It also was able to participate in nearly all major financial undertakings because of its close working relationships with Baring Brothers in London and J. P. Morgan in New York. After the turn of the century and in particular following World War I, though, the firm's position began to wane as financing of large-scale enterprise shifted to New York, its client base narrowed, and it began to lose out to more aggressive New York investment bankers. While Kidder, Peabody carried on successfully during the 1920s, and actually expanded its retail sales organization geographically, once the stock market collapsed and asset values fell, the firm was unable to cover investor withdrawals and soon found itself insolvent. During the 1920s, it had also succumbed to some of the new ways of Wall Street by becoming involved in setting up an "acceptance corporation," an organization originally designed to provide commercial credit, but one that came to be used to launch its own high-leverage closed-end trusts, which, following the crash, sank faster than the market as a whole.[50]

The firm's salvation came from a variety of sources, including its rival but close associate, J. P. Morgan. The House of Morgan arranged a loan in which it and Chase National Bank each contributed $2.5 million, while another $5 million was raised by three New York and four Boston banks. All of this was contingent upon finding another $5 million from among Kidder, Peabody clients or friends. After closer inspection of the firm's declining assets, even more was needed. While a group of Boston businessmen made a sizeable contribution, the major impact was made by Edwin S. Webster, a firm client and the cofounder of the Boston-based engineering company Stone & Webster. Webster was more than familiar with investment banking as his own firm had set up such services for its own clients, for whom Stone & Webster constructed and operated electrical generation and distribution facilities. In time, the Morgan firm would ask Webster to reorganize Kidder, Peabody.

Webster ended up contributing $1.6 million in cash and another $3.56 million in Stone & Webster stock, while his son-in-law Chandler Hovey committed $425,000, and a young former Goldman, Sachs employee, Harvard-trained and Boston native Albert Gordon, put in $100,000. Gordon was the classmate of Edwin S. Webster Jr. at Harvard Business School a decade earlier, and although the elder Webster had intended to have his son jointly manage the company, a severe injury prevented the young Webster from taking on responsibilities for several years. In the meantime, Hovey managed the Boston office while Gordon, then not yet thirty years of age and with little investment banking experience, took over the New York office, which would now become the headquarters for the firm.

The new managers quickly reduced the size of their offices, from 170 to 100 in Boston, and 300 to 150 in New York, and narrowed the focus of the firm to the selling and distribution of securities (and later a commission and bond-trading business), leaving other formerly profitable activities in foreign exchange, letters of credit, and trusts for others. By late 1931, the new Kidder, Peabody had, at the suggestion of J. P. Morgan, also acquired a New York brokerage and banking firm, which provided important good will for the firm's redirected business as well as income from new clients, and left Gordon with more time to focus on business creation. Gordon and others also sought ways to stem the firm's declining business and continuing portfolio losses, which remained high. While there were few major underwritings in the early 1930s, New Deal legislation soon provided at least one unexpected opportunity for the rejuvenated company. Following the passage of the Glass-Steagall Banking Act of 1933, commercial banks were forced to end their investment, trading, and underwriting activities. This, in turn, provided Kidder, Peabody with a supply of securities specialists for the restructured firm, and allowed Gordon and others to focus on selling and distribution. As Gordon later noted, "We felt that if we were to recover the standing of Kidder, Peabody, we would have to do something new and that was build a securities distribution capability. This was a time of retrenchment on Wall Street and we took advantage of it."

Gordon also realized that Kidder, Peabody could not be the underwriter of former days, at least for the foreseeable future, so he sought to participate in syndicates that were managed by other firms. Kidder worked hard at becoming an originator for the issues of small companies with growth potential, which were usually ignored by other major distributors. Gordon likewise worked hard to develop a national distribution channel through the establishment of local sales branches in key cities. Although the new Kidder, Peabody had difficult years in the early 1930s, and its profits were wiped out in the 1937 downturn, the firm gradually rebuilt its business, which grew to include private placement financings on the eve of World War II. With most of its senior management left intact during the war, it was well positioned to take advantage of opportunities in the prosperous postwar era with two New York–based Bostonians, Edwin Webster Jr. and particularly Al Gordon, at the helm.[51]

The histories of these two Boston houses epitomize the story of investment banking in Boston: they rivaled any company, including those in New York, during the nineteenth century because they invested in manufacturing, mining, and railroads—the growth industries of the day. Indeed, even during the era of great consolidations and mergers at the end of the nineteenth century and beginning of the twentieth, Boston houses and capital were actively involved in many of the most important of them, such as the Chicago Union Stockyards, American Sugar Refining, Westinghouse, P. Lorillard, United Fruit, New England Cotton Yarn, and U.S. Smelting, Refining and Mining. By 1900, however, the underwriting and syndication of newer, large-scale industrial enterprises was coming from New York, and Boston firms felt compelled to open offices there to be a part of the activity.

Ironically, investment banking in Boston reached its heyday in a spurt of activity from about 1900 to the middle or end of World War II, but it was not from the corporate world but rather in the underwriting of municipal bonds for cities and towns across the country. During that period, probably as many as fifty brokerage/investment banking firms in Boston were involved, combining their underwriting and brokerage functions in financing and then selling these securities. In this smaller pool of investment opportunities through underwriting, Boston commercial banks like Shawmut, and trust companies such as the Old Colony Trust Company, were also active, while others like First National developed affiliated investment banking corporations to make offerings until they were dismantled in the New Deal legislation of the 1930s. Nevertheless, by the 1920s, only Kidder, Peabody and Lee, Higginson could be considered houses with a national distribution system as well as the ability to originate major issues and underwrite them. As events following the crash played out, Boston investment banking houses of their proportions came to an end. And unlike in New York, the events of that era also reconfirmed Boston as more a buyer of investment products than a seller.[52]

CHAPTER 5

Developing New Investment Ideas, Information, and Services in Boston

Testamentary trusts or trusts under a will had become a way of life by mid-nineteenth century Boston, and they also acknowledged the pervasiveness and influence of the Boston trustee at the time. During much of the nineteenth century, however, the trust in Massachusetts developed in other ways and was slowly evolving into what became the Massachusetts business trust, a new and important investment vehicle. While this trust was first used in the 1890s, its popularity did not expand until after World War I with the rise of interest in investing by the general public, in Boston and elsewhere. By 1924, the Massachusetts business trust was used to create the Massachusetts Investors Trust (M.I.T.), the first open end "Boston-type" mutual fund.

As these developments were taking place, Boston's role in the business and investment world also attracted a number of individuals who became pioneers in the collection and publication of business and investment news, information, and data. One of them, Clarence W. Barron, acquired and saved the struggling Dow Jones Company, which had only recently started publication of *The Wall Street Journal*. Boston also attracted numerous young men, many just out of college, like Roger Babson, who invented new investment services. Another young college graduate in Boston tinkered with an idea that eventually became investment counsel. The idea, which had originated in Boston in the 1910s and early 1920s, soon spread across the country and helped to build the investment profession. A few years later in 1924, three men in Boston created the first mutual fund by means of a deed of trust, a concept developed in the 1890s and sanctioned by law in Massachusetts in the 1910s. Boston had become an unusually fertile place for investment ideas and services.

From Voluntary Associations and Copartnerships to Investment Trusts: The Evolution of the Massachusetts Business Trust

As noted in chapter 3, although no equity jurisdiction existed in colonial Massachusetts, equity powers were gradually added to Massachusetts courts throughout the early 1800s, first in the field of trusts and then expanding to other areas. At the same time, there was a parallel or corresponding rise throughout the commonwealth of "voluntary," nonincorporated business associations, which passed through a period where they were known as partnerships before some of them were further distinguished as Massachusetts business trusts.

The evolution of that latter development is a somewhat complex puzzle, not altogether clear but possible to piece together. It started in the postrevolutionary era with the persistent and unique way Massachusetts created business corporations. Like many other transitions after 1776, the power to incorporate various enterprises moved from the British Crown to the state legislatures. The Massachusetts General Court took its power of incorporation as a serious prerogative, and over the next five decades from 1780 to 1830, the legislature incorporated more business corporations than states such as New York and Pennsylvania with much larger populations. But the incorporation movement, which crested in the mid-1830s, was accomplished only through the passage of special legislative acts in each individual case—a tedious, long, and competitive process that was largely confined to banking, insurance, and public utility (including transportation) enterprises. And although Massachusetts was at the locus of American industrial development in the early 1800s, it did not end, or rather slow down, the practice of required special legislation until a general incorporation law was enacted in 1851.[1]

During the early decades after 1780, most charters were handed out to various governmental entities—towns, districts, parishes, and so forth—that is, to "municipal corporations" as known in English law. The work of the General Court, however, increasingly involved what gradually became known as business or private corporations, which, with little English law to draw upon, became largely the province of new and developing American law. While some acts of special legislation provided corporations with immunity from nuisance suits, or gave them eminent domain powers or a monopoly to run a railroad between two locations, those powers could also be taken away. Furthermore, there was no uniformity of privileges bestowed from charter to charter. More importantly, the charters did not provide corporations with important special powers like limited liability.

Indeed, the full significance of incorporation law did not begin to take shape until after the *Dartmouth College* case in 1819, in which the U.S. Supreme Court held that the corporate charter was an inviolable contract and prohibited state legislatures from interfering with chartered rights of private corporations. To make the process of incorporation in postrevolutionary Massachusetts even more inscrutable, there was no correlation between incorporation and the number of new enterprises, the scale or scope of the enterprise, or the people involved in incorporated or unincorporated enterprises.[2]

Since incorporation offered few advantages to a private corporation's shareholders in the 1820s, is it easy to understand why nonincorporated, private, but voluntary associations were used to make a profit for partners. Business trusts (i.e., an entity created by agreement of its partners) were common in all but name in Boston in the early nineteenth century in many areas of commerce. For instance, the proportion of mercantile partnerships engaged in overseas trade increased from 31 to 38 percent from 1800 to 1820, before it dropped in succeeding decades. By 1840, however, a quarter of Boston craftsmen and manufacturers were involved in partnerships, and the number of them was rising in relation to the total population. In all, the ratio of partnerships to all individuals working in occupations rose modestly over the antebellum decades, starting at 5.5 percent in 1800, exceeding 7 percent by 1840, and then dropping to 5.7 percent by 1860, despite the population growth of the era. Although a small percentage, it represented a significant and constant number of individuals in the community over time.[3]

While these partnerships were small, generally involving just over two individuals on average, they did practice and maintain certain formalities and constraints—partnership agreements, a fixed period of life for the partnership, procedures for termination, and, like corporations of the time, no limited liability.[4] This was all accomplished without going through the rigid, time-consuming process of incorporation by special legislation. And while these small partnerships had few legal advantages over single proprietorships, they offered the partners an opportunity to avoid long-term relationships of dependence, and provided young men with the opportunity of leaving partnerships after a certain period of time if they so desired. Additional evidence seems to suggest that, as opposed to other areas of the country, New England partnerships, which extended into major manufacturing concerns, were more likely to have multiple ownership, as new partners could be tapped to supply additional capital for the enterprise.[5]

The voluntary association/partnership had other benefits unavailable to corporations. Corporations were prohibited from developing, holding, managing, or leasing real estate, and the legislature refused to grant charters for

real estate, which probably led to the growth of real estate trusts in the nineteenth century. Furthermore, corporations had specific minimum and maximum capitalizations, which could severely handicap various kinds of enterprises, and the commonwealth required corporations to make onerous annual
filings of its assets and liabilities. These were all reasons why a merchant, a
small manufacturing partnership, or even a large mill enterprise would likely
avoid the incorporation route for their businesses. And so, while voluntary
associations, created by agreement among people who capitalized an enterprise and acquired transferable shares of ownership in it, were common in
Massachusetts by the late eighteenth and early nineteenth centuries, such
forms did not appear in the law until 1827.[6]

In that year, an obscure case argued in the Massachusetts Supreme Judicial
Court called *Alvord* v. *Smith* was decided involving a distillery in western
Massachusetts owned by partners who had signed a copartnership (occasionally also called a coproprietorship) agreement. Gaius Alvord had sold his share
in the distillery to the two defendants—Zebina Smith, who was the "clerk of
the proprietors," and Ralph Morgan—on condition that they would pay "any
arrearages which were then or might thereafter become due from him, as one
of the proprietors." Nevertheless, Alvord ended up paying for arrearages that
were supposed to be paid by the new proprietors. The result of the case hinged
on when the sale actually took place, which the court determined occurred at
the initial discussion and agreement, not when the share certificate was phys-
ically conveyed, thus giving Alvord the victory. The court further stated that
"we think the certificate not material to the sale, for although by the articles
of association it is provided that certificates should be made and filed by the
clerk, yet this is for the convenience of the company, and the omission of it
cannot prevent the right of an owner to sell his interest."[7]

While the outcome of the case was hardly dramatic, it helped to lay out some
of the elements of the voluntary association/partnership that would reappear
in other cases later in the century. It was duly noted that Alvord and others had
"formed an association in 1817, by an agreement under seal, for the purpose of
setting up and carrying on a distillery." Shareholders had provided the capital
for "the distillery, land and buildings connected therewith," and were free to
sell their shares to others through the office of the clerk of the proprietors, or,
more informally, as the court stated, simply by the action of a buyer and seller.

Massachusetts courts continued to view voluntary associations/partner-
ships as distinct from corporations over the next sixty years. In one Civil War–
era case, the court noted that "the originators of this scheme have endeavored
to avail themselves of the advantages of a corporation, under an association
as partners."[8] But it was not until the 1870s before the tax consequences of

these organizations generated actions before Massachusetts courts in larger numbers. In 1885, for instance, in *Ricker* v. *American Loan & Trust Company,* a case concerning taxation of an association set up to buy, sell, and lease railroad rolling stock, the Massachusetts Supreme Judicial Court held that "there is no intermediate form of organization between a corporation and a partnership, like the joint stock companies of England and of some of the United States, known to the laws of this Commonwealth. Since this association is not a corporation, its members must be partners," and not co-owners.[9]

In 1890, the Massachusetts courts recognized a third organization somewhere between a corporation and partnership, yet containing many of the same elements as a voluntary association, which later became known as the Massachusetts business trust. As in the previous cases discussed above, partnerships had been set up with transferable shares under a declaration of trust, but in *Mayo* v. *Moritz,* the court ruled that the organization in question was not a partnership but a business trust: "The deed of trust does not have the effect to make the scrip-holders partners. It does not contemplate the carrying on of a partnership business upon the joint account of the grantor and the scrip-holders, and in this respect the case is unlike Gleason *v.* McKay, 134 Mass. 419, and Phillips *v.* Blatchford, 137 Mass. 510. The scrip-holders are *cestuis que trust,* and are entitled to their share of the avails of the property when the same is sold."[10] In this case, an inventor by means of a deed of trust assigned his invention to trustees, who then managed it and sold scrip (shares) to investors, including themselves and copartners. When the trustees failed to pay a bill, however, the inventor sought to find out the names and addresses of the copartners so that they could be made parties in the case.

The court decided in favor of the trustees by neither requiring them to disclose the names and addresses of all of the copartners nor making them pay for the debt, because the rules to reach the debtors' property were not applicable when dealing with the property of a trust. The court's position on the role and power of the trustees also established another significant change: there was no association of shareholders in this case, just a common interest among them, as in an ordinary trust. The journey from partnership and voluntary association to business trust had taken more than sixty years to complete, but it was well established by 1890 and became more firmly set in place in the decades thereafter.[11]

The outcome of *Mayo* had a strong and almost immediate impact on the development of the Massachusetts business trust. As noted earlier, Massachusetts law forbade the incorporation of organizations that dealt with real estate, so organizations that invested in real estate had been set up as trusts. *Mayo,* however, likely emboldened some to expand on the concept. Three years after the decision, the Boston Personal Property Trust was formed by a group of trustees, who included John Quincy Adams, Moses Williams, William Minot, Abbott Lawrence Lowell, and Robert Sedgwick Minot, many of whom were also Boston trustees. The trust made investments in real estate "in the cities of the United States of America, for the purpose of leasing the same upon long terms, or ground rents" and held "bonds and notes or obligations secured upon real estate." Before long, it became the model of the Massachusetts business trust, and a similar arrangement was applied in many areas of investment and commerce.[12]

The trust contained features already found in voluntary associations, as well as others that would be common some thirty-one years later with the creation of the first mutual fund. The declaration of trust gave all funds and property to the trustees "for the benefit of the Cestuis Que Trustent, and it is hereby expressly declared that a trust, and not a partnership, is hereby created." In other words, neither the trustees nor the Cestuis Que Trustent or the trusts' beneficiaries would be personally liable as partners would be in a partnership. Furthermore, the trustees had "full power and discretion, as if absolute owners, to invest and reinvest the Trust Fund." They had power to "sell, transfer, and convey . . . any part or all of said Trust Fund," and "absolute control over and power to dispose of all real estate." They could borrow money and mortgage the trust's real estate, and sign contracts, conveyances, and transfers relating to the fund. The eighteen articles in the trust included an initial selection of a depository—State Street Safe Deposit & Trust Company, which would later be the same custodian for the first mutual fund—to keep the trust's documents and records, and it included a provision that allowed the trustees "from time to time [to] hire suitable offices for the transaction of the business of the Trust, appoint, remove or reappoint such officers or agents . . . as they may think best, define their duties, and fix their compensation." The trustees decided and declared on at least a quarterly basis the dividends for the beneficiaries from the net income of the trust, and decided whether brokers' and agents' commissions were to be charged against income or capital. They were responsible for distributing an annual accounting to the beneficiaries. The trustees were a self-perpetuating body, and as trustees either died or retired, their vacancies were filled by the remaining trustees. Finally, the trustees could increase the size of the trust by accepting additional cash or property.

While about half of the trust's provisions dealt with the duties, powers, and liabilities of the trustees, the others focused on the beneficiaries. If "any *Cestui Que Trust* neglects to pay any installment within the time specified," that person might forfeit previous payments. Beneficiaries were issued certificates for each $1,000 they paid into the trust fund, and were issued scrip for each $100, which could be converted into certificates when scrip amounted to $1,000.

Beneficiaries could sell their certificates "at not more than the last preceding appraisal made by them" to the trustees, who could then reissue those interests to a new beneficiary. If trustees failed to acquire them within ten days after being offered them in writing, beneficiaries apparently could sell their interests on their own. Beneficiaries also had the right to inspect the books of the trust. The trust terminated twenty years after the death of the last survivor of a list of twenty individuals, presumably all beneficiaries, noted in the document. At that time, the trust could be terminated, and the proceeds would go to the beneficiaries "being first duly indemnified for any outstanding obligation or liability, and shall thereupon be forever discharged."[13]

The Boston Personal Property Trust contained all the features that would later be associated with the mutual fund. The trustees were "masters" or owners of the trust property, making all of the decisions and acting as a self-perpetuating body. Investors, by their purchase of certificates, scrip, or shares, received dividends on a quarterly or more frequent basis, and could sell their interest within a short period at the last appraised rate, akin to what is now referred to as a mutual fund's net asset value (NAV). Beneficiaries also received annual reports on the financial health of the trust. Assets of the Boston Personal Property Trust grew from about $104,000 in 1893 to about $2.8 million in 1928, when the number of shareholders reached 550. During this period, it paid dividends varying between 4 and 8 percent, with a dividend of 50 percent in 1902.[14]

It would be some time before the Massachusetts business trust as exemplified in the Boston Personal Property Trust would be used to form investment trust companies. But because, unlike corporations, the business trust had no maximum capitalization, it soon became a popular form of organization for many enterprises, such as street railway companies and gas and electric utility companies. A young local securities salesman at the time, Roger Babson noted that many street railways were consolidated under the Massachusetts Electric Companies, a trust created to acquire shares in street railway and other companies. The legislature had passed laws against the incorporation of holding companies for railroad, street railways, and public utilities to prevent the sale of often scandal-ridden securities they would offer: "The most conservative and aristocratic law firms, however, quickly got around this legislation by forming 'trusts.' The special trust in question was named 'Massachusetts Electric Companies.' Instead of a *company* being incorporated, a *trust* was organized, and the swellest blue-bloods of Boston became the trustees of the Massachusetts Electric Companies. Common stock and four-per-cent preferred stock were issued. This later sold at par and was bought by the most conservative investors because of a non-taxable feature and the names which appeared as trustees."[15] Investment companies would later have much in common with both real estate trusts and utility holding companies, in that all three pooled their assets and trustees issued dividends derived from their management of those assets. Furthermore, none of these trusts actively operated a business or engaged in a trade.

Despite its popular success, the Massachusetts business trust was attacked in the legislature and courts. In 1912, the legislature directed the state tax commissioner to investigate voluntary associations that did business under "a written instrument or declaration of trust, the beneficial interest under which is divided into transferable certificates of participation or shares" to determine their legal status and whether further regulation of them was advisable. Like Babson's criticisms, the legislature was concerned that these organizations were unregulated—they acted like corporations with none of the corporation's legal responsibilities: Furthermore, "there was no legal entity in such organizations and they could not sue or be sued in a common name."

In his report, the tax commissioner noted that "the voluntary association in this country has received its greatest development in Massachusetts, and has come to its present status by adopting and utilizing many of the attributes characteristic of corporations." After reviewing the history of associations in Massachusetts, he responded to the resolve of the legislature as to whether associations "should be prohibited or further regulated by statute" by stating that "to say, then, than they should be prohibited would be an unwarranted interference with the right of contract, and would raise serious constitutional questions. My opinion is that since large amounts of capital have been put into these associations and they have already been recognized by law it would be wise to subject them to further regulation by the State especially such of them as own, hold or control stocks of public service corporations."[16] Thereafter, the commission made several regulatory reforms, including one that limited the amount of securities of public service companies held by an association or an express trust to 10 percent of their assets.[17]

A year later in 1913, in several cases involving municipal governments following the *Mayo* case, the Massachusetts Supreme Judicial Court ruled that business trusts organized for investments in real estate should be taxed as trusts rather than as partnerships. The trust in question was, again, the Boston Personal Property Trust, set up consciously as a trust only three years after *Mayo*. The court in *Williams* v. *Inhabitants of Milton* noted that taxes had been assessed by the municipalities "on the theory that the property held by the plaintiffs under that trust was partnership property" which was to be taxed where the "partnership (if there was a partnership) had its place of business." While the trust did not deny it might owe taxes, it insisted that, as a trust, it should be assessed under other provisions and payable to other persons. "The right to tax property as trust or as partnership property depends upon what the character of the property taxed really is."[18]

The court then recited the string of cases involving partnership in Massachusetts and how *Mayo* differed from them. "In the former cases," the court noted,

> the certificate holders are associated together by the terms of the "trust" and are the principals whose instructions are to be obeyed by their agent who for their convenience holds the legal title to their property. The property is their property. They are the masters. While in *Mayo* v. *Moritz* on the other hand there is no association between the certificate holders. The property is the property of the trustees and the trustees are the masters. All that the certificate holders in *Mayo* v. *Moritz* had was a right to have the property managed by the trustees for their benefit. They had no right to manage it themselves nor to instruct the trustees how to manage it for them.[19]

The court carried the distinction between the two lines of case law one step further, noting, as American courts only occasionally did by this time, that there was a three-decade-old precedent in English case law that made a similar distinction between partnership and trust. The court concluded by stating that the Boston Personal Property Trust "is in every respect an investment trust and nothing more."[20]

With the *Williams* decision, it soon became clear that businesses in Massachusetts could be legally organized as corporations, as voluntary associations/partnerships, or as business trusts, the latter in many ways similar to partnerships with an important exception that assets were owned by the trustees, not the individual members, partners, or stockholders. The significance of the Massachusetts business trust had been given further weight two years earlier in 1911, when the U.S. Supreme Court ruled that a trust formed in states like Massachusetts "where statutory joint stock companies are unknown . . . is not within the provisions of the Corporation Tax Law." In addition, the language in the *Williams* opinion, emphasizing that trustees are "masters" of the trust, is reminiscent of the independent judgment Judge Samuel Putnam gave to Boston trustees in his opinion in *Harvard College* v. *Amory* more than eighty years earlier.[21]

Massachusetts business trusts not only became recognized as legal entities but soon grew in number. As Austin W. Scott noted in the *Harvard Law Review* in 1920, "the Massachusetts device of creating a trust for the carrying on of a business is rapidly growing in popularity," even beyond the borders of the state. In 1912 alone, the Massachusetts tax commissioner found that there were some 103 real estate trusts filed in his department, and such trusts in Boston alone held property

Later, some other organizations acted like investment trusts but held very narrow classes of assets. The Boston Personal Property Trust is considered by some to be the first investment trust, and one that functioned along the lines of the modern investment trust. But its investment was limited to a single type of security, real estate. Another Boston-based investment group, the Railway and Light Securities Company, founded in 1904, made investments only in street railway companies and public utilities. This company was operated by Stone & Webster, a Boston engineering and construction company founded in 1889, which built various urban transportation and utility systems throughout the country or acquired and then reorganized and developed their properties for temporary or long-term investments. As a result, the company had a financial interest in the stocks of a large number of transportation and utility companies, and eventually created a securities department for the sale of stocks and bonds of public utilities as well as an investment banking arm, Stone & Webster and Blodget, Inc.[27]

Nevertheless, these and other proto-investment trust companies had certain characteristics in common. Most were local and relatively small, and had been created at different times for specific investor bases. There was little interest in publicizing them, perhaps because popular interest in investing in them was still in the future. There was no effort to create a diversified portfolio of securities or one that focused on common stocks, as mutual funds did when they arrived in the 1920s.[28]

It is difficult to determine why investment trusts were not developed in the United States before the 1920s. Some scholars have suggested that investment banking, a unique U.S. institution, supplied the needed funding into the twentieth century, and that it was not until the United States shifted from a debtor to a creditor nation during World War I that interest in creating investment trusts took place. Indeed, after the war, there was even federal legislation to encourage the development of investment companies to help finance postwar Europe, but it created little interest—at least in overseas investment. Instead, it appeared to one contemporary that American financiers seized upon the "new idea" and developed "its potentialities with rapidity and skill . . . without paying much attention to the original purpose which brought it into being."[29]

The rise of investment trusts began after the brief depression of 1920–1921, and was a product of changes in investing habits of many Americans, discussed in more detail below. The trusts, mostly modeled after British trusts, offered investors ownership in an often diverse portfolio of securities, and their numbers increased rapidly over the decade. From 1921 to 1924, 139 such trusts were formed, after which they grew more briskly: 140 in 1927, 186 in 1928, and 265 in 1929. By that last date, there were a total of 677 investment trusts, each with assets of more than $500,000 and aggregate assets of $8 billion. By

contrast, only 19 of them were open end mutual fund companies whose combined assets were a mere $140 million.

The pioneer and largest U.S. trust of this era was the International Securities
Trust of America, which was organized in April 1921. It was the earliest member
of what became the Founders Group, a pyramided system of several investment
companies. Although it was patterned after the British trust model, with its complex capital structure and substantial leverage, it was formed in Massachusetts
as *initially* a Massachusetts business trust, as were some other early trusts, suggesting that this form of organization was widely known in the Boston financial community at the time. It issued bonds and preferred and common stock
through dealer contacts, and employed a fiscal agent to sell its securities and
provide investment information and accounting services. Securities (totaling at
least 400 issues) were bought and sold by the trustees on the basis of an analysis
of the company's statistical staff. Reorganized in 1923 and incorporated in 1927,
its assets by that latter date were more than $33 million. In 1926, the Second
International Securities Corporation was established and financed by the
American Founders Trust (established 1925), another Massachusetts business
trust, which became a corporation in 1928. Two other Massachusetts business
trusts, the Bond Investment Trust of America and the Bond Investment Trust
(1923), were formed by Harris, Forbes & Company of Boston.[30]

Each trust had unique features, but a few examples from New York, where
they were more prominent, help to indicate what most of them were like. One
was the "bankers' share" trust, which acquired high-priced securities that were
deposited with a trustee, bank, or trust that, in turn, issued low-priced certificates of pro rata ownership to investors against that deposit. The United
Bankers Oil Company, for instance, issued certificates based on holdings of
shares of ten Standard Oil companies (1924); another called Industrial Trustee
Shares (1924) issued certificates based on common stocks held in ten companies in different industries. Diversified Trustee Shares (1925) based its certificates on shares of twenty-four companies, while another trust of the same
name (1927) held shares of twenty-four other companies. Investors in bank
shares usually paid a premium of about 10 percent on the value of the shares,
and sold them on the overall value of the shares as a whole. Another example was the United States & Foreign Securities Corporation (1924), the first
diversified investment trust organized on a large scale and sold to the public. The high leverage of the sponsor's common stock gave it control over the
trust. This dominance was expanded further through provisions in the trust
that allowed it to participate in syndicates, promotions, and underwritings; to
make secured and unsecured loans; and to participate in almost "every kind"
of undertaking in the United States or abroad.[31]

As these examples suggest, investors had a variety of investment trusts available to them in the 1920s. Some of them had pyramided capital structures, some had a single share class while others had leverage, some restricted management while others allowed them to do virtually anything, some revealed their holdings while others did not, some had fixed security investments while others could buy and sell trust securities, some had easy redemption methods while others required sale via exchanges, and some invested in foreign securities while others made only domestic investments. These closed-end investment and holding companies also had the potential to perform badly in rapidly declining markets.[32]

The Hub of Business and Investment News and Information

Boston became not only a locus of asset management but also a center for investment and business news. Perhaps the most influential figure of the late nineteenth and early twentieth centuries was Clarence W. Barron, who was born in Boston's North End and was probably the foremost exponent of modern financial journalism. Barron's father was a teamster, and Clarence grew up in working-class Charlestown. Through the help of family friends, he was able to attend the more polished Boston English High School (also the alma mater of J. P. Morgan two decades earlier), where he was an excellent student and won essay prizes. With a keen desire to become a reporter at the age of fifteen, he apprenticed himself to a court reporter so that he could learn shorthand, a skill he believed was more valuable than the study of Greek or Latin. As a journalist, he was able to develop fuller, more detailed, and interesting stories because of his shorthand skills. He later hired the best stenographers available and trained them into newspapermen in his own image.

Described as a "short, rotund powerhouse," an exuberant man who weighed 300 pounds and stood only 5 feet 5 inches tall, Barron was at first a general news reporter at the *Boston Daily News*. From 1875 to 1887, he worked at the *Boston Evening Transcript* where he became financial editor and made his mark as a business journalist. While still a general news reporter after coming to the *Transcript,* he wrote one of his early Boston exposés about the Boston Port Authority, which was losing nearly $1 million a year because it did not collect a transit fee on imports passing through Boston on their way to the West. A short while later, Barron reported to his supervisors that he thought "it was absurd to give the quotations of Boston securities and every transaction, yet never give the news under the fluctuations." Barron "believed there was a news item every day in State Street that might be picked up." They agreed with his suggestion, and he was "asked to annex that to [his] daily duties." Barron shot back saying, "Give me my whole time for the new project," and his request was granted. As a result of this unexpected encounter, he created the financial section of the paper, and while the *Transcript* was Boston's most important newspaper of the day, allegedly read by "everyone," within a few weeks of his starting the financial section, the paper's circulation rose by 15 percent. Barron's special reports were occasionally of historic proportions, such as the one he wrote on Alexander Graham Bell's telephone demonstration before Boston's American Academy of Arts and Sciences in 1877, which predicted the potential importance of the invention.

Barron left the *Transcript* in 1887 after writing a controversial article about Henry Villard, president of the Northern Pacific Railroad. Barron soon founded a news service called the Boston News Bureau, which published handbills containing bulletins of local business news, generally issuing twenty-five or thirty of them a day. The handbills were distributed by messenger boys to businessmen who subscribed to the service for a dollar a day, and was operated much like Dow Jones's new news bulletin service in New York. On July 27, 1887, two days after the first handbills were printed and distributed, Barron expanded his operation by launching a newspaper under the same name, *The Boston News Bureau,* consisting of two columns on the front and back on a single sheet containing the same bulletins printed in chronological order. Barron soon referred to his newspaper as "The Financial Bible of New England." Next Barron provided a telegraph stock-market ticker service for his customers. A decade later, he founded the *Philadelphia News Bureau,* which supplied business news bulletins to the Philadelphia market. In the meantime, Barron became the *Wall Street Journal's* first out-of-town correspondent in 1889, the year the New York paper was founded. From 1887 to 1889, Barron had supplied Boston news articles by telegraph to the Dow Jones's *Afternoon News Letter,* a publication similar to Barron's *Boston News Bureau,* which sent him news from Wall Street in return.

In 1902, Barron became further involved with the *Wall Street Journal,* when he—or rather his wife, Jessie Waldron Barron—purchased Dow Jones & Company for $130,000 after the death of it cofounder Charles Dow. Jessie Barron, a prosperous boardinghouse keeper where Barron had lived for fourteen years before they were married, is said to have made a cash payment of $2,500 for the company, while her husband provided some sixty-three personal notes. As a result, she acquired nearly 90 percent of the Dow Jones stock. For about ten years after the acquisition, Barron remained in Boston and did not take charge of the company or the *Journal.* Instead, his wife moved to New York to serve as his representative. In 1912, however, he made himself president of Dow Jones and editor of the *Journal,* and merged his Boston and Philadelphia organizations into the newspaper. Between that date and 1928, he expanded the *Journal*'s circulation fivefold to over fifty thousand. He enlarged his journalistic empire with *Barron's National Financial Weekly* (later *Barron's Magazine*), a newspaper for investors, in 1921. Following his death, two books based on his notes—*They Told Barron* (1930) and *More They Told Barron* (1931)—revealed the breadth and depth of his connections with financiers during his years in New York.

Always a reporter, one of Barron's hallmarks was his journalistic scrutiny of corporate financial records, as was demonstrated in testimony he provided to a government inquiry about a New Haven Railroad slush fund and in his investigation for an exposé he published on Charles Ponzi, a Boston financial swindler, prior to the man's arrest and conviction. Barron also wrote books on various subjects like the Boston Stock Exchange, the war with Mexico, and financial aspects of World War I and its aftermath. One of his personal maxims described what he believed to be the purpose of financial journalism: "If we are live wires, we can so project financial truth that it will, at times, illumine the path of the investor. We should not usurp his prerogative of selecting, guessing or predicting but should steadily seek to illuminate his forward path."

Barron lived at the couple's Boston mansion at 334 Beacon Street, or at their summer estate in Cohasset, Massachusetts, where he was commodore of the Cohasset Yacht Club, when he was not at their suite at the Waldorf-Astoria in New York or on trips to Europe or to John Kellogg's health food sanitarium in Battle Creek, Michigan. Following his death a year before the stock market collapse, his estate was bequeathed to his adopted daughter, Jane, who lived in Boston and had married into the patrician Bancroft family. That family retained control of Dow Jones & Company until 2007, when its interest was sold to Rupert Murdoch's News Corporation.[33]

A Bostonian more in the investment and education fields than in financial journalism was Roger W. Babson, mentioned earlier. Babson was born in Gloucester, Massachusetts, a tenth-generation descendant of that Yankee family on Cape Ann, and studied at the Massachusetts Institute of Technology (MIT). After graduation in 1898, he worked selling bonds, typically the new transportation, utility, and industrial bonds then coming into the market, for several investment firms in Boston, New York, and Worcester. He was dissatisfied, however, with the methods they used and prices they charged their clients. Following his marriage and convalescence from a bout with tuberculosis, Babson decided to begin a business that would provide a central clearinghouse for information on investment information and business conditions. He intended to sell his analyses of stocks and bonds in newsletters to an investing public. The initial idea for his company was to collect, analyze, and disseminate information that bond houses already received, and that each house statistician, like Babson, simply duplicated:

> The bond houses used to issue offering circulars, and the statistician from each office would call on every other bond house each month to collect these circulars. These were then indexed separately by each house, so that when the firm desired to purchase or sell any inactive bond, it could look up and ascertain the name of the firm last offering or bidding for it. . . . The thought occurred to me that one person, with some assistance, who concentrated on this one job, could do it more efficiently and at much less cost to each house if he did it for the entire group. This was the idea that gave me a start. I saw no reason why it could not be done at Wellesley as well as in New York or Boston. The results could be mailed to the different banking-houses, in either card or circular form.[34]

Other ideas on how to provide useful business and investment information efficiently to investment managers and investors in general soon followed. "Our underlying purpose was to furnish protection to the investor in relation to his capital and income," Babson later remarked.

With only $1,200 as an initial "investment," Babson founded his business advisory company in 1904 in Wellesley Hills, Massachusetts (later the home of many Boston-area venture capital and private equity companies), which he called Babson's Statistical Organization. The company published *Babson's Reports,* its best-known service and one of the oldest investment letters in the United States, from 1918 to 2001. The company eventually changed its name to Business Statistics Organization and then to Babson's Statistical Reports; later it became Babson-United Investment Reports. In 1912, he also founded the Investment Bankers Bureau, which later became the United Business Service Company.

Even though investment by the general public was just coming into its own, the company reported annual revenues in the millions of dollars during its first decade (1904–1913). Following the Panic of 1907, Babson focused on counseling the public about when to buy and sell stocks through various publications. He also worked with an MIT engineering professor to develop the "Babsonchart" of economic indicators, applying Sir Isaac Newton's Third Law of Motion ("actions and reactions") to economics to assess current and future business conditions. While predicting the future proved to be more complex, Babson's analysis allowed him to become one of the first forecasters of the stock market collapse and the depression that followed. On September 5, 1929, he gave a speech stating that, "sooner or later a crash is coming, and it may be terrific." Later that day, the stock market declined by 3 percent, which became known as the "Babson Break." The stock market collapse took place a month later.

Besides providing advice, Babson used his fortune to develop and finance new public health and safety products, ranging from hygienic products to fire sprinklers and traffic signals. Babson also found additional ways to broadcast his investment insights and experience before the general public. From 1910 to 1923, he was a regular columnist in the *Saturday Evening Post,* one of the most popular magazines of the age. He also wrote weekly columns for the *New York Times* and the Scripps Syndicate, and then formed his own publication syndicate called the Publishers Financial Bureau from which he spread his writings to a broader group of newspapers across the country. While his choice of topics went beyond business and investment to, among others, education, health, politics, and religion, the focus of his message was on individual and social betterment. He was a popular lecturer on business and financial trends. Babson acquired the *United States Bulletin* in 1919 from the federal government, which he renamed the *United Business Service,* a weekly bulletin of commodity and investment information.

Over the course of his career, Babson wrote forty-seven books, including several on "business barometers" that went through multiple editions, and his autobiography, appropriately called *Actions and Reactions.* But perhaps his most permanent achievement was his founding in 1919 of the Babson Institute (in 1969 renamed Babson College), in the Babsons' former home on Abbott Road in Wellesley Hills. The college began in 1908—the same year Harvard Business School was founded and only eight years after the first graduate school of management was established at Dartmouth College—when Babson offered a correspondence course on how to sell bonds through Babson's Statistical Organization. This soon expanded to other courses in economics, finance, and distribution. Sensing the need for a private college that specialized in business education, Babson founded his institute after World War I. The curriculum, which did not include a liberal arts education, was divided into four major subject areas—practical economics, financial management, business psychology, and personal efficiency—and focused on actual business training as well as classroom work. Another important accomplishment was Babson's early interest, as described by a former colleague, in the belief that "it was more important to give information than to sell bonds," a view that was important in the creation of investment counsel.[35]

Boston Invents Investment Counsel

Not all business news and investment ideas in Boston appeared in newspapers, magazines, or books. Several investment concepts were developed by a new generation of asset managers looking at alternate ways to sell services to a rising middle- and upper-middle-class clientele. Before the 1920s, investment management was largely the province of professional managers, such as trustees, investment bankers, brokers, trust bank officers, and a few others, and investors had few choices in investments. As those choices broadened, however, from manufacturing, banking, and railroad stocks of the nineteenth century, to bond, stock, and preferred stock investments offered by an expanding number of new industrial organizations in the early decades of the twentieth century, investors' options theoretically widened, and their need for help in selecting them became more crucial.[36]

But that expansion of investment opportunities was largely theoretical. For decades, stocks in particular were looked upon as poor investments because the corporate managements that issued that stock provided the public with little but the most flattering information about their companies. As Theodore Scudder later noted, "Prior to 1900 corporate morals were so low that common stocks of practically all publicly-held companies could be considered nothing more than outright speculations." Yet all of this was changing, and as Scudder recalled, by about 1912 or 1913, "public corporate financing and corporate ethics had reached a point where some investors were beginning to recognize that common stocks held a real place in the individual investment program." While the advancement of corporate financial reporting would extend beyond that period and into the 1920s and 1930s, as more thorough accounting practices took hold and stock analysts started making "investigation" trips to company headquarters, the situation was improving.[37]

Stocks were rising in popularity for other reasons as well. The long-prevailing view that bonds provided a better long-term investment than stocks was being overturned during the 1920s with the help of a book called *Common Stocks as Long Term Investments,* written by Scudder's New York friend and collaborator Edgar Lawrence Smith. In his publication, Smith provided a number of "test" investment portfolios between the Civil War and 1923 which showed that common stocks had been a better investment than high-grade bonds.[38]

Another postwar catalyst was the rise of a broader investing public. During 1917–1918, when the United States was actively involved in the war, the American public participated in five Liberty Bond and Victory Loan drives. Some 21 million individuals, or one-fifth of the country's population, took part in the final drive. All told, the drives sold some 12 million bonds worth $24 billion, equivalent to about one-third of the country's national income in 1920. Following the war, the public continued to invest, redeeming the government bonds for corporate stocks and bonds, and a rising number of new corporate issues, which nearly quadrupled in value, from \$2.7 to \$9.4 billion, between 1919 and 1929. At the same time, disposable personal income was growing, up nearly twofold in the 1917–1921 period, then rising a little over one-third more in the decade that followed. The sweep and scope of these changes, many starting before the war, took years to mature and sink in.[39]

Scudder had graduated from Harvard in 1911, and during the next few years worked in several jobs, slowly developing his skills in selling and gaining confidence in his abilities. By 1912, he returned to Boston where he worked as a bond salesman. He did well in his new occupation but realized that "it did not take me more than three months to come to the conclusion that although I was selling securities in exactly the same way as other salesmen, I was not doing a good business." Even if he sold one customer the best and cheapest bond of its type, it could have very different, perhaps drastic effects on the portfolios of two different clients. Yet "under the selling methods of the day," bond salesmen sold bonds, and only those available at the time, not portfolio advice with those bonds. Upon further reflection, Scudder began to "analyze what investing was, what constituted the real objective of the investor, what the tools were that he had to work with, what the defects and advantages of these tools were and how they could be utilized to accomplish [the investor's] real objective. This led me to the simple economics on which our later work was based."

Scudder continued to work on the conceptual underpinnings of what would become "investment counsel" and discussed his ideas with clients as early as 1912 and 1913. The next year, he had a conversation with another client, Frederic H. Curtiss, chairman of the Boston Federal Reserve Bank, to whom he had come to sell some bonds. "Have you looked all over these bonds," Curtiss asked Scudder, "and do you think they are perfectly good?"

> Of course, [Scudder] had. They were very careful about that. And then I said, "Well, how do you know that is what I need? That is, the bond maturity and the amount and all that sort of thing." Well, [Scudder] hesitated and said of course he didn't. He said, "I don't know unless I see your list of securities." Then [Scudder] said, "What is needed here is a separate agency that will give advice and that would have no interest in the things they have to sell." And I said, "Well, of course, that means you are not going in and buying into any underwritings." [Scudder] said, "Yes, I believe in that," and that is what he did.

Curtiss went on to tell Scudder, "I'd be willing to pay for unbiased advice if I could find it."[40]

Scudder continued his study of business, investing, and economics, concluding that "the time had come when there was a pressing need for a strictly professional class who, over the years might become expert in the business of investing and to whom the investor, both corporate and individual, could turn for unbiased, expert advice." As a result of these reflections, Scudder began in 1914 to attempt to "educate my customers to what I believe to be sound investments and the other to be impartial in the selection of securities, irrespective of whether or not I made a profit. I found this course of action was appreciated by people with whom I did business." Soon Scudder was on his own as an independent securities salesman, but with the beginnings of an investment counsel philosophy and practice. Five year later, he started his own firm, Scudder, Stevens & Clark, with F. Haven Clark, an engineer and in-law of Scudder, and Sidney Stevens, an older man, neighbor of Clark, and former mill manager, who was interested in becoming an investment banker for manufacturing enterprises. They set up their office in Boston's Exchange Building.[41]

At its beginning in 1919, the firm started out in investment banking to stay in business in a postwar world still filled with uncertainty and to satisfy the interest of Stevens, who provided half of the capital for the company. "Scudder conceived the idea of starting a firm which would look at the investment from the investor's point of view," Clark would later write. "He suggested that [we] unite to form a firm which would advise clients how to invest money in an intelligent way. The question was how to make any money out of it. We decided to go into the investment bankers business but to give investment counsel." Stevens's underwritings of several companies proved to be disastrous and reminded Scudder of his years as a bond salesman when he made money at the expense of his clients. Yet how could the company create a profitable business by providing investment counsel, which Scudder had offered to his clients since 1914 as a free service? Would clients be willing to pay for investment counsel and on what basis would fees be determined?[42]

Scudder set up investment counsel methodically and intimately by talking with about twenty people. Would they trust him with knowledge about their complete portfolio as well as other pertinent facts like life insurance coverage, real estate mortgages they owned, what they needed yearly to live on, and similar information? "We would then diagnose their situation and suggest to them what we believed to be a sound investment program to follow." In return, clients of the firm agreed to pay a fee of 1 percent of the value of any securities they bought or sold on the advice of the firm. Brokerage charges would be paid by the firm from the fees it collected, leaving even less for the partners. As Scudder did the selling and Clark the bookkeeping, Stevens became disenchanted, viewing the outlook of investment counsel "too far away." He soon became a limited partner in the firm. Scudder and Clark, on the other hand, went to work giving the service a more detailed description and name.

By the summer of 1921, they had written a detailed statement in the form of a business prospectus called "Fundamental Problems of the Investor and Their Solution." The five-page document focused first on the declining value of the dollar in terms of purchasing power, and then moved on to discuss investment bankers, whose interest was more in selling their securities than in counseling their customers. Investors needed to move beyond them to find some "unbiased expert advice." Scudder created a plan for a diversified portfolio in which the investor placed 40 percent of his capital in fixed income securities and another 40 percent in a broad range of common stocks. The remainder was left liquid in a variety of forms. Yet having created a plan, Scudder stated that investment counsel was more than a diversified portfolio; it needed to be constantly supervised and refined as the economy and business conditions warranted.

Scudder had by mid-1921 laid down the elements he had been discussing for almost a decade—experienced advice, knowledge of the client's financial situation, a start-up investment plan, and constant supervision of its content. A few months later, one of Scudder's young consultants and salesmen, A. Vere Shaw, coined the term "investment counsel." In 1922, Shaw also helped to write a small promotional book entitled *Investment Counsel,* which the company used for many years. Up to 1925, the idea of investment counsel was "hard sledding," Clark later said. "Everybody on the Street said that we were bound to fail—that we had a good idea but that there was no money in it." Some people thought it was just another Ponzi scheme. "Half the people thought we were not honest and that we must be making money in some other way." And yet by 1927, investment counsel was given notice and a long article in *The Nation,* which branded it as "The New Profession." It was in that same year, 1927, that Clark would later note, "the volume of business reached the point where people began to take notice of us and realized that we were here to stay and had a business that had much appeal to the public."[43]

The firm began to flourish and expanded nationally, with Scudder himself moving to New York to set up operations there by 1923. The New York office grew "like wildfire," one young associate later recorded, because of Scudder's "amazing vitality and wide interest. . . . We became identified quite rapidly in New York with important people." The company soon had offices in Providence (1925) and Philadelphia (1929), as well as correspondence relationships with companies and individuals in Cincinnati (1924) and Los Angeles (1929). By 1924, if not a little earlier, Scudder also faced its first encounter with competition as several firms, most notably Eaton & Howard, entered the business.[44]

Charles Freedom Eaton, whose family had been in the lumber business in eastern Maine, spent several years in his youth at Massachusetts General

Hospital recovering from polio, then went on to Exeter and Harvard, which he left before graduating. He ended up, like so many young men of his generation and the one that followed, working at Boston's First National Bank, which served as a nursery for new investment service enterprises like investment counsel in the 1920s. "The First National Corporation at the time was a mere baby with almost unlimited capital," he later said, "a great opportunity to experiment and develop in the financial field." By 1924, however, Eaton decided to start "an investment firm of a different type" with John G. Howard, a man ten years older and more experienced, with "relationships around the street, around town and with the trust companies." Like Scudder before him, Eaton sensed that "no investment house was taking the point of view and working exclusively for the best interests of the investor." When the firm opened its doors in the First National Bank building on December 1, 1924, Eaton & Howard was only the third investment counsel firm in Boston and among a half dozen or fewer such firms around the country.[45]

Looking back thirty years later, Eaton recalled that finding "good investments had been more or less an individual affair, known mostly to bankers, trustees, or people with large sums to invest." Furthermore, investment options had become more numerous and complex, and required the skills and developed policies of an investment management organization. "No one person or few persons could cover the field involved. There was a place for organizations which would explore the subject of investing in a large and growing capitalistic society; weigh its risks and its opportunities; in fact, try to delve into the whole philosophy of investing and evolve practical investment procedures; and which would then make the results of their work available to people of all types with money to invest."[46]

Eaton & Howard proved to be ahead of the Scudder organization in finding a more objective way to charge fees, basing them on a percentage of a client's principal, rather than a charge for buying or selling securities. And while Scudder developed more offices or correspondence relationships in the 1920s, Eaton & Howard was the first investment counsel firm on the West Coast. It opened its San Francisco office in September 1929, only a month before the stock market crash, and continued to do well despite the changing economy. In 1931, Eaton himself visited the California office where he expected to acquire several thousand dollars of assets, but ended up securing $4 million. Eaton believed the reason for his success was that "we were young, different, came from the East—from Boston. Believe me if we came from New York they wouldn't have listened to us. From Boston, we must be pure. That made a difference, believe it or not, that made a big difference in those days."[47]

The profession grew slowly during the 1920s but then expanded broadly during the early 1930s, growing during a period of economic decline. Up through 1929, there were only twenty-four such organizations, but during the next three years alone, the numbers increased by thirty-nine. Based on a 1940 census of the profession, there were approximately 104 investment counsel organizations by that time, some of which had offices in several locations. Boston had thirteen of them, but New York, which had expanded into the field rapidly in the early 1930s, as selling advice became more viable than selling securities, had thirty-four. A number of the new companies were started or manned by Scudder alumni, such as A. Vere Shaw, Charles Brundage, Dwight C. Rose, Imre DeVegh, and Dean Langmuir.[48]

During the 1930s, the investment counsel profession, just like investment companies generally (see chapter 6), were under increased scrutiny, which led to an investigation by the Securities and Exchange Commission (SEC) and increased regulation by Congress. The warnings were clear enough for the early leaders of investment counsel to form a professional group, the Investment Counsel Association of America, in 1937. A year later, the SEC began public hearings "concerning the possible need to regulate investment counsel firms." Unlike the investment company industry as a whole, however, the SEC failed to examine individual investment counsel firms or discover any abuses. When the hearings eventually took place in 1940, many Boston investment counselors were in attendance as the congressional committee formulated a bill to register and regulate investment companies and investment advisers. The portion affecting investment counsel, Title II, soon became a separate piece of legislation.

To some it seemed that the draft legislation was moving beyond its original intent of providing guidelines for professional "good behavior and honesty" to one that would soon give the SEC "broad but unspecific power to investigate and perhaps to regulate any investment adviser." David Schenker, chief counsel for the SEC investment trust study, which became the basis for both the Investment Advisers and the Investment Company Acts of 1940, discussed the bill with Hardwick Stires, an investment counselor at Scudder who happened to be in Washington, D.C., at the time. Schenker said to Stires, "Don't you think it's about time for you fellows to throw in the sponge and realize that there is going to be a bill and that we are going to have, as a minimum, a registration of investment counsel? So why don't you tell your group to stop thrashing and get together and write a simple bill that I feel sure we can all agree on?"[49]

Stires accepted the invitation, and a night later, he and a small group from the Investment Counsel Association, along with Scudder's legal counsel, redrafted the legislation, which "to the surprise of all participants in the exercise . . . turned out to be a compromise" between the SEC and the profession.

The revised legislation quickly received approval from the association and Congress, and was signed into law in August 1940. As a result, Scudder and a small group of firms almost singlehandedly drafted the legislation that came to regulate their own profession. The act helped to clarify the meaning of investment counsel, restricting it to "rendering investment supervisory service" and to the giving of "continuous advice as to the investment of funds on the basis of the individual needs of each client." These restrictions actually helped the profession by limiting the use of the term *investment counsel* to only those registered advisers whose principal business was investment counsel.[50]

Investment counsel continued to grow over the next three decades until a changing economy and new opportunities compelled many in the profession to move in a different direction. During the period from about 1940 to 1965, the profession flourished, became stronger, and better defined though still small in size. It dealt with an increasing amount of legislation and restriction, which in many ways helped to separate the business from the work of less credentialed or experienced financial advisers who soon began to multiply in numbers. Some new investment counsel firms were formed like David L. Babson & Company, established by Roger Babson's cousin David and associates from Babson's Reports in 1940. David Babson's strategy was "using an approach that would communicate useful background information to clients through a weekly letter (The Babson Staff Letter), but focus on personal advice tailored to each client's needs." The firm became well known during the postwar boom. Based on a study it made and published in its Staff Letter on September 17, 1951, the firm became a pioneer in growth stock investing through its counsel advice and its Babson Growth Fund, focusing on new industries involved in pharmaceuticals, data processing, research and development, and other areas of economic expansion.[51]

The 1960s caused new problems for investment counsel. By the mid-1960s, as the stock market roared and the Go-Go era took off, larger financial institutions, such as trust companies and commercial banks, realizing the importance of investment counsel firms to their overall growth, began to acquire them. The first of these takeovers occurred in 1962 when DeVegh & Company was acquired by Winthrop & Company in New York. But the movement soon spread to Boston, where Bailey & Rhodes was acquired by the Boston Company, a holding company of Boston Safe Deposit & Trust Company, and Loomis Sayles & Company became part of New England Mutual Life. Meanwhile, the New York insurer Marsh & McLennan approached David Babson in the mid-1960s to see if he would sell his firm. A parallel merger movement in Boston's mutual fund industry would also take place during this period and into the 1970s and early 1980s (see chapter 6). A second blow to the investment counsel profession occurred during the mid- to late-1970s in the wake of the enactment of the Employee Retirement Income Security Act (ERISA) of 1974. The act quickly transformed the pension industry for both individuals and employees, and soon led to the staggering growth of pension funds during the next several decades. As a result of this, many investment counsel firms effectively gave up managing individual accounts in favor of taking on institutional clients, particularly large pension funds in those organizations. The rewards there proved to be more substantial, but the opportunities to manage them became less certain because of the growing importance of measurable investment "performance" required by those institutions. Furthermore, institutional clients tended to divide up their expanding assets among a number of asset managers, and were advised by third-party "consultants" who helped them to select those asset managers. (For more on the pension revolution, see chapter 9.) Other Boston investment counsel organizations were acquired near the turn of the last century—Scudder by Zurich, a Swiss financial services company, in 1997, and then by Deutsche Bank in 2002, while Standish, Ayer & Wood, founded in Boston in 1933, was merged into another, larger financial service provider, Mellon Financial, in 2001.[52]

The Coming of the Open End Mutual Fund

While Scudder and Clark were perfecting their idea of investment counsel, others in Boston's financial district were putting together the first mutual fund. The innovation was the work of an unlikely trio of bond salesmen at a small Boston firm called Learoyd, Foster & Company, which had been founded more than a decade earlier in 1912. The two firm principals were Charles H. Learoyd, born in Taunton, Massachusetts, the son of a clergyman, and Hatherly Foster Jr., a native of upstate New York who had graduated from Harvard in 1907. While neither was by any stretch a Boston "Brahmin," they were joined in about 1923 by a third outlier of even more distant origins, Edward G. Leffler. Born in Milwaukee, Wisconsin, in 1892 of Swedish immigrant parents, Leffler graduated from Gustavus Adolphus College in Minnesota in 1915. Following college, he held a number of jobs in the Midwest selling everything from shoes to pots and pans, and then ended up with his first securities job selling bonds for temperance hotels in the region. After the hotels went bankrupt, he moved to Boston where for six years, he sold stock for an automobile finance company, though neither proved to be very successful.

Many give credit to Leffler for the invention of the mutual fund, but the story is more complex than that. While Learoyd, Foster & Company was not likely struggling for business in 1924 amid the bull market of the 1920s, they were selling a rather conservative investment product and missing out on more lucrative sales in some form of equities. Selling shares in an investment trust was probably a more exciting prospect and profitable line of business than what they had been doing, and they may have seized on the idea after talking with Leffler, despite the midwesterner's largely unsuccessful sales career. There was no doubt that Leffler was pivotal, because he had tried out his ideas on others in Boston. But only Foster and Learoyd were interested in transforming those ideas into an investment product—and had the experience to do so. While Leffler had spent six years in Boston, which allowed him the time and location to learn about the Massachusetts business trust, the Boston Personal Property Trust, and the International Securities Trust of America—all useful local background needed to create the first mutual fund—this was local knowledge available to many Bostonians, including Foster and Learoyd, who had collectively been in the securities business for several decades. Foster was also a long-standing member of the Boston Stock Exchange. Leffler was more a catalyst than a creator in a collaborative effort with others who knew securities and Boston better than he did.[53]

When the three men and their lawyer set up their investment trust in early 1924, it was remarkably similar to the Massachusetts business trust. Their common law trust was managed by three trustees who had "absolute and uncontrolled discretion" to invest the trust's funds "free from the control of the Shareholders." They were a self-perpetuating body and were only liable for "willful default or neglect." Shareholders were protected from any personal liability for any debt, obligation, or act of the trustees. The trust was originally capitalized at $50,000 with shares valued at $50 each. Perhaps the most important feature in the original trust was the continuous offering of shares to the public. While the trustees fixed the number of shares from time to time, they could also issue "additional shares ranking with the same rights and privileges as existing shares," and they had the "right to sell, exchange, or to otherwise dispose of such additional shares upon such terms and conditions and for such prices as they may determine" to individuals who held no outstanding shares. The trustees' compensation was, like Boston trustees, a small percentage of the trust income, and State Street Trust Company served as both custodian and transfer agent. This investment trust was named the Massachusetts Investors Trust (M.I.T.). It was obliquely called a mutual fund for the first time in March 1925, when M.I.T. referred to itself as a "mutual investment association" in its sales literature. The phrase continued to be used in newspaper advertisements and other marketing materials for several years, and was gradually shortened to simply "mutual fund."[54]

The deed of trust was an important but not perfect document, and over the next few years, amendments helped to shape some aspects of the first mutual fund, many of which were responses to features of early rival funds. One of the most important was the gradual development of the redemption principle—one of the mutual fund's most important features—from a passive, indirect, and permissive feature to one that occurred automatically on demand. By 1929, M.I.T. shareholders could, with a small redemption fee, redeem their shares at NAV; earlier, shareholders had to make a good faith effort to find a buyer before selling them back to the trust. Despite the changes in the language of the deed of trust, M.I.T.'s sales force as a matter of policy had redeemed shares of the trust without any delay.[55]

For Learoyd, Foster, and Leffler, the idea behind creating M.I.T. was largely to have a product they could sell, not manage. Indeed, the selling side of mutual funds proved to be the more lucrative end of the business for almost five decades. During the summer of 1924, Leffler resigned his position as trustee to go back to Learoyd, Foster & Company and sell shares of the fund. Soon Foster followed him. Learoyd remained as a trustee and held other trust management positions for the next decade, and in doing so, straddled the functions of both management and distribution for much of the remainder of his career. Foster stayed with Learoyd, Foster & Company and its successor companies until the 1960s when he retired. While Leffler returned briefly to Learoyd, Foster & Company, he soon moved on to form his own sales organization, then worked with M.I.T.'s two major Boston competitors, Incorporated Investors and State Street Investment Corporation, in efforts to create nationwide distribution for mutual funds.[56]

All of the elements were there in Boston in the 1920s for anyone to use—the Massachusetts business trust, examples of that trust like the Boston Personal Property Trust and International Securities Trust of America, a rising investing public, and many new investors who looked for investment services and products. The fact that two other major mutual funds were created at nearly the same time as M.I.T. suggests that the idea was in the air, and had been for some time. Looking back to the 1820s and going forward through the mid-twentieth century, if not later, trusts have played an important part of Boston life. In 1936, *Time* magazine noted that "trusts in all their variations are woven into the whole fabric of Boston life. A Bostonian who is not either a beneficiary or trustee of at least one personal trust fund is liable to find himself at a distinct social disadvantage." The emergence of investment counsel and the mutual fund merely exposed Bostonians to a broader array of fiduciary relationships.[57]

CHAPTER 6

The "Boston Type" Investment Trust

New ideas spread quickly. As Charles H. Learoyd, Hatherly Foster Jr., and Edward G. Leffler were setting up the Massachusetts Investors Trust (M.I.T.), other Bostonians were developing their own versions of what became known as the mutual fund. Based on such historic models as the century-old Massachusetts business trust, and more modern examples like the 1893 Boston Personal Property Trust, it is not surprising that other funds would follow in rapid succession. Indeed, M.I.T. had two early and major rivals, the State Street Investment Corporation, which was incorporated in July 1924, four months after M.I.T.'s deed of trust was signed, and Incorporated Investors, which was organized in November 1925. All three reflected Boston's expertise and strength in evaluating equities by becoming diversified common stock funds. This was at a time when conventional investing in the United States still primarily relied on fixed assets like bonds.

Each of these investment companies had distinctive characteristics, including different corporate structures, and each was faced with dissimilar and contrasting challenges over the next decade and a half—a time of boom then bust in the economy, eventually culminating in the enactment of the first federal legislation affecting mutual funds, the Investment Company Act of 1940.[1] M.I.T. was created by three sales people, who largely wanted to remain on the selling rather than management or trustee side of the business. While Learoyd remained an M.I.T. trustee into the 1930s, and continued with the trust in other capacities for a few years thereafter, Leffler and Foster resigned almost immediately to return to selling the fund.[2] The three original trustees were gradually replaced by a more permanent group, including Merrill Griswold, who arrived in the summer of 1925. Even so, the actual investing side of M.I.T.'s business was not that actively managed. The number of stocks held in the fund grew from 45 in 1924 to over 130 by 1927, becoming, in effect if not in name, something like an index fund (an average return from a widely diversified portfolio). This investment strategy would actually help to soften the blow of the crash still several years away, but eventually M.I.T. would have to focus on research and a more disciplined investment approach, which it started to do in the early 1930s (fig. 7).

Unlike the other two funds, M.I.T. was divided into two distinctive—and separate—entities: the trustees who managed the fund and a distribution organization that sold it through an eventually nationwide network of brokers and dealers. That distribution organization was originally Learoyd, Foster & Company, but as new people and investors came in, it changed its name, becoming Slayton-Learoyd in 1928, Massachusetts Distributors in 1934, and then Vance, Sanders & Company in 1944. Because both Learoyd and Foster hailed from and were familiar with the Boston brokerage community, they were able to establish a distribution system of broker-dealers with whom they were familiar and that dominated the sales of most mutual funds for more than fifty years.[3]

The second oldest company, the State Street Investment Corporation, was originally set up to invest the family assets of its three founders—Richard Paine, Richard Saltonstall, and Paul Cabot. Before setting up their fund, they had worked in the credit departments of Lee, Higginson and Company, Merchant's National Bank, and the First National Bank, respectively. All of them were interested in the stock market, and by 1923, they were meeting weekly at the Parker House to "yak about common stocks." Even though their fund began about four months after the M.I.T. deed of trust was signed, it remained private until January 1927. At State Street, both the fund—State Street Investment Corporation—and fund management—State Street Research and Management Corporation—were run by its founders/officers, who were themselves investors, making the fund more actively managed than either of the other two. But the officers were reluctant to spend time or money selling the fund, and thus created no sales organization—or much growth—for several years.[4]

Incorporated Investors was founded by George Putnam, William Amory ("Brother") Parker, Edward G. Leffler (after he left Learoyd, Foster & Company), and John T. Nightingale, who collectively discussed and studied "the merits and demerits of the plan as formulated by the officers of Massachusetts Investors Trust" throughout 1924 until they decided to start their own company a year later. At Incorporated Investors, both management and distribution were in one company (sales was a subsidiary of the management company), and the fund was in a second company, though managers could participate in all three entities. Unlike the other two funds, Incorporated used national advertising

from an early date, and soon created a national market for its product. As a result, assets rose from $5.4 to $45.7 million between 1927 and 1928. By contrast, during those same years, State Street, with its emphasis on research, tripled its assets from $4.3 to $12.8 million, while M.I.T., with neither a superior investment strategy nor a large-scale and national marketing plan, grew the slowest, from $6.5 to $10.9 million.[5]

Like most innovations, the distinctive features of the open end or mutual fund evolved slowly over time into the kind of financial product we know today. Unlike closed-end funds, the mutual fund had a simple capital structure with only one class of security, common stock, and it was believed that new shares were issued continuously to meet the demand.[6] This second principal, however, was not tested. During the mid- to late 1930s, State Street and Incorporated Investors halted the sale of new shares, and there was much discussion in the fledgling industry about the "optimum size" a fund could achieve and still remain a viable investment vehicle. As a result of such thinking, these two funds did not expand their number of shares and became a little more like closed-end funds, with limited numbers of shareholders. Consequently, both investment companies fell behind M.I.T. as mutual fund sales continued to grow throughout the decade.[7] Another commonplace notion was that mutual funds could be redeemed "on demand," a concept that took some time and competition to be fully developed.

From the beginning, mutual fund shares could be redeemed for their "net asset value" (NAV) and, usually, a small sales charge. This was a step forward from the closed-end fund, where the seller had to find a buyer, much like a stock sale.[8] During the earliest days of the mutual fund, the question was not so much redeemability but rather under what conditions shares would be redeemed. It took four amendments to M.I.T.'s Deed of Trust to create the kind of redemption privilege we would recognize today. Even influential fund trustee Merrill Griswold was opposed to the idea, thinking it was "bad business and bad law." Indeed, the redemption feature came from the same group who created the fund, the distributors at Learoyd, Foster & Company, who believed they could make a market by buying back shares then reselling them. Slowly the trustees amended the trust document, first agreeing to buy back shares within seven days at book value less $2.00 after shareholders had exhausted other alternatives. In 1929, to compete with Incorporated Investors, an amendment was added making it a right, not a necessity, to sell shares to the trust. In the meantime, Learoyd, Foster & Company continued to do well buying and reselling the bulk of these shares by themselves, until the direct effects of the stock market crash hit them—and hit them hard.

The flood of redemptions following the crash swamped the sales company, forcing it to raise a substantial sum to keep afloat. But it also provided M.I.T. with a reason to adopt a more liberal voluntary repurchase clause in the trust agreement. Furthermore, it made the trustees more responsible for backing up the redemption process. The new provision, adopted in 1931, gave the shareholders 99 percent of the NAV of their shares on the day they were assigned over to the trustees, rather than wait for seven days to expire. Another amendment expanded the number of banks where shareholders could take their shares for redemption. Other funds likewise used their own new redemption features to compete with M.I.T. What began as an acknowledgment of redemption gradually became an "on demand" right of shareholders.

While the redemption feature was shaped to an extent by competition, it proved to be an important feature of the security as the U.S. economy declined and the trustworthiness of financial organizations came under greater scrutiny. The ability of shareholders to sell their shares back to the investment company at current value might have presented a potential fatal flaw for mutual funds because it provided a way for customers to quickly get rid of their shares, but the redemption feature actually helped to strengthen public confidence in them during the depression.[9]

Riding out the Storm: The Impact of the Depression

Each of Boston's three major mutual funds fared differently during the depression, and in ways that contrasted from the boom times of the 1920s. At the height of the bull market on September 30, 1929, M.I.T., then the smallest of the three funds, had about $17.6 million in assets from its 3,500 shareholders. By the end of that year, following the crash, its assets had diminished to $14 million, but the number of its shareholders had grown to 5,000. A combination of the distributors' redemption policy and M.I.T.'s more diversified portfolio helps to explain, if only in part, why that fund did relatively well. During the next crucial period of the depression between 1931 and 1932, M.I.T. continued to do better than its rivals, with its assets declining only 23 percent compared with State Street and Incorporated Investors, whose assets fell 78 and 75 percent, respectively. Some temporary factors helped to cushion M.I.T. during this period, but structural changes in the investment company—merging the assets of other funds and enlarging its independent distribution resources—were also beginning to show their mark.

By 1935, M.I.T. had created a research department, focused investment on 77 rather than 132 securities, promoted a nationwide distribution system, and grown by acquiring smaller funds. Gradually, M.I.T. increased the size of its asset base compared to its two major rivals. At the end of 1928, for instance, M.I.T.'s share of the business had been lopsidedly small, only 16 percent of the whole or $10.9 million compared with Incorporated Investors' $45.7 million. By 1932, M.I.T.'s share had grown to 28 percent, to 44 percent in 1935, 50 percent a year later, and 60 percent by 1940, when it had $105 million in assets compared with Incorporated Investors' $38.5 million and State Street's $33.6

million. On a broader scale, U.S. open end funds, about 18 in number, had grown from about $140 million in 1929 to 80 funds and about $532 million in 1940, in contrast with closed-end companies, which had assets of close to $7 billion in 1929 but declined to about a tenth of that or $784 million in 1940, only to be surpassed by the aggregate of mutual fund assets in the next few years.[10]

Boston and Its "Conduit" Theory

Although the depression had an impact on the leading companies in Boston's fledgling mutual fund industry, it also created a sense of camaraderie and solidarity, especially in the face of intense government scrutiny of the investment industry and an expectation that restrictive legislation might soon come about. Following passage of the Securities Act of 1933 and the Securities Exchange Act of 1934, Congress enacted the Public Utility Holding Company Act of 1935. This last act provided the legal foundation for a five-year investigation by the Securities and Exchange Commission (SEC) of the investment company industry, and was particularly interested in the role of closed-end companies in the economic collapse. As a result of this study, the commission transmitted to Congress between 1938 and 1940 an exhaustive report on the industry. Commonly known as the "Investment Trust Study," it laid the foundation for the Investment Company Act of 1940, the major piece of legislation that has shaped the mutual fund industry ever since.[11]

The industry's most immediate challenge from Washington, however, came a year after the study commenced, when Congress was preparing to enact the Revenue Act of 1936. President Franklin D. Roosevelt had proposed significant increases in corporate tax rates, including for investment companies. These companies would be severely hit, with the possibility that they would be taxed at three distinct and separate levels—the portfolio company, the investment company, and the fund shareholder. The small mutual fund industry was without a trade group or association, and in the face of higher taxation, the separate fund companies had to work things out by themselves. Leadership came from Boston. Spokespeople from each of the three major mutual fund companies—M.I.T., State Street, and Incorporated Investors— met with Roosevelt in the summer of 1936. Employing his legal and negotiation skills, Merrill Griswold of M.I.T. wrote to the president to ask him to give special consideration to mutual fund companies for more equitable tax treatment for both themselves and their shareholders. Paul Cabot proposed a meeting in Washington where he could discuss with the president the impact that triple taxation would have on open end investment companies. The third member of what became this Boston group was William Tudor Gardiner, the former governor of Maine, who was chairman of Incorporated Investors and who knew Roosevelt personally. All three came to Washington, arriving at the White House on June 3, a sweltering summer day, to encourage the president to endorse what Griswold called the "conduit theory" of taxation.

Adoption of the "conduit theory" would exempt investment companies from taxation of their income (except for income that was withheld) if they distributed their taxable income to shareholders, who, in turn, would end up paying the tax. The tax implications, in effect, passed through the investment company to the shareholder. As a result, investment companies could pay out higher dividends to shareholders, enhancing the mutual fund as a viable investment product. Income not handed out as dividends remained liable for taxation.

Despite their resolve, the three almost missed out on their scheduled meeting. As the three Bostonians were being invited into the Oval Office for their ten-minute meeting, Roosevelt received an important telephone call that used up all of the men's time. When the president's secretary tried to usher the three Bostonians out, Cabot turned to the president and said, "Mr. President, this is a damned outrage. It is true we were promised only 10 minutes, but you wasted the entire 10 minutes talking to that man on the telephone." Roosevelt "threw back his head and laughed. 'All right, boys,' he said, 'you can have another 10 minutes.'"

Thirty years later, Cabot recalled the details of that meeting. "I told him what we wanted and why." The president, Cabot went on, "understood what it was all about better than anybody—mind you I was prejudiced against the guy—he understood it better and quicker and asked more intelligent questions about it than anybody I had talked to in Washington and I was amazed. Then he said, I'm all for you, I agree with you, what can I do to help you."[12] At the end of their brief meeting, the president promised to see what he could do. Cabot mentioned "great difficulty with the Treasury Department," but by the time he revisited the department, he found a previously strained relationship had turned into a cooperative one. Although none of the three could discern any specific action that the president had taken on the bill, it passed in their favor.[13]

The Revenue Act's provision, however, specifically affected only open end companies, which were largely in Boston, and not the closed-end companies primarily located in New York. The group had emphasized before the president the assumption that open end funds were small investor funds that had to be protected from the peril of extensive taxation. Cabot later recalled that "the New York group had no or very little knowledge that the three of us . . . were down in Washington working on this thing" with Massachusetts

the detriment of shareholders, issuing securities with inequitable or discriminatory provisions, setting up irresponsible management, using unsound or misleading ways to compute earnings and asset values, changing the character of the company without investor consent, or pursuing excessive leveraging. The law also required full and accurate disclosure about the company and its sponsors. To these ends, the act required safekeeping and proper valuation of the fund's assets, greatly restricted transactions with affiliates, limited leveraging, and instituted governance requirements to safeguard fund management.[20]

The Act of '40 had much more impact on closed-end trusts, whose number and assets had fallen precipitously from pre-crash levels, so that by 1940, closed-end assets were only slightly greater than open end fund assets. This change of direction for mutual fund assets would continue on during the war, and then accelerate in the postwar economy. By 1966, open end fund assets accounted for 82 percent of all investment company assets.[21]

Following the act's passage, the government took little further notice of the mutual fund industry until the 1960s, when the SEC prepared reports and sponsored research as it looked into potential conflicts of interest between fund shareholders and fund management companies. As a result of these reports, delivered in 1962 (Wharton School's *A Study of Mutual Funds*), 1963 (*Special Study of Security Markets*), and 1966 (*Public Policy Implications of Investment Company Growth*), the first significant amendments to the act were passed in 1970. The amendments addressed potential conflicts by requiring that independent directors on the fund boards be disinterested, or not connected to the interests of the management company or investment adviser, and required from the fund adviser a fiduciary duty regarding fees and other compensation received from the fund. In effect, these changes strengthened the independence of boards of directors and restricted sales charges and fund expenses. Other issues came up in the 1960s and 1970s. For instance, shareholder suits were brought against fund advisers over excessive fees, but in nearly all cases, courts ruled against the shareholders for not meeting the burden of proof in those charges.[22]

Other Boston Funds

Other Boston investment companies started after 1925 played an important part in the early history of mutual funds, and in some cases, would later come to surpass the size and scope of the city's early industry leaders.[23] While most were common stock funds, the Great Depression influenced the development of additional types, including the "balanced" funds (with shifting proportions of stocks, bonds, preferred stock, and cash, as conditions changed). These funds came to dominate most companies' sales in the 1930s, 1940s, and into the 1950s. There were also a few bond funds, some growth funds like M.I.T.'s Second Fund (created in 1934),[24] and a variety of income funds by Keystone, primarily for retirement-focused accounts but also a more speculative fund called S-4.

The Keystone Company actually started out in Philadelphia in 1932 but moved to Boston in 1939. For many years, Keystone was run by S. L. "Skid" Sholley, who, like Leffler, was a master salesman from Minnesota. The move to Boston was seen by many in the local mutual fund community, like S. Whitney Bradley of Eaton & Howard, as an attempt by Sholley to give Keystone a tone of "respectability." Even Paul Cabot later noted, when comparing New York to Boston, "I think there was a feeling on the investors' part that they didn't trust the New Yorkers quite as much as they did Boston because Boston had the reputation of the old Boston conservative trustee and New York had the reputation of the slick Wall Street fellows who take the shirt off your back. I think . . . Keystone moved from Philadelphia up here entirely for that reason. The atmosphere had the appearance at least of being better here than it was in those bigger cities."[25]

The Keystone funds were set up as eight different fixed trusts in 1932, but three years later, they were replaced by a new series of ten open end funds, including four bond funds, two preferred stock funds, and four common stock funds (S-1 through S-4, the latter employing an innovative approach with higher-risk categories based on the stocks used), all of them varying in the types of securities they held and their investment objectives. This array of specialized funds, individually or in combination, made it possible to solve a variety of investment problems, and surpassed a single fund that provided similar results to investors regardless of an individual's financial circumstances or investment objectives. Each fund was widely diversified and represented a "carefully supervised invested position in the securities of its particular characteristics" to solve the unique needs of an investor's own individual investment problems. Keystone, like other investment companies, developed periodic investment plans for investors to help create "a properly balanced investment program" with Keystone funds, individual securities, or a combination of both. This made the Keystone funds the most diversified and perhaps the most sophisticated set of mutual funds until nearly all fund companies started to expand their offerings in the 1960s and 1970s.[26]

Century Shares Trust was begun in 1928 by New York's Brown Brothers & Company (later Brown Brothers Harriman & Company) but was based in Boston and run primarily by Boston trustee attorneys. Unlike Keystone, it had a singular focus. It invested only in foreign and domestic insurance companies, banks and trust companies and their subsidiaries, or any company whose principal business was in the management of one or more insurance or banking businesses that it controlled through direct stock ownership. The fund viewed these stocks as growth vehicles because a larger portion of earnings was not paid out as dividends but rather was used to finance additional business that was expected to produce additional profits. Another company established that year was the Pioneer Fund. It was founded by Philip L. Carret, a native of Lynn, Massachusetts, who completed Harvard College in three years, substituting his senior year in college with a year at Harvard Business School. Carret started managing money for family and friends in a pooled investment trust in 1924 while working as a reporter and feature writer at *Barron's*. He ran Pioneer for fifty-five years and was known as a value investor who held stocks for long periods of time. Carret used his *Barron's* articles as the basis of *The Art of Speculation* (1930), a classic book on investing.[27]

The Boston Fund was started in 1932 as a closely held fund of five individuals associated with Stone & Webster, but it became a corporation in 1936 and thereafter offered shares to the wider public.[28] In 1938, the fund had only 740 shareholders and assets of $160,000, but by May 1958, it had 30,000 shareholders and $153 million in assets, while outstanding shares grew from 183,000 to 10.1 million.[29]

In 1937, George Putnam founded his conservative balanced fund. At the time, Putnam was a partner in Townsend, Anthony & Tyson, a brokerage firm. He brought in several other Incorporated Investors alumni, including Charles M. Werly and Spurgeon Cunningham. The name of the fund, the George Putnam Fund of Boston, was chosen to highlight Putnam's considerable investment reputation and to give it a more approachable and personal appeal than other funds, which were assigned names like "Second Trust," Fund "A," or "stock fund." Cunningham suggested that "of Boston" be attached, believing, according to his son, that "Boston belonged to the mutual fund like a top hat and shawl to Abraham Lincoln." Putnam became a major company after the war, particularly after the 1960s when it launched its aggressive growth fund.[30]

Another company that would later become a dominant player in Boston and the mutual fund industry was Fidelity Fund, Inc. Originally organized in 1930 by the Boston brokerage firms of Taliaferro, Millett & Company and Anderson & Cromwell, it was run in its earliest years by Richard N. Taliaferro. A change in management took place in 1943 when Edward C. Johnson II was elected president and a director. Johnson, a lawyer at Ropes & Gray with an interest in investments, served in several positions at Incorporated Investors and managed his own personal and family's holdings, following the sale of the family business, C. F. Hovey, to the Jordan Marsh Company.

Until the 1960s, Fidelity's assets grew gradually, overtaking some Boston fund companies during those intervening decades. By the beginning of 1940, for instance, Fidelity was the tenth largest fund or fund complex in Boston, with a little over $4 million in assets under management (AUM). By 1959, assets had climbed to $491 million, and its distribution group was the eleventh largest in the country. While it was much smaller than the dominant Boston firms at the start of World War II, its distribution arm had surpassed Incorporated Investors, Eaton & Howard, State Street, Putnam, Scudder, and Colonial by 1960.[31]

While Colonial did not become a major Boston mutual fund company until after World War II, it had started out in 1931 as the Investment Service Corporation, when the engineering and utility construction company Stone & Webster sold its investment corporation subsidiary to a former employee, James H. Orr, and others.[32] Under Orr's reorganization, the company's initial client was the Railway & Light Securities Corporation, which had begun as a closed-end trust run by Stone & Webster in 1904. The 1904 company had invested in the securities of street railways, interurban transportation, and electrical utilities. When it was reorganized as the open end Colonial Fund in the early 1940s, it became technically the oldest investment company operating as a mutual fund.

In 1945, Orr's company changed its name to Colonial Management Associates. Four years later, it launched its first public offering, the Gas Industries Fund, and a year after that, it had twenty-three clients including four mutual funds and four institutional accounts. As its business shifted into the mutual fund industry, the company was renamed in 1954 the Colonial Fund, with its investment counsel group retaining the name of Colonial Management Associates. In 1956, Colonial added its first corporate pension fund client, and by 1957 the company had three mutual funds, including a fixed-income fund called the Bond Investment Trust of America.[33]

Some smaller Boston fund organizations included the General Capital Corporation, which was started in 1927 and reorganized two years later to manage mutual funds. The firm grew slowly, but in 1943 acquired all of the assets of the Old Colony Investment Trust for shares of its stock. Another small open end investment company was the New England Fund, which was created as a Massachusetts common law trust in 1931. The fund was organized by several Boston trustee lawyers and investment counselors. While originally a common stock fund, it became more diversified and balanced following the downturn of 1937, after which "cash, notes, bonds, and preferred stocks [were] used for greater stability of income and capital." Like many Boston open end funds, the New England Fund had a voluntary investment program by the 1950s in which investors set up investment accounts and contributed at their own pace. The New England Fund trustees also served in the same role for the General Investors Trust, which was created in 1932 by some Boston trustees. In 1934, the trust acquired the assets of several companies, and then those of the Franklin Mutual Fund, a year later. Another small fund was the Investment Trust of Boston, which was originally set up in 1931 as the World Finance Investment Trust. It ended share sales in 1938, and had only $118,000 in assets in 1940.[34]

In a few cases, Boston closed-end funds transitioned to mutual funds, particularly following the crash and depression. An example of this transformation was the Bond Investment Trust of America. It was originally organized as a closed-end fund in Boston in 1926 by a group of trustees and lawyers as a common law trust, to pool the funds of clients and friends for investment in bonds, notes, and debentures, but in 1942, it became an open end investment company.[35]

One of the interesting facets of the early Boston mutual fund industry was how closely its major players worked with their counterparts. For instance, O. Kelley Anderson, who was president of the New England Mutual Insurance Company, was also a trustee of the Century Shares Trust and president of the Boston Fund, while Edward C. Johnson II was both president and director of Fidelity at the same time that he was vice president and treasurer of Incorporated Investors. Charles Eaton, who headed his own investment counsel firm and its mutual funds, served as a trustee of Boston Management and Research's Boston Fund. This type of practice, common in the 1930s through the 1950s, would change as the competition in the mutual fund industry shifted from other types of financial products in banking and insurance to a more head-to-head competition among the funds themselves in the 1960s.

While a number of trust companies were set up to create early mutual funds, other financial service firms in Boston soon created their own funds to sell to new or existing clients. Although Scudder, Stevens & Clark pioneered the investment counsel business in 1919, it likewise created its own mutual fund, later named the First Investment Counsel Fund, in 1927. The fund provided some additional income for the firm (it had both sales charges and redemption fees during its early years). But it also provided an easy way to manage small, time-consuming investment counsel accounts and to give the families and employees of wealthy investment counsel clients a way to invest for themselves. As one early partner later noted, "By 1927, it was apparent that the cost of continuous supervision of the smaller accounts was more than the client should be asked to pay and less than the firm could afford to receive." While the firm made no attempt to sell the shares in the fund, after a few years, it issued and redeemed them at net asset value without a selling commission or redemption penalty.

In 1928, Scudder set up two other funds, the Second Investment Counsel Fund, a "risk-security" fund that did not survive the depression, and the Third Investment Counsel Fund, which later evolved into the Scudder, Stevens & Clark Common Stock Fund. Into the post–World War II era, therefore, Scudder had essentially two funds, the First Investment Counsel Fund, which became a balanced fund, and its stock fund. Like most other Boston investment companies, Scudder mutual funds came in only two varieties—balanced and stock funds—until the 1960s.[36]

Another Boston company that came to mutual funds in the same manner was the investment counsel firm of Eaton & Howard, founded in 1924. Like Scudder, Charles F. Eaton Jr. saw mutual funds as "investment management for the smaller people." At first, Eaton & Howard funds had no sales company and none were actively sold. As Eaton said of his early experiment in mutual funds, "we were trying to do something . . . not *sell* something. We were managers, not merchandisers." According to Eaton, the funds "were originally formed solely for the purpose of managing smaller accounts, or amounts of money, of clients of the firm desiring Eaton & Howard management—accounts of a size which did not appear to warrant being handled as individual accounts."

After the Act of '40, Eaton's company decided to sell the two funds more broadly, "to make the funds more of a public vehicle for investment." This required some restructuring, including a change in the composition of the fund trustees, a majority of which were no longer affiliated with the fund's managers or underwriters. Another change was to apply a "reasonable sales charge" as well as a quarterly management fee, and a redemption fee when sold. Other investment counsel firms like Scudder and Loomis, Sayles & Company, founded in 1926, had more modest charges placed on their funds, but despite this, Eaton & Howard had more fund AUM into the 1950s than either of the other two companies.

Eaton & Howard created in 1929 four somewhat experimental funds, only two of which survived the depression. One was set up for clients of moderate means whose assets were well below those of investment counsel clients. Two of the others were stock funds, and a fourth was mostly invested in stock but with some fixed income assets. Through mergers and liquidation, and changes in the types of securities that the funds held, Eaton & Howard ended up with two strong funds by 1940, which were renamed the Balanced and Stock Funds. Despite the economy, Eaton & Howard funds grew throughout the 1930s, reaching $1 million in AUM in 1935, $2.5 million in 1937, and $3.5 million in 1939. Rival investment counsel firm Loomis, Sayles set up its first mutual fund in 1929.[37]

Thus by 1940, and certainly by the end of World War II, mutual funds had not only grown in size and numbers but had also become more highly specialized funds. During the 1930s, companies began to offer funds invested in bonds of varying grades; funds with holdings of bonds and preferred stock with common stock, though they were generally classified as common stock funds; funds that were balanced, which usually included about half high-grade senior securities and common stocks; and funds that were specialty funds, that is, invested in certain industries or classes and grades of securities. Now fully established, mutual funds would see greater growth during the war and especially in the postwar years, with increasing rivalry and competition.

War and Recovery

Following passage of the Act of '40, leaders in the fledgling mutual fund industry created their first trade organization. It started out as a permanent committee that would serve to work with the SEC to formulate rules and regulations to comply with the act and was originally called the National Committee of Investment Companies. The committee also sought to follow changes in state and federal tax legislation that would affect mutual funds. The first committee had many Bostonians—Paul Cabot, Charles F. Eaton, William Tudor Gardiner, Merrill Griswold, and James H. Orr, while Warren Motley, a lawyer from Boston who worked with mutual fund companies, was one of two counsel to serve the committee. In October 1941, the committee became the National Association of Investment Companies (NAIC), which was renamed the Investment Company Institute (ICI) in 1961. Charles F. Eaton became chairman of the ICI's Board of Governors in 1963.[38]

The war years had witnessed modest but progressive growth of mutual fund assets, rising from about $500 million to approximately $1.2 billion by the end of 1945. Boston claimed eighteen of eighty-six funds in January 1940, and 50 percent of the industry's assets. By war's end, Boston's concentration increased to about 56 percent of all fund assets perhaps the most impressive lead since the 1920s. The growing popularity and rising success of the funds, however, led to a geographical spread in the industry. By 1946, New York had established a presence, occasionally by converting its closed-end funds into mutual funds. Its first open end fund was set up in 1929, followed in 1932 by a burst of five more funds. Most of the rest were founded later in the 1930s or in 1940. Once the closed-end fund center, New York open end funds provided a platform for more extended growth as various financial intermediaries became involved with mutual funds in the 1960s and 1970s.[39]

As the popularity of mutual funds continued to grow in the postwar era, Boston investment companies, as well as the whole industry, were faced with new problems and opportunities. There were few new developments in the industry itself. Before the 1960s, growth could not be attributed to the creation of new types of funds, new distribution methods, or changes in investment company shareholder services.[40] The key to expansion was to sell more shares to the potential customer base. All of the investment companies had long faced state compliance regulations, known as "blue sky" laws, but a significant number of states had even banned sales of fund shares altogether.[41] In these jurisdictions, fiduciaries were only able to acquire for their clients securities that were on a state-mandated "legal list" or "legal standard." Gradually, however, through legislation and court decisions, those same investment advisers were permitted to follow what became known as the "Prudent Man Rule" (with a slightly different meaning from the original term), which allowed them to acquire mutual funds for their clients' portfolios. In 1950, only twenty of forty-eight states followed this practice, but over the next quarter of a century, the influence of the rule was greatly expanded at both the state and federal levels.[42]

Another important development was the growth of mutual fund savings programs ("contractual plans") for individuals. These plans spawned others. At Putnam, for instance, the early 1950s saw the launch of several new sales promotions that included the Monthly Cash Withdrawal Plan, the Putnam Plan with Life Insurance, and the Putnam Program for Profit Sharing Retirement— all of them employed to gradually increase their customers' investments in the company's mutual funds. In the end, these individualized saving programs, as well as future retirement accounts, weaned customers from traditional savings and retirement accounts. In 1949, there were less than $2 billion in mutual funds compared with $50 billion net reserves in life insurance companies, $55 billion in individual deposits in banks, and $56 billion in outstanding savings bonds. But those numbers would soon change. Furthermore, as *Time* magazine noted in 1959, mutual funds were creating a way for people to invest in the stock market rather than tying down their money in savings accounts: "No one doubts that by luring people's savings into stocks the funds have broadened the base of corporate ownership. Two-thirds of all mutual fund holders live outside the Eastern Seaboard; about a third do not own other stocks, [and] would probably not otherwise put their money into the market."[43]

Efforts also occurred to expand the "institutional" market, that is, to interest various organizations in mutual funds. These would include business

By late 1957, however, Putnam had also launched a second fund, the Putnam Growth Fund, owing to the pressures of fund dealers and investors who regarded the original fund as "too conservative for their needs in these boom times." The Putnam Growth Fund (known later as the Putnam Growth and Income I Fund) was established despite the founders' concerns that it would dilute the management and sales of the first fund and a belief that "the balanced concept was best for most investors." To keep with Putnam's conservative image, the new fund was to be used by investors "who wished to create their own balance through the ownership of tax exempt bonds or real estate." Despite starting out just after a stock market decline, the fund's assets rose from $179,000 to $20 million by 1960.

The Growth Fund only continued to do better in the early 1960s. Its assets rose almost 40 percent in 1961, as the shares were actually split twice that year, with a 50 and then a 100 percent stock dividend. The boom also spread over into the original fund, so that Putnam assets as a whole grew to $1.067 billion in 1964. Putnam briefly swung back in a more conservative direction when it established in 1963 an Income Fund, which grew modestly during the 1960s. After mid-decade, Putnam found itself "late in the . . . parade" for several innovative products—an exchange fund and a duofund, for investors interested in diversifying their stock holdings or wanting to combine both income and growth features in their investment. Still, the company offered the Putnam Equity Fund by the fall of 1967, which reached its peak in assets of $163 million the following year, before the decline that eventually ended the Go-Go years. The company also began marketing other growth (i.e., "performance") funds in 1968 (Putnam Vista) and 1969 (Putnam Voyager and Putnam Mariner), only shortly before the whole company, Putnam Investments, was sold to New York insurance underwriter Marsh & McLennan. By 1970, Putnam had $1.696 billion in AUM, which continued to rise to $2.328 billion in 1972, before falling to $1.435 billion in 1974, and then not rising to 1972 levels again until 1980.[47]

Perhaps the most interesting developments in these years happened to one of Putnam's rivals, Fidelity Investments, which was also on the rise in postwar Boston. Fidelity's upward movement initially came through growth funds and somewhat awkward transition to a new generation of management. Fidelity launched its Fidelity Capital Fund, an aggressive growth fund, in the 1950s, and by 1964, the fund had spawned no less than eighteen imitators. The fund would come to reflect changes in the industry broadly, and, specifically, how important the fund's portfolio manager was to an investment company's success. Investment decisions would be made less and less by investment company committees than by "star" portfolio managers. This era's growth funds also intensely focused on performance, particularly in relationship to that of other funds. Indeed, at the time, the word *performance* was used interchangeably with *growth* to describe these funds. Performance funds not only accounted for a large proportion of new fund sales, but, as John Brooks, a financial writer and historian of the period, noted, "It appeared that by picking your [growth] fund at random you could still make 40 percent on your money in a year's time." "Swingers," or high-flying stocks, such as Polaroid and Xerox were far outperforming old-line blue-chip companies such as AT&T, General Electric, and General Motors, which were only increasing at rates of about 15 percent a year.[48]

Fidelity's direct links to the Go-Go years began in 1952, when its president, Edward C. Johnson II, was asked by a friend at Scudder, Stevens & Clark to interview "a clever fellow" for whom they had no place at that time. The young man was Gerald Tsai Jr., who was born in Shanghai of westernized Chinese parents, and who came to New England to study first at Wesleyan and then Boston University. Bright, articulate, and ambitious, Tsai worked in business and finance for a couple of years before becoming interested in the stock market, which seemed to bring out some of his best talents. Edward Johnson was an Orientalist by avocation. He saw Tsai as a kindred spirit, and hired him as a stock analyst. By 1957, Tsai had built up a close enough working relationship with Johnson to ask if he might start his own growth fund. Johnson agreed, saying, "Go ahead. Here's your rope,"—meaning either here's your opportunity to succeed or to hang yourself. Tsai succeeded, establishing the Fidelity Capital Fund.

Tsai's success was accomplished by unorthodox methods. For one thing, Tsai bought and sold large quantities of stock, usually 10,000 shares or more. Also, his portfolio turnover generally exceeded 100 percent a year, then an unusual practice. The fund did well, and new money rapidly came into it. Even at the time of the Cuban missile crisis, following the largest single day drop in the stock market since the crash, Tsai was able to recover by injecting large amounts of capital and getting his fund's NAV to rise almost 70 percent within three months.

Such results, of course, did not go unrewarded, and by 1963, Tsai owned 20 percent of Fidelity Management and Research, or half the amount owned by Johnson. In the years that immediately followed, the Fidelity Capital Fund continued to do well, rising almost 50 percent in 1965 on a turnover of 120 percent, while the Dow rose only 15 percent that year. That same year, Tsai pressed Johnson on succession in the firm. The competition was between Tsai and Johnson's son Edward ("Ned") C. Johnson III. While Ned was slightly junior in age and experience, and more self-effacing than the mysterious, self-confident, highly publicized, and dazzling Tsai, Ned was a highly competent man who had done as well or better with his own growth fund, the Trend Fund, which he started managing in 1961, than Tsai had done with the Fidelity Capital Fund. Still, firm associates were unsure what kind of a leader Ned might someday become. Even close Fidelity confidant Caleb Loring Jr. noted that "Nobody suspected that Ned had the kind of mind he turned out to have."

Blood proved thicker than water. Tsai resigned in 1965 and then left for New York to begin his Manhattan Fund. Tsai's spectacular success at Fidelity contained a lot of good luck and timing. The Manhattan Fund got off to a great start, raising $247 million by the day of its official opening, and continued to do well until 1968, when assets were over $500 million. After that, the fund went into a tailspin, declining along with the market at the conclusion of the Go-Go years.

Looking back, Tsai had done much for Fidelity, whose assets rose from $86 million in 1952, the year he joined, to $2.3 billion in 1965, the year he left. His legacy was to insure that in the future, funds would be "performance driven," and to enshrine the role and importance of the fund's portfolio manager in that process. Ned Johnson's test would come later, after he succeeded his father in 1972, at a time when Fidelity's assets had declined 40 percent from the high established by his father, and after both the Fidelity Capital and Fidelity Trend Funds had dwindled to fractions of their former sizes. He would require something more than just the ability to pick good stocks, a facility that both he and Tsai had proven to have.[49]

While investment companies were pleased with the growth of assets in the 1950s and 1960s, the industry then went into a tailspin with many destabilizing consequences. A sales and redemption frenzy, which began in the late 1960s, became a net redemption phenomenon throughout most of the 1970s. At Eaton & Howard, for instance, sales had been strong in the 1960s and culminated in 1968 and 1969 with net gains (sales minus redemptions) of almost $41 and $34 million, respectively. Then came the 1970s, with net losses for every year to 1977 of often large redemptions, reaching almost $32 and 30 million in 1972 and 1973, respectively. At Putnam as elsewhere, there were losses, too. Whereas the multiple of redemptions over sales averaged 1.62 (or $16.20 in redemptions for every $10 in sales) at Eaton & Howard from 1970 through 1976, conditions at Putnam were almost as bleak, where that same multiple of redemptions over sales averaged 1.52.[50]

The Go-Go years and its aftermath not only rattled Boston investment companies, but also brought into play several forces that helped to change the mutual fund industry in the city. One of the most notable changes on the local landscape was the demise of Incorporated Investors. Part of Incorporated's problem was its investment policy; in the postwar years, it had tended to invest heavily in a relatively small number of companies. This approach actually worked well until the business recession of 1957–58 and the rise of growth stocks. Another key factor was the retirement in the late 1960s of William Amory Parker, who had run Incorporated from its beginnings in 1925. Parker was the first of a generation of founders of the industry whose death or retirement would soon affect other firms. Another early leader, Charles F. Eaton of Eaton & Howard, prolonged his retirement into the late 1970s, yet provided no opportunities for younger employees to buy into the firm and take it over gradually. This situation unfolded just as the decline in fund assets became a serious concern for the firm and its value as a company. In the end, Eaton decided to cash out, perhaps the most inappropriate choice he could make as an investment counselor, but the only option he left open for himself.[51]

Eaton's suitor was Vance, Sanders & Company, the successor of Learoyd, Foster & Company, the bond company that invented the mutual fund in 1924. For years, Vance, Sanders was largely a distributor of M.I.T. and several other funds, becoming by 1959 the second largest mutual fund distributor in the country. Thereafter, Vance, Sanders started changing course, entering fund management through exchange or "swap" funds it created in the early 1960s. While income from fund sales declined in that decade, Vance, Sanders was shocked in 1972 when M.I.T., by then part of Massachusetts Financial Services (MFS), announced that it was going to create its own mutual fund sales force and sever its nearly fifty-year business relationship with its distributor. It took several years for Vance, Sanders to recover from this sudden loss, but in 1979, it merged with Eaton & Howard to create Eaton Vance. The merging of traditions—investment counsel and mutual funds with a company that specialized in fund distribution—eventually helped to create one of Boston's most creative investment management companies. MFS, which undid its relationship with Vance, Sanders, had been under pressure to cut costs, but, ironically, it never quite recovered and had to merge with Sun Life (now Sun Life Financial), the Canadian insurance company, in 1982.[52]

In the midst of all of this local squalor, Boston's position as the center of the mutual fund industry was also being challenged, not only by New York but by the nation. While data is somewhat impressionistic as to the cities' relative strengths in the postwar period, New York was definitely becoming more influential. As noted earlier, in 1945, Boston controlled 56 percent of open end mutual fund assets. By 1956, a business article reported that Boston had thirty-eight mutual fund investment companies with assets of $2,939,198,000, which represented 36 percent of all mutual fund company assets nationwide. Despite this shrinking percentage, Boston funds had greatly increased in size in the previous fifteen years, from twenty-seven investment companies and

CHAPTER 7

The Rise of Venture Capital in Postwar Boston

I nvesting in companies in their "early stages" of development was not new in Boston—or elsewhere for that matter—after World War II. Such investing had been going on for ages, even by Massachusetts investors, when they set up textile mills or other industries a century earlier. Venture capitalists like to say that Christopher Columbus was the first venture capitalist, but even high-risk, potentially high-reward projects that venture capital represented were likely familiar to some centuries earlier, even as far back as Hammurabi's time.

What was new about this kind of investment in the 1940s was its location, focus, the kind of training and experience it required, and the results it offered. Some aspects of the venture capital process had been developed over previous decades, while others were discovered through the efforts in Boston of the first working venture capitalist firm, American Research & Development (AR&D), and still more came about a decade or so later, when the business model for the venture capital firm was restructured and transformed into its modern form.

By the early 1980s, however, venture capital as practiced in the Boston area came to a crossroads in its development, as firms shifted into later-stage and "special situations" investing, and leveraged buyouts—"private equity" investing as it became known. Although Boston and the East Coast had never engaged in venture capital as strictly a pure investment form, it had by the early 1980s come to represent one of several asset classes. On the West Coast, where venture capital came to dominate local investing, it remained a distinct cultural force. This chapter describes Boston's brand of venture capital, including the unique role of bank lending; the following chapter elaborates on that journey to private equity over its first several decades.[1]

Over the years, venture capital came to embody a number of characteristics expansion of industrial jobs in the Midwest where new or expanding companies were manufacturing radios, automobiles, and other consumer durables. Aware of the decline even before the Depression, local Boston business, political, and education leaders, under the guidance of Lincoln Filene, founded the New England Council in 1926 to find ways to improve regional conditions. During the next couple of decades, the council, which represented industry, government, and academic viewpoints, advocated regional economic revitalization by encouraging the settlement of branch plants of national companies, providing access to academic research for product development, and promoting local enterprises financed by local capital. This last undertaking, which focused on finding long-term capital for small businesses, would eventually become the mantra for venture capital and especially the Small Business Investment Company Act in the late 1950s.[11]

This effort to help finance small business was renewed again in the late 1930s when the council established a new products subcommittee. Its membership included MIT President Karl Compton, a strong proponent of technology-based revitalization of the New England economy, and Georges Doriot, a Harvard Business School professor, best known for his manufacturing course and, in time, his interest in military planning and its applications in business. Both men would help the effort to establish and develop the first venture capital firm in 1946. The subcommittee's report, which appeared in 1939, advocated support for sunrise industries, that is, helping to form new industries or assist existing firms upgrade their businesses, rather than sunset industries, like shoes and textiles, which were declining and leaving the state. The emphasis was on new companies creating and marketing new products that could in turn create new industries in New England. Just how this new organization would function, besides providing capital and perhaps some business and technical advice, was never fully developed before World War II intervened.[12]

In the early 1940s, Compton proposed the formation of the New England Industrial Research Foundation. Convinced that enough venture capital was available in New England, he wanted to create an organization that would have the expertise to evaluate opportunities presented to it—projects or technologies that would be funded by New England groups which would each subscribe $100,000. Income for the foundation would come from evaluation fees, and the reports and services it would provide to companies that would be funded. Both it and its similarly named New England Industrial Development Foundation never went beyond the planning stages, most likely because of the demands and effects of the war effort in the region.

During the war, the concept of an organization to help small and new business was expanded by another new products committee member, Ralph E.

FIGURE 8. Ralph E. Flanders (*Boston Herald-Traveler* Photo Morgue, Boston Public Library)

Flanders (fig. 8). Later serving in the U.S. Senate from Vermont and perhaps better known as the senator who introduced the motion to censure Senator Joseph McCarthy in 1954, Flanders played a pivotal role in developing the venture capital concept and then organizing and presiding over its corporate embodiment, AR&D, when it was established in 1946. Son of a subsistence farmer and lacking higher education, Flanders apprenticed as a machinist and draftsman, then went on to edit *Machine,* a machine tool magazine, traveling widely to report on developments in that industry. Gradually he also became a self-taught scholar on many subjects.

Flanders next became president of a successful machine tool company in Vermont, developing new machinery and about two dozen patents. During the Depression, he turned to addressing issues of economic policy, serving on the federal Business Advisory Council of the U.S. Commerce Department, where the committee he chaired came out in favor of addressing unemployment both geographically and by industry. Later in the 1930s, he served on Vermont committees to modernize the dairy industry and another to work out a way for New England states to share costs for a system of flood control dams. Flanders took these experiences in 1940 to the New England Council

TABLE 3. Investor Groups in American Research & Development in 1947

INVESTMENT GROUP	SIZE OF INVESTMENT	PERCENTAGE OF TOTAL INVESTMENT
Investment Companies	$1,340,375	38.6%
Insurance Companies	$300,000	8.6
Educational Institutions	$225,000	6.5
Individuals	$1,610,500	46.3
Totals	$3,475,875	100.0%

Sources: Compiled from Table 1 in David H. Hsu and Martin Kenney, "Organizing Venture Capital: The Rise and Demise of American Research & Development Corporation, 1946–1973," *Industrial and Corporate Change* 14, no. 4 (2005): 591, which is based on AR&D, *Annual Reports*, 1946 and 1947; Hugh Bullock, *The Story of Investment Companies* (New York: Columbia University Press, 1951); John C. Bogle, "The Economic Role of the Investment Company," A.B. thesis, Department of Economics and Social Institutions, Princeton University, 1951.

investment companies, which, as table 3 shows, were disproportionate to other kinds of investors and very different from the kinds of investors that would later participate in venture capital. Still, these groups of investors followed Flanders's view that the development corporation should be financed by conservative fiduciary interests like trusts, investment firms, and insurance companies as well as private individuals, and, at the same time, be managed and directed by capable individuals in business and technology fields.

In the years to come, as AR&D would need additional capital for its portfolio companies, it faced some difficulties. In 1949, for instance, despite numerous and glowing articles in several business publications, it could not find an underwriter and was able to sell privately only 43 percent of a $4 million offering. In the 1950s, opportunities to sell additional shares to increase the company's capitalization were for the most part disappointing until 1959. By 1960, however, with some success and increasing net assets, the company was able to persuade Lehman Brothers to underwrite another offering that netted it about $8 million. As a culmination of its success, its growing asset base, and as the country's only publicly traded venture capital firm, AR&D stock was at last officially listed on the New York Stock Exchange in 1962.

The General

It was not long before Georges Doriot became the central figure of AR&D (fig. 9). Doriot, a Frenchman who came to the United States to attend Harvard Business School in the 1920s, soon became a professor at the school in industrial management, and during World War II was made a naturalized citizen so that he could serve in the Quartermaster Corps in Washington, D.C., where his expertise could be put to best use. Doriot's wartime career was brilliant, and in 1945, he was promoted to the rank of brigadier general, an unusual dis-

FIGURE 9. Georges F. Doriot (left) at the 1968 Annual Meeting of American Research & Development (*Boston Herald-Traveler* Photo Morgue, Boston Public Library)

tinction for an officer in the corps. Doriot continued to serve in the reserves for decades, and for the rest of his life, everyone—students, colleagues at AR&D, and outsiders—affectionately referred to him as "the General."

Doriot quickly came to personify venture capital and develop key characteristics of the profession. As Charles Waite, his former teaching assistant at Harvard who became an AR&D staff member in 1960, noted, "Doriot took the first steps toward institutionalizing venture capital. . . . He was, more than anything else, a teacher. He was in business to test a thesis. Making money wasn't really a higher objective. He wasn't opposed to it, but the salaries were modest. There was no ownership in the company for anybody." Doriot's approach to new ideas, developments, products, and lines of research had been the basis of his well-known manufacturing course at Harvard Business School for decades, but it was his work in the military that provided the kinds of experiences useful for the emerging profession. During World War II, Doriot served in the Military Planning Division of the Quartermaster Corps, which consisted of four main subdivisions—research and development, operations, requirements, and machine tabulating branches—in a multifaceted approach to problem solving. In this position and using those approaches,

Doriot tackled a number of stubborn problems, such as finding substitutes for raw materials and developing innovative products ranging from materials for military clothing to compact food—ideas that were later institutionalized by the U.S. Army Soldier Systems Center in Natick, Massachusetts. Doriot's practical application to problem-solving during the war became a template for analyzing potential investment ideas after he came to preside over AR&D following his military service.[19]

Another aspect of Doriot's character, which manifested itself in the growth of venture capital, was his patient approach to investing. Results, if any, might take a decade, which is why he often referred to his portfolio companies as his "children." In 1952, Doriot noted to a reporter,

> When you have a child, you don't ask what return you can expect.
> . . . Of course you have hopes—you hope the child will become
> President of the United States. But that is not very probable. I
> want them to do outstandingly well in their field. And if they do,
> the rewards will come. But if a man is good and loyal and does not
> achieve a so-called good rate of return, I will stay with him. Some
> people don't become geniuses until *after* they are 24, you know. If I
> were a speculator, the questions of return would apply. But I don't
> consider a speculator—in my definition of the word—constructive.
> I am building men and companies.[20]

Doriot also prescribed to a style of active management with his children, meaning sitting on their boards to monitor and, when necessary, to become involved in the managerial direction of the company.

Doriot's pedagogical approach to many issues and projects—leading discussions in front of his colleagues, who were largely his former students—led "the great man" or the "enquiring mind," as he was sometimes called, to be stubborn in his opinions from time to time. He could think years ahead in wanting to conduct a study on building a tunnel under the English Channel even though there would be no profit in it. He could also be very patient with an early portfolio company like Tracerlab, which included radioactive isotopes and radiation detection equipment, realizing that there would be few commercial markets for their products but knowing that it would eventually be important for universities and would spawn other companies that might make different applications of the technology to create commercial products.[21]

The Broad Context of AR&D's Venture Capital Investing

Once established, however, AR&D led a less than predictable investment life during its most active years, 1946 to 1973, suggesting that venture capital is a more complex, highly opportunistic activity than might be supposed, and one that required a period of growth before it acquired maturity. For instance, despite early and close connections with Harvard and MIT, no more than 10 percent of AR&D's portfolio companies came by way of those two institutions, and this was only in its earliest years. Instead, it was AR&D's investment officers who accounted for 40 percent of the portfolio companies at the beginning, but this figure declined by half in the 1960s and through to 1973, when AR&D was merged into another company. Investment banks and brokerages accounted for from a quarter to half of all deals. The use of coinvesting with or referrals from other venture capital firms, practices common with private venture capital firms in the 1960s and 1970s, were not common at AR&D.[22]

One of the initial objectives of all venture capital firms is to review and selectively choose business plans, recognizing that the firm can only fund and actively manage a few projects at a time. Over the years, AR&D accepted no more than about 4 percent of the plans that were submitted or found, often even less. This selectivity was probably due to a growth in the number of business plans available for review over time, and changes in the general economy that encouraged or discouraged new plans. While venture capital has been largely perceived as emphasizing high-tech and research- and development-intensive enterprise, there is little in AR&D's record to suggest that this kind of portfolio company was typical over the long run. In fact, its involvement in these types of businesses actually declined over time, even though its most critical successes were ultimately in computer hardware, medical technology, and similar fields. AR&D's early ventures emphasized chemical and professional service equipment companies, while in later years, education, media, electronics, and scientific instruments prevailed. In large part, the variations were likely due to the opportunities that became available and the changing expertise of the AR&D staff.[23]

Even early-stage investing, a practice that has become synonymous with venture capital, was only gradually introduced by AR&D's investment choices. Initially, only about one in five portfolio companies could be described as an early-stage investment, but this figure almost tripled later in AR&D's history. The reason for this was likely that early-stage investing, with its time horizon of about a decade, placed greater—perhaps almost fatal—pressures on AR&D when it came to providing dividends for shareholders, whereas later-stage investment, with far fewer years to reach profitability and marketability, gave the venture capital company a greater chance at success and ability to spread interest in the concept as a whole to the investment community. Furthermore, managing long-term investments in portfolio companies required a knowledge that would require some time to develop.

Another deviation from general expectation was the assumption that because of AR&D's location in Boston, venture capital would primarily benefit local small businesses. Instead, like nineteenth-century Boston investment in railroads, investors went to where the opportunities were; they were not necessarily in business to transform the local economy. During its life as an independent corporation, AR&D's investment in Massachusetts companies reached to about 45 percent during the early part of this period, then declined to about 30 percent with a low at less than 10 percent in the early 1960s. Nevertheless, time would prove that AR&D's most significant investments were closely identified with Route 128 companies (that is, high-tech companies situated on the beltway around Boston) and the Massachusetts minicomputer boom of the 1960s.[24]

Indeed, it was the variety of enterprises that AR&D was funding that caught the attention of *Fortune* magazine in 1949, when an article on AR&D marveled at the diversity of the corporation's undertakings, which ranged from shrimp fishing and processing to a manufacturer of detergent for automobiles and another developing applications based on generating high-voltage electricity. By that time, some three years after its establishment, AR&D had invested in eleven companies, six of which were making money, four were being "nursed," and only one was seriously in the red. The article noted that AR&D took a minority, but sometimes a controlling, interest in its portfolio companies, and that it had helped in efforts at deregulation, obtaining permission in four states to allow investment trusts to acquire interests in companies that were less than three years old, even though in more than half the states, insurance companies still could not make a legal investment in AR&D.[25]

By 1952, another *Fortune* article noted that the corporation was investing in sixteen major "situations," financing "such scientific gadgetry as radioactivity meters, high-voltage particle accelerators, spectrochemical instruments, automatic weapon-control systems, radar gear, liquid-fuel rocket motors, precision timing devices, and a plastic membrane to turn sea water into fresh." That March, AR&D acquired its first wholly owned subsidiary, Natural Gas Odoring. This Houston-based concern produced an odorant used to detect leaks in natural gas lines. Despite the diversity of AR&D's operations, the business community remained uneasy about a lack of a dividend after six years of operation. Doriot's response was that AR&D did not invest in "the ordinary sense"; rather, "it creates, it risks. Results take more time, but the potential for ultimate profit is much greater."[26]

Even before AR&D reached the end of its first decade, it had developed a few characteristics and procedures that would become common in the venture capital world. Merrill Griswold, for instance, noted that while some of the corporation's early ventures included two fishing companies, it was the more esoteric technological, or "long-hair," enterprises for which they were most criticized. "Some of our friends began to say, 'Oh, Lord, not another long-hair project. Why doesn't A.R.& D. back something commercial and make some money?' We learned our lesson. Now we realize that our best things are longhair. If they click we're not trying to do something that everyone else can do." Another rule that AR&D followed was to invest some of its funds in portfolio companies as notes or debentures and the remainder in voting stock that amounted to a 25 to 30 percent investment. It also fixed its management fee at 4 percent of its investment.[27]

While AR&D was quite successful by the early 1960s because of the maturity of its portfolio companies, rising net assets, and growing stock price, the company and industry will always be linked to its backing of a single minicomputer manufacturer, Digital Equipment Company ("Digital" or DEC). In 1957, some of the younger men at AR&D—Hoagland, William H. Congleton, and Wayne Brobeck, an AR&D technical advisor who was on the MIT faculty—met early on with DEC's founders, Kenneth H. Olsen and Harland E. Anderson, about their desire to secure venture capital backing to start their proposed company (figure 10). Despite skepticism of Doriot and others at AR&D about early computer technology, Hoagland and Brobeck helped to prep the two entrepreneurs for their presentation to the AR&D board. According to Olsen,

> They gave us three bits of advice. One was "Don't use the word computer because *Fortune* magazine said that no one was making money in computers and no one was about to." So we took that out of our proposal . . . and they said "Don't promise five percent profit. . . ." The staff continued that if you're asking someone for money, you've got to promise better results than that. So we promised ten percent. And we made about ten percent most of our history. The third thing was "most of the board is over 80, so promise fast results." So we promised to make a profit in a year. The other side of that story is that we really did, after 12 months, make a profit.[28]

The two men, who had changed the name of their company from Digital Computer to Digital Equipment Company, so impressed the board with their presentation that they were given $70,000 for an equity position—which turned out to be about 78 percent of the company's value—and another $30,000 in a line of credit. The two rented space in an old woolen mill in Maynard, Massachusetts, at 25 cents a square foot, and brought in lawn furniture and an old roll-top desk to set up their business.[29]

In 1959, AR&D made another $100,000 investment in DEC to help develop the Programmed Data Processor 1 (PDP-1) mainframe computer. Easier to use and priced lower than the IBM mainframe, sales of the PDP-1 for DEC reached

the separation of First National Bank from First Boston following the passage of the Glass-Steagall Act in 1933. But a couple of Boston banks—First National and New England Merchants Bank—came to specialize in loans to unique, usually technologically oriented, businesses. At the time Peter Brooke and Arthur F. F. Snyder represented transitional figures, who started their careers in commercial bank lending, but as the investment environment changed, ended up involved in something closer to venture capital. Unlike venture capital, these loans provided the banks with interest and repayment of the loan, not an actual ownership interest, which could increase the reward many times over if the company proved successful. Still, they represented a profitable business for the banks.

Peter Brooke, later the founder of TA Associates and Advent International, began his financial career, after Harvard Business School and the U.S. Army, in the loan department of Worcester National Bank. After about six months, he came to First National Bank of Boston and their "Special Industries Section," headed by Serge Semenenko. This section was part of the bank's lending department and operated more or less strictly in that capacity. Unlike venture capital, it did not spend time working with a company's management. Nevertheless, Brooke was keen on helping the bank to succeed in this area and focused on economic development in the Boston area. He noted, "It seemed obvious to me that the business of the bank should be to finance the only valuable raw material we had in the region—namely brains. I felt that the bank shouldn't go around the country syndicating credits for General Motors and other national companies—it should concentrate on the core strength in the region in which it operated."[36]

In the late 1950s, following the launch of Sputnik, Brooke wrote a paper to the head of his department in which he sought to develop a program for lending that would focus on local economic development and advancing technology, and also one that would rely on government contracts at MIT (which would provide the collateral) and technology-based enterprises spawned by MIT. In turn, the bank set up a "High Technology Lending Group," operated by William H. Raye Jr., the senior credit officer; Bill Brown, later president of the bank; and Brooke, "the youngster." One of the basic points of Brooke's analysis was that investing in businesses outside of New England had only limited impact on Boston, but in lending to small technology firms in the area, there would be a multiplier effect that would provide a needed local stimulus.

Brooke scoured Cambridge and the Route 128 area, calling on virtually every small company that had spun out of MIT or Harvard. Brooke's lending section started with about $20 million in capital—a vast sum in its day, but small compared to the combined assets of First National, one of the largest commercial banks in the country. He went around soliciting business using the Standard Industrial Classification (SIC) system to identify electronics companies in the Boston area. There was little risk in these investments (the section lost perhaps $5,000 out of its $20 million pool) because it lent against government contracts as collateral, and became an active force in the growth of these businesses. As a result of Brooke's work, he missed out on very little business, except for perhaps DEC. While the bank did not get the high risk/high rewards of early-stage venture capital with an ownership share when they were sold, the bank made profitable loans because of the interest they generated. Some of the businesses Brooke helped to finance were Wang Laboratories, Unitrode (which was later sold to Texas Instruments), Damon Engineering (the subject of a leveraged buyout), and Worcester Controls. Many other successes were sold and quickly lost their identities as they merged into larger companies. Despite the success and profitability of these loans, very little attention was given by business historians or writers to this activity or to the activities of bank-affiliated SBICs (small business investment companies, discussed in the next chapter), because the capital commitments for these operations were so small that they escaped the attention of bank annual reports.

Brooke's transition from lending to venture capital came when he decided to leave for New York to head the venture capital operations of the Phipps family's Bessemer Ventures in 1961. Bessemer had at the time the largest portfolio (though not the largest amount of capital) of any venture capital organization in the country, but it needed someone to develop a rational approach to diversification of its investments. While it was technology-oriented, it spanned various areas from computers to medical devices, electronic peripherals to the health sciences. Brooke was determined to diversify it and included companies that spread from early- to late-stage development, or what he called "a balanced portfolio," a notion that he would someday incorporate into his own venture capital firm. Brooke never moved to New York but commuted each week from Boston. In 1963, however, he decided to come home. He accepted a position with Tucker Anthony and R. L. Day, a Boston brokerage firm in which he became half owner of TA Associates. That company would soon become a private venture capital and, later, private equity firm.[37]

While no other Boston banks had a high-tech team like First National, one other bank lender competed with Brooke: Arthur F. F. Snyder, a loan officer at New England Merchants National Bank. Bill Egan, who later founded the Boston-based private equity firm Alta Communications, regarded Snyder and Brooke as the two most important people in the development of venture capital in New England. Brooke himself called Snyder "a powerhouse on his own, and he was my only competition." Of course, Brooke could "beat him to death" because First National had so much more money, but Snyder picked up many good clients. Both men liked technology companies, and were often seen, the story goes, with Brooke on one side of Route 128 talking to prospective clients while Snyder was on the other side doing the same. Occasionally, they ended up on the same side of the highway. Brooke once recalled, "I knew I'd found a good one if I saw Arthur's car in the parking lot. We were out there slugging it out for business when no other banks had the imagination or nerve to back great new enterprises like Damon Engineering and Unitrode. Arthur Snyder was a visionary and a formidable competitor."

Snyder, a native of Philadelphia, came to New England and eventually was hired by Shawmut Bank's trust department around 1950. He was given a copy of "Shattuck on trusts," read a few trusts, and was then sent out to "sell the trust department." He brought in a lot of business but received only a meager raise. When he mentioned how productive he had been to his boss, the boss said that Snyder had just been "lucky." Spurned by the comment, he decided to go see Mark Wheeler, president of New England Merchants National Bank, who immediately increased his salary by about 50 percent.[38]

At Merchants, Snyder shifted from the trust to the loan business, making loans up and down Route 128. Aside from First National, Merchants was the only Boston bank at the time interested in making "technical" loans, that is, loans to technology companies. Snyder, by then vice president of commercial lending at Merchants, "regularly took out full page ads in the *Boston Globe* showing himself with an aircraft or missile model in his hands, calling upon high-technology enterprises to see him about their financial needs." He also set up the bank's venture capital small business investment company (SBIC). Egan ended up heading the bank's SBIC, the New England Enterprise Capital Corporation (1961), which Snyder had previously "run out of his hip pocket," making loans and possibly acquiring pieces of equity in businesses. Like Brooke, Snyder left Boston briefly to become president of a Detroit bank, but returned to New England as chairman of a manufacturing company. He then went to Commonwealth Bank in Boston, which he ran successfully for four years. After its sale, Snyder next moved on to the Boston bank U.S. Trust Company, where he returned to the lending business.[39]

Snyder's most significant triumph was his close and early relationship with Continental Cablevision, undeniably the most important Boston venture capital investment after DEC and one that came to involve much of the venture capital community in Boston. "Continental Cablevision never would have happened without Arthur," noted that company's cofounder, Amos Hostetter. "He made an outrageously risky term loan to us in 1963 when nobody was making term loans to cable companies, and very few people even knew what cable companies were all about. When we sold the company in 1996—33 years later—we had over 10,000 employees. These were all jobs that Arthur created."

The loan to Hostetter did not, however, come easy. In 1962, Hostetter and Snyder both worked on State Street and carpooled from their homes in Marblehead, Massachusetts. Over that summer, Snyder asked Hostetter how the cable deal was going, and after a few months, Snyder told him what he was going to do: "I want you to talk to everyone else who might be a potential lender to this. At the end of that come tell me what you've got, and we'll see if I can do better." Throughout the rest of 1962, Hostetter visited "every bank in New York, Chicago, and Philadelphia that might have some knowledge of cable television. In every case we got the same answer: 'It sounds like a great idea. After you get it up and running and you have some positive cash flow, come see us, and we'll talk about lending you some money.'"

In the end, he returned to Snyder, who "spared me the embarrassment of asking what the next best offer was, because there wasn't one." Hostetter brought his loose-leaf notebook, which contained the prospectus for the company, and a goal of someday reaching as many as 25,000 customers. Snyder took the notebook away from him, ceremoniously dropped it into the waste-paper basket, and said, "Now tell me about your company."

> He didn't want to see anything in writing; it was all face-to-face and eye-to-eye. He then laid out the provisions for the potential term loan. We need $600,000 and he said. "I will loan you half the money, if you get $300,000 in equity first."
> "Will you give me a letter to that effect?" I asked.
> "Yes, I will."
> Based on the strength of that letter, we were able to raise the equity, and the company got started.[40]

As Brooke and Snyder continued to help finance new local businesses, venture capital activities in Boston were beginning to take place in banks, investment companies, and, shortly, small private venture capital firms as well.

CHAPTER 8

The Growth of Venture Capital and Emergence of Private Equity

While American Research & Development's (AR&D) organization and structure would later lead to its own undoing, and Peter Brooke's and Arthur Snyder's activities largely remained on the cusp of venture capital, a more reliable source for funding and structure for venture capital firms came into being with the passage of the federal Small Business Investment Act of 1958. The act was passed to improve the general economy and especially the prospects of small business "by establishing a program to stimulate and supplement the flow of private equity capital and long-term loan funds, which small-business concerns need for the sound financing of their business operations and for their growth, expansion, and modernization, and which are not available in adequate supply."

The legislation encouraged the creation of small business investment companies (SBICs) to make loans to small businesses. The SBICs were monitored, funded, and licensed by a division of the Small Business Administration, a federal agency that was itself only five years old. Of fundamental importance to Boston and the Northeast as a whole, the act allowed commercial banks to set up their own SBICs by providing them with certain exclusions or exemptions from the Securities Act of 1933, the Trust Indenture Act of 1939, and the Investment Company Act of 1940. What made these SBICs unique was that the federal government loaned them substantial sums of money, which, in turn, could be used to leverage the funds that the SBICs might acquire on their own.[1]

Passage of the act represented a confluence of certain policy concerns about economic growth that dated as far back as the depression, when governments were looking for ways to stimulate their economies. The act was seen as a way of meeting the equity capital and long-term credit needs of small businesses, a serious issue for many years. But it was more likely seen as an incentive to aid new, entrepreneurial, and technological companies, driven by the launching of Sputnik a year earlier, the rising competitiveness of the Soviet Union, and fear that the United States might be falling behind.

The Rise of SBICs in the Late 1950s

Traditionally, small- to medium-sized businesses had difficulty gaining access to long-term capital. The first formal recognition of this problem occurred in the early 1930s, when it was discussed in a report by the British Parliamentary Treasury Committee on Finance and Industry, chaired by Hugh Pattison Macmillan but largely written by economist John Maynard Keynes. In its report, the committee noted that "it has been represented to us that great difficulty is experienced by the smaller and medium sized businesses in raising the capital which they may from time to time require even when the security offered is perfectly sound." Noting the difficulties of raising capital through stock offerings for the small sums these businesses needed, or to interest investors in such offerings, "the only other alternative would be to form a company to devote itself particularly to the smaller industrial and commercial issues. . . . We see no reason why with proper management and provided British industry in general is profitable, such a concern should not succeed." This problem of inadequate capital for small business, as outlined in the report, subsequently became known as the "Macmillan Gap."

While this proposal made little headway during the depression and World War II, in 1945, Parliament created the Industrial and Commercial Finance Corporation, which went on to provide long-term and permanent capital in modest amounts to British businesses "where the existing facilities provided by banking institutions and the Stock Exchanges are not readily or easily available." Although the British corporation and its successor proved less successful than venture capital in the United States, their focus on developing new ways to deal with the shortage of risk capital and long-term capital needs for small businesses eventually led to the creation of SBICs, and later to private investment firms modeled (and improved) in a variety of ways after AR&D.[2]

The idea of a federal government program to promote the financing of small business had started with studies in the Commerce Department in the 1930s. No action took place until the 1950s, however, and then it came from several unlikely sources. In 1950, Alabama Senator John Sparkman proposed his "Small Business Investment Act," which would have used "capital banks" to carry out the program. While one small step in that direction came about with the creation of the Small Business Administration (SBA) in 1953, nothing happened to

Sparkman's bill until Senator Lyndon B. Johnson, looking for ways to develop support for his run for the presidency in 1960, convinced House Speaker Sam Rayburn to endorse the bill. The measure easily passed Congress, and President Dwight D. Eisenhower signed it into law in August 1958.

These SBICs, or private investment companies, were given borrowing rights from the SBA, thus leveraging their own resources, and also certain tax benefits. An SBIC's "statutory capital" consisted of the twenty-year subordinated debentures the SBA would purchase, which was matched by private capital up to $150,000, giving the SBIC a total of $300,000 for investment. SBICs could deduct losses from convertible debentures or stock received as ordinary losses, which were deductible from ordinary income. Furthermore, SBICs were allowed to invest only in companies with a net worth of $2.5 million or less and assets not exceeding $5 million. Of singular importance to Boston, commercial banks were allowed to invest up to 1 percent of their capital and surplus in an SBIC. This allowed them to circumvent the exclusion from owning industrial corporations, and was the first time they could make equity-type investments since the passage of the Glass-Steagall Act almost twenty-five years earlier. All major New England banks, particularly those in Boston, soon set up their own SBICs, while some twenty-six smaller area commercial banks were involved in a single Boston SBIC.

There were some serious weaknesses in the original act. The requirement that SBICs invest only in convertible debentures was quickly changed to include collateralized debentures. Also abandoned was the SBICs' obligation to remain small with only a maximum of $300,000 in capital. This former situation had meant that in order to repay government loans, SBICs had to invest in the form of debt or debtlike securities, making it impossible to invest in start-up companies that could not quickly generate cash. In addition, both the SEC and IRS needed to make new regulations for SBICs, which were operating in conflict with already established regulations. The number of SBIC license approvals grew from 16 in 1959 to as many as 298 in 1962 before beginning to slide until none were approved by 1969. After the program was changed to address new problems and opportunities, it was able to attract new interest in the 1970s.

During this period and well into the future, there were four different kinds of SBICs. First, some were publicly owned, although none raised more than about $100 million. Next, there were also small private SBICs, about forty or so in number, as well as real estate SBICs, firms that were not intended with the passage of the act but that were not excluded.[3] Finally, there were bank SBICs. Bank-affiliated SBICs became a significant source of venture capital funding in the 1960s and 1970s. Some were successful, like the one created by First National City Bank (later Citibank) and others by Bank of America, Chase Manhattan,

First Chicago, and Security Pacific. Many SBICs that were formed in the late 1960s, however, did not survive the intense economic downturn in the 1970s.[4]

One of the first SBICs in Boston was the Boston Capital Company, headed by Joseph W. Powell Jr. and formed in 1960. A Princeton and Harvard Business School graduate, Powell worked for the National Shawmut Bank and Standard Brands in Boston before he became vice president of AR&D, second to General Doriot, from the time of the company's founding in 1946 until 1953. In that year, Powell moved to Cleveland to become vice president of the Harris-Seybold Company, a printing equipment manufacturer, before returning to Boston less than a decade later. Perhaps Boston Capital's most significant investment was in Continental Cablevision. Powell and Merchant Bank's Arthur Snyder provided Continental with the seed money it needed; as a result, Boston Capital probably owned 40 to 50 percent of Continental Cablevision at one time. By the early 1970s, however, Boston Capital, originally devoted to investment in small businesses, transformed itself into BBC Industries with operations principally in the medical and dental fields. As a result, by 1971, Boston Capital's venture position in Continental Cablevision was bought by Vin Ryan's Boston venture firm Schooner Capital.[5]

As noted earlier, every major Boston bank had its own SBIC, and, in some cases, these banks were also stakeholders in other SBICs financed by syndicates of (often smaller) local banks. In 1961, First National Bank of Boston, apparently encouraged by Brooke's "High Technology Lending Group," set up the first bank-affiliated SBIC in New England, the First Small Business Investment Corporation of New England. In November of that year, Richard Farrell became its first full-time employee. The corporation became the venture capital arm of the bank at the time. Farrell had come to First National in 1956 as an investment analyst for the Old Colony Trust Company (the two companies had been "consolidated" in 1929, though each carried on separate financial activities until they merged in 1970). First National had a long record of making nontraditional investments, perhaps the best known of which were those of Serge Semenenko, senior vice president of the bank, who had funneled more than $2 billion into Hollywood films since the 1930s as part of his "Special Industries" portfolio. In 1956, he had also agreed to buy a majority of stock in Jack and Albert Warner's motion picture studio, Warner Brothers.[6]

Farrell and his corporation had no connection with Semenenko and his widespread lending operations at the bank or with Peter Brooke's "High Technology Lending Group," even through all three were doing similar work. Within a short time, other banks followed suit in setting up SBICs, such as Merchants Bank's New England Enterprise Capital Corporation (run by Arthur Snyder, William Egan, and later Jay Patterson) and Federal Street

Capital Corporation (sponsored primarily by Shawmut, State Street, and Merchants Banks and run by Jack Lamott), among others.[7]

Farrell's first investment was with the Hitchner Manufacturing Company, which made metal castings—an investment that illustrates how venture capital in the early days was somewhat dependent on what opportunities existed and the need to find partners to spread the risk and cover the investment. Other financial sources for the deal included Boston Capital, run by Joe Powell, and several local wealthy families, including the Coolidges and Putnams, who would continue to play a crucial role in venture capital over the next two decades.

Although Hitchner was a traditional manufacturing company, Farrell actually did mostly early-stage high-technology deals. Damon Engineering, a highly successful laboratory testing company, turned a $300,000 investment into a $10 million IPO. Other significant investments included Codex, a data communication firm in Mansfield, Massachusetts, which was acquired by Motorola, and the Hollis Engineering Company of Nashua, New Hampshire, which was bought by another midwestern company. During this era and into the 1970s, Boston area computer "hardware" companies—Wang, Data General, and Prime, for instance—received venture capital investments, while software companies did less well in Boston, particularly under the scrutiny of bank-owned SBICs. Software and semiconductors soon received significant investments from West Coast venture capital firms and helped to create a distinction in the kinds of companies in which each region would invest.

Sometime after 1967, when Semenenko left First National, his "Special Industries" and the bank's SBIC were brought closer together, each reporting to Bill Brown, who headed the bank's "High Technology Lending Group." With Special Industries' aggressive lending in the movie industry, it soon moved on to investing in the communications field with cable, radio, television, and eventually cell phone development. Few other banks loaned to cable companies, but First National and many Boston venture firms, including the First's SBIC, invested in Continental Cablevision, a business that was always raising money and expanding, and was probably the largest and most widespread investment by the venture capital businesses in Boston. In order to take on a broader role in venture investment, First National decided in the early 1970s to use the holding company platform to create the First Capital Corporation of Boston so that it could take an equity position in its portfolio companies, an action that was prohibited to SBICs.

Even though venture capital was always risky, Farrell's group was able to achieve some level of success with at least one out of every three companies in which it invested. While the early 1970s were hard on venture capital, Farrell and his associates continued to invest in high-tech, and eventually did well.

The bank's SBIC began with $250,000 in assets but had risen to about $50 million by the time Farrell left in 1980. Over the years, First National used its profits from its SBIC to fund the bank's charitable activities. In 1980, Farrell and Harry Healer, his associate since 1969, founded a private firm, the Venture Capital Fund of New England, in Wellesley, Massachusetts, with their first fund reaching $19 million, even though they had initially anticipated only about $10 million.[8]

Another early pioneer in Boston venture capital was Rick Burnes. After completing college in 1963, he was hired by National Shawmut Bank and began a fifteen-month training program before being assigned in February 1965 to a venture capital subsidiary owned by forty other Massachusetts banks. Although owned by many, the Massachusetts Small Business Investment Company (later renamed Federal Street Capital Corporation) was effectively run by its largest stockholders—Shawmut, State Street, and Merchants. After his appointment, Burnes was sent to learn from Arthur F. F. Snyder, who had "cut his wings" with Shawmut earlier before going to New England Merchants, where he made loans to fledgling local high-tech companies.

While Burnes was at the Massachusetts Small Business Investment Company, it invested in "funny little companies . . . before it was identified that technical companies were the way to go." There was also a development side to the company, and Burnes looked for opportunities that would employ people as well. Still, the companies that he oversaw covered a wide array of businesses—furniture rental, security guard services, electronics components manufacturing, and even a diamond grinding mill company—with investments ranging from $50,000 to $250,000. Over time and with the encouragement of members of the company's board, Burnes was able to find a number of quite successful technical companies in which to invest, like Computervision. By the time he left, he had received his board's approval for a $100,000 investment in MCI–New England, even though the deal was never consummated.

Shortly before that, however, Burnes received a call from John H. ("Jack") Carter, an MIT administrator and founder of Itek, a high-tech company involved in optical disk technology, computer-aided design systems, and camera systems for spy satellites. Carter had the scientific and technical knowledge to understand new startups and was interested in creating a university-affiliated venture firm, but he did not have experience in the venture business. Carter had been a successful investor in Data General, the proceeds of which he planned to use to set up the new venture capital firm. Carter's plan was to create an academically oriented organization, perhaps more like AR&D than a modern venture capital firm, which had six professors who would serve as special limited partners. Burnes would provide the investment expertise.

Together they founded this private venture capital firm in the late 1960s, sub-sequently called Charles River Ventures (described later in this chapter). Work in a bank-affiliated SBIC prior to founding one's own venture capital firm was typical at that stage in the growth of the industry.[9]

While many of Boston's private and most of Boston's bank-affiliated SBICs were established in the early 1960s, SBICs formed later and in other locales had an uncertain future. By 1962, a total of 585 SBICs were licensed, with nearly 700 of them organized and running by the mid-1960s. But the rate of increase was steadily declining. While 298 new SBICs were established in 1962, only 101 were founded in 1963, and a mere 10 in 1966.[10] Heady growth then decline was followed by financial disaster for many SBICs. By 1966–1967, an increasing number were cited for financial mismanagement, self-dealing, and corruption, with some 232 SBICs classified as problems by the Small Business Administration. In many of these cases, SBICs exploited the interest spread of the borrowed federal funds with the money they lent. Because of the constant need to repay the government loans, most of these small, private companies made few high-risk, long maturity high-tech investments. New regulations reduced their number to only 250, and by 1978, they represented a mere 21 percent of available venture capital in the country. This trend away from SBICs to private venture capital firms could be seen by the start of the 1970s. Of the 190 independent venture capital organizations active that year, 32 SBICs and 20 private firms were formed between 1959 and 1965, while 10 SBICs and 119 private firms were established between 1966 and 1970.[11]

Besides the financial mismanagement, the dwindling number of SBICs was due to economic developments in the late 1960s and early 1970s. First, the general economic decline in the late 1960s, the failure of both stock and bond markets to perform generally throughout the 1970s, and the rampant rise of inflation late in that decade and lasting into the 1980s created difficult economic conditions. These conditions did not generally bode well for venture capital unless investments were in place beforehand, so that venture capitalists could recoup their investments at the end of the declining cycle. The debt service and repayment requirements of federal government loans made it difficult for SBICs to survive in that climate. But many of the new private limited partnership venture capital firms could and did survive, bringing their portfolio companies to fruition at the end of the 1970s, when the stock market started to improve. These firms had already emerged by the late 1960s, and by 1968, alone had surpassed the SBIC industry in total capital under management. Despite their frailties, SBICs helped to train a large number of venture capitalists and to fund many new startups in the 1960s, particularly on the West Coast.[12]

Furthermore, SBICs were important because they provided capital, which remained scarce until the late 1970s. In 1967, for instance, the 791 licensed SBICs had invested more than $1 billion in small businesses. They, like AR&D, provided important lessons—some of them negative—in how to create a venture capital firm. Because they used debt rather than equity, SBICs could only finance companies in relatively stable, non-high-risk industries. Furthermore, they usually could only provide money, not industry experience, for their clients. Part of the answer in overcoming these obstacles was to establish a better organizational structure, the limited partnership, for venture capital.[13] The SBIC program went through another period of growth in the early 1980s, then a rash of failures and liquidations in the late 1980s; the program was again overhauled and revived in the early 1990s.[14]

The Development of Limited Partnership Venture Capital Firms

While the fortunes of many SBICs in the 1960s and 1970s were grim, starting a private venture firm during the same period was also problematic, particularly after 1969, when the economy started to fail. For those lucky enough to begin operation before the downfall, and with capital and patience to wait out the storm, it was an excellent time to acquire equity interests in portfolio companies on favorable terms and with low equity values. Following recovery, these ventures would likely sell as market conditions for IPOs improved. For others interested in starting a venture business, however, capital commitments in the fledgling venture capital industry dropped steadily through 1977, and reached a low of about $10 million in 1974–75. The private limited partnership structure not only helped to compensate its partners adequately but also created a stable organizational structure with about a ten-year lifespan to insulate the company from having to meet short-term profit expectations. Nevertheless, talk of the period frequently focused on the imminent "death" of venture capital as the industry virtually shut down.[15]

The fledgling industry was eventually helped by legislation. Venture capitalists made their money as capital gains, and although capital gains had had preferential status in the U.S. tax code since 1921, much of it was taken away by the so-called tax reforms of 1969 and 1976, which raised the effective minimum rate for capital gains from 25 to 49.5 percent. The nearly twofold tax increase dried up sources of venture capital and substantially shrunk the number of public issues available. More favorable events were soon on their way, however. In 1978, the Revenue Act reduced taxes on capital gains to 28 percent, which created a tenfold increase in capital commitments to venture capital funds a year later. Far more important was the Department of Labor's liberalization of the "prudent man rule" for the Employee Retirement Income Security Act (ERISA), which had become law in 1974.[16] Previously, pension fund managers were prohibited from investing their funds in venture capital or other high-risk investments. After the change, they were allowed to invest up to 10 percent of their capital in venture funds.[17] This change opened the floodgates for the funding of venture capital but also changed the collegial, noncompetitive nature of their business, shifting it away from wealthy individuals to institutional client partners.[18]

Several other pieces of federal legislation enacted in the early 1980s also helped to promote venture capital. Under the Small Business Investment Incentive Act (1980), venture capital firms became business development companies, thereby avoiding having to register as investment advisers with the SEC and deal with related regulations. Also that year, the Department of Labor's ERISA "Safe Harbor" regulation stated that venture capital fund managers were not to be considered fiduciaries of the pension fund assets that were parts of the fund pools they managed. Again, venture capital was spared serious risk exposure and given more freedom to operate. Finally, the Economic Recovery Tax Act passed in 1981 again lowered the capital gains tax, this time to 20 percent, which helped to increase venture capital fund commitments twofold that year.[19]

The other major development at this time was the emergence of the limited partnership. Developed from similar structures created in the oil and gas industry a decade earlier, the limited partnership had many advantages. Profits passed directly to investors without being taxed, while general partners received management fees for overhead expenses (thus eliminating pressure to get them from dividends or interest income) as well as shares of the capital gains. The structure also ensured that, with a business life of about ten years, limited partners would not expect dividends or interest, only long-term returns. Partners would have no role in the management of the fund, and the fund would eventually be self-liquidating. The first such limited partnership in the venture field was formed by Draper, Gaither & Anderson in Palo Alto, California, in 1959. The first Boston limited partnership was Greylock in 1965.[20]

Boston Venture Capital Firms

From 1965 to the end of the twentieth century, a number of private limited venture capital partnerships were founded in the Boston area. Some like Greylock and the Palmer Organization (William H. Congleton and John A. Shane, 1971) could trace their roots back to AR&D, as many alumni of that organization founded or joined new firms. Others like Charles River Ventures (1970) and Fleet Venture Partners were founded by individuals who had trained in Boston SBICs, or been connected to Boston-based insurance or brokerage firms.[21]

In addition, there were a number of other Boston venture firms that had different origins, changed their names, or failed to survive. One was Faneuil Hall Associates, established in 1975 by the Kendall family, while another was the Massachusetts Small Business Investment Company, which became the Federal Street Capital Corporation in 1970 and was owned by twenty-six banks, with Shawmut, State Street, and Merchants having the most ownership interest in the enterprise. Hellman, Ferri Investment Associates (1977) was renamed Matrix Partners in 1982. Other companies included the Massachusetts Capital Corporation; the Massachusetts Venture Capital Corporation, "a minority enterprise SBIC formed by 14 institutional investors in 1973"; and the Urban National Corporation, the first purely private sector venture capital fund to invest in minority businesses. During the 1970s, the First National Bank created or renamed two other venture organizations, the First Capital Corporation of Boston and the First Venture Capital Corporation of Boston as part of its new bank-holding structure.[22]

Greylock

From 1965 through the early 1970s, a number of Boston private venture capital firms were established largely by alumni of AR&D. The first of these was Greylock, founded in 1965 by William Elfers and others who had spent their apprenticeships in Doriot's firm. Elfers had joined AR&D in 1947 and had served as senior vice president since the early 1950s. By 1965, he had realized that his chances of ever running the venture capital firm were becoming more limited. Greylock's general partners in Greylock & Company, the original limited partnership, included Elfers; Daniel S. Gregory, who founded the firm with Elfers in October 1965; Charles P. Waite, who came on in 1966; and Henry F. McCance, who followed in 1969. The new firm was also assisted by David E. Place of Ely Bartlett Brown & Proctor (later Gaston Snow & Ely Bartlett), the first of many Boston law firms involved in Boston's private venture capital industry. Greylock's first offices were in a cramped conference room of Ely Bartlett in the Old South Building on Washington Street. The close conditions helped to encourage everyone to go out, meet people, and look for prospects. Over time, those early general partners and their successors came to specialize largely in health care and medical products, computer software, and telecommunications.[23]

Greylock's original limited partners were five "founding families"—the Cornings-Murfeys (the Corning trusts, primarily from Cleveland, Ohio), Edward and Landon Thorne (of Greenwich, Connecticut), Thomas J. and

Arthur K. Watson, Sherman Fairchild and Walter Burke Jr., and the Louis F. Polk family (of Dayton, Ohio)—that Elfers had come to know largely through connections he had established over the years. The Watsons and Fairchild both had large financial holdings in IBM, and Fairchild, an inventor and businessman, founded Fairchild Camera and Instrument Company, which soon became a major player in the semiconductor industry and the development of Silicon Valley, as well as many other enterprises. Greylock was the first private venture firm to use a multifamily approach instead of a single limited partner. Its plan was to invest in special situations and ventures, that is, investments in which events impact on the value of that opportunity or where the ultimate outcome is uncertain or risky. The families proved to be great investors, especially because they "knew what to expect . . . [and] to be patient."[24]

Greylock & Company (1965–1977), Greylock's first partnership, a $10 million fund, soon moved to a small office in the new State Street Bank building at 225 Franklin Street. It invested in cable television, an industry that some, including AR&D, concluded might be upstaged should a technological breakthrough make underground cable obsolete. Greylock's initial investments in small cable companies proved unsuccessful, primarily because of problems with those companies' management and insufficient prospective markets. This situation changed, however, when the fund became involved with Continental Cablevision as an investor through Boston Capital, which was selling its interest in venture businesses to become a division of another company. Continental Cablevision's strategy was to acquire franchises away from large, competitive urban areas. Despite the intensive use of capital, the cable television industry was able to maintain extreme leverage because it had a predictable cash flow. Continental proved to be an important early win for Greylock, which continued to invest more money in the enterprise in two successor partnerships.

Greylock's most substantial early investment was in International Equipment Company of Needham, Massachusetts. Like most early deals, Greylock worked with an investment team of two family offices, one in Boston and the other in New York, and the Massachusetts Small Business Investment Company, the same bank-affiliated SBIC that Rick Burnes worked for at this time. While International Equipment's owner family wanted to sell the business, which made medical centrifuges, to its management, Greylock suggested merging the company with the Damon Engineering Corporation, also located in Needham, which made military high-frequency filters but needed to expand its product base if it wanted to grow into a major company. The merger proved to be another success for Greylock and helped it to develop its expertise in management-led buyouts.

Greylock worked with Peter Brooke's TA Associates to devise a plan for a private common stock issue for Wang Laboratories. Likewise, collaborative arrangements with other venture groups moved Greylock into new investment areas. When the Rockefeller family venture office bowed out of a project involving the Worthington Biochemical Corporation in New Jersey, they invited both J. H. Whitney and Greylock to help out the company. Besides taking on directorships, both firms worked to fashion a public offering in 1971 to assist the company with a facility expansion. Later, when the owner-scientist wanted to turn his company over to professional managers, they facilitated its acquisition by the Millipore Corporation. Besides offering an almost classic example of tasks performed by venture capitalists, Greylock's exposure to Worthington provided it with firsthand experience in the biotechnology field, one that would provide many additional opportunities over the years.

New projects made other demands on Greylock. During the late 1960s, for instance, the firm became involved in efforts to rationalize the mom-and-pop clinical laboratory business into one organized and run by a nationwide business entity called Biomedical Resources. Rather than buy up the small concerns, Greylock and its partners decided to build their own more efficient and controllable laboratory facilities. But the venture proved costly in time, eventually leading to a sale to a pharmaceutical company. In another project involving the women's hair fashion business, Greylock soon realized that it had bought the interest at the height of the market and knew too little about the industry to overcome that mistake.

Many of the opportunities that Greylock developed in the 1960s and 1970s involved working with their legal and business contacts, nurturing young venture capitalists taking on new industries and specialties, and helping companies in unexpected ways. While the firm was unable to assist a New Hampshire machine tool company in diversifying its product line, Greylock aided the company in succession issues through buyouts to change top management and ownership. In another instance, Greylock helped with the management and some liquidity problems of a specialty chemical company in the electronics industry. Eventually its owners decided to sell their interest to a company with substantially more financial resources so that it could effectively compete in its market worldwide. Greylock's patient help with that company over the years yielded $15 for each original dollar invested. In another instance, the firm and its partner, Fidelity Ventures, tried to expand the business of a door-closer manufacturer. While marginally successful, the venture capitalists realized that management could go no further with diversification efforts. The management of the company also resisted several mergers. In the end, the venture capital firms created an IPO to provide liquidity for management and shareholders, and to develop new opportunities for the business.

Greylock's first partnership focused on the developmental capital phase for its portfolio companies (i.e., a second round of financings for emerging companies), in a venture program consisting of four different stages—"start-ups, developmental capital, buyouts, and public stock of unrecognized companies." By and large, Greylock felt that start-ups were disappointing and too much of a gamble. The firm did develop confidence in buyouts and taking stock positions in nonpublic companies. According to Elfers's colleague Charlie Waite, despite his early training at AR&D, "Elfers preferred at first to avoid startup investing. . . . In the 1960s and even well into the 1970s competition was so rare that investors had the luxury of waiting until a company was at least off the ground to make a commitment that paid off handsomely." Gradually, however, Greylock became "an eager and respected participant in startups," as it "was finally forced to change its strategy by the growing competition and rising prices for second stage deals."[25]

During the 1970s, Greylock fashioned two other partnerships, Greylock Investors & Company (1973–1985) and Greylock Partners & Company (1979–1989). Under the new partnerships, the size of the fund increased, as did the average size of investments in the portfolio company. One West Coast family and four universities—Dartmouth, Harvard, Duke, and MIT—came on board as limited partners (later joined by Stanford and Yale), and more activity was done with companies in the start-up and buyout phases, and some new industries. In addition, Elfers decided to assume a special limited partner status to let the others—Gregory, Waite, McCance, and Henry Cox—take on greater executive responsibilities and receive larger financial rewards. Elfers's decision had much to do with the history of AR&D, where key personnel had had to leave in order to find more remunerative work. That judgment was also likely the reason why Greylock never lost a general partner in more than twenty years.[26]

The firm made investments in Brookstone, a New Hampshire mail order and retailer of unique tools and gifts, in 1972. This enabled the husband-and-wife team of owners of this well-run and growing company to liquidate their holdings for shares in the large-scale business that acquired it. Greylock also invested in WellTech, an oil- and gas-well servicing company in 1973, with Fidelity Ventures; the Stryker Company, which made surgical saws and other surgical and medical products the same year; and in 1977, Prime Computer and several computer software companies (such as the Cullinane Corporation and McCormack & Dodge), which were later merged with Computer Associates and Dun & Bradstreet, respectively. These last connections provided experience in computer software that became important in later partnerships, as did investments in a number of biotechnology start-ups. By the end of the 1970s, Greylock was developing a strong position in the telecommunications industry; close collaborative relationships with other Boston venture capital firms, especially Fidelity Ventures, which, according to Elfers "share[d] the same philosophy and way of venturing"; and a growing number of deals with West Coast venture capital firms where Charlie Waite was spending more time each year.[27]

TA Associates

Peter Brooke worked a dozen years in high-technology lending and gained experience with high-tech companies at First National and Bessemer Ventures in New York, where he helped the family investment operation diversify its portfolio. When he returned to the Boston financial district in the 1960s, he had a definite idea of the type of venture capital firm he wanted to create. He found a partner in Tucker Anthony and R. L. Day, a brokerage, investment counsel, and investment banking company, to help realize it. Tucker Anthony had already set up a shell of a company, called Tucker Anthony & Company, which Brooke used to create a series of venture capital (although some might call them investment banking) private placements of companies. These were then sold to individuals he knew from previous work experiences or who were Tucker Anthony clients. While this proved very successful, eventually the IRS ruled that the company could not hold the capital and required that he declare a liquidating dividend. Brooke convinced the partners at Tucker Anthony and R. L. Day, who were shareholders in this enterprise, to take enough money to pay for the taxes but to leave the rest for seed capital in a venture capital limited partnership called the Advent Company. Eventually, in 1968, that seed capital, along with money from other investors, became Advent I, which was managed by TA Associates, the latter half owned by Tucker Anthony and R. L. Day partners and half by Brooke.[28]

Brooke had a portfolio approach to investing based on a diversified collection of companies according to business sector and their stage—early, middle, later, and mature—of development. His portfolio included a broad mix of older companies, such as those in the furniture business; profitable middle-market companies like New England Business Services in the business supply and equipment field; emerging small technology companies that were selling products but not yet profitable; and other companies that required seed capital. Larger companies needing expansion capital represented about 35 percent of the portfolio, while middle-market companies were another 35 percent. Emerging companies accounted for about another 20 percent of the portfolio, and seed capital only 10 percent. The latter two categories were primarily technology-based in semiconductors, computers and computer peripherals, medical devices and equipment, and one start-up dealing with character

by John H. ("Jack") Carter, a successful high-tech investor and special assistant to President James Killian of the Massachusetts Institute of Technology (MIT); John T. Neises, an alumnus of Xerox marketing and sales; and Rick Burnes from the Federal Street Capital Corporation, the SBIC of Shawmut Bank as well as other local banks. While remaining for the most part in venture capital, the firm over the years has made a transition from providing capital for a diversity of businesses to one that focuses on communications and information technology—a specialization that has taken hold in many venture capital firms.

Carter's idea of creating a venture capital firm was to tie it closely with MIT.[33] When some sort of formal connection proved impossible, he set up the first partnership in Cambridge with five MIT professors serving as limited partners and advisers, a recognition that some venture capital firms in the 1960s had principals with no business operating experience to guide them in decision-making. Each of the limited partner professor-advisers pledged to give back 15 percent of the gain to MIT. The first fund of $4.5 million (with a second infusion of $2 million in 1972) turned out to be "a curious variety of what we thought were technical growth companies." They ranged from auto component businesses to "two investments in innovative methods of pig farming." "Didn't work, and there were a lot of things like that," noted Burnes. At the beginning, CRV was also a development company interested in a variety of investments "all over the country." Charles River Partnership I (CRP I, 1970) proved to be a modest success despite "losses from dumb investments," because those investments also included some in the emerging electronics industry, particularly in Storage Technology, a data storage management company founded in 1969 by IBM engineers, and Avantek, a microwave communications company. CRV's early investors included the Insurance Company of North America, the Mellon and Freuhof families, and First Chicago Corporation.

By CRP II (1977), the professors were no longer involved with the partnership, and the fund of $7.5 million was modestly larger. Just as CRV obtained ten partnership commitments for this fund, the U.S. Supreme Court ruled that such partnerships were required to have from twelve to fifteen limited partners. Having to give back cash commitments that had taken a year or so to raise, CRV ultimately leveraged that commitment with the SBIC program one for one, bringing about $14 million into the fund. By CRP II, investors also included a number of educational endowments like the University of Rochester, Notre Dame, and Boston University. Other investors that later came into the CRP funds included Harvard, Stanford, and Carnegie Mellon, as well as pension funds.

According to Burnes, CRV's investment strategy started to change by the late 1970s. "There was a debate as to whether we should focus on specific industries and market segments, developing real expertise, or remain opportunistic." In CRP III (1980), which raised about $25 million, an investment was made in Amgen to determine whether CRV should consider focusing on the biotech industry, but by the late 1980s, after selling their position before the company's performance shot up, the firm decided to look elsewhere due to a lack of experience. By the early 1980s, investments in Summa Four, a New Hampshire–based manufacturer of microprocessor-controlled telephone switches, proved to be a successful, if frustrating, investment, ultimately acquired by Cisco Systems. Four more IPOs followed for Bytex, Xyplex, Chipcom, and Cascade, all in the communications sector. Chipcom was eventually sold to 3Com for almost $1 billion, and Cascade brought in over $100 million return to CRV. CRP IV (1984) raised $45 million, and CRP V (1986) had assets of about $95 million. The debate on the "soul of the firm" continued through the 1980s, and the diverse portfolio reflected the partners' indecision. Even the choice to specialize was not resolved until about 1990, when it became difficult to find backers for CRP VI. "We looked carefully at where we had made our money," Burnes noted, "and realized we should focus on early-stage information processing and communications companies." Eventually, after twenty years, it became more specific—electronics and communications technology.

During the 1970s, venture capital had been a close-knit group of only about thirty or forty firms. None of them had enough capital, and they relied on each other for support. By the 1980s, however, that trend was reversed, and CRV took leadership positions rather than joining syndicates of other venture capital firms—especially in post–CRP VI funds. Like other venture capital firms, over the years CRV has increased the size of each partnership, put more money into each stage of growth, and limited the number of coinvestors; in the process, it cut down the number of portfolio companies.[34]

Fidelity Ventures

Although he had been with Doriot during the war and afterwards for two decades at AR&D, Harry Hoagland decided to leave that company in 1969. Shortly after his retirement, he was invited by Edward C. Johnson III to consult with Fidelity Management and Research Corporation (FMR) on starting a venture capital unit. Fidelity had been involved in some venture investments before that time, but formally entered into the business that year, following recommendations made by Hoagland. Fidelity subsequently created a private investment partnership in 1971, which was called Fidelity Ventures Limited Partnership and headed by Hoagland. By 1973, the unit was known more familiarly as Fidelity Ventures Associates, which became the name of the management company of the partnership when it was incorporated in 1978.

Until 2010, it was known as Fidelity Ventures, when it became an independent venture capital firm called Volition Capital.[35]

In 1971, Hoagland brought in Samuel W. Bodman III, another alumnus of AR&D with a background in chemistry from MIT. Bodman later served as president and CEO of Fidelity Investments, and eventually became secretary of energy in President George W. Bush's administration. During the 1970s, Fidelity Ventures was involved in the capitalization of about a dozen companies, the most important of which was MCI New England, the local subsidiary, as part of the expansion and unification of William G. McGowan's MCI Communications Corporation, which became at the time one of the most profitable companies in the telecommunications industry. Fidelity also invested in Continental Cablevision in 1972, and in 1975, put $300,000 in Atari, the maker of the first generation of personal computer and video game systems. After a successful IPO for Atari, Fidelity Ventures worked with Sears, Roebuck & Company to set up a distribution system for Atari products.[36]

The Emergence and Growing Acceptance of "Alternative Investing" by the 1980s

Venture capital, as well as the whole U.S. financial industry, had gone through a traumatic experience in the early to mid-1970s, but slowly came back to life in the late 1970s and early 1980s with the rebound of the stock market.[37] Prior to 1970, new venture capital small business issue underwritings reached a high point in 1969 of $1.4 billion for 698 companies, but by 1975, it was only $16 million for 4 companies. As part of that decline, limited partnerships emerged as the dominant organizational structure for venture capital. In 1970, the venture capital landscape consisted of about 375 SBICs—25 publicly held and 75 affiliated with commercial banks—with the balance privately held or affiliated with some other organization. There were 5 publicly held companies, with AR&D being the largest at $400 million; about 50 to 75 private partnerships and family investment firms; 25 to 35 venture capital divisions in large corporations; 20 to 25 venture companies affiliated with investment bankers; and 5 publicly held letter (or unregistered) stock and combination venture capital funds. The number of private partnerships grew from about 75 in 1970 to 225 in 1979 and 658 by 1988, at the same time other organizations seriously declined in numbers. Indeed, by the 1980s, 80 percent of the funds used for venture capital investing came from limited partnerships. The number of companies in which venture capital invested rose from 375 in 1979 to 797 in 1981, and then took off with 1,320 in 1983 and 1,729 in 1987, before contracting at the end of the decade.[38]

During the 1970s, the "wilderness" period for venture capital, the industry created its own group, the National Venture Capital Association, in 1973, and by 1979, *Venture* and *Inc.* magazines started publication. In 1977, Stanley E. Pratt in Wellesley Hills, Massachusetts, took over *Venture Economics* and the *Venture Capital Journal,* and expanded news about the industry with other publications. Prior to this time, little general information was known about the industry. It had been identified through the work and activities of Chicagoan Stanley M. Rubel, who started writing a newsletter, *SBIC–Venture Capital Service,* for venture capital in 1961; gave occasional speeches on the subject (including his first seminar on venture capital in 1970); and subsequently became executive director of the National Venture Capital Foundation.[39]

The venture industry was still quite small in the 1970s, with the real surge taking place in the 1980s, when the cumulative capital rose from $4 to over $35 billion.[40] New capital commitment rose gradually, from $200 million in 1978 to $3.4 billion in 1983. It remained roughly at that level, except for a rise to $4.2 billion in 1987, and then declined before starting to rise again in 1992. The cumulative effect of venture capital, however, had more impact, rising from $4.0 billion in 1978 to $24.1 billion in 1986, and climbing to $35.9 billion in 1990 before declining slightly to $35 billion in 1991. Most of this transition was powered by a strategic shift in the sources of funding for venture capital pools. In 1978, 32 percent of those funds came from wealthy families and individuals, while only 15 percent were from pension funds. A decade later, pension funds made up 46 percent of those funds, while families and individuals contributed only 8 percent. No wonder Bill Elfers referred to this period of venture capital investment as the "roaring eighties."[41]

Growing Recognition of Venture Capital's Economic Success

Although little was known about the venture capital industry even in 1970, its impact on the economy became more broadly recognized by the 1980s. One often-cited study published in 1980 was based on a sample of 110 private equity investments between 1960 and 1975, ranging in size from $1,000 to $1.11 million. The data were supplied by three venture capital firms, one a publicly held SBIC, another a wholly owned SBIC subsidiary of a large bank holding company, and the third "a partnership holding seats on major stock exchanges and engaged in a wide spectrum of activities related to securities, including underwriting, market making, and retailing." As a whole, these three firms were not representative of those set up in the late 1960s and throughout the 1970s, but this was the first major study on the impact of venture capital on the economy. Of those 110 investments, 6 were total failures whereas 11 produced rates of return of 50 percent or better. The annualized rate of return generated by all of them over the fifteen-year period was 18.9 percent. The study suggested that performance was lessened because SBICs as a whole did not perform well and only half still existed. Nevertheless, the research concluded that well-diversified venture portfolios could generate attractive rates of return over time, and that adequate diversification might require greater minimal capital levels than in portfolios with more marketable securities of mature enterprises.[42]

Despite this somewhat pessimistic view of venture capital from an earlier SBIC-dominated period, a far different picture was emerging from other studies. While venture capital was just beginning to take off in the early 1980s, it had already demonstrated to the U.S. General Accounting Office (GAO) that "this small segment of the U.S. economy has produced disproportionately large benefits to the Nation's productivity and economic well-being." The GAO study "showed that even though venture capital was relatively scarce during the 1970s, it contributed significantly to the Nation's economic and productivity well-being." The study was based on data of 1,332 venture capital–backed companies in which investments of $1.4 billion were made between 1970 and 1979. The GAO focused on the seventy-two companies that had gone public by 1979 to "demonstrate benefits to the Nation's economy and productivity that are disproportionately large when compared with the amounts of capital invested." The $209 million invested to create those companies had in 1979 combined sales of $6 billion. "Growth in annual sales averaged 33 percent a year and, in the process, these firms created (1) an estimated 130,000 jobs, (2) over $100 million in corporate tax revenues, (3) $350 million in employee tax revenues, and (4) $900 million in export sales. Moreover, most products were productivity enhancing, such as computer related equipment, fiber optics, industrial controls, lasers, robots, word processors, and numerous others." While the results were impressive even in down periods like the 1970s, venture capital did not always guarantee great success and public acclaim. At that time, the general rule of thumb was that 20 percent of venture-backed companies achieved wide, public market success; about 40 percent of them were merged into larger companies; another 20 percent continued to operate as small, privately held businesses; and the last 20 percent were considered failures. As venture capitalists had earlier noted, one large success could more than make up for any number of mediocre or poor investments.[43]

A Note on Silicon Valley

While venture capital was invented in the Boston area and a key to the region's post–World War II financial history, it has also long been associated with the San Francisco Bay area, generally in the region referred to as Silicon Valley.[44] In fact, the size of Silicon Valley's venture capital operations actually surpassed Boston sometime before the 1980s, and is currently several times larger there than it is in eastern Massachusetts.[45] While a purpose of this chapter is not to focus on other parts of the country or analyze why this shift took place, a few words should be said about how venture capital differs between the two regions, and what this tells us about both.

Venture capital actually got started in the San Francisco area as early as 1957 when Arthur Rock, then an investment banker at Hayden, Stone & Company in New York, came out to make investments, which eventually led to a venture partnership, Davis & Rock, in 1961. Davis & Rock made an early high-tech investment in Fairchild Semiconductor and later in Intel, Scientific Data Systems, Teledyne, and Apple. Meanwhile, Draper, Gaither & Anderson became the first venture capital limited partnership in 1958, and it was followed much later in the early 1970s, by many other well-known venture firms such as Sutter Hill, the Mayfield Fund, Kleiner Perkins Caufield & Byers, and Sequoia Capital, some of which were founded by former students of Georges Doriot. Not only did venture capital become larger in northern California, but by 1992, nearly half of venture capital disbursements were invested in that region, while the Northeast accounted for only 20 percent of the invested capital. Perhaps the symbolic shift took place in 1979, when Bill Egan left TA Associates to establish Burr, Egan & Deleage, the first bicoastal venture capital firm.[46]

Despite Boston venture capital's historic ties to Harvard, MIT, and other universities, those educational institutions largely stayed out of venture activity in the region, having little, if any, direct impact on AR&D and firms like Greylock and Charles River Ventures. MIT, for instance, saw its role as to "enhance the technological capacity of local industry by infusing it with new ideas," rather than a more direct participation. On the other hand, the University of California and, especially, Stanford University took active roles in creating high-tech startups from their inception as well as supporting the venture capital industry to finance them. Stanford's Engineering School maintained a close relationship with local industry for decades under Frederick Terman, whose mentor and thesis adviser had been Vannevar Bush at MIT. But Terman went beyond his teacher to become an active consultant to industry, and through his students, helped to build new companies from technology developed at the university.[47]

These distinctions in venture capital also played out in the types of companies, technologies, and even products both regions developed, and the associated technological changes that subsequently occurred. One well-known study focusing on cultural, social, and regional disparities has noted "the significant differences between highly networked technical persons in Silicon Valley firms and more isolated individuals in Route 128 companies." While both cultures boomed in the late 1970s and early 1980s, this analysis took place in the mid- to late 1980s, when there was a decline in microcomputer manufacturing (DEC,

Prime, General Data, and Wang) along Route 128 and a decline in computer chip manufacturing in Silicon Valley. Despite the downturn, the Silicon Valley appeared to be more resilient and "laid back," and adapted to the change better than the more formal, "button-upped" Route 128 culture. Accordingly, "by the late 1980s the locus of technological innovation in computing had shifted decisively to the West." It had become "the national center of computer systems innovation . . . more specialized chips, and computer-related specialties." While this popular viewpoint never took into account events after about 1990, when there was explosive growth in software and biotech in Massachusetts, there is no question that high-technology companies in the two regions were and still remain different—with Route 128 companies centering on corporate applications of technology, whereas Silicon Valley businesses focus on peripherals and popular consumer end products. Such distinctions also reflect different venture capital focuses.[48]

The Expansion of "Alternative" Investment

Boston, as compared to Silicon Valley, has had a very different financial tradition going back to family fortunes, collateral-backed bank loans, and even "balanced" venture capital portfolios. Boston was more reluctant to go into early-stage investing, preferring to see a product on the market that it could finance. Venture capitalists in the West have come out of technology companies, and have been more operationally or technologically, rather than financially, driven. They were likely more adventuresome, but their precision was sometimes comparable to throwing darts at a board. Unlike the West, Boston is primarily not a "start-up," long-term investment culture, but one that sees venture capital as an important but not exclusive asset class. Even AR&D wanted quicker returns with later-stage portfolio companies, if only to reassure its stockholders they were doing their job and to confirm its ability to secure additional funding from new investments.[49]

By about 1980, as the second major cycle of venture capital was peaking, massive new amounts of capital—especially from ERISA and "new" wealth created in the post–World War II era—were entering the market, but to many investors, there were other ways than venture capital to make money. Although venture capital funds increased significantly in the 1980s, interest throughout much of Boston shifted to private equity as an increasing number of new or younger asset managers turned to more focused investments. Private equity investments were nontraditional by definition, generally illiquid, and usually made outside the structure of public markets. That decade soon became an era of buyouts, as private equity capital was used to gain ownership control or a strategic acquisition, or to change the capital structure of selected businesses. Others became involved in special situations investments (often with both venture capital and buyout characteristics), such as financial backing of an experienced management team to buy a business, or building a dominant company in a fragmented industry. They also involved previously ignored companies with undervalued assets. Alternative investments of all types grew and included real estate holdings, timber properties, oil and gas exploration, and mezzanine (or subordinated) debt to provide, in part, the leverage for leveraged buyouts as well as venture capital, all of which have become commonly recognized components of sophisticated portfolios within the last thirty years. In 1980, alternative investments amounted to only about $2 billion under management, but by the end of the decade, it was more than $70 billion.

By about 1980, this blurring of the line between venture capital and private equity in the Boston area was complete. Unlike the past, ventures were different, with new, usually institutional, investors; there was a growing specialization by growth stage, industry, and region. The business had a more formalized and less collegial atmosphere; there were more precise evaluation and pricing techniques. Above all, there were larger funds, and far more money, which created more competition. On the other hand, private equity investment focused on later-stage company developments, which created higher and more immediate payouts during the 1980s. Some Boston private equity firms invested in troubled companies or turnarounds, while others focused on profitable and established companies, where they could still make outstanding profits. All of these conditions helped to push Boston venture capitalists into other alternative investments in private equity, which are viewed more closely later in this book.[50]

Although the line between venture capital and other alternative investments was becoming less clear, the former developed a distinctive culture that time and circumstance did not replace. Stanley E. Pratt, a Boston venture capitalist and longtime observer of the venture capital scene both in Boston and around the country, noted that "venture capital is the business of building businesses," a reaffirming business that adds value rather than restructuring or removing it. He also described venture capital by what it was and what it was not—value creation, not value extraction:

> The venture capital business is very different from any other professional skill-set. It is not stock picking, trying to identify successful businesses to invest in for the future. It is not commercial banking, lending money to growing businesses. It is not investment banking, structuring and doing deals—it must not be transaction oriented. It

is not management consulting, providing advice, but not accepting responsibility.

Venture capital is becoming a partner with a management team in a five to seven year relationship that can be far more difficult than marriage. It is teamwork, often with very smart, very driven and very difficult partners. Its long-term orientation is different from any other capital markets. We must learn to live with successes and failures. Venture capital is a combination of all of the above skills.[51]

CHAPTER 9

Rising Assets to Manage

The economic highs and lows of the 1960s and 1970s not only wreaked havoc on traditional financial institutions; they also created a climate in which new and more highly specialized ones could grow. Banks and insurance companies, once the only financial service firms to provide pension programs and act as investment advisers for institutional clients like companies and labor unions, were overtaken in the 1970s by smaller money managers, many of whom had been advising wealthy individuals for decades. The endowments of institutions of higher learning, which had largely been managed by the trustees, treasurers, or financial offices of the universities and colleges, soon turned to more professional investment management as word got around that private money managers could increase endowments substantially—as the contrast between two of them, Harvard and Yale, dramatically showed. The rise of pension and endowment funds and their managers also spawned the growth of a counterweight, third-party consultants, who advised pension fund sponsors, foundations, and institutions of higher learning on the hiring of investment managers.

The Revolution in Pension Funding

These new-found assets came from several sources, including private wealth and the growing endowments of institutions, but the most important were pension or retirement funds, which began to take on significance after World War II, stimulated by legislation favorable to their accumulation. Even though the Social Security Act of 1935 is generally viewed as the watershed event in U.S. pension history, the development of private pension plans began

FIGURE 11. President Gerald R. Ford signing the ERISA bill into law, 1974 (Courtesy Gerald R. Ford Presidential Library)

effect.[5] Another notable addition came with the Taxpayer Relief Act of 1997, which created the Roth IRA, which participants acquired by using after-tax income but would not be taxed when redeemed, provided that the Roth IRA was held for a five-year period. Throughout this period and into the twenty-first century, Congress has also enacted numerous provisions affecting and enhancing these pension programs, such as the Economic Growth and Tax Relief Reconciliation Act of 2001, which allowed for an increase in contribution limits on 401(k)s and other deferred compensation pension plans developed over the preceding quarter century, such as the 403(b) plans (tax-exempt organizations), 457 plans (state and local government employees), and SIMPLE (savings incentive match for employees of small companies) plans. The 2001 act also allowed for "catch-up" IRA contributions for older individuals, among other changes.[6]

These private, publicly subsidized, and regulated employer plans covered about half of the U.S. labor force by the early twenty-first century. Early on, nearly all of them were "defined benefit" pension plans, meaning that the employer promised to pay a specific monthly benefit to the retiree, which was based on a formula that included the former employee's age, service, and earnings history, and often included his or her final salary figure. In other words, the employee's benefit was "defined" because he or she knew what that benefit was in advance. Gradually, however, as pensions became more the responsibility of employees, many company pensions came to be called "defined contribution" plans, as employers agreed to make specific contributions but not guarantee what that actual benefit might be in the future. This change, which was well under way during the 1980s, along with the rising numbers of participants in the growing number of legally sanctioned private pension plans, became two important shifts in direction for U.S. pensions in the last half century.[7]

The impact of the surging numbers of participants and pension plans was noted in 1969 when the Internal Revenue Service (IRS), faced with an overload of applications for pension and profit-sharing plans, started to relax its regulations by allowing small- and medium-sized companies to set up their programs in more streamlined prototype employee-benefit plans sponsored by investment middlemen, like mutual fund companies. "For years," *Business Week* explained, "the only way corporations could set up programs was to pay wads of fees to lawyers, accountants, and benefit plan designers to tailor a maddeningly complex package of trust agreements, plan provisions, and actuarial formulas. Each plan had to be approved individually by [the] IRS. The whole process could take eight months." The IRS preapproved plans were "likely to shake up the entire employee-benefit plan field" because they could be set up in "as quickly as 18 minutes," and "are just the sort of products that ordinary stock brokers and insurance and mutual fund salesmen can peddle without knowing much about them." The magazine calculated that only 15 percent of the nation's 1.3 million corporations had existing retirement plans, so the prototype plans helped to open up a vast market for an increasing number of financial salespeople.[8]

Furthermore, existing retirement plans were not necessarily immune to the new competition. As a new investment magazine, *Institutional Investor* noted two years earlier in 1967, "The big pension money had been controlled mostly by banks, which have powerful credit relationships with corporations, and, to a lesser extent, by insurance companies, which have batteries of pension specialists and, of course, captive sales forces. But the banks and insurance companies have had notoriously mediocre investment results," and investment *performance* had become and would continue to be a major issue in the investment world during the 1970s and beyond.[9]

Many factors facilitated postwar growth of the private pension system. The proliferation of pension programs was encouraged by federal legislation (which regulated plans and became guarantor of benefits) and supported financially by employers, the rising mobility of the workforce, and the shift to (more commonly) multiple employers over the course of an employee's career. In addition,

TABLE 4. Private Pension Retirement Plan Assets, 1950–2000
($ in billions)

TYPE OF PLAN	1950	1960	1970	1980	1985	1990	1995	2000
Private Trusteed	$7.1	$38.1	$112.0					
Defined Benefit				$401.5	$814.0	$896.0	$1,440.0	$2,014.0
Defined Contribution			$162.1	$417.0	$676.0	$1,312.0	$2,272.0	
401(k)					$91.8	$384.9	$863.9	$1,739.0
Private Insured	$5.6	$18.9	$40.8	$158.2	$346.7	$636.1	$871.3	$1,527.5
State & Local Governments	$4.9	$19.7	$60.3	$197.6	$398.7	$800.6	$1,308.1	$2,124.3
IRA/Keogh				$38.6	$234.7	$636.0	$1,288.0	$2,629.0
Totals	$17.6	$76.7	$213.1	$958.0	$2,302.9	$4,029.6	$7,083.3	$12,305.8

Source: Ken McDonnell, "Facts from EBRI [Employee Benefit Research Institute]: The U.S. Retirement Income System," *EBRI Notes* 26, no. 4 (2005): 10 (Figure 7), which is based on EBRI, *Pension Investment Report,* Federal Reserve Board, *Flow of Funds Accounts,* www.federalreserve. gov/releases/Z1/Current/data.htm; and U.S. Social Security Administration, *2004 OASDI Trustees Report,* www.ssa.gov/OACT/TR/TR04/. This chart does not include his figures for Social Security and federal government retirement plans because neither fund was managed by professional investors.

as structural changes in the twentieth-century economy took place, the role of Big Labor and Big Business, major pension players of an earlier age, diminished, while self-directed individual (or "household") accounts began to take on greater significance. As a result of such developments, "the pension emerged as a huge economic institution in the third quarter of the twentieth century." As table 4 shows, the greatest pension growth rates occurred in the decades of the 1950s (426 percent), the 1970s (450 percent), and the 1980s (421 percent), while the 1990s were somewhat less (305 percent), and the 1960s even lower (279 percent). Despite the fluctuations, these were sizeable and newly created pools of investment funds, and as they compounded over the decades, they helped to transform part of Boston's growing asset management industry.[10]

As viewed from a 1990 perspective, pension assets had grown six times faster than the economy as a whole during the previous four decades, and had transformed the U.S. money management industry. Since 1974 when ERISA was created, pension fund assets in 1990 as a whole had risen 16 percent per year, while the share of household financial assets managed by investment advisers had increased from 12 to 28 percent. Not surprisingly, the number of investment advisers had grown threefold in the 1980s alone. While this great transformation was well under way by 1990, it had started in Boston much earlier.[11]

The pension revolution and the rise of institutional and mutual fund investing also dramatically changed traditional relationships. For instance, for over 180 years, the New York Stock Exchange had acted as a privately regulated cartel, charging high, fixed commissions on all purchases and sales of securities listed on its board, and prohibiting the brokerage affiliates of institutional investors from becoming members. By the 1960s, however, there was growing pressure on the exchange to charge negotiated or discounted commissions rather than permit price competition among its members. That pressure came from government, institutional investors, public critics, litigants, and even some exchange members, who saw that the monopolistic ways of the exchange only helped to enrich the members of the "club." After constant pressure from many quarters, and its inability to deal with its shortcomings and to adjust to changing circumstances, the practice of fixed commissions was abandoned on May 1, 1975, a date that came to be known in the brokerage community as "May Day." The arrival of the institutional investor also highlighted the rise of the computer and new technology generally, which made the purchase and sale of large holdings of securities more efficient transactions, as it had for NASDAQ (National Association of Securities Dealers Automated Quotations, later Nasdaq), the electronic exchange of over-the-counter stocks, which started in early 1971. Life under the exchange's ancient regime had been during a long era when transactions usually involved small investors and small orders, which presumably justified relatively high fixed commissions. But that era no longer prevailed when institutional investing came to rule the roost. Banks were the initial winners in the war with the exchange, but soon they were supplanted by smaller and more nimble investment companies and their money managers, and mutual funds.[12]

Transforming Boston Money Management

Before the pension revolution, employee benefit fund management in Boston was run by trust companies and commercial banks. In 1968, for instance, five of them were among the top forty employee benefit fund institutions nationwide, and included (with their rankings) Old Colony Trust Company (14), First National Bank of Boston (16), State Street Bank & Trust Company (25), New England Merchants National Bank (30), and National Shawmut Bank (31). Collectively, they managed 1,372 employee benefit funds, 829 of which were the fund's sole trustee. These institutions managed just $2.5 million in employee benefit assets, only a fraction of their total private trust accounts, but as a congressional report earlier in 1968 noted, employee benefit fund management "is by far the fastest growing institutional investment area in the country."[13]

By the end of the 1970s, Boston had a more significant place in the field of pension management. While insurance and trust companies continued to hold commanding positions in the business, ten of the top fifty U.S. pension managers in 1976 were Boston (or, in one case, Massachusetts) companies. They

funds of its regional government, union, and corporate clients. Soon Scudder's institutional business eclipsed its traditional personal investment counsel business. In 1970, for instance, 70 percent of its business was with its traditional high–net worth individual clients, but by 1979, 80 percent of Scudder's assets under management (AUM) came from institutional clients as the traditional investment counsel business dwindled to a shadow of its former self. Pension funds offered enormous future opportunities both from potential growth and also from the appreciation of assets. As Scudder's president, George Johnstone, noted in 1974, "It will not be long in some situations before the net worth of a company's pension fund is greater than the market valuation of the company's outstanding stock. Also, it may not be long before the net worth of the pension fund is greater than the book value of many U.S. corporations."[19]

The stories of some other Boston firms—some old, some new—also show the transformative power of the pension fund revolution and how that revolution changed Boston's investment community permanently.

State Street Research and Management

Perhaps one of the first Boston money managers to notice the pension fund shift, or at least to act upon it, was George Bennett of State Street Research and Management. Bennett had started in investment banking in Boston around 1933, and then switched to the "buy side" at State Street Research a decade later, becoming an analyst primarily in the utilities field.[20] Bennett was a protégé of Paul Cabot, who had helped to create one of Boston's early mutual funds in the mid-1920s and managed State Street Research from about 1934. After World War II, Cabot served simultaneously as Harvard treasurer until 1965 and head of State Street Research until 1958; Bennett eventually also served in both of those positions. By the time Bennett became managing partner in 1958, his influence was quite visible: The State Street Investment Trust portfolio was worth about $160 million, with over 20 percent in utility stocks and another 20 percent in energy stocks.[21]

While still regarding itself as a family-owned investment company, with State Street Investment Trust and Harvard as its only business, State Street Research started acquiring small investment companies in the 1950s. By 1961, it had set up its first exchange (or "swap") fund, the Federal Street Fund, which quickly added about 50 percent to the company's AUM. Bennett then continued to focus on growth of State Street Research, and following the creation of a second exchange fund in the mid-1960s, moved into the pension field:

> After we did the exchange funds and had done these acquisitions, I
> was trying to figure out how we could continue growing our assets

and our income without going public in the funds and having a lot of
sales problems—not become the slaves of the wholesalers, but at least
beholden to them in a way that we didn't want to be. So it seemed
like the pension and foundation business were a good direction to
go in, and so we went into it all over, so to speak. In a few years, we
had seven of the largest ten corporations as clients. And the Harvard
relationship was helpful in that, no question about it.

In order to transform the company's business, Bennett developed relationships
with companies both by taking over Cabot's board memberships, such as at the
Ford Motor Company, but also by reaching out to other companies—Hewlett-
Packard, Monsanto, John Hancock, and various utilities nationwide. Bennett
brought financial knowledge and experience to the boards, "so if one of those
directors sat on a board of a foundation or a corporation and they were looking for a[n investment] manager, we would talk and that would give me an
introduction."[22]

Within a short time, the firm was chosen by a number of blue ribbon clients—General Mills, Monsanto, Ford, Mobil Oil, Atlantic Richfield, Kroger,
Philip Morris, IBM, and Exxon—to handle their pension funds. "George was
very entrepreneurial and very expansion-minded and did an outstanding
job of pulling us into the pension fund business," a former colleague later
noted. By the time State Street Research was acquired by the Metropolitan Life
Insurance Company in 1983, the partnership had grown from about twelve
partners in 1960 to twenty-six; AUM from pension funds and foundation
endowments greatly exceeded its other assets—the State Street Investment
Trust and two exchange funds—by six to one, according to one estimate.[23]

In order to create its pension and endowment business, State Street Research
brought in top talent from the big New York banks, which included Peter H.
Vermilye, who had started out at age thirty as vice president for pension investments at J. P. Morgan, just at the time when General Motors was starting to
demand that its pension funds move more into equity investments. Before he
left Morgan in 1964, Vermilye was regarded as the largest manager of equities
in the country. As one contemporary at the firm noted, "corporations, up until
the mid-'60s, would only have their pension fund managed by very large major
city banks, particularly the New York banks. . . . J. P. Morgan, of course, had
an absolutely blue-chip list of pension fund clients and Peter was Mr. Pension
Fund U.S.A. as a result at that time."[24]

The following year, Vermilye moved to Boston, where he developed the company's pension business until 1970. Before his coming, State Street Research
"had no pension business, no connection with the pension business." But business followed him, and while he was there, six major companies asked him

to manage their pension funds. Vermilye was actively soliciting prospective pension clients by 1967. He was also identified with growth stocks in the 1960s, which at that time proved an important attraction for institutional investors used to dealing with conservative, often sleepy banks to manage their pension money. Vermilye's successor in State Street's pension business, Charles Flather, later noted that Vermilye did more for the company "than anybody but the three founders because he got us into the corporate pension business." After Vermilye left, State Street managed to hold on to almost all of its pension clients and continued to grow the business with new ones like Merck, Inland Steel, International Harvester, Standard Oil of Indiana, Shell Oil, and some state and local government funds. The business was becoming so big that when one portfolio reached $1 billion, Flather noted, "Our computer people had to reprogram the portfolio forms to handle more columns."[25]

State Street Research's role as adviser to Harvard diminished when Bennett gave up his treasurer's post in 1973. His successor, George Putnam Jr., helped to create the Harvard Management Company a year later, making that entity Harvard's investment manager. The change, while momentous, opened up more "capacity" at State Street Research to move it into the pension business. With Harvard's departure, "we cleared half the factory floor for full-rate work and we got a lot of calls from companies at the time," particularly from "people who just plain wanted to step into Harvard's shoes." Harvard's assets had once been half of State Street Research's AUM, but within a year or two of the university's departure, "we replaced all the assets for much higher fees."[26]

Wellington Management Company

State Street Research entered the pension business as strictly a mutual fund company with a highly regarded investment research capability. It had no individual accounts or investment advisory services per se, except perhaps Harvard University's annual payment of about $35,000 for advice and management of its endowment.[27] A more usual approach to the pension business came from a background of investment counsel and mutual funds, the two major businesses of companies like Wellington Management.

Wellington's early history began in Philadelphia in 1928 when Walter Morgan, an accountant, created an early (some say the first) "balanced" mutual fund, using equities and fixed assets, which was later renamed the Wellington Fund. The following year, he set up the Financial Power and Securities Company to manage the mutual fund, renaming it Wellington Investors in 1935 and eventually the Wellington Management Company in 1959, to provide professional advisory services to investment companies. It became a public company in 1960.[28]

Wellington's rise as a Boston investment manager began in 1959 when four young men—W. Nicholas Thorndike, Robert Doran, Stephen Paine, and George Lewis—all from the Boston area, but with different educational and business experiences in Boston's financial community (mutual fund, brokerage, and counseling), started up an investment club called Professional Investors. Each of the four men, all under thirty years of age, pooled $2,000 into their venture, which grew to $250,000 within a year through the financial support of friends and relatives. As a result of their success, they incorporated Thorndike, Doran, Paine & Lewis in November 1960 as an investment counsel firm, and opened a small, somewhat obscure office at 1 State Street. "We needed the State Street address for respectability," one of the partners later exclaimed, even if people had some difficulty finding it. Investment counsel was, of course, not a new field; it had been invented in Boston over forty years earlier. But most of those Boston firms were older, having been organized in the 1920s and 1930s, and this was thought to be the first new one since that time. As Robert Doran later noted, "obviously, our youth distinguishes us immediately" from the rest. Also different was the new firm's focus on research; all four principals continued to work as analysts but looked at prospective investments along five broad categories (utilities, finance, basic industries, consumer and service, and applied science and research) that were more in line with future economic developments than the traditional industry categories like automobiles and chemicals used by others. A year later, they began their no-load, open end growth fund called Ivest, which soon led to the development of an advisory service; this, in turn, provided research services that expanded to other mutual funds.[29]

In October 1966, Thorndike, Doran, Paine & Lewis agreed to merge with Wellington Management, which had offices in Philadelphia. The two companies appeared to be a good fit: the Philadelphia company had an effective distribution system for mutual funds, while the Boston company provided strong, new leadership and a significant growth mutual fund for the merged firm. The name of the Boston part of the firm gradually disappeared by the mid-1970s, becoming known simply as the Wellington Management Company. During the late 1960s, the new firm created several new mutual funds, including the Gemini and Explorer Funds in 1967, the W. L. Morgan Growth Fund in 1968, and the Wellesley Income Fund in 1969. By about 1970, Wellington had hired a partner that ran only international stocks, making it one of few firms in the era to do so.

In 1974, Wellington began to unravel. In 1951, Morgan had hired John C. Bogle, a young college graduate, who later succeeded him as chief executive and chairman of Wellington in the late 1960s. Because of friction with the Boston group due to differences in management styles, however, Bogle was let go in early 1974. Nevertheless, he remained as president and chairman of the eleven Wellington funds, and ultimately gained control of fund distribution and servicing functions. Quite undeterred by his removal, Bogle formed the Vanguard Group of Investment Companies late in 1974, which included, by then, fourteen Wellington funds. Those same fund trustees who voted to retain Bogle as head of the funds also continued to use Wellington Management as an investment subadviser for their funds.

Wellington Management found itself at a critical crossroad. It could continue to act as a subadviser for Vanguard, but there was no guarantee that Bogle's new organization would continue to give them contracts for the work. Indeed, by 1976, Bogle had launched a low-cost fund strategy that focused on nonactively managed index funds. To diversify the business and make it less dependent on a single large client, Wellington needed to expand its base of companies that required the services Wellington could perform. Despite the turmoil over the Vanguard relationship, subadvisory services grew. By the late 1980s, it constituted about two-thirds of Wellington's business and made the firm the largest subadviser in the world for about 250–300 mutual funds.

While growing that business played on Wellington's strengths, getting into the pension business was a little more formidable. Nicholas Thorndike, one of the firm's partners, described the kinds of changes taking place at Wellington during the mid-1970s:

> The investment counsel business was relatively small at that point in time. It was mostly personal business. It wasn't really until the middle-to-late '70s that the investment counseling, investment advisory business took off, and that was when pension funds started to become a big factor in the industry as well as endowments and then that business took off in the '70s and '80s. . . . Endowments [started] waking up to the fact that they needed to be more aggressive in terms of their investment management. That business really took off big time, in the late '70s and '80s.

Although Wellington Management had the experience in personal investment counsel and the investment advisory business, it still needed a major pension client to gain a foothold in the burgeoning pension industry.[30]

That opportunity came along in 1977, when the Massachusetts Institute of Technology chose the company to handle its $575 million in pension and endowment funds.[31] "It probably was the largest shift of funds to a single new investment manager in recent history," noted the *Boston Globe,* as it beat out other Boston money managers—Fidelity Management Company; Standish, Ayer & Wood; and Colonial Management Company, which had previously managed the funds—in stiff competition. "We had been losing Vanguard assets, as Jack Bogle had found new managers," Thorndike later noted. "We needed something to bring a spotlight on us and our getting that MIT account was it." The relationship became more important over time. In the beginning, Wellington employed a team of four people to run MIT's funds; two decades later, the Wellington team was handling a much more complex portfolio run by over twenty individuals. As a result of the MIT relationship and other pension and endowment clients that were soon added, Wellington created in 1978 Wellington Investment Advisors, an investment counsel unit to serve a very small group of large institutions that sought high income returns. In 1982, it set up Wellington Trust Company to provide specialized investment products and services for employee benefit plans and other tax-qualified investors.[32]

In October 1979, Wellington's outside shareholders approved a plan to sell their voting shares to a management group of twenty-nine partners, after which Wellington became a private general partnership. The reenergized company soon adopted a broad diversification strategic plan—one that emphasized delivering "any product [to] any client anywhere in the world." Through its portfolio managers and analysts, Wellington developed a broad range of product types (only fixed income and equity investments, however; no private equity investment) that it could deliver, and started to create a track record by selling them. In the 1980s, the company began a quant (quantitative analysis) group and created research portfolios and sector funds. From a core of about 20 to 50 fixed or equity products, it expanded its product mix to 50 to 150 funds over the course of a decade and a half. Many of these were related products, with a lot of them coming from client suggestions. Later, Wellington moved into asset allocation and then into alternative investments, such as hedge funds in 1994, and generally created more product sophistication and specialization. The asset base remained essentially pension and endowment funds, although sovereign funds and high net-worth individuals became a factor later on.[33]

The company opened its first foreign office in London in 1983, and while not immediately successful, Wellington moved ahead in the late 1990s with overseas expansion, beginning in Singapore in 1996, Tokyo and Sydney in 1997, Hong Kong in 2003, and Beijing in 2007. In 2011, a Frankfurt, Germany, office was opened by its London-based affiliate, Wellington Management International Ltd. Wellington's expansion was due to the rising number of foreign securities, which were becoming more and more important in asset management. The U.S. share of equity markets in 1969 was 70 percent, but by 1980 it had declined to 50 percent, and by 1989 it was only 29 percent. In order to cover those non-U.S. securities, Wellington had to expand globally. Wellington also needed to tap an international talent base to get this broad investment coverage. The only way clients would take this kind of coverage seriously was for the firm to have a physical presence overseas. Overall, Wellington grew from 189 employees and $25 billion in AUM in 1986 to 2,000 employees and $630 billion in AUM in 2007. The last vestige of Wellington's original and personal investment counsel business (separately managed accounts for individuals) left the firm in the 1980s.[34]

Batterymarch Financial Management

Another important Boston money manager of the era, Batterymarch Financial Management, combined important innovations into a Hub financial power-house. Begun in the late 1960s by Dean LeBaron, a media savvy former Keystone mutual fund employee, Batterymarch became within a decade one of the largest independent (and solely owned) money management firms in the United States. The company was best known for its early indexing of funds and heavy reliance on computer technology. LeBaron's extensive use of the computer made him not only one of the prophets of quantitative investing, but also served, according to some critics, as an important marketing ploy. As a result, the small, low-overhead staff, as described in the company's annual report, was "less a group of money managers than a highly disciplined team of computer scientists using 'interactive programs' and 'market war games' to 'test hypotheses' before feeding their idea into the great maw of the Batterymarch mainframe." Topping it all was the LeBaron "mystique"—"his carefully cultivated reputation as a thinker on the cutting edge of money management science." Taken together, all of these features were viewed as "masterstrokes of a superb marketer."

LeBaron, along with other Keystone employees and some backers, started Batterymarch in 1969, but the company went into a nosedive and limped along during the early 1970s, having only about $48 million in assets in 1974. Then, as the market started turning in its favor, the company started introducing small cap funds. Batterymarch came up with the idea of an indexed small cap value fund at a time when indexing had only been introduced by about three other companies, but preceded Vanguard's well-known strategy by several years. As a result, Batterymarch avoided growth stocks and the "Nifty Fifty," an unofficial group of stocks from large capitalized companies known for their solid earnings and growth during the 1960s and 1970s, and followed an indexed second-tier small- and medium-sized company stock investment strategy niche that other investment companies shunned. The idea proved powerful by the mid-1970s, bringing a "rush of funds into passive accounts [that] would finally enable Batterymarch to establish its credibility in the pension market." It was also a strategy conceived and executed more by manual calculation than the use of a powerful computer. As Batterymarch grew, it attracted other pension funds from institutions that felt the company was "big enough to manage their money." Later, LeBaron was successful in moving clients to actively managed and more lucrative investment accounts.

In the meantime, however, indexing attracted clients, with assets multiplying sixfold to just over $1 billion two years after introducing the concept. Another former Keystone employee, Evan Schulman, who joined Batterymarch in the mid-1970s, participated in the firm's rapid rise in AUM: "For the first seven years, assets doubled every year, starting at 100 million when I joined—the jump from 100 to 200 million isn't bad, but that last 7 to 14 billion was a big step. . . . We went from 100 million to 14 billion in seven years. That's basically a doubling every year." By 1978, Batterymarch had surpassed the S&P 500 by more than 20 percent over the two previous years. Another transition was Batterymarch's shift in the late 1970s from a boutique firm managing personal accounts into one that managed pension and endowment funds for institutional clients. "After that was successful," Schulman continued, "[we] took the individual accounts and put them in a mutual fund that was administered by Vanguard but run by Batterymarch. . . . That was Dean's solution to having the batch of individual accounts."

LeBaron looked into ways to improve efficiency with the computer, running his index product on it, running quantitative stock screenings, and seeking ways to improve the company's trading activity and lower transaction costs. The LeBaron business model—"a few senior people and one big machine"—was beginning to change how the firm was operated and how to develop a broad investment strategy approach while handling more and more money. By the early 1980s, however, Batterymarch's early success in indexing started to underperform, primarily because it focused only on the largest capitalization stocks to complement its actively managed program, which focused on smaller companies. Eventually, he got out of indexed funds entirely. Further aspects of LeBaron's approach—value-oriented and contrarian investing—lost their luster as other money managers adopted them as well. LeBaron tried new approaches but by the mid-1980s, Batterymarch's fortunes had declined consecutively for several years and it was losing institutional accounts. The company continued to develop new fund areas, including non-U.S. developed markets in 1978, and in 1987 became an early U.S. institutional manager to invest in emerging equity markets. Nevertheless, LeBaron was not able to repeat his earlier successes. In 1995, the company became a subsidiary of Legg Mason, a Baltimore asset management company.[35]

Grantham, Mayo, Van Otterloo & Company

By the late 1970s, there was a proliferation of new investment boutiques in Boston with money managers who had developed their talents in other shops.

Among those Boston boutiques was Essex Investment Management Company, founded in 1976 by Joseph McNay and Walter Goehring, who had honed their skills at Endowment Management & Research, a college and university endowment fund manager. Essex's clients soon became a geographically dispersed group of individuals, educational institutions, and pension and profit-sharing plans in both the United States and abroad. Jeremy Grantham and Richard Mayo, two founding partners of Batterymarch with ties also reaching back to Keystone, founded Grantham, Mayo, Van Otterloo & Company (GMO) in 1977 with Eyk Van Otterloo, another Keystone manager. Both of these new firms believed that they could make more money for their clients because they were more flexible, simple, and specialized. Furthermore, they became established at a time when many larger investment companies had weak investment results because of narrow investment focus, and when ERISA's apparent restrictions on the use of small investment companies for pension management was beginning to wane. Early on, the particular interests of GMO were to find out-of-favor and less-well-followed stocks, to develop bigger, more contrarian investment ideas, and to find value added from the smaller area of institutional stocks—the kinds of investment focus that small firms would want to pursue, and many of the same types of ideas they had developed at Batterymarch.[36]

Grantham and his partners focused on traditional stock picking and judgment, using some dividend discount models rather than elaborate computer models as a starting point. They picked a group of only twenty-five stocks for their portfolio, which grew 8 percent a year during its first nine years, besting their new rivals, Batterymarch, year after year. GMO limited the fund to a manageable $250 million. Van Otterloo moved the firm internationally by creating the first machine-readable database of foreign securities, from which they picked securities and secured nearly every client they solicited to join the fund. GMO epitomized a shift taking place in the money management industry of the early 1980s by moving into this vast new and still little explored world of international investing. In 1980–1981, GMO became the first investment company to sell Harvard, Yale, and Princeton their first international portfolios, and became one of the first two value-based international managers and probably the first institutional value manager.

GMO was also one of the earliest two or three quant firms, moving the company into various growth, value, international, and small and large cap product options as opportunities developed. By about 1988, GMO was asked by a client to develop asset allocation models, that is, forecasting what is the best mix of assets to have at any given time or time period. Two decades later, asset allocation had become the firm's largest division, with 40 percent of GMO's business.

The company suffered during the peak of the dot-com bubble, with assets declining about 30 percent, from $31 billion to $20 billion by mid-2001. This was largely due to Grantham's refusal to buy more technology growth stocks at a time he believed they were overvalued, a conviction that was soon born out. Instead of cutting costs and reducing staff, Grantham decided to make investments in client service (staff who worked directly with their pension clients), sales, and marketing. He increased the size of staff by 50 percent and diversified the business into eight hedge funds, a fund of funds, an emerging markets debt fund, as well as other funds with different strategies, and also acquired $300 million in timber assets. (Grantham had also tried this strategy before the 2000 bubble, but clients did not like his bearish stance and pulled out.) As a result of his loyalty to the value "mantra" and the new offerings, he attracted more clients. Assets rose to $27 billion by the end of 2002, and then climbed to $55 billion the year after, reached $155 billion by 2006, only to fall to about $105 billion in mid-2011. The changing size of AUM had something to do with performance and cold spells with clients, but it was also Grantham's strong belief that the size of a fund has a strong impact on that performance. "You need to close everything down at an appropriate size," he noted, or else you will lose value in any further purchases because you have attracted new buyers of the stock, and thereby diminished the value of your original investment decision. Ideal size rather than continuous asset growth matters at GMO. Besides recognizing the ineluctable ups and downs of his business, Grantham has also been looking ahead at where his company might be a decade or two into the future, in light of more recent, possible, or impending changes in the pension industry.[37]

State Street Bank & Trust Company

Trust companies and banks generally fared badly as the pension revolution began to take off in the 1960s and 1970s. The oldest Boston trust company, New England Trust Company, merged with Merchants National Bank in 1961, becoming New England Merchants National Bank (renamed the Bank of New England in 1982), only to fail in the late 1980s when the bank overextended itself. One prominent trust company, Boston Safe Deposit & Trust Company, changed its name to the Boston Company before it was sold to Shearson Loeb Rhoades (1981), which was then bought by American Express, before it was eventually sold to Mellon Financial for $1.45 billion in 1992.[38] Another formerly prominent Boston trust company, Old Colony Trust Company, had a long association with First National Bank before they merged. Later known as BankBoston, First National merged with Fleet Financial Group in 1999, which became part of the Bank of America in 2004 in a $48 billion merger.

A trust-like organization, the Massachusetts Company (formerly known as the Massachusetts Hospital Life Insurance Company, established in 1818), was acquired by Travelers Insurance in 1969, which was merged with Keystone Custodian Funds in 1979, creating The Massachusetts Companies. This was followed by a Keystone buyback from Travelers in 1989, while the other half, then called The Massachusetts Company, was acquired by PNC (formerly Pittsburgh National Bank) from Travelers in 1993.[39] Over time, the trust work of all of these institutions became a less appreciated component part of constantly changing and evolving organizations that were continuing to grow and expand the scope of their financial services in the post–Glass-Steagall era. That decline in the importance of trust work was also the result of these institutions' tendencies, with a few exceptions, to invest in conservative fixed assets when newer rivals were involved in equity investments and investment performance.[40]

The only major Boston trust company player not to follow this model was State Street Bank & Trust (State Street or State Street Corp.), which moved in two different directions during the late twentieth century, becoming one of several internationally prominent custodial banks and, in a separate subsidiary known as State Street Global Advisors (SSgA), becoming the world's largest money manager and also the world's largest manager of institutional assets. State Street's rise from custodial bank for the first mutual fund in 1924 to its more current achievements is perhaps one of the most important and intriguing Boston financial stories of all time.

For years, banks and their trust companies had had their own way, managing investments and acting as custodians for securities and recordkeeping. But as a change in this relationship approached, many of them resisted. "There were many banks that would not act as custodian" for Boston money managers "if they were not also the manager. We had a lot of trouble with some of the bank custodians who really didn't like the business," one State Street Research partner later recalled. Others, however, saw a "huge opportunity and that with the right fees, they could gather assets and maybe even sell other services." One of those few was State Street.[41]

The State Street Trust Company was founded in 1891 and its rise in the Boston banking community came through the acquisition of some thirteen other trust companies and commercial banks, one dating from 1792, to form State Street Bank and Trust Company in 1961. Its leader for most of that period (1911–1950) was Allan Forbes, the grandson of Captain Robert Bennet Forbes whose exploits in the China trade of the early nineteenth century, along with those of his brother John Murray Forbes, were explored in an earlier chapter. During Allan Forbes's period, State Street became best known for and was long after remembered because of its collecting habits of Boston and New England history and artifacts. The bank was associated with his series of illustrated historical booklets, some thirty-nine publications by the time of his death, on Boston and New England history with such titles as *State Street* (1906) and *Old Shipping Days in Boston* (1918). Forbes also constantly collected antiques, relics, historical prints, paintings, and ship models, and even created historical banking rooms; these mementos of the past decorated new offices as the bank grew and number of branch offices increased. As Walter Muir Whitehill, a close friend of Forbes, later wrote, "In the banking rooms flagstone paving, granite counters, oak and pine paneling, antique lanterns, ship models hanging above the tellers' cages like votive offerings in a Basque fishermen's church, innumerable prints and ship portraits, tavern chairs, trestle tables, and pewter inkwells combined to create an atmosphere unique in Boston business."

As for Forbes himself, "he would be ensconced in a low-studded room of seventeenth-century inspiration, with heavy beams, and a great kitchen fireplace, suggesting that he might be about to roast a haunch of venison or cook a mess of succotash. Seated in a Carver-Brewster chair, originally from the tap-room of the Wayside Inn, surrounded by ship models and prints, with fire buckets for waste baskets and a sea chest serving as a wood box, Allan Forbes would deal with an extraordinary variety of twentieth-century business in the course of a day."[42]

Forbes's love of local history or the smart marketing ploy of identifying his institution with Boston's rich past (it was often referred to as the "ship model bank"), however, was soon eclipsed by State Street's steady growth. When Forbes became president in 1911, the bank had $13 million in deposits. By 1925, this had risen to $57 million, and three decades later in 1955, State Street deposits exceeded $187 million, just before its merger with the Second National Bank of Boston, which increased deposits to almost $319 million.[43]

Nineteenth- and early twentieth-century Boston banks had strong personalities, largely because there were so many of them and they developed their customer bases from the industries and ethnic ties that surrounded them. The merger with the Second National Bank brought to State Street a strong commercial lending bank, which had prominence in two important local industries: the wool trade, in which Boston served as the worldwide center, with relationships from Australia to Europe, and the grain trade, in which Boston served as the critical nexus of a business that started in the American Midwest and ended in Europe. While State Street had operated at a retail level with checking and trust accounts, and had done work in the mutual fund accounting and custody business, the Second was a wholesale operation and worked with important companies in New England, New York, the western United

States, and abroad, something that became more important as the pension revolution began to unfold in the 1960s.[44]

Perhaps the most visible sign of change of the newly enlarged State Street Bank & Trust occurred in 1966 with the completion of its new headquarters at 225 Franklin Street, the first modern bank building in Boston, with its name clearly visible on the city's rising skyline. Although the construction of bank buildings was nothing new in other major U.S. cities, Boston banks had largely housed their businesses in less ostentatious structures, mimicking the old Boston make-do adage: "Buy our hats? We have our hats." But Boston's financial community was changing, and 225 Franklin proved to be a major event in the Hub as other banks—among them, First National, Shawmut, and Merchants—followed State Street's lead in the 1970s.

After it moved into its new headquarters, State Street started to develop a new infrastructure for its custody business, constructing in 1969 the Quincy State Street South office complex to handle it. By the mid-1970s, State Street had $30 billion in mutual fund assets under custody, about 30 percent of the market. The modern custody business involves several functions, including holding securities, keeping track of their market values, apportioning those holdings to various accounts, and issuing account statements and other status reports. The bank also made strides in developing its pension fund and profit sharing businesses (the latter supplanted by 401[k] plans) as it serviced manufacturing company bank customers, correspondent bank pension plans, and companies that had oversubscribed pension funds. It soon started creating its own investment products, including stock and balanced mutual funds as well as the fourth oldest index fund, and then others such as international funds.[45]

Despite its gains in custody and pension businesses, State Street went through a period of heavy losses in commercial lending in real estate (with the worst loan record of any Boston bank), a lack of success in developing a diversification program by acquiring or leasing nonbanking ventures, and the experience of a lowering on the rating of the bank's notes. By 1975, the bank's board appointed fellow member William S. Edgerly as president. The MIT-trained engineer had a Harvard MBA and was financial vice president of a Boston manufacturing company. He immediately focused on building on the company's strength, its custodial or securities servicing capabilities, even though it was the fourth largest bank in the city. In another move, he set up in 1978 a separate subsidiary from the trust company portion of the business to form State Street Global Advisors to develop institutional asset management. In turn, the personal trust business was sold off. By the time Edgerly left in 1991, the bank was engaged in three spheres, including custodianship, asset management, and traditional commercial banking and lending businesses. But Edgerly's successor, Marshall

N. Carter, sold off that third portion to commercial banks in town. By March 2011, custodianship and asset management provided State Street Corp. with $22.6 trillion in assets under custody and administration, $2.1 trillion in AUM, and a position of world leadership in both.[46]

State Street Corporation. Edgerly had strong views about where the bank should head, believing that if a firm cannot be first or second in a line of business, it was best to sell it off or discontinue it. He was more concerned about earnings per share as a sign of success than he was about the number of AUM or, by the 1980s, growth through the acquisition of other banks. He moved to sell off the retail commercial banking and credit card businesses as well as its affiliated community banks, and got rid of the bank's international loan business, believing that the custody business was the place to be. While Edgerly's predecessor, George Rockwell, had made a number of disastrous business decisions, he had been a former IBM marketing manager and helped to beef up the custody business through better computer technology and by establishing State Street's data processing operation at a complex ten miles away in Quincy, Massachusetts. These moves into a deeper commitment to the custody business came at a propitious time, just as ERISA became law and pension funds needed more accurate recordkeeping, and as assets started rolling in at an accelerated pace. From about 1978 through 1981, Edgerly and others at the bank developed a one-page State Street Plan, a guide that sought growth in high-priority innovation through systems development (low-cost, high-volume processing), sustainable real growth in earnings per share (with a goal of 18 percent return on equity and 20 percent dividend payout without increasing the number of shares), with a bold strategy to compete in regional, national, and international markets successfully.

By the mid-1970s, State Street had about 30 percent of all U.S. mutual fund processing business, or about $17 billion under custody, but the entire pension market at the time amounted to $700 billion. Although State Street had a technological edge, in order to gain a share of the new market and create a fundamental shift in the pension business as a whole, it had to overcome any reluctance pension plan sponsors might have about separating custody and recordkeeping from investment management. It was a hard sell at first, but by the end of the 1970s, it started to pay off as a number of blue-chip clients came on board with their custody business. By the end of the decade, State Street was also ahead of its rivals in developing crucial master-trust software, which gave them an advantage well into the 1980s.

State Street's next big step was to go international in the 1980s. Without overseas branches like its competitors, it developed an elaborate subcustodial network of local banks in sixty-eight countries to handle local clearing and settlement of trades to help it build scale in its international operations. Another development was Prism, an early multicurrency accounting system, an important nexus because asset management included not just securities but also cash management. As a catalyst, Prism also led to the gradual development of an entirely new transactions processing system, merging and integrating record-keeping with multicurrency accounting as well as data on mutual funds and pension funds on a global scale. This project first developed as an upgrade of the then-current system called Horizon in the mid-1980s, and in the early 1990s, became a wholly new architecture called Global Interchange with full interoperability by State Street staff. In the meantime, State Street was by 1986 in first place in mutual fund processing and the U.S. pension fund master-trust business. By the end of the 1980s, assets under custody went from $64 to $787 billion.

During the 1990s and into the twenty-first century under Marshall Carter's direction, State Street moved from its core custody business into one that offered a broad range of value-added ancillary information services, which were largely based on its technological innovations. "We determined," Carter later noted, "that our business is based on technology, and is not a business that just uses technology." He launched efforts to cross-sell each division's products, "re-engineer anything" to cut costs, embark on further international expansion, and support efforts to add value to products and develop new ones. The focal point of the business turned to giving customers more data and information for "customer empowerment," that is, providing more timely information about a customer's assets to help the customer do his or her job. At the same time, Carter continued the work begun by Edgerly to move out of commercial banking. At the time Carter took over, a quarter of the bank's revenue came from commercial lending, but by the mid-1990s, the bank was virtually out of it. Carter also sold the last of the bank's branch operations to Citizens Financial a few years later.[47]

All of these actions helped move State Street into an important global custodian bank as the number of custodial banks, which often serviced only local clientele, gradually became smaller, more globalized, and consolidated. By the time some of the first global industry rankings became available in the 1991–1992 period, State Street Bank & Trust was already ranked sixth worldwide in assets under custody, while Boston Safe Deposit and Trust Company was twelfth. By 2000, the four largest global players were Chase Manhattan Bank, Bank of New York, Deutsche Bank, and Citibank, which were followed by State Street and in eighth place the Mellon Group, which included the custody assets of the old Boston Safe Deposit & Trust Company. State Street's position as a global custodial bank continued to rise when, in 2003, it acquired Deutsche Bank's global custody business for $1.1 billion. Deutsche's $2 trillion in custodial assets pushed State Street's total to $9 trillion and ahead of its two arch rivals, Bank of New York's $8.9 trillion and J. P. Morgan Chase & Company's $8.3 trillion. But this would not last for long. In late 2006 and 2007, Mellon merged with the Bank of New York (BNY Mellon) in a $16.5 billion takeover that combined the second and eighth largest global custodian banks. According to one ranking service, in 2011 BNY Mellon ($25.5 trillion) was ranked first in assets under custody worldwide, followed by State Street ($16.692 trillion), J. P. Morgan ($16.6 trillion), and Citi ($12.6 trillion), after which there were a number of much smaller foreign custodial banks. While second in total assets, State Street remains first in many asset and client categories, such as endowment/foundation assets, while BNY Mellon's assets include those of several former Boston companies including Boston Safe Deposit & Trust and Standish, Ayer & Wood.[40]

State Street Global Advisors (SSgA). The second prong of Edgerly's strategy for the State Street Corporation was to create in 1978 a separate asset management division, which was based originally on its former personal trust business. That division soon launched three index funds (domestic, international, and short-term investment), becoming an early leader, for the bank's large custodial clients. It also brought together the use of information technology, a knowledge of quantitative finance (more efficient and less costly securities picking by the numbers), and marketing with a focus on its growing institutional business. In 1986, it became the largest U.S. manager of international pension assets and international indexed assets. By 1989, the division had $53 billion in AUM. A year later, the division was made into a separate entity, State Street Global Advisors, and was given a mandate to expand internationally. It quickly set up offices in London, Brussels, Hong Kong, Toronto, Paris, Sydney, Tokyo, Dubai, San Francisco, Montreal, and Atlanta, and eight others between 1995 and 2007. The company's assets rose to $161 billion in 1994, and by 1999 had grown fourfold to $667 billion. By the end of 2003, assets totaled $1.1 trillion, making SSgA the world's largest asset or money manager. In the 1990s, it invented the exchange traded fund (ETF), and during the 2000s, SSgA sought to increase its client base outside the United States and developed actively managed institutional products. It also created other important products and services, including customized investment strategies for institutions through commingled funds (common trust funds), various ETF products and mutual funds, and a partnership with local investment companies to develop investment strategies for clients.

SSgA's rise to prominence as one of the world's leading money managers was symbolic of the growth and significance of Boston firms generally during the past forty years. While Boston institutions had been major players as investment managers for pensions, endowments, and foundations in the 1970s, their role became even more noticeable by the 1990s. According to one rating publication, *Institutional Investor*, Fidelity Investments ranked first in the world as money manager in 1992, a position it held for the next eleven years (1992–2002). By 1993, Fidelity was followed by State Street Corp. (fifth), and then two companies with significant Boston subsidiaries, Travelers (Keystone and the Massachusetts Companies, seventh), and Mellon (which included $40 billion in assets from the Boston Company, eleventh).

Aside from a constant Fidelity, there were some year-to-year fluctuations, with Mellon rising to third place and State Street moving up to fourth, then the two reversing their positions, and State Street gradually moving up. By 1998, *Institutional Investor* noted the change that had taken place in money management since its original ranking in 1975: "The ranks of our original top ten in 1975 were dominated by insurance companies and bank trust departments, which soon fell back as the mutual fund and defined contribution revolutions took hold in the 1980s."[49]

But notice of Boston's growing importance in money management had already taken place. By 1996, several publications and research companies ranked Boston as the fourth most important money management center in the world, behind only Tokyo, London, and New York—and piling up assets faster than any other city on their lists. Using a broad measurement of money under management that included stocks, bonds, and cash, Boston managed $1.4 trillion, with New York at about $2.6 trillion. Three of the city's giants— Fidelity, State Street Global Advisers, and Putnam—saw their assets climb by $125 billion in the first nine months of 1996, while the AUM by all of the city's investment firms in 1975 was only about $80 billion.[50]

By the end of the twentieth century and the beginning of the next, Boston had more and more highly ranked money managers, including Putnam Investments, Scudder Kemper Investments, Wellington Management, United Asset Management, State Street Research and Management, Old Mutual Holdings (including United Asset Management and some other Boston investment managers), Evergreen Investments (part of Wachovia Bank), FleetBoston Financial, John Hancock, and CDC IXIS Asset Management (which included Loomis, Sayles & Company), all of which scored among the top fifty companies by AUM.[51]

In 2003, SSgA became the world's largest money manager, followed by a second fund "indexer," Barclays Global Investors, with Fidelity falling to third. Besides indexing, the new frontrunners also used active quantitative strategies and employed hedge funds, which helped to increase assets faster than

Fidelity. During the first decade of the twenty-first century, a few more Boston or Boston-affiliated companies grew into the rankings, but most of the action was near the top with further consolidation among some of the larger players. All of this activity culminated in 2009 when BlackRock acquired Barclays Global Investors for $15.2 billion. As a result, by 2010 SSgA became the second largest money manager in the world at $1.9 trillion to BlackRock's assets of $3.3 trillion, with Fidelity in third place at $1.4 trillion. While nothing lasts forever, in the money management world as in the custodial banking world, it appears that the large companies are only a merger away from being on top.[52]

The Expansion of Institutional Endowments

College and university endowment funds as well as those of other nonprofits and foundations have been managed almost hand in hand with pension funds by Boston money managers since before the 1960s. Early on, they represented a significant portion of funds managed in Boston. In 1972, for instance, Robert Lenzner, financial columnist of the *Boston Globe,* noted that "more college endowment money is handled here than in any other city."[53]

Since World War II, college and university endowments have also grown exponentially. It is not possible to track that growth precisely in aggregate figures because, until more recent times, some institutions kept better records than others. One important study compared the size of endowments of 104 colleges and universities in 1962 and 1987. Over those twenty-five years, endowments at those schools increased from $6.734 to $39.510 billion, roughly sixfold. Another study focused on the top twenty-five college and university endowments (in size) showed that they increased from $21.837 billion in 1986 to $201.819 billion in 2007. There are, of course, thousands of institutions of higher learning in the United States with endowment funds, so these figures, impressive as they are, can only offer an impression of the overall size these funds constitute. Another and more recent study states that the size of endowments held by some 850 colleges and universities in 2010 was $346 billion.[54]

Despite their growth and increasing importance, college and university endowments were in dire straits less than fifty years ago. By the end of the 1960s, there was growing concern about their fate due to the widening revenue-expense gap in which many nonprofit organizations, particularly institutions of higher learning, found themselves. The need to spend more money for education, classrooms, and research facilities put a strain on colleges and universities, which, at the same time, used traditional approaches when it came to investing their rising endowments. According to one influential study, the

reiterated, would lead "to the slow strangulation of Harvard's goose that has laid so many golden eggs over past years."[58]

Cabot's ideas of fiscal prudence included the creation of a reserve fund whereby endowment earnings were not committed until the following budget year, and a prohibition on the use of the endowment for large capital projects, which Cabot saw as a slippery slope of robbing the future to pay for current needs. Despite the fact that the market value of the endowment doubled between 1955 and 1965 under his direction, expenditures increased even faster. Harvard received most of the difference through government-sponsored research projects and a rise in tuition, not from the Cabot-managed endowment.[59]

George F. Bennett, Cabot's colleague at State Street Research and Management Company and deputy treasurer since 1948, took over in 1965. Bennett's tenure occurred during a rough period for the university, including student unrest during the Viet Nam War, and he resigned in the fall of 1972. He was eventually replaced by George Putnam Jr., a long-serving member of Harvard's Board of Overseers, whose immediate family was involved with Putnam Investments in Boston. Severing of the dual role of financial chief and investment manager took place with Bennett's departure. Putnam endorsed the idea of setting up a separate operation for the Harvard endowment, which he and his successors would only monitor. The plan was apparently first suggested by Bennett himself and discussed in a 1970 Harvard Governance Committee report called "Harvard and Money." In 1974, the Harvard Management Company was created, a wholly owned subsidiary of the university and the first of its kind. The company was set up to deal with the size and complexity of modern financial markets, and employed a small team of investment professionals who managed a significant proportion of the endowment in the treasurer's office at 50 Federal Street in Boston. The company also worked with five outside investment groups, representing different approaches, which invested a part of the endowment but also provided information and strategic inputs.

Filling the role of the company's first president was Walter M. Cabot, a nephew of Paul Cabot and, ironically, the former manager of the George Putnam Fund at Putnam Investments. Walter Cabot had more recently been a partner at Wellington Management Company. He recruited eight partners for the organization, consisting of Harvard MBAs and personnel from Boston investment companies. In reviewing its activities during its first decade, the company noted that it

> has been a leader, breaking new ground in many previously untested
> and profitable investment areas including stock and bond loans,
> options, financial futures, bond and stock arbitrage, real estate,

venture capital, leverage buyouts, risk arbitrage, indexed portfolios, and a variety of new fixed-income instruments. The growth of the endowment and the continuing diversification and integration of the financial markets required that the Management Company expand its staff and change its mode of operation. The Company has grown from the original group of nine to almost one hundred professionals and staff.

The growth of the organization and the complexity of the financial markets necessitated a management structure that provided for investment decision making at both the macro and micro levels. Consequently, separate pools of capital have been established with specific objectives. These pools are the responsibility of individuals inside the organization, supported by a team of analysts or professional investment managers employed by the Management Company. The results of these pools of capital are monitored closely and evaluated often to ensure that the prescribed objectives are being met. The allocation of the capital pools is performed by a committee of top management personnel. Daily and monthly meetings of investment professionals to exchange ideas and financial data support the investment decisions of the Company. In addition, the constant information flow from Wall Street and other investment professionals and experts augments the internal decision making. This management structure provides the creativity and flexibility required in today's rapidly changing, complex investment environment.[60]

Pioneering various investment approaches for a nonprofit, including security lending, venture capital, options, and the use of arbitrage, and making investments that came to be called alternative, Cabot and his successors were able to increase the size of the school's endowment to $19.2 billion by 2000, far ahead of any other university. So successful was Harvard Management in its work that steadily rising salaries and bonuses among investment partners became a source of complaint at Harvard, especially from its faculty.[61]

Harvard's initial success in growing its endowment led Harvard's great rival—Yale University—to try to create another successful investment organization, also in Boston. Yale's hobbled endowment had been run by members of the Yale Corporation and a single manager in New Haven until 1967, when the university decided to establish an investment company outside of New Haven that employed professional investment management. Surprisingly, they set up their company, Endowment Management & Research, in Boston, selecting Roland D. Grimm, a Yale graduate and former vice president at Fidelity Management & Research and manager of the Contra Fund, as its chief executive officer. Grimm and his two Boston colleagues owned 50 percent of the firm and had a reputation of being aggressive stock pickers.

An article in *Institutional Investor* ten years later discussed in part why Yale chose Boston for its investment operation:

> Boston, of course, was the Camp of the Other Guys, but "I have my own untutored, unprofessional reasons for wanting it there," says [Yale President] Kingman Brewster. "They might as well put up *two* thermometers on the Boston Common." Ultimately it was because the finalists in Yale's management derby—Bostonians all—wanted to stay there that Endowment Management settled there. "I told them," says Roland Grimm, "that Boston was the finest financial center in the country. Those people in New York see only black and white; when they're bullish, they're totally bullish; when they're bearish, they're on the windowsills. This is a better place for perspective."[62]

Shortly thereafter, the company acquired portfolios from eight other universities, including Tufts and the California Institute of Technology, and by 1972, Yale's finance committee had broken up the university's portfolio into four categories—appreciation, income, restricted, and real estate—to help give each clearly defined objectives. It also developed a screening process with nine criteria to help judge investment risk. In 1972 and 1973, Yale divided part of its endowment among two other investment managers that included T. Rowe Price and U.S. Trust of New York.[63]

The move to ship part of the endowment to other managers was generally seen as the result of poor performance by Endowment Management after 1968, its first year, albeit also a poor time for many investment managers. By the early 1970s, a number of portfolio managers and analysts had left the company, and its new Omega fund fared badly in that decade. By 1977, much of the company's early leadership had left to found new ventures of their own, and the company was eventually sold to a U.S. subsidiary of Baring Brothers & Company.

It was not until about 1985 when Yale began to develop a new course of action and move its endowment ahead from decades of underachievement. At that time, the university decided to manage its endowment internally, and appointed David Swensen as its chief investment officer. Over the next several decades, Swensen shifted a lackluster investment policy to something more like what Harvard had done under the management of Cabot and Harvard Management. He raised Yale's stake in private equity from 3.2 to 20.2 percent, increased real assets (including timber and real estate) from 8.5 to 29.3 percent and hedge funds from nothing to 25.1 percent, and, for the most part, got out of domestic stocks and bonds, which declined from 71.9 to 14.1 percent. Swensen discussed much of this publicly in his *Pioneering Portfolio Management: An Unconventional Approach to Institutional Investment,* published in 2000. Nevertheless, in developing new areas for universities to invest in—international securities, private investing (like security lending), venture capital, oil and gas ventures, and the beginnings of private equity—Harvard was a decade or more ahead of Yale.[64]

Following Walter Cabot's tenure, there were significant changes at Harvard Management Company. While the types of investments did not materially change, the value of the endowment accelerated. The size of the endowment when Cabot's successor, Jack Meyer, took over in 1990 was $4.7 billion, and by the time Meyer left in 2005, it had quintupled to $22.6 billion. Meyer's success was largely due to the development of a model portfolio with specific weights, more control of investment from the center, and spreading the endowment out to a variety of outside investment managers. Meyer, who resigned in 2008, was followed by the short, two-year tenure of Mohamed El-Erian, and then the temporary management of the company by two others. By this time, 70 percent of the Harvard endowment was in the hands of outside managers. Harvard Management's unique model of investment has evolved over time: during its early years, nearly 90 percent of the endowment was run internally, but in more recent years, this has declined to 50 and then only 30 percent, as the company has hired specialized investment adviser talent to invest an increasingly larger proportion of the endowment. This model of highly paid internal fund managers combined with the use of outside managers is generally considered unique to Harvard; most other universities with large endowments choose their outside managers but do not run their money internally.[65]

Harvard and other elite universities led the focus away from holding traditional securities to what have been called alternative investments—hedge funds, real estate, venture capital, private-equity funds, and natural resources, among others. The move to these kinds of investments was not generally recognized until after the stock market crash following the tech bubble in the spring of 2000, and endowments saw that investments in alternatives did reasonably well. The change was gradual but unmistakable. In 1995, for instance, endowments invested less than 10 percent in alternatives, but by 2008, that had climbed to an average of over 30 percent, although some went much further.[66]

Another innovation that the Harvard Management Company brought was the development of third-party consultants in the endowment, foundation, and nonprofit institutional investment management business, and of the preeminent company in that field, Cambridge Associates.[67] In the spring of 1973, at the time George Putnam was setting up Harvard Management, he hired a couple of independent consultants, James Bailey and Hunter Lewis. Graduate students both, they were asked to help choose outside investment managers from about one hundred applicants, and to set up an index to measure their investment performances. Bailey was also allowed to use the data he collected—information on asset classes, investment managers, and institutional investors' best practices—to provide a basis for a new business. That business later became Cambridge Associates, which sought to advise other groups on how they should invest their endowments and whom they should hire to do it. As Bailey later noted, while several companies had been founded a few years earlier to act as consultants for pension funds, "no one had focused on [educational institutions] as a class of institutional investors before, so we thought they deserved focus." Since its founding, Cambridge Associates continues to be the largest adviser for school endowments and foundations in the country.[68]

Over the next year and a half, Bailey and Lewis helped to develop for Harvard Management a set of investment objectives and asset allocation policies, and the kinds of strategies to pursue those objectives; they also established performance measurements, investment accounting, and other monitoring systems. Essentially, they sought to separate this set of functions and the selection of investment managers from a second function, the selection of individual securities. In sum, the two consultants came to collect information on institutions, asset classes, and investment managers; offered advice; and provided performance measurement services.

As Cambridge Associates shifted from working with Harvard to other university or college endowments by the early 1980s, they moved their clients from a strictly balanced approach of U.S. stocks and bonds, long the model for investment by many of these institutions, to new asset classes, ranging from venture capital and hedge funds, to foreign stocks and bonds, distressed securities, real estate, oil and gas, timber investments, and a panoply of other alternatives. Through study and reports, each new asset class was explored to determine any legal issues it might have as an investment and whether each was of institutional quality. From a 50/50 approach, the company went to a roughly 60/40 stocks-to-fixed-assets allocation, with small percentages in other asset classes that included some foreign stocks and real estate holdings. Over time, this changed again so that by the 2000s, about 90 percent of all investments were in various types of equities—about 15–20 percent in U.S. stocks, another 15–20 percent in developed or emerging non-U.S. stocks, 15 percent in venture capital and private equity, 20–25 percent in hedge funds, and 10–15 percent in real assets—with only about 10 percent in fixed assets.

By 1975, Cambridge Associates had a base of twelve clients, including six colleges and universities in New England but several others as far away as the West Coast. This group expanded to some thirty institutions by the early 1980s but continued to grow so that by the end of the 2000s, there had about nine hundred clients. In the meantime, the company began to accept other kinds of clients, including government and pension funds, family groups, and sovereign wealth funds, and to expand to several locations in the United States. By the 1990s, it moved internationally, establishing offices in London, Singapore, Sydney, and, in 2011, Beijing. Today, over three thousand foundation and endowment managers make visits to Cambridge Associates a year.[69]

Boston money management over the last fifty years has been a series of spinoffs and a generational phenomenon as well. Large money managers with good performance records like Fidelity and SSgA attracted more and more money to Boston. This, in turn, helped to create investment opportunities. As one long-time Boston money manager exclaimed, "Any company that wants to raise money has to go through Boston." But attracting money and talent to the Hub has also led to other consequences. New firms spinning off from others have brought additional energy and strategies to investing, which have nurtured and attracted new talent and clients. What had once been only a narrow focus in money management in such areas as personal investment counsel and management of mutual funds has spread to opportunities in institutional investing for pension funds or endowments as well as the management of family wealth and hedge funds, both discussed in a later chapter. As money management opportunities mature or become routine and predictable, new ones seem to emerge, become attractive, and strive to succeed in Boston.

CHAPTER 10

The Transformation of the "Boston" Open End Mutual Fund since 1970

The economy of the 1970s had a devastating impact on the growing mutual fund industry. But the downturn also created new opportunities that helped to transform that investment vehicle into a competitive force in the U.S. financial system. Before 1970, commercial banks, savings or thrift institutions, and pension funds largely dominated the economy. By contrast, mutual funds played a minor role. But as they began to take off again in the late 1970s, the growing market for mutual funds was accompanied by changes in laws and regulations affecting finance, an increasingly global economy, new financial instruments, major transformations in the structure and nature of financial institutions, and a profound shift in the bearing of financial risk—from institutions to individuals. All of these factors would have an impact on mutual funds, an instrument that adapted easily to these changing conditions.[1]

Economic adversity helped to create diversity, first in the types and number of funds that became available—including money market, tax-exempt, specialty, or index funds—and then, as the economy improved, investment companies found new ways to advertise and distribute them. Some of these new funds offered more convenience to investors with special fund features; they also expanded the number of choices, which helped to create more diversity in the investors' ever-widening portfolios. Investment companies even provided financial research for the new investment world in which the individual became more responsible for his or her own financial future. Where mutual funds had been largely the domain of broker-dealers working with moderately wealth individuals, events in the 1970s created a leveling—and an expansion—of access to investing that became more apparent in the decades that followed. Indeed, Arthur Levitt, chairman of the U.S. Securities and

Exchange Commission, noted in 1998 that, "as recently as 1980, only one in 17 households invested in mutual funds; today that number has risen to more than one in three."[2]

Boston had been the center of the mutual fund industry from its beginning in 1924 and continued in that role into the postwar years. Because of the growing success of the industry and increased national competition, however, Boston's predominance gradually receded. This shift requires considering the industry from a national perspective. In 1945, for instance, a little over a dozen Boston investment companies held about 56 percent of all mutual fund assets. By January 1965, Boston investment companies or complexes ran 27 of 103 mutual funds in the industry, which accounted for a little over 30 percent of the assets. While Boston's predominance in the industry was shrinking, it was and would continue to remain the industry's center with no other geographic location rivaling its position. Still, things did not remain the same even in Boston. While M.I.T. with its sister fund, the Massachusetts Investors Growth Fund, remained the largest fund complex in Boston in 1965, with $3.4 billion in assets under management (AUM), the previously little-known investment company called Fidelity Investments, now sponsoring the two high-flying growth funds managed by Gerald Tsai and Edward ("Ned") Johnson III, was in second place with nearly $1.3 billion in AUM. Like Fidelity, another fund company, Putnam Investments, was also on the move with its balanced George Putnam Fund of Boston and the new Putnam Growth Fund. While there would be ups and downs for both of these companies in the decades ahead, the two would come to dominate Boston's mutual fund industry from the 1980s through the early 2000s. Both investment companies had strikingly different corporate cultures and pursued divergent strategies in their drive for success. And because of their size, they also would soon become important institutions in the dispersion of trained talent into new Boston asset management businesses, where their influence has been felt for decades.[3]

Resilient Fidelity: Confronting the Downward Spiral

Many people largely viewed the 1970s as a "nowhere" decade; by the various economic and market measures of the time, it certainly seemed that way. The Standard and Poor's 500 industrial average went from 102 in early January 1970 to only 120 at the end of the decade, having declined by almost half during 1973 and 1974. The Dow Jones Industrials were at 809 at the beginning of the decade but only inched up to 824 on the last day of 1979, having risen to 1,031 then declined to 633 in the interim. Fund assets for the industry

and in 1980 $10.1 million, as assets rose from $375 million to $2.6 billion over the corresponding period.[8] Even after 1980, when Congress removed earlier regulations and passed legislation that allowed banks to offer negotiable order of withdrawal (NOW) accounts, which paid interest like that of money market funds, it did little to stop the flow of money to mutual fund companies.[9]

The younger Johnson's tinkerings were transformational. As Peter Lynch, one of Fidelity's soon-to-be star fund managers, would later note, it was one thing to have a vehicle individuals or small businesses could use to temporarily park their cash, but quite another to provide it with a check-writing feature. The latter enhancement "gave the money-market fund universal appeal as a savings account and a checking account," and would give the shareholder not just 5 percent interest but rather the best short-term rates, which increased to about 20 percent by the early 1980s.[10]

One of the unintended—but necessary—consequences of Fidelity's move into and success in money market funds was a change in its basic fund distribution system from broker-dealers and their sales commissions (loads), which the company had maintained since the 1930s, to the direct marketing of their products (with no loads) to the general public. Briefly, paying a commission would take away the fund's yield advantage, making Fidelity's fund much less attractive to the investor. But the shift to direct marketing required large investments in new technology—computers, phone systems, shareholder information systems—as well as traditional print and other media advertising, all coming at a time when Fidelity and its competitors were struggling to survive. Several large or growing investment companies made this change. Fidelity was a leader in the shift, combining it with low-cost brokerage to gather and retain customer assets under management.[11] Other companies used different strategies. Vanguard, a Pennsylvania investment company, focused on low-cost investments for its customers through direct market sales (begun in 1977) and on lower cost index funds. Putnam Investments' owner, the New York insurance broker Marsh & McLennan, "favored the no-load concept in principle, [but] was disturbed that establishing direct distribution would entail considerable advertising and other expenses at a time when the fund business did not appear to be growing. Fund-owned Vanguard and privately held Fidelity, Dreyfus and others went fully or partially no-load but not many other major firms followed." As George Putnam Jr. noted, "The principal problem we saw was that to go into competition with our former distributors could mean large scale redemptions of existing shares as our erstwhile dealers sought to keep the shareholder money that they had placed in the Funds under their control."[12]

While money market funds changed Fidelity and soon made it into a mutual fund powerhouse, that success had been the byproduct of a number of decisions made in the downward spiraling 1970s—all of them epitomizing a favorite word in the industry lexicon, *diversification*. Fidelity had long been known as an equity shop, but when stocks and stock funds sold as poorly as they did in the 1970s, Johnson looked to other products to pull Fidelity out of its predicament. Fixed-income products began in the 1970–1971 period with a bond debenture fund. This was followed by the Fidelity Municipal Bond Fund, the first no-load municipal bond fund, in 1976, which required a limited partnership structure in order to pass on the tax-exempt income to shareholders. Although remaining largely an equity shop, Fidelity would continue creating new fixed-asset products, particularly single-state muni bond funds, throughout the 1980s.[13]

The lull of business activity in the 1970s and the fact that Fidelity was a private company answerable only to Johnson also allowed him to begin to invest in technology for the near future—not only to keep up with the demands of the business but also for future marketing needs as Fidelity's business shifted to direct marketing. As C. Bruce Johnstone, a close confidant of Johnson during these years, remarked, "all the time Ned was willing to spend more money than most thought appropriate in technology. Nobody else was doing this. No one else was putting money in marketing like we were. In 1975–1982 we were in the black, but did not make a lot of money because we were preparing for better times." Indeed, Johnson became so involved in these efforts that there were stories of his sleeping overnight on the phone room floor because so many IT projects were going on at once (fig. 12).[14]

Johnson's push for technology was also marketing related, and came at a time, at least the early stages of it, that coincided with his decision to create and launch the Daily Interest Income Trust and shift to direct marketing. As Johnstone related, Fidelity was "the *first* to go 24/7 on the phone, the first." This happened in 1979, when Fidelity set up the first computerized, automated telephone system for price and yield quotes. Soon, "a whole floor at 82 Devonshire [Street] was devoted to nothing but phones." Success with money market funds led to more technology spending—$25 million in 1982, $35 million in 1983, and then in 1984–1985 about $175–185 million a year. All of this gave Fidelity a significant competitive advantage over the competition. "It was like Star Wars!" "We spent money to get ourselves ready," exclaimed Johnstone. The results of this investment in technology were impressive, too. Customer calls to Fidelity skyrocketed from about 16,000 a day in 1981 to 114,000 in 1986, and the number of shareholder accounts rose from 1 to 4.7 million over the same time period. In addition, Fidelity was so successful with its technology strategy that by the end of the 1970s, it had already removed its 8 percent sales charge on most funds. Meanwhile, Fidelity began to bring critical activities in-house;

FIGURE 12. Edward C. Johnson III (Courtesy Fidelity Corporate Archives Services)

in 1970, for instance, it became its own transfer agent and took over its back office shareholder record-keeping work and set up FMR Service Corporation to handle these and other tasks.[15]

Another direction pursued by Johnson was a series of acquisitions and ventures in nonrelated businesses, which perhaps only a privately held company could have done at the time. In 1971, before the decline in the mutual fund business, Johnson created a private investment partnership, first called Fidelity Ventures Limited Partnership and later Fidelity Ventures Associates, then simply Fidelity Ventures. The company invested in cable television and the telecommunications industry. In starting his venture operation, Johnson hired Harry Hoagland, with long experience at the country's first venture capital firm, American Research and Development (AR&D), and Samuel W. Bodman, also from AR&D, who soon became president and chief operating officer of Fidelity Investments. In 1978, Johnson started Fidelity Brokerage Services, a discount brokerage service. Only three years earlier, on May 1, 1975, the New York Stock Exchange had stopped enforcing a system of fixed-rate brokerage commissions, not only cutting investment companies' costs in trading stocks but allowing Charles Schwab and later Fidelity to compete directly with long-standing brokerage firms like Paine, Webber, Dean Witter, and Merrill Lynch to sell shares to the public at substantially lower costs. The discount brokerage business also played to strengths Johnson was creating in communicating to his fund customers through advertising, telephone, and direct-mail efforts by providing another, related service they might want to use.

Fidelity diversified into other kinds of businesses. Its constant need for more office space in downtown Boston soon led it to form its own real estate company, Fidelity Capital Real Estate Investors, now called Pembroke Real Estate. By 2006, it owned over 3.5 million square feet of office space in Boston and more than 1.5 million square feet of commercial and residential space in London, Tokyo, Paris, Stockholm, Brussels, and Washington, D.C. Other ventures included BostonCoach (1985), a limousine and bus shuttle service company; a catering and café chain; *Worth* magazine (1991); and companies specializing in construction supply, executive recruiting, and event planning. These companies were put under an umbrella organization, Fidelity Capital, in 1987. By 2005, half of Fidelity's annual revenue came from divisions not part of money management.[16]

Johnson took the financial lull of the 1970s as a time to explore opportunities overseas and begin to create an international presence, even though the rewards of this activity took some time to develop. Fidelity opened its first international office in Tokyo in 1969, and in London ten years later, when Bill Byrnes, a longtime Fidelity executive, was sent there to create a British version of Fidelity Management and Research Company. This was followed up by outposts in Hong Kong, Canada, and a few other locations. Success outside the United States was hard to find in the early years—there were only a few international institutional clients—but Fidelity created at the time a promising International Fund at a time when the U.S. dollar was weak. After advances and retreats, Fidelity was able to expand in Europe, creating dozens of mutual funds and an institutional business in those countries.[17]

By the early 1980s, the growing success of Fidelity's new products helped to create an atmosphere at the company best described by contemporaries as exhilarating. "There was an enormous sense of ferment within the firm," one account described, "which flowed from Ned Johnson's wispy, suggestive, elliptic sentences and spread to every corner of the company. Money was pouring into the firm's money market funds, but that was only part of it. People at Fidelity felt they were in the middle of a grand experiment, in which anything was possible, and nothing was too crazy to be tried once." Out of this experimentation, a new kind of mutual fund company—indeed, a new kind of financial services company—was gradually taking shape, one aimed not at the financial cognoscenti but at everyone. This was the kind of firm that would prosper in the 1980s.[18]

Repositioning for the Future: August 12, 1982

While Fidelity's money market funds and Johnson's interests in new or other parts of the business helped to turn the company around, it was the rise in the stock market and economy that put everything firmly on a new course. Over thirteen years, from 1969 to 1982, the stock market stayed, in effect, the same, with the Dow Jones Industrial Average never rising above 1,000 points. Thereafter, it took off. Although the shift was barely noted for some time to come, the economy was on its way up again, beginning in the late summer of 1982, and would continue to climb, except for a momentary, two-year setback in 1987, until early 2000.[19]

While boom times in the past had created widespread popular interest in investments and investing, during this nearly twenty-year period, the United States would experience the rise of popular capitalism through the sale of mutual funds and other investment vehicles that had never been used before in this fashion. What had been only about $49 billion in mutual funds in 1980 reached over $7 trillion—in the form of direct investments, 401(k)s, IRAs, and other savings or pension instruments—by the end of 2000, with stock funds alone rising from $100 billion in 1995 to $4 trillion by 2000. Within a year of the market's rise, the *Wall Street Journal* would report that fund assets had risen by almost 61 percent, and that top-performing funds, that is, stock funds, had grown more than fivefold since the market started to climb.

During this period, the industrial average rose from a mere 777 points to a high of over 11,900, while Nasdaq (the National Association of Security Dealers Automated Quotations) rose thirty-fold from 166 to above 5,000 points. The largest leaps took place in the late 1990s. The industrial average had risen from 1,000 to 4,000 between 1982 and the beginning of 1995, but it went past 6,000 in October 1996, 7,000 in February 1997, 9,000 in the spring of 1998, and over 11,000 by January 2000. Nasdaq's gains were even more dramatic—from below 2,000 in November 1998 to above 5,000 by March 2000. Both markets crashed in early 2000, starting in January, with the slide ending in mid-April of that year.[20]

If there was any single individual who came to personify this long bull market, it was Fidelity's Magellan Fund manager, Peter Lynch. And perhaps no other fund better demonstrated such a dramatic shift to success. An actively managed equities fund, Magellan had started life as Fidelity's International Fund when it was launched in 1963 and at a time when the U.S. dollar was weak overseas. Several years later, however, Congress passed an equalization tax law, effectively discounting what shareholders paid for it. No longer a viable fund, it soon changed direction but gained little momentum. Under the management of Ned Johnson from its inception, it limped along, like many funds, through the 1970s and amassed only $20 million in AUM until Peter Lynch took it over in 1977. At the time, the public did not invest in Magellan; the fund only serviced Fidelity and Johnson family money. It was reopened to the public in the summer of 1981, and when Lynch ended his reign as portfolio manager in 1990, Magellan had grown to a staggering $13 billion.[21]

After spending a brief internship at Fidelity after college, Lynch returned in 1969 and became an industry analyst before his rise to director of research in 1974. Three years later, he was put in charge of Magellan where he created a portfolio of stocks that grew from 40 to 1,400. Besides great financial success, Lynch developed investment techniques and an investment philosophy that were easy for investors to follow and emulate. In books he wrote about his experiences, Lynch described those investment techniques necessary to build an investment portfolio, and later analyzed the stock picks he had made to illustrate how he went about it. Perhaps the most impressionable point made to his largely nonprofessional investing audience—who had little knowledge or inclination to read financial reports or delve into a quantitative analysis of stocks—was that they could invest for themselves through the "power of common knowledge": "Twenty years in this business convinces me that any normal person using the customary three percent of the brain can pick stocks just as well, if not better, than the average Wall Street expert."[22] Lynch employed the mantra "invest in what you know," and demonstrated it using his own experiences with his family and shopping at the mall to drive across his point: "If you stay half-alert, you can pick the spectacular performers right from your place of business or out of the neighborhood shopping mall, and long before Wall Street discovers them. It's impossible to be a credit-card-carrying American consumer without having done a lot of fundamental analysis on dozens of companies—and if you work in the industry, so much the better. This is where you'll find the ten-baggers [company stocks that earn a tenfold return on investment]. I've seen it happen again and again from my perch at Fidelity." In the end, Lynch carried on the role of star portfolio manager, first made important by Gerry Tsai at Fidelity in the early 1960s, and also helped to brand a singular mutual fund that continued on long after he left it. At the time of his departure, one out of every one hundred families in the United States had an investment in Magellan.[23]

AUM at Fidelity started to take off in the late 1970s. The year 1974 was catastrophic for Fidelity, the first (and only) year the company not only lost money but also went into the red, a situation that resulted in the firing (a "massacre" according to contemporaries) of sixteen fund managers. During that year, assets hit their lowest mark since 1966, when they were just $2.9 billion, although they gradually rose to $5.4 billion by 1978. Thereafter, they rapidly increased, rising from $7.9 billion in 1979 to $14.9 billion in 1981, and then roared on to $75.3 billion by 1987, even with the stock market recession of that year. Assets in Fidelity's Cash Reserves Fund helped to carry the investment company's total assets higher in the early 1980s, constituting almost 21 percent of them by 1982, while Magellan's contribution increased to over 10 percent of all Fidelity mutual fund assets by 1987. This became the start of Fidelity's long progress upward, as AUM rose to $1.6 trillion by 2007.[24]

Money market funds reached their highest yields just before the industrial average shifted its course in 1982, and soon investment companies were looking for new ways to keep their existing customers and attract new ones. While some effort was made to develop funds that might interest money market shareholders, most of the attention and effort was given to creating funds for new investors who were entering the market or interested in new products. In Fidelity's case, the company created a line of fixed-income funds as a backstop to the decline in interest for money market funds; assets in those funds increased twofold between 1980 and the end of 1983. During the same period, Fidelity also began handling more money from institutional clients, increasing from 20 to 35 percent the proportion of Fidelity's assets derived from that client base. Long known as an equity shop, Fidelity focused attention on developing new equity funds. By the mid-1980s, assets in these funds surpassed assets in its money market funds for the first time since 1974.[25]

The number and types of funds began to rise by the late 1970s, expanded significantly in the 1980s, and rose again in the 1990s. Fidelity was a microcosm for the whole industry. The company had maintained a single fund until 1947, and this number only increased to four by the late 1950s, then nine in 1965, sixteen in 1970, and eighteen in 1975. Thereafter, the climate changed. The company created the first no-load open end municipal bond fund in 1976, and in 1979, two money market funds were added, Fidelity Cash Reserves and the Fidelity Tax-Exempt Money Market Trust, which became the first such tax-exempt U.S. fund.[26] As the objectives of these funds suggest, Fidelity and other fund managers were creating new vehicles for a changing economy, and by 1980, Fidelity had twenty-nine different funds. In 1981, Fidelity created its Select Portfolios, funds that acquired stock in specific industries—from electronics to natural resources. Much of the initiative was coming from Johnson, but some of the impetus flowed from Fidelity's large and expanding marketing department, with training in sales and distribution, and "an intensive strategy of splitting the market into many, many segments." In 1985, Fidelity had 101 funds under its brand and in 1990, that number had climbed to 182. During the 1980s, the company had also developed funds for sales through broker-dealers

(Plymouth Investments, which was expanded and renamed Fidelity Advisor Funds in 1992) and the Spartan Funds for long-term, high-asset investors in 1989. By 2005, the number of individual mutual funds had grown almost two-fold to 331.[27]

On a much less grand scale than Fidelity, other Boston investment companies were broadening and diversifying fund offerings. Massachusetts Financial Services (MFS), for instance, maintained only two funds, dating back to 1924 and 1934, respectively, until 1971, when it launched three more with different investment objectives. By 1991, the investment company had thirty-three different funds in ten different categories: Growth (5), Growth and Income (2), Total Return (1), Bond (4), Global Bond and Total Return (2), Government (3), Municipal Bond (2), Money Market (2), Tax-Free Money Market (1), and State Municipal Bond (11) funds. Meanwhile, Colonial Management, another Boston company, created fewer but more innovative funds during the period. In 1969, it brought out the Colonial Income Fund, one of the first bond or income funds, and in 1978, it introduced its Tax Managed Trust, a fund that enabled shareholders to accumulate income on a tax-deferred basis.[28]

Besides individual investment organizations, the industry was also shifting from classifying funds in a few broad categories, such as domestic equity, international equity, bonds, and money market funds, to something far more specific, emphasizing different investment styles and different kinds of capital-specific industries. By the late 1980s, Morningstar, the research, reporting, and rating organization, began to create new categories for funds, like growth and value funds, and small, mid-, and large domestic equity funds. From 1990 onward, funds often were style-specific, such as asset allocation funds. In Fidelity's case, they included the Freedom Funds (initially set up for customers who would cash out of the fund in specific decades from 2010 to 2050, and then each half decade between), 529s (for college tuition and expenses set up for separate states), Income Replacement funds, and Asset Manager funds. In addition, many of these products were sold to specific markets—retail, adviser, and VIP customers. In a word, during the more recent period, from about 1970 until today, funds have become more specific, often reflecting current economic conditions, and are packaged to sell to very specific client bases.[29]

As data gathered by the Investment Company Institute (ICI) shows, before 1970, there were balanced funds (many of them in Boston) and some bond funds, but most were equity funds. ICI added "hybrid" funds to the mix in 1984, although as a group, they never amounted to more than about 8 percent of all assets in a given year. During the 1970s, equity funds declined, and although bond fund assets increased to almost a quarter of all assets, it was money market funds that transformed the industry. Beginning in 1978, they accounted for 19 percent of all fund assets and this rose to 57, 77, and then 74 percent of all assets in 1980, 1981, and 1982, respectively. As Matt Fink, former president of ICI, has noted, "money market funds totally changed the fund industry" by bringing more individuals into mutual funds and creating an alternative to equity funds, which long dominated the industry.[30]

In the 1980s, money market funds declined in assets but still managed to account for at least 41 percent of all assets during that decade. During the same period, from 1980 through 1989, bonds represented as much as 34 percent of all assets, and, as in 1988, accounted for more fund assets (32 percent) than equity funds (23 percent). During the 1990s, that pattern changed with equity funds reaching 59 percent by the end of the decade, while money market funds maintained 24 percent of all fund assets. By comparison, hybrid and bond funds represented only 5 and 12 percent of fund assets, respectively. During the 2000s, except for 2008, equity fund assets dominated, reaching as high as 57 percent in two years, while bond funds languished in the mid-teens, and money market funds ranged from a quarter to a third of all mutual fund assets.[31]

During the 1980s, Fidelity responded to the changing landscape in the mutual fund industry not only by creating new funds but also by improving customer service and reaching new customers. The investment company created a group of private label money market funds that banks and savings and loan companies could sell, growing this into a $1.3 billion business between 1981 and 1983. Fidelity pitched new products to institutional investors, quickly increasing that proportion of Fidelity's institutional assets. As a result, it established Fidelity Investments Institutional Services in 1985 to focus on selling to institutional markets and their customers.

Recognizing the economy and flexibility offered by offices outside of Boston in building a nationwide business, Fidelity established its first regional office in Dallas, Texas, in 1983. This was followed by another in Salt Lake City (1986), Cincinnati (1987), and then in the 1990s in Covington, Kentucky (1993), Marlborough, Massachusetts (1995), Merrimack, New Hampshire (1996), and Smithfield, Rhode Island (1998). Fidelity's geographical expansion was a mixed blessing. While this was a normal practice for a national company, it was a recognition that Fidelity was also concerned about the risks of being too concentrated in a single location, Boston, and the high operating costs of the city.

Johnson's expensive investments in technology continued to provide competitive customer service into the 1980s. These improvements had begun in 1979 with the first computerized phone system, which provided price and yield quotes on a twenty-four-hour basis. In 1982, the Fidelity Systems Company was established to oversee company computer and telecommunications operations. The new system provided automated telephone service with access to account balances and exchanges. By 1986, Fidelity offered hourly pricing for its Select Portfolios, an industry first, as well as providing live representatives on a twenty-four-hour basis.[32]

Another factor accounting for sales at Fidelity and other investment companies in the 1980s was the growing market for Individual Retirement Accounts (IRAs). Although U.S. tax law allowed tax-deferred pension accounts for self-employed individuals and small businesses as far back as 1962 with the Keogh Plan, the Economic Recovery Tax Act of 1981 permitted any working person to transfer $2,000 of their annual income and place it into tax-deferred IRAs. It took several years for the idea to catch on, but once it did, following heavy advertising by Fidelity and other investment companies, there was no turning back. Congress repealed the IRA tax benefits for many in 1986, but by then, the public had become heavily involved in the pension/savings program. IRAs continued to drain money from banks, thrifts, and nonbank institutions, and into mutual funds.[33]

The 1980s were not without some backward steps for Fidelity and other mutual fund companies. Following the stock market plunge of October 19, 1987, assets and company revenues collapsed, and Fidelity suffered its second worst year after 1974. It took two years to recover lost assets, which meant it had to cut costs and jobs all over the company. Just as things began improving, the savings and loan (S&L) crisis appeared, creating problems for banks in the Boston area and elsewhere, and leading to the demise of the prominent New England Merchants National Bank (called by then Bank of New England) in 1990. It was not until a year later that Fidelity began its second and most explosive phase of growth, which continued until early 2000.

By the 1980s, Fidelity and other investment companies were running into competition from several sources. One was the large financial service firms, such as insurance companies, that had acquired investment companies like Massachusetts Financial Services and Putnam in the late 1960s and 1970s. Newer and more lethal competition also came from investment banks and brokerage firms—or at least those few Wall Street giants like Merrill Lynch that survived the long bear market of the 1970s, the end of fixed commissions, and multiple mergers. As one 1981 article in *Forbes* magazine noted, "almost everybody seems to be cracking into the money management business," including "the so-called department store of finance that American Express, Merrill Lynch and Sears, Roebuck are building toward." Merrill Lynch, which had not even been in the mutual fund business before the mid-1970s, had by far more AUM than any other company by 1981. During the 1990s, even newer competition came from large national commercial banks, which with the virtual demise of the Glass-Steagall Act, allowed those institutions to sell and operate funds, many of which they acquired from smaller private companies. By 1993, over one hundred banks offered mutual funds, which accounted for a tenth of all fund assets.[34]

As a result of Fidelity's success and broader changes in the industry, Boston's mutual fund landscape had changed considerably by the mid-1980s. In terms of Boston investment companies, perhaps the most noteworthy decline was M.I.T., which had been restructured into Massachusetts Financial Services in the late 1960s. With assets in its funds already losing about 10 percent each year by the time of the reorganization, things only got worse in the 1970s and early 1980s. Under Merrill Griswold's successors, as *Forbes* magazine commented, "Mass Financial became threadbare and undistinguished." Although the company did have remarkable success in the variable annuity tax-deferred annuity business, which soon accounted for 40 percent of its revenues, the Internal Revenue Service ruled in 1981 that only insurance companies could sell that kind of product. One competitor diagnosed MFS's decline as coming after "an extended period of marketing and performance stagnation resulting in part from their fund trustees' reluctance to accept newer philosophies, particularly in the marketing area." In 1982, Sun Life Assurance Company of Canada bought the ailing investment company at the bargain-basement price of $45 million.[35]

By 1985, the early postwar Boston investment company community had shifted considerably, with Fidelity ($35 billion in AUM) clearly ahead of the pack. It was followed by up-and-coming Putnam ($10.4 billion), then Keystone ($8.8 billion), Massachusetts Financial Services ($6.87), Colonial ($4.8 billion), and Pioneer ($3.5 billion). Boston's place in the whole industry was also getting smaller. In 1981, for instance, Fidelity was only the fourth largest complex in the country (behind Merrill Lynch, Dreyfus Management, and Federated Investors) with less than 5 percent of all mutual fund assets under its management. Still, such figures can be somewhat misleading, only providing a temporary snapshot of Boston's position in the industry.[36]

Although Boston investment companies were not the largest in the industry, they still continued to be the locus of the largest concentration of mutual fund management activity in the country. At the end of 1991, for instance, 21 Boston companies offered nearly 550 mutual funds with assets of about $288 billion. This amounted to about 23 percent of all fund AUM in the United States, and these figures do not include eight other Massachusetts companies outside of Boston with 43 funds and about $2 billion in AUM. In addition, some Boston investment advisers managed the portfolios of fund sponsors located outside of the commonwealth, such as Wellington Management's management of several Vanguard funds, which accounted for almost another $40 billion in AUM. Besides the investing side of the business, Boston companies handled the back office operations of Boston and non-Boston mutual funds, which included custodianship, account maintenance, and other customer services. While some companies like Fidelity and Putnam had decided early on to set up their own back office operations, others used outside services like State Street Corp. and the Boston Company (formerly Boston Safe Deposit Company), the industry's first and third largest custodians, which at that time serviced assets of $623 billion in 2,165 funds. By 1991, Boston was the home of the largest mutual fund family, Fidelity, with 176 funds and assets of $155 billion; Putnam (12th largest complex of funds); Massachusetts Financial Services (15); and Scudder, Stevens & Clark (16). As these and other statistics seem to suggest, there were ups and downs of particular companies over time, but from about 1970 to the present, Boston companies have managed roughly 25 percent of all mutual fund assets, give or take periodic fluctuations in the economy and industry.[37]

Takeoff and Expansion in the 1980s and 1990s

Just as money market funds helped to expand the rising mutual fund industry in the late 1970s, other changes helped to promote funds in the buoyant economic times that followed. Besides the increase in the number and variety of mutual funds in the early 1980s, there were other, structural alterations in the industry that encouraged their sales.

One important change was advertising. Until the 1970s, the SEC, under the Securities Act of 1933, did not allow mutual fund investment companies to offer shares of their funds through advertising since it represented a breach of the act's prohibition against the use of the mails and interstate commerce. By 1972, however, the commission had become concerned about the domination of the industry by broker-dealers and their load funds, and it sought to develop less costly methods of fund distribution. Gradually the commission moved to make advertising of funds more permissible, first by allowing the placement of so-called tombstone ads in newspapers and other publications with some general information about the investment company and fund's attributes but something short of a full-scale advertisement. By the mid-1970s, the SEC had continued to broaden its tombstone rule, allowing companies to provide more background information "but not directly or indirectly relating to past performance or implying achievement of investment objectives." By 1977, following a series of Supreme Court cases involving commercial free speech and investors' interest in seeing fund performance data, the commission again modified its restrictions.

In 1979, it adopted what became rule 482, which permitted fund companies to use any information, including performance, in print advertisements, with no restrictions as to length, and also allowed advertisements on radio and television. This change was a boon to direct marketers of mutual funds such as Fidelity, as the percentage of no-load equity funds and no-load bond funds grew over the next two decades, rising from 34 and 47 percent to 58 and 64 percent of all offerings, respectively. Three major investment companies moved from load to no-load in the 1970s, including Fidelity, Vanguard, and Dreyfus, so that by 1980, sales of no-load funds and no-load share classes reached 30 percent for equity sales and 40 percent of bond fund sales.[38]

Another response to the 1970s' economy and growing need to diversify mutual fund holdings in the 1980s was the development of tax-exempt funds, particularly state municipal or "muni" bond funds. Before passage of the Tax Reform Act of 1976, the few municipal bond funds available were fashioned after a cumbersome limited partnership. Under the new law, investment companies were allowed to create funds with tax-exempt securities issued by states and municipalities across the country and led to several unexpected results. One was single-state muni funds, which enabled investors living in that state to have tax-exempt status at both the state and federal level. By the early 1990s, Boston's Eaton Vance developed the largest single-state muni funds of any company in the country. Another unexpected tax-exempt development was the creation of short-term tax-exempt instruments. The first tax-exempt money market fund was created and sold by Fidelity in 1980.[39]

A further innovation of the period was index funds. By the early 1970s, a number of academics, as well as banks and pension consultants, called for the development of index mutual funds as a way of providing a less expensive mutual fund for the investor.[40] These funds would invest in the stocks of a market index, such as the S&P 500, and weight those stocks according to each security's outstanding capitalization (or some other factor like sales, earnings, book values, or dividends), and thus required no active management. By 1976, Vanguard, a Philadelphia area–based mutual fund company, brought out its version of the index fund, and over the years, was very successful at marketing them. Although at least one Boston money manager, Jeremy Grantham, later a founder of Grantham, Mayo, Van Otterloo & Company, pioneered the idea of an index fund in 1971 while he was at Batterymarch Financial Management, this type of fund never caught on in Boston, where most of them are actively managed by portfolio managers, a style of successful investing characterized by the Magellan Fund and Peter Lynch during the 1980s.[41]

An additional significant change was the adoption of Rule 12b-1 by the SEC in 1980, making it legal for a fund to use some amount of shareholder assets to finance fund distribution, so long as a number of specified conditions were met. Before the change, all distribution expenses (advertising, sales commissions, and any other marketing costs) were paid by the management company out of the fee the fund provided for administrative and advisory services. The rule helped to provide more money for these expenses and opened up the number of distribution avenues for funds. One of the most successful mechanisms was the so-called contingent deferred sales load, or spread load plans, which created three different classes of mutual fund shares. Class A shares had a traditional front-end load and an annual 12b-1 fee of .25 percent. Class B shares had an annual 12b-1 fee of 1 percent per year and a redemption fee if the investor sold his or her shares within five or six years; these shares automatically converted to Class A shares in the sixth or seventh year. A third class, C shares, required payment of a 1 percent charge annually and an additional charge if shares were redeemed within the first year. The 12b-1 fees were also used for other purposes, such as paying for brokers, pension fund administrators, and the expenses of fund supermarkets. Over time, share classes became more and more complicated but provided customers with options that encouraged sales. By mid-1993, funds with 12b-1 plans accounted for 54 percent of all funds tracked by the ICI (2,359 funds in all), up 7 percent from 1988. Like all sales features, however, their fortunes changed along with the economic environment, particularly after 2000.[42]

The development of new fund products, new distribution systems, and new legislation, which provided opportunities for investment companies and incentives for prospective customers, propelled mutual funds into becoming the world's largest financial industry by 2000, even surpassing the U.S. banking system in size. Ten years earlier, the industry had come to dominate the U.S. financial industry according to both its admirers and critics, as its funds drove stock, government bond, short-term commercial paper, junk bond, and even foreign stock and derivatives markets. On some days, Fidelity alone was reported to be responsible for about 10 percent of the volume on the New York Stock Exchange.[43]

The mutual fund's perceived significance was reflected in its staggering growth. Total assets begin to rise by 1979, almost doubling from $55.84 to $94.51 billion within a single year. The steady rise in assets from the early 1980s onward was strongly influenced by changes in pension laws. By 1979, mutual funds had become a legitimate vehicle for retirement investment under the Employee Retirement Income Security Act (ERISA) of 1974, and under the Tax Reform Act of 1981, everyone with earned income could invest in an IRA using mutual funds.[44] By 1999, almost 40 percent of all mutual fund assets represented some form of retirement savings, either as IRAs or employer-sponsored defined contribution plans.[45]

There were few mutual funds available for investors before the 1980s. In 1940, there were only 68, 103 in 1951, 204 in 1967, and by 1980 the number was still under 500. As table 5 notes, the number of funds available for investors also rose from 857 in 1982 to 1,528 three years later. Thereafter, the number of funds doubled by 1990 (3,079) and again in 1996 (6,248), eventually reaching 8,305 different funds in 2001, before the number started to gradually decline over the rest of the decade. By 1996, assets in mutual funds matched those of banks ($3,000 billion for each), after which mutual fund assets continued to rise steeply.

The "Ascent of Once Sleepy Putnam"

Despite the level of and intensity in the mutual fund industry in the 1980s, Fidelity more than held its own, becoming the largest U.S. mutual fund complex by the mid-1990s, beating out archrival Merrill Lynch, and closing in on the leader of the discount brokerage business, Charles Schwab. Fidelity's ability to provide customers with a broad, diversified, one-stop shopping experience became a hallmark of its new-found success, and provided a blueprint for new markets overseas.[46]

Despite these results, Fidelity was not the only model for success in the mutual fund industry. Putnam Investments, founded by George Putnam in 1937, had remained a relatively small and, as a 1996 *Fortune* article described it, "sleepy" investment company until the 1980s. A decade later, it had become a powerhouse. By the end of the 1990s, Putnam was the fourth largest mutual fund complex in the United States but had achieved its success in ways very different from its downtown rival, Fidelity. Putnam retained its broker-dealer distribution system and was unable to exploit the dynamic money market fund growth. Instead, it concentrated on an institutional customer base and helped to develop a consulting profession that advised institutional (businesses, labor unions, nonprofit) clients on whom they should hire to manage their pension funds. By following this strategy and with the help of effective marketing, Putnam was able to grow as this important client base developed. Between 1970 and 1990, the percentage of institutional assets to total company assets rose from only 11 to over 25; during the 1990s, that figure again doubled.[47]

Putnam's involvement with institutional pension funds began in the mid-1950s when Ohio State University asked it to manage some of its assets. The business became more formalized later in the decade. By June 1968, as pen-

TABLE 5. Mutual Fund Growth in Net Assets, Number of Funds, and Number of Accounts, 1970–2008

YEAR	TOTAL NET ASSETS ($ IN BILLIONS)	NUMBER OF FUNDS	NUMBER OF SHAREHOLDER ACCOUNTS (IN 1,000S)
1970	$47.62	361	10,690
1971	$55.05	392	10,901
1972	$59.83	410	10,635
1973	$46.52	421	10,331
1974	$35.78	431	10,074
1975	$45.87	426	9,876
1976	$51.28	452	9,060
1977	$48.94	477	8,693
1978	$55.84	505	8,658
1979	$94.51	526	9,790
1980	$134.76	564	12,088
1981	$241.37	665	17,499
1982	$296.68	857	21,448
1983	$292.99	1,026	24,605
1984	$370.68	1,243	27,636
1985	$495.39	1,528	34,098
1986	$715.67	1,835	45,374
1987	$769.17	2,312	53,717
1988	$809.37	2,737	54,056
1989	$980.67	2,935	57,560
1990	$1,065.19	3,079	61,948
1991	$1,393.19	3,403	68,332
1992	$1,642.54	3,824	79,931
1993	$2,069.96	4,534	94,015
1994	$2,155.32	5,325	114,383
1995	$2,811.29	5,725	131,219
1996	$3,525.80	6,248	149,933
1997	$4,468.20	6,684	170,299
1998	$5,525.21	7,314	194,029
1999	$6,846.34	7,791	226,212
2000	$6,964.63	8,155	244,705
2001	$6,974.91	8,305	248,701
2002	$6,390.36	8,244	251,123
2003	$7,414.40	8,126	260,698
2004	$8,106.94	8,041	269,468
2005	$8,904.82	7,975	275,479
2006	$10,396.51	8,117	288,596
2007	$11,999.52	8,024	292,624
2008	$9,601.09	8,022	264,499

Source: Investment Company Institute, 2009 Investment Company Fact Book, 110, www.ici.org/pdf/2009_factbook.pdf.

sion funds grew, the investment company established Putnam Advisory, an incorporated, wholly owned subsidiary of Putnam's management company, under which clients could receive more specialized advice. The organization's first client was Brown University. By the end of 1969, Putnam Advisory had eleven clients and $150 million under management. By 1973, it had over $1 billion in advisory assets and increased the minimum size of accounts to $10 million. Assets reached $5.4 billion in 1980. In the years that followed, much of Putnam's activity was divided between the fund and advisory sides of the business, with each developing different personnel, skills, and operations. By 1985, advisory assets accounted for $7 billion, or 36 percent, of all Putnam AUM; by 2000, advisory assets reached $101.2 billion but represented about 27 percent of the company's assets. During that whole period, advisory assets accounted for slightly less than a third of the total.[48]

Putnam's advisory business had once been the province of commercial banks, but during the 1970s, companies like Putnam and many investment counsel businesses were turning to the management of pension funds as a new or growing business. In many cases, Boston investment counsel firms simply shifted from serving individual clients to institutional clients. The economic downturn of the 1970s and the poor investment performance that followed offered pension funds an opportunity and a reason to look elsewhere for advice and management, and many came to companies like Putnam. This shift was not because of any change in the law but rather the growing belief that selection had to be based on a company's performance as a manager of pension funds and how faithful that manager was to the pension fund's investment objectives. Pension funds often looked to several asset management concerns to fulfill their overall investment goals.[49]

Like other investment companies, Putnam created a number of new funds in the late 1970s, including some income funds like the Putnam Daily Dividend Fund (1976), Putnam Tax Exempt Income Fund (1976), Putnam Option Income Trust (1977), and Putnam High Yield Trust (1978). Despite the repeal of the Interest Equalization Tax Act of 1964, Putnam also launched in 1978 the Putnam Equities Fund, renamed the Putnam International Equities Fund, which invested up to 70 percent in foreign assets. This interest in foreign securities helped lead Putnam to opening offices in London and Tokyo in 1982 and 1983. By the early 1980s, Putnam started up two specialty funds in health care and information sciences, which were soon followed by several state muni funds. The Putnam Health Sciences Trust, introduced in 1982, was regarded at Putnam as the first new mutual fund in the industry in a number of years, and became, at the time, the "biggest new offering of a mutual fund ever," raising $427 million on the day of its launch. Putnam discovered that new products created a buzz and an involvement with their brokers that off-the-shelf products could not do—an important lesson in selling mutual funds during the next two decades.[50]

From 1982 to 1987, Putnam's net assets (sales minus redemptions) grew by $25 billion, although following the 1987 downturn, it lost a net of about $3.5 billion over the next three years. By 1988, three-quarters of Putnam assets were in fixed-income holdings and only a quarter in equities. As income-oriented funds did progressively worse by the mid- to late 1980s, Putnam turned to creating and marketing equity funds, beginning a trend that by 1999 accounted for three-quarters of the assets in its funds and advisory business—a complete reversal from the past. It also started some new closed-end funds beginning in 1987. Putnam was successful in developing 12b-1 sales options for its funds; the different classes of shares, as well as the advent of the so-called fund supermarkets, in which fund companies selling competitors' shares blurred the line of distinction between load and no-load funds, helped companies like Putnam. Indeed, as George Putnam later pointed out, the 12b-1 sales alternatives "probably made the greatest change in fund marketing in the industry's history and ... brought the industry enormous growth in the 1990s."[51]

Throughout the period, Putnam Investments increased its share of the retirement plan business, primarily through 401(k) plans. Such plans were well suited for companies like Putnam with well-established families of mutual funds, reflecting various investment styles and strong fund administrative resources. A pioneer in corporate profit-sharing and Keogh plans in the 1960s, IRAs in the 1970s, and 401(k)s by the 1980s, Putnam remained one of the leaders in the retirement business at the end of the century, when approximate a fifth of its $300 billion of fund assets was in 401(k) plans alone.[52]

In 1993, *U.S. News & World Report* ranked Putnam as one of the top four families of mutual funds in the United States, along with Fidelity, Vanguard, and American Funds. Three years later, *Fortune* magazine commended Putnam for its fund consistency, an important feature in the retirement plan field: "Consistency helps Putnam's stable of U.S. diversified stock funds stand out," hewing "more closely to their stated objectives than those of any other big-fund group." As a result, Putnam was "an appealing choice for financial planners, who rely on a fund's declared objectives when making asset allocations decisions, and to managers of 401(k) plans, in which individuals can't be expected to keep tabs on a fund's stylistic dalliances." Putnam's diversified equity funds "walk[ed] away with top honors among the ten largest fund groups for the one-, three-, and five-year periods."[53]

Much of Putnam's growth occurred under the careful watch of Larry Lasser, a Harvard Business School graduate who came to Putnam in 1969 as a research analyst. By 1972, he was appointed assistant director of research and then its director in 1975. He became executive vice president of the Putnam Management Company in 1980 and then chief investment officer of the company in 1981. In 1985, he was made CEO of the Putnam Companies, which included both advisory and fund operations. Even before that, Lasser made significant improvements to the company's sales organization and marketing, with led to strong sales in its new special and tax-exempt funds. Under Lasser's watch, Putnam launched some forty-five funds from 1982 to 1992. This then marked the beginning, according to Lasser, of the ascent for the company, "from quite ordinary and inconspicuous to quite exceptional, important, large, high profile, and highly profitable."[54]

Lasser was reputed to rule autocratically. He "eschews stars and gets results." According to "the Lasser Way," as his management style was called, "those who fail are fired or quit. Insisting on a team approach, he refuses to nurture a star system for money managers. But, when would-be stars leave for work elsewhere, he rarely lets go without a struggle." Whatever his methods were, they seemed to get results as Putnam grew to become only second to Fidelity in size and by 1994, to provide Marsh & McLennan, Putnam's owner, with $670.3 million, a third of the parent company's operating income. Lasser's greatest strength, some called it his genius, seemed to be in marketing, and he was successful in selling funds through banks and giant fund retailers like Merrill Lynch. By 1994, Putnam was managing the retirement plans for some 523 companies. Lasser later noted that during his tenure as head of Putnam, from 1985 to 2003, the company produced aggregate earnings in excess of $6 billion for Marsh & McLennan, which had bought the company in 1970 for only $30 million.[55]

Lasser believed that Putnam's golden age was in the 1990s, when it had what he thought was the strongest group of people in the industry—the best marketing, the best back office, and the best management. He also thought that his most important contribution was in seeing Putnam in terms of three distinctive areas of activity—products and performance, customer service, and marketing—all of which were equally important. Within retail, Putnam had three separate sales forces: a broker sales force, a bank sales force (starting in the 1990s), and independent brokers. In the institutional business, Putnam had a consultant group, a corporate group, a public funds group, and a separate marketing force that sold corporations on hiring Putnam for full-service 401(k) business. In the customer service or back office part of the company, Putnam created Putnam Investor Services, which Lasser considered the "crown jewel" of Putnam. It could handle millions of customer accounts and provide customers with help from service centers. While Putnam might not be able to guarantee investment performance, it could assure customer service using state-of-the-art technologies, not only to individuals but also to brokers, who helped Putnam get their new clients.[56]

By the end of the century, Putnam had 116 separate funds and nearly $400 billion in total assets, about $300 billion of which were in mutual funds, and had grown from just over 400 employees at the beginning of the 1980s to about 7,000. Referring back to the early 1980s, Lasser noted that "no one that I ever met in the investment business in Boston in that period ever imagined a firm of that type could grow large by today's measure." Likewise, he observed, "Did anyone imagine you could get a firm to $10 billion? Maybe. But not bigger than that. . . . [It was] not a practical aspiration."[57]

Despite their different ways of getting there, Fidelity and Putnam were Boston's largest investment companies by the mid-1990s and the only two Boston companies in the top ten (then managing a total of $1 trillion in assets) in the country. In Fidelity's case, it was also the largest investment company in the country.[58] Another listing, prepared a short while later, identified twenty-seven investment companies with assets of over $20 billion and showed Fidelity as the first and Putnam as the sixth largest complexes in the country, with two others from Boston finishing substantially lower.[59] Getting to the top, as Fidelity did, was not without complications. By 1996 and 1997, as it increased its AUM to $500 and then $635 billion, Fidelity was suffering from some of the problems of growing too fast: twenty fund managers left or were fired within sixteen months, its fund performance plummeted, and the company shifted from the retail customer to the corporate administrator and retirement businesses, which by this time constituted some 54 percent of Fidelity's assets. Such were the rewards and consequences of success.[60]

The New Century

All good things must come to an end, and in the late winter and early spring of 2000, the bubble created by high-tech and telecom stocks burst. The New York Stock Exchange and Nasdaq fell precipitously, ending a spectacular and unprecedented run up over the two previous decades. Investment companies in Boston and elsewhere were both affected by this crash, as values declined, redemptions went up, and new opportunities like the money market funds of the 1970s remained elusive. Interestingly, the decade of the 2000s was much like the 1970s in that the industrial averages and Nasdaq tried to regain the highs achieved just before the dot-com bust, with only the former able to achieve a brief, fleeting recovery to that level.

While Boston investment companies suffered immediately after the crash, many managed to recover within a couple of years and move forward. Fidelity, for instance, had $977.6 billion in AUM at the end of 1999, which declined to $812.4 billion in 2002, and then started an upward climb that reached $1.597 trillion in 2007. Eaton Vance, another Boston company, had $49 billion in AUM at the end of October 2000, about six months after the crash, but through a variety of new investment products and services—including new fund offerings, retail managed accounts, and exchange funds, all with a focus on high-net-worth individuals—was able to increase its assets to $129 billion by 2007. The aftereffects of the 2000 bust were more acutely felt in the corporate world, which was exposed to major stock and accounting scandals that led to the Sarbanes-Oxley Act, than in investment companies.[61]

But while things gradually returned to normal for many Boston investment companies after the turn of the century, some new problems developed affecting a few of them. This happened in 2003–2004 when revelations of illegal market timing and late trading in mutual fund shares were made, involving almost two dozen fund complexes and setting off what was called the worst scandal ever in the fund industry. These developments surfaced on September 3, 2003, when New York Attorney General Eliot Spitzer revealed that "four big-name mutual fund companies had cut secret deals allowing a New Jersey hedge fund to profit from short-term trading at the expense of ordinary investors." The SEC and other state regulators followed with investigations into a growing list of abuses. Customer reaction was swift as they took money out of the funds of the accused. Among the hardest hit mutual fund companies were Janus Capital Group, Strong Capital Management, and Boston's Putnam Investments, while new or transferred cash moved into unscathed firms like Vanguard, Fidelity, and American Funds.

Congress soon held hearings, and the SEC passed or proposed new rules on fund governance, pricing, and disclosure. Many funds, unaffected by the scandal, nevertheless implemented changes, including a reduction in management fees. Much of the scandal involved late trading and market timing—placing same-day orders after the official 4 p.m. deadline and making short-term investments that exploited differences between a fund's daily price and the value of its holdings.

At Putnam, a small number of customers had timed their purchases and sales of fund shares to take advantage of stale stock prices overseas to the detriment of other Putnam investors. But Massachusetts regulators soon learned from tips that some Putnam employees were also making excessive short-term fund trades, for clients and themselves. By October 2003, SEC and Massachusetts officials charged Putnam with fraud by allowing their employees to trade rapidly in its funds. Six were later fired. By the end of the month, the Commonwealth of Massachusetts withdrew $1.7 billion of its state pension fund from Putnam. In November, Putnam reached partial settlement with the SEC, promising to enforce its own rules better and restrict employee trading. By March 2004, the SEC filed a brief calling for a $138 million fine for Putnam's fraud. In the interim, Putnam's enigmatic CEO, Larry Lasser, was forced to resign. In 2007, Marsh & McLennan Companies, Putnam's owner since 1970, sold the company to the Canadian-based Power Financial Corporation.[62]

At the time of the scandal, Putnam was the fifth largest mutual fund complex in the country. Besides the exiting of pension fund monies, the revelation of impropriety led angry institutional clients to pull substantial assets out of Putnam, and for brokers and advisers to steer retail investors away from the company's products. Within a year or two, over $100 billion in assets walked out of the company, and between 2000 and 2006, Putnam assets dropped from $437 to only $179 billion. It was also soon revealed that Massachusetts Financial Services was involved in soft dollar payments, arrangements in which fund companies pay brokerages higher commissions if they direct more business to them in exchange for goods and services. MFS eventually agreed to pay $225 million to settle these allegations of improper trading practices, and its top management resigned. Thereafter, it struggled with sales and the declining popularity of some of its largest offerings.[63]

Where, then, does the Boston mutual fund industry stand at the end of the first decade of the twenty-first century? Its geographic concentration in the national industry remains essentially the same as it has over most of the period covered in this chapter, despite the number of new local players, the changing fortunes of old-line firms, and the growth of the industry nationally Above all, it has been a dynamic period with much in play.

The decade of the 2000s saw significant changes in Boston's mutual fund industry, including large drops in assets following the dot-com crash of 2000 and, for a few of the Boston players, significant asset losses following the insider trading scandal of 2003. Yet nothing is forever. While Putnam's fall was deep and profound, the investment company climbed back to the top in *Barron's* annual survey of fund families in 2010 after making significant management and product changes in recent years. This may be the start of a comeback for Putnam. Other Boston investment companies like Eaton Vance, unaffected by the scandal, made a 267.3 percent total return (compared with an S&P 400 Financials Index of total return for mid-sized U.S. companies of only 69.11 percent) for the entire decade ending on December 31, 2009, as it continued to grow yet remain independent.[64]

Firms like MFS and Putnam may rise again as they have recently, but perhaps the more common development was merely a recasting or reshuffling of the current players. For instance, net fund flows to local fund firms between 2001 and 2006 showed drastic declines for MFS Investment Management of $10.5 billion and a more astonishing $105.6 billion for Putnam Investments. On the other hand, a few large firms grew, such as Fidelity by $77.3 billion in net fund flow and $46.2 billion by State Street Global Advisors. In addition, there were many smaller firms that did well during this period, including Grantham, Mayo, Van Otterloo ($22.4 billion), John Hancock Funds ($15.5 billion), Eaton Vance ($8.7 billion), Ixis Asset Management ($5.4 billion), Evergreen Investments ($4.2 billion), and Columbia Management Group ($1.56 billion). While various fund complexes rose and fell, there was a persistent growth of other local companies, which helped to maintain Boston's concentration in the mutual fund industry.[65]

Table 6 gives an impression of Boston's position in the mutual fund industry over the last quarter century, and despite year-by-year changes, Boston larger complexes have maintained control of between 20 to 25 percent of the industry's assets, even following dramatic events like the insider trading scandals of 2003.[66] Some Boston complexes have merged with others from different regions, and their Boston portions may be somewhat less than stated here in the table. Nonetheless, while Boston investment companies may be acquired by outside companies, most of their asset management business remains in Boston.

Many new and current players manage the assets of older Boston companies. Natixis, a French investment management company, forms an umbrella for several Boston money managers, including Loomis Sayles and New England Financial mutual funds, and employs over 1,100 people in Boston. Ameriprise Financial, an American Express spinoff, recently took over the Boston-based Columbia Management mutual fund business, which was owned by Bank of America until 2009 and included mutual fund families created by FleetBoston Financial Corporation and Colonial Management. That expanded business remains in Boston.[67] Other recent ownership changes in Boston's mutual fund companies include the sale of State Street Research to BlackRock in 2004, Manulife's acquisition of John Hancock and its mutual fund business also in 2004, and the merger of Evergreen into Wachovia (2009), which was followed by the merger of Wachovia into Wells Fargo. The names change, but the place remains the same.[68] In addition to the investment companies, themselves, Boston continues to supply account ancillary services like custodianship, shareholder services, and many independent research and data services, such as State Street Corporation, Boston Financial Data Services, and Financial Research Corporation.[69]

The concentration of the mutual fund industry in Boston has also enhanced

TABLE 6. Boston's Position in the Mutual Fund Industry, 1985–2009: Boston Investment Companies among the Fifty Largest U.S. Complexes

1985	1990	1995	2000	2005	2009
3. Fidelity	1. Fidelity	1. Fidelity	1. Fidelity	1. Fidelity	1. Fidelity
12. Putnam	12. Putnam	6. Putnam	4. Putnam	6. Columbia	5. BlackRock / State Street Research
18. MFS	16. MFS	17. Oppenheimer / Mass Mutual	16. MFS	10. Oppenheimer/ Mass Mutual	12. Wells Fargo / Evergreen
20. Keystone	19. Scudder	18. Zurich Scudder	25. Evergreen	17. Putnam	13. Columbia
21. Scudder	27. Keystone	21. Scudder	37. Fleet	24. MFS	16. Oppenheimer / Mass Mutual
22. Colonial	32. Colonial	23. MFS	50. Eaton Vance	26. Evergreen	21. John Hancock
27. Pioneer	33. Eaton Vance	33. Colonial / Liberty Finance		30. John Hancock	27. Hartford
36. SteinRoe / Liberty Mutual	37. Pioneer	35. New England		48. Eaton Vance	28. MFS
37. Eaton Vance	48. New England	36. Eaton Vance		49. Pioneer	37. Natixis
49. New England		38. John Hancock			40. Putnam
		43. Pioneer			42. Eaton Vance
		47. Keystone			
10 Top 50 complexes; 326 complexes in all	9 Top 50 complexes; 326 complexes in all	12 Top 50 complexes; 371 complexes in all	6 Top 50 complexes; 431 complexes in all	9 Top 50 complexes; 358 complexes in all	11 Top 50 complexes; 331 complexes in all
Boston complexes with 17% of industry AUM	Boston complexes with 12% of industry AUM	Boston complexes with 23% of industry AUM	Boston complexes with 21% of industry AUM	Boston complexes with 21% of industry AUM	Boston complexes with 25% of industry AUM

Source: Compiled from data supplied by Douglas Richardson, Research Department, Investment Company Institute, Washington, D.C. Information based on December 31 of year used.

the city's position as a center for investment management. In the early 1990s, A. Michael Lipper of Lipper Analytical Services, a mutual fund rating organization, stated that "Boston is still probably the single most important [mutual fund] location, and that's out of proportion perhaps even to its assets, because it has a large number of successful groups." By 2003, following the Fleet Bank merger with Bank of America and the consolidation of its asset management unit in Boston, some viewed Boston as the premier location of asset management in the country (with over $2 trillion in AUM at Fidelity Investments, State Street Global Advisors, and Bank of America), in contrast to Charlotte, North Carolina, the retail banking center of the United States, and New York,

except in retrospect. As Kevin Landry of TA Associates noted, "Around 1989, we looked at our data and realized we had always made more money investing in profitable companies than in early-stage companies. . . . So we decided to do only profitable-stage investments." In addition, as the buyout business grew, it created and developed new, innovative, lower-cost debt instruments. While the Boston venture capital firms described in chapter 8 had moved from early-stage venture capital to late-stage private equity financing during the 1970s, some new Boston firms in the 1980s and later would move beyond late-stage financing to that expanded definition of private equity involved with company buyouts.[3]

The late twentieth century also witnessed what has been described as the wealth "explosion." In Boston, this meant not just the continuation of old, traditional family offices but new ones as well as multiple-family offices set up by individuals, investment professionals, law firms, and other organizations to assist in managing several generations of New Economy wealth from the Hub's high-tech businesses. So widespread had these asset managers become by the early twenty-first century that it was hard to distinguish a small or specialized asset management business from a family office, except perhaps that the center for the latter activity was around Post Office Square in Boston's financial district. Indeed, Boston seemed to be growing not just assets but asset managers, many of whom had come from one of the city's most important incubators, the mutual fund industry.

From Managerial to Financial Capitalism: The Development of Private Equity

Of course, private equity as a concept goes back much further in time than simply the post–World War II era. Indeed, the large-scale industrial consolidations of the late nineteenth and early twentieth centuries, culminating in the creation of companies like U.S. Steel, are earlier examples of private equity. The only major difference is that, in the earlier era, private equity was used to build larger companies out of smaller ones, while in more recent years, private equity has often been used to buy companies to break them up into more valuable stand-alone assets. In addition, during the late twentieth century, buyouts took on many more forms than in the past. They included privatizing public companies, often followed by large-scale divestitures; buyouts by company managers with the help of private equity financing; the merging of companies in the same industry, often accompanied by the spinoff of peripheral businesses to more specialized companies; and many other buyout strategies. Another aspect of private equity has been the so-called leveraged buyout. While leveraged buyouts still continue to be made, their heyday was in the 1980s, when private equity investors could contribute only 10 to 15 percent—in some cases as little as 1 to 2 percent—of the capital needed for the acquisition and borrow the rest, which, in turn, created the leverage. Since 1989, investors have had to invest more of their own capital.

Unlike other developed countries in Europe and especially the United Kingdom, the United States never utilized what has been called merchant banking to finance private equity projects. Until the 1950s, most of these enterprises were financed by wealthy individuals and families, such as the Rockefellers, Whitneys, and Vanderbilts, many of whom invested in venture capital as well. During the 1960s and 1970s, corporations and financial institutions also became involved financially. All of this changed, however, by 1979, when a favorable interpretation of ERISA allowed pension funds to invest in private equity funds under the act's "prudent man" rule. As a result, between about 1980 and 1999, the private equity market grew from $4.7 to $400 billion in assets, although it remained small compared with the public equity market of $17 trillion in 1999. Still, private equity was growing and provided an alternative to raising public equity, issuing public debt, or arranging a private placement of debt or a bank loan. And in doing so, it allowed a company with a poor or nonexistent financial record to participate in forms of financing otherwise unavailable or too expensive, to expand ownership without going public, or to take on the fixed cost of debt financing, among other alternatives.

The mechanics of private equity are similar to venture capital. Most private equity investments are made through limited partnerships, which have a fixed life, often ten years, with returns not usually expected until after there is an IPO for the business. Likewise, private equity companies exercise control over their portfolio companies by representation on company boards. Private equity firms charge investors a fee in the range of 1.5–2 percent of assets under management (AUM) and 20 percent (a formula known as "two and twenty") of all fund profits (the 20 percent is often called "carried interest"), subject to a minimum rate of return for investors, which they have agreed to beforehand. In addition, interest on any debt taken out by the acquired company in these leveraged buyouts is treated as a business expense and can be used as a deduction against income made by the leveraged company. Of course, none of these measures insures positive or successful results. The fortunes of company acquisitions have run the gamut, as one writer has noted, ranging from "The Good" to "The Bad" and "The Ugly."[4]

While there were scattered examples of company buyouts in the 1950s and 1960s, it was not until the mid-1960s, when Jerome Kohlberg Jr. and Henry

Kravis, both then working at Bear Stearns, along with Kravis's cousin George Roberts began investing in family-owned businesses with succession issues, that buyouts started becoming more commonplace.[5] Too small to go public yet too proud to sell their firms to competitors, company owners found an outlet through private equity arrangements, which allowed them to retain family control. Beginning with their first important buyout in 1964 of Orkin Exterminating Company, the trio continued making successful investments until 1976, when they decided to form their own firm, Kohlberg Kravis Roberts & Company (KKR). The new firm received help from wealthy family investors, and by the late 1970s, it was able to raise its first institutional fund with pension money available because of changes in ERISA regulations. In 1978, it acquired Houdaille Industries, a publicly traded company that made pumps, machine tools, and other products for industry, for $380 million, the largest company to be taken private to that time. Meanwhile, Bostonian Thomas H. Lee founded his investment firm of the same name in 1974 to acquire companies through leveraged buyouts. He became one of the earliest proponents of acquiring more mature companies rather than making venture capital investments in growth companies.[6]

While buyouts began to become attractive in the 1960s and 1970s, it was not until the 1980s that they started to take off. This was largely due to the easy availability of funds, including the new source, pension funds; a government hands-off policy toward antitrust regulation, which had made the merger of two companies in the same industry virtually impossible during the preceding 35 years; and the declining fortunes of business conglomerates, many of which were destined to fail. They became targets of private equity, which sought to break them up and sell their divisions to buyers in the same industry. Ironically, many large businesses in the 1960s had little choice but to buy unrelated businesses with their spare cash. Had they acquired similar businesses, they likely would have helped to raise their companies' market share. A mere point or two—from 5 to 7 percent market share, for instance—could subject a company to years of antitrust prosecution. But during the Reagan administration, antitrust enforcement virtually disappeared. Tax law also became an important motivator for private equity. There was the disparity in tax treatment that favored interest paid to bondholders rather than dividends paid to stockholders. As a result, private equity investors used leverage to reduce their taxes. Following the Tax Act of 1981, the top capital gains rate was reduced from 28 to 20 percent, which also encouraged high-risk investments. (Since that time capital gain rates have declined to 15 percent, while earnings from public companies have been taxed at a much higher rate.) Changes in corporate governance (specifically managerial and shareholder interests) and banking, which came to provide more investment funds for buyouts, were also factors in private equity's rise. As a result, the locus of control shifted from management to shareholders (private equity and investors in its funds)—from managerial to financial capitalism—a phenomenon not seen since the late nineteen and early twentieth centuries.[7]

The growth of takeovers in the 1980s changed the U.S. economy. While there had been noteworthy waves of mergers and acquisitions between the late 1890s and early 1900s, the 1920s, and 1960s, during this period the impact was more widespread. A total of $1.3 trillion in assets changed hands, while in the same period, 28 percent or 143 of the 500 largest industrial companies were acquired. The leveraged buyout boom began in 1982 with the acquisition by a group of investors of the Gibson Greetings Company. Only $1 million of the $80 million acquisition price was reportedly contributed by its investors, while the rest was borrowed. By the middle of the following year, the company completed a $290 million IPO for the business. In 1989, at the end of the decade, KKR acquired RJR Nabisco for $31 billion, the largest leveraged buyout until the mid-2000s. The fight for RJR Nabisco involved several private equity suitors and their entourages of advisers and financiers, including Morgan Stanley, Goldman Sachs, Salomon Brothers, and Merrill Lynch.

During the 1980s, over two thousand leveraged buyouts took place, including those of numerous well-known public companies like Atlas Van Lines, Beatrice Companies (Tropicana, Sara Lee, and others), Sterling Jewelers, Revco Drug Stores, Safeway, Federated Department Stores, and Uniroyal Goodrich Tire Company. Some buyouts were known as hostile takeovers, which were conducted by corporate raiders or takeover artists, who might employ greenmail, money paid to a raider to avoid a corporate takeover, but were not usually associated with most private equity investors or investments. Those practices were epitomized by Philadelphia businessman Ronald Perlman's takeover of the cosmetics company Revlon, the first hostile takeover of a major public company using junk bonds (high-risk but high-yield securities), which potentially put any company at risk and raised the price of buyouts. Many corporate raiders were also clients of investment bank Drexel Burnham Lambert and its star operative Michael Milken, who pioneered high-debt or junk bond financing for their buyouts. Still, many private equity companies were seen essentially as asset strippers that acquired companies, often under siege, sold off good assets for quick profits, and left the rest of those companies burdened with heavy debt.[8]

By the late 1980s, the industry was in a credit crunch. The RJR Nabisco deal of 1989 proved to be the last significant buyout transaction of the decade, but provided KKR with only negligible returns over the next six years—a sign that the driven-up acquisition price could not easily sustain a good return for investors during a recession. At about the same time, Drexel Burnham Lambert, under constant scrutiny for several years by federal and state authorities, was forced to close down many of its operations and eventually filed for Chapter 11 bankruptcy protection. The high-yield or junk bond debt market of the 1980s, which had created about $20–40 billion in new issues between 1986 and 1988, also collapsed, drying up before the end of 1989. In 1990, only $1.4 billion in new junk bonds were sold. Soon junk bond default rates dramatically increased, accompanied by a credit lockdown in 1991 and 1992 due to the credit crisis in the savings and loan industry. Deregulated during the 1980s, that industry was a large recipient of these bonds. As a result, a shakeout of private equity firms occurred, with the emergence of new ones leading to a constellation of companies of similar size that would come to dominate the industry in the 1990s.

Within a short time, conditions for private equity were on the rebound. By about 1992, it began to enter a second growth period or boom, which effectively lasted to the end of the 1990s. During that period, private equity funds grew from about $21 billion raised in 1992 to over $300 billion by 2000. Private equity also took on a more positive, respectable, and legitimate role than it had had in the 1980s. In the previous era, many buyouts involved industrial conglomerates, ready and waiting to be acquired, broken up, and resold using a high proportion of leveraged debt. Often these transactions led to asset stripping, employee layoffs, and plant closings as investors walked off with enormous profits made from borrowed money.[9]

By the 1990s, private equity investors became more concerned with the long-term development of companies they acquired, as well as in making buyouts more attractive to shareholders and managements. Debt levels of acquired companies declined from the high of 95 percent down to the 20–40 percent range, as lenders demanded that buyers put up 20–30 percent or more of the entire price in equity, rather than just 5–10 percent as had been common in the 1980s. This helped to sideline many of the corporate raiders, who required large amounts of funding from firms like Drexel. Buyout firms would accept companies more or less as they were, and make them dig deeper into their operations to make them worth more. Value creation became the new mantra. Emblematic of this change was Boston's Thomas H. Lee Partners' acquisition of Snapple Beverages in 1992, a deal discussed later that helped to bring the private equity industry back into a more favorable limelight.

Another shift was the source of buyout backing, from insurance companies and banks to state and local government pension funds, as they sought to adopt modern portfolio theory, which emphasized nontraditional investments in venture capital, buyouts, hedge funds, and real estate. Pension funds provided as much as half of the investment capital in the private equity industry by the end of the century. Some of the important buyouts of this era included Duane Reade (drug store chain), Sealy Corporation (mattress manufacturer), J. Crew (apparel maker), Domino's Pizza, and Oxford Health Plans. By the mid-1990s, private equity activity moved from investments in old-fashioned industrial businesses to high-tech and the new economy of telecommunications, cable, and the internet, with such companies as Netscape, Amazon, and eBay.[10]

Private equity, like other financial services areas, suffered in the aftermath of the dot-com bust or internet bubble of 2000, but after 2002, activity began to rise steadily. Telecommunications, a strong private equity area of investment in the late 1990s, collapsed in the early years of the new century, including such companies as WorldCom, Adelphia Communications, and Global Crossing. Technology and internet companies were also hard hit, bringing a number of prominent private equity companies to their knees. But following a few painful years, there was a brief, five-year resurgence of private equity. Between 2002 and 2005, fundraising for private equity firms quadrupled, and by 2007, some firms raised from $15 to over $20 billion. During the period 2003–2007, thirteen of the fifteen largest leveraged transactions in the United States took place, leading to a major expansion of the industry and its primary firms. The industry also became more widely dispersed in the United States. Instead of a few well-known companies in the 1980s, there were two dozen well-financed firms by the 2000s. In addition, private equity transactions worldwide increased from a mere $28 billion in 2000 to $502 billion in 2006, and then reached $501 billion during the first half of 2007. Deals during this period reflected a change in acquisition patterns over the previous three decades—from unrelated business units in 1960s-style conglomerates to the acquisition of entire public companies.[11]

The new era thrived on decreasing interest rates, which actually encouraged high-yield debt as well as loans from banks or syndicates of banks with few restrictions on collateral, payment terms, and income qualifications, and a weakening of lending standards and changing regulations for publicly traded companies. This in turn made private equity ownership of public companies more attractive. Some early acquisitions in this period included Burger King and Houghton Mifflin (both by Boston's Bain Capital and with Thomas H. Lee Partners involved in the latter), Toys 'R Us, Metro-Goldwyn-Mayer, and the Hertz Corporation. By 2006 and 2007, the buyout boom hit its stride. Over an eighteen month period, a number of large-scale buyouts were made, affecting companies as widely diverse as Georgia-Pacific Corporation (lumber),

Albertson's (groceries), Equity Office Properties (office buildings), Harrah's Entertainment (gambling), and Chrysler (automobiles). On a broader scale of activity, private equity acquired more companies and raised more capital for private equity funds than it had in the past, and became a global, not just an American, phenomenon, with buyout expansion in Europe and Asia. As public interest in private equity expanded, several leading private equity firms decided to sell portions of ownership to the public and created funds that would allow the public, not just limited partners, to invest in them. It had become private equity's moment.[12]

The 2007 turndown in the mortgage markets soon also affected private equity and its high-yield debt markets, to the point that by the fall of the year, some major deals struck during the earlier boom time had to be withdrawn or renegotiated, and many lenders became involved in significant debt write-downs due to credit losses. While there was apparently no single event causing a downturn, it was disastrous for private equity's investment banks. During this decline, private equity firms invested in other buyouts, moved into other asset classes, or invested in publicly traded debt funds, all of which proved to be bad bets. Exacerbating these developments, pension fund investors were not only tapped out of further investing funds but also needed to sell off investments in stocks and bonds to meet the cash needs of pension fund retirees. In addition, private equity firms had only to look a few years into the future when their rising amounts of debt would have to be refinanced.

Since 2009, there has been some recovery and rebuilding. Private equity has been better off than many other suppliers of capital, such as commercial and investment banks, and is constantly changing. More currently, its focus has been on buying up distressed debt at highly discounted rates, and has drawn back pension funds in search of better investments; its investment funds are estimated to be about $500 billion. Private equity remains a changeable and cyclical industry, but one that finds different kinds of investment needs in different parts of the business cycle. Nevertheless, its huge returns of previous decades may become more elusive as market efficiency has largely eliminated the opportunities available the 1980s and 1990s: there are simply fewer prospects for big deals, less debt available, and greater regulation, and it is proving more difficult to sell companies that have been built up by private equity firms. Nevertheless, private equity funds have grown substantially. Among big public-employee pensions alone, private equity investment was about $220 billion in late 2011, up from a mere $1 billion for all pension funds with $1 billion or more under management a decade ago.[13]

The Expansion of Venture Capital: Private Equity in Boston

Because of its interrelationship with venture capital in Boston, private equity in the Hub stretches back to the late 1940s and 1950s with American Research & Development and to the 1960s and 1970s with such firms as TA Associates and Thomas H. Lee Partners. Boston's position as a center for private equity has grown stronger over time. For instance, one 2007 survey of the fifty largest international private equity companies showed that five of them—Bain Capital, Thomas H. Lee Partners, TA Associates, Advent International, and Summit Partners—were in Boston, and they held 7 percent of the total equity of the fifty. By 2011, that same survey source reported that those five firms, each one larger and much higher in the rankings, held 10 percent of the total equity. The Hub was outnumbered only by New York with twelve and London with eight firms. Another recent research survey noted that Massachusetts is behind only California and New York in the total number of private equity firms, and has two of the top ten private equity firms based on total funds raised over the decade of the 2000s.[14]

Aside from TA Associates and Thomas H. Lee, most major Boston private equity firms were founded in the mid-1980s. For instance, Summit Partners, a firm that handles leveraged buyouts, recapitalizations, venture capital, and mezzanine capital, was founded in 1984 by E. Roe Stamps and Stephen Woodsum, who had both worked in venture capital and at TA Associates. From 1984 to 2008, Summit raised fourteen private equity funds. Another firm, Berkshire Partners, was also founded in 1984, and it has raised eight funds, which have grown in size from $59 million (Berkshire Fund I) to $4.5 billion (Berkshire Fund VIII). Over that quarter century, Berkshire Partners' diverse investor base has included endowments (25 percent), public pensions (16 percent), financial institutions (10 percent), foundations (10 percent), sovereign wealth funds (8 percent), Berkshire partners (8 percent), family offices (7 percent), corporate pensions (6 percent), insurance companies (6 percent), and special relationships (4 percent). Even though both of these private equity firms were created by former employees of other firms, this practice appears to be the exception, at least in Boston. Continuity and longevity seem to be important characteristics of the business in Boston. Several early Boston private equity firms are described in more detail below.[15]

Thomas H. Lee & Company

One of the earliest private equity firms in Boston specifically involved in leveraged buyouts was founded by Thomas H. Lee in 1974. Over the next quarter century, Thomas H. Lee & Company produced probably the best returns among top-tier private equity funds at over 40 percent. Better-known rivals like New York's KKR produced only half that amount. In 2005, the company was renamed Thomas H. Lee Partners, when Lee left to form Lee Equity Partners in New York, which was interested in growth capital transactions rather than leveraged buyouts. Later, he also went into the hedge funds business through another company, Thomas H. Lee Capital Management. The 2005 separation had been planned for some time, as Putnam Investments had acquired a 25 percent interest in the Boston firm in 1999.

Following his graduation from Harvard College in 1965, Lee became a securities analyst in the institutional research department at L. F. Rothschild in New York. Thereafter, Lee returned to Boston to work in the highly diversified loan department at First National Bank of Boston for eight years. This was in the High Technology Lending Group that Peter A. Brooke had helped to set up back in 1958, and where Lee became an "angel banker" for small Route 128 companies. In 1974, Lee established his own firm, investing $150,000 seed money in it from an inheritance. He founded the firm with J. Christopher Clifford, who was then working in Boston for a small New York investment bank following stints at Harvard Business School and then in the Army Reserve during the Vietnam War. By 1974 and with the help of Greylock, the venture capital firm, Clifford was responsible for setting up the IPO for Prime Computer, a local company that became the best performing Nasdaq stock in the 1970s. That same year, Clifford received a call from Lee, an acquaintance he had come to know in the Boston investment community. Lee told Clifford that he was thinking of leaving the First, and with his own experience in commercial banking and Clifford's in investment banking, he wanted to set up "a little boutique firm to advise small, moderate size companies." They opened their office in September 1974.

For the next several years, according to Clifford, "our business was just Tom and myself and a secretary advising small and medium size companies on how they could either finance their growth or optimize their balance sheets, things of that sort." In the course of dispensing that advice, clients would sometimes give them equity in their business rather than cash. Typical of their early clients was a Pennsylvania tube manufacturing company that had run out of money to buy copper. Unlike at New York firms, where the possible solution might have been seen in a financial engineering of the company, the pair took a management consulting approach, which became common in Boston private equity: They rethought how the owners could change the business and do away with such cash-flow bottlenecks. Lee and Clifford then found people who could better manage the company and took an equity position in it rather than a fee.

Their overall approach became the way much private equity would be handled in Boston: less orientation toward the financial engineering aspect of private equity—perhaps in large part because there was so little investment banking in Boston—and more of an emphasis on the dynamics of a particular business or industry in determining whether a business was worth pursuing for a particular private equity transaction. Wealthy families contributed to early deals, but as time wore on, commercial banks and especially institutional money in the city provided the key financial infusions for Boston private equity, just like they had with venture capital years earlier.

Thomas H. Lee & Company's first leveraged buyout took place their first year in business. While this was not the first ever leveraged buyout to take place, as similar transactions had been made in the 1950s and 1960s, it may have been the first leveraged buyout so named. It involved the David Clark Company of Worcester, Massachusetts, which was owned by Munsingwear, a clothing and undergarment manufacturer in Minnesota. Begun in 1835, the Worcester company had been in the textile business for most of its life, but it had gradually shifted over to aeronautic flight suits in World War II and then into space suits, and eventually into communication devices and systems for the military, general aviation, and other customers in the decades that followed. It became a profitable Munsingwear division. Two employees, however, were interested in buying the company but were unsure how to proceed. Through a friend, they were put in touch with Lee and Clifford, who started putting together a plan whereby the prospective new owners could borrow money from a bank to provide some equity. By early 1975, they were in negotiations with Munsingwear and were able to acquire the business for $5 -8 million. The company remains profitable to this day.

Throughout the rest of the 1970s and into the 1980s, deals were largely bootstrap operations, in which Lee's and Clifford's company received new capital for companies by borrowing against the assets—receivables or inventory—of the client. Unlike KKR, most deals did not involve family succession issues. By the 1980s, companies they serviced were growing rapidly, but they needed capital. Clifford noted that Lee bootstrapped LBOs by using his own money and bringing in institutional investors. By the end of the 1980s, the company found financing from the secured lending departments of Boston commercial banks—First National and Leo Breitman at Merchants, in particular—or from insurance companies like Prudential or even Westinghouse, which had a venture capital–type component in its business, that were beginning to see these investments as important parts of their portfolios. University endowments and sovereign debt funds would become other sources of finance in the years to come, but pension funds never played an important role in the business.

and expanded globally, setting up offices in London, Munich, San Francisco, and Tokyo. Banking its reputation on the results it gave its clients, Bain & Company would often take equity positions in companies instead of fees. The step of moving from management consulting to private equity seemed to be only a matter of time.

That came in the early 1980s, when Bill Bain decided to form a new venture that combined the company's consulting expertise with investments in companies that were underperforming or showed promise. The new company was Bain Capital. It was independent of Bain & Company and did not provide management consulting services. It "would buy companies, retool them with Bain techniques, and resell them at a profit." The new company was formed in 1983, and Bain put Romney in charge of it. With two other original partners from Bain & Company, T. Coleman Andrews III and Eric Kriss, Bain Capital was in operation by the following year. The company was at first conceived as both an equity start-up and leveraged buyout fund, suggesting again how wide open the term "private equity" was during the 1980s. But in time, Bain Capital became widely known for its buyouts. By the middle of 1984, the company had raised its first fund of $37 million from individuals. Since then, Bain Capital has used its private equity funding for more than two hundred companies. In addition, it has moved into other investment strategies through affiliate companies and their public equity (Brookside Capital), high-yield debt obligations (Sankaty Advisors), venture capital (Bain Capital Ventures), European-focused funds (Bain Capital [Europe] Limited), and absolute return funds (Absolute Return Capital), managing as a whole about $66 billion in assets by 2011.[19]

Romney and Bain Capital got off to a slow start, but during Romney's fifteen-year tenure, he helped to increase assets to $4 billion and doubled the company's return on realized investments every year. Even crosstown rival Thomas H. Lee acknowledged that Bain Capital's performance under Romney was "one of the great stories of American capital." The opposite of a swashbuckling deal maker, Romney was a conservative and cautious investor, who worked closely with his investors and partners, and developed a painstaking analytical approach—traits that quickly defined Bain Capital as well. As late as 1986, Bain Capital had made few investments, but momentum was about to shift when it put $650,000 into a small start-up called Staples, an office supplies business. The Bain Capital funding helped to launch the company's first store in Brighton, Massachusetts, in May of that year. Many scoffed at the venture, believing that few would find saving a few cents on boxes of paper clips that important. But the job market was beginning to shift toward more independent workers, and small stationery stores soon were exposed to competition from larger business supply stores that could efficiently deliver what was needed. Bain Capital continued to invest in Staples over the next few years in what soon became a $2.5 million stake in the new enterprise. It eventually came away with $13 million, a more than fivefold return on its investment. Staples expanded from a single store in 1986 to almost 1,700 of them twenty years later. Romney and his company could later look back on Staples as a forward-looking, job-creating enterprise, but in reality it was a small venture capital project. Like other Boston equity firms, Bain Capital would soon move on to late-stage investing or leveraged buyouts, where much more money could be made and which also played to the company's analytical strengths.

An early example of the shift was Bain Capital's purchase of the wheel-making division of the Firestone Company in 1986, which Bain renamed Accuride. Using its analytical skills, it changed production methods and executive pay, and created loyalty discounts to customers who gave them all of their business—adjusting conditions and behaviors that Bain & Company had previously written up in numerous case studies. Accuride's earnings soon rose by 25 percent, and less than two years later, that company was sold for $120 million on Bain Capital's $5 million investment. With results like this, Bain Capital was not only doing well in private equity but also undoubtedly influencing the industry as to how private equity should be conducted in the post–hostile takeover era of the 1990s. One level of analysis of a company often led Romney to a further level of analysis with even more significant results. One such case involved Bain Capital's prospective purchase of the Gartner Group, a high-tech research firm. That further analysis led Bain to change Gartner's focus as a business, and this eventually resulted in a 1,500 percent return on Bain Capital's investment, a figure rarely realized in the world of general investing. In the end, Bain Capital's original fund of $37 million returned more than $200 million.

Bain Capital's second fund was about three times larger, totaling more than $100 million, and again came primarily from wealthy individuals. At first the fund grew slowly, but in the end, did quite well. One deal in 1988 of Specialty Retailers involved junk-bond financing by Drexel and Milken, a connection that later created public relations problems but no financial issues. Another involved the purchase of Damon Engineering Corporation, a Needham, Massachusetts, medical testing firm, which later pled guilty for defrauding the federal government for billing unnecessary blood tests. Nonetheless, in the end, Bain Capital tripled its original investment in Damon.[20]

Not all investments proved beneficial to companies and their employees. While the acquisition of American Pad & Paper, or Ampad, in 1992 made money for Bain Capital's investors, it served the company's employees poorly and bankrupted the company. Following Ampad's acquisition, Bain Capital embarked on a roll-up strategy to buy up other office supply makers, which helped to expand revenues and cut costs. As Ampad bought up those other companies, its debt grew from $11 million in 1993 to almost $400 million by 1999. While sales grew at first, the industry was quickly overrun by foreign competitors and, ironically, office supply superstores like Staples. As a result, Ampad's revenues dropped, and the company was unable to pay its rising debt service. It then plunged into bankruptcy, with a loss of jobs for workers and shareholder value. In the meantime, Bain Capital made money off management fees, fees for arranging an IPO, and revenue from selling some of its Ampad shares.

Throughout the 1990s, Bain Capital raised several funds, and acquired, sometimes with funding from other private equity companies, many well-known U.S. brand names. They included Domino's Pizza, from which it received a 500 percent return on its investment; Experian, the credit reporter, from which it earned $200 million in just two months' time; and the Sealy Mattress companies. Among the hundreds of other companies Bain Capital invested in or acquired were Bright Horizons Family Solutions, Brookstone, and the Sports Authority. By the early twenty-first century, Bain Capital was managing $50 billion in assets and held positions in companies like Toys 'R Us, Burger King, and Unisource. Other investments have included AMC Entertainment, Aspen Educational Group, DoubleClick, Hospital Corporation of America, Warner Music Group, and the Weather Channel. The decade of the 2000s has seen a number of successful deals for Bain, such as the purchase and transformation of Bombardier's recreational products division into a new company (2003); the acquisition of Burlington Coat Factory Warehouse and its 360 retail stores from shareholders (2006); and the purchase of the semiconductor division of Royal Philips Electronics (in a private equity consortium, 2006), which became NXP Semiconductors. That same year, Bain Capital and Thomas Lee Partners acquired Clear Channel Communications for almost $19 billion and, with another private equity consortium, a one-third share in Home Depot Supply, the wholesale construction supply business of Home Depot. In 2007, Bain Capital and a Chinese networking company purchased 3Com for $2.2 billion.[21]

During the 1980s, Bain Capital faced many challenges, including the one-client-per-industry restriction Bain & Company had promoted since its inception, and competition from other firms that quickly adapted to Bain Capital's implementation-focused strategy. Bain Capital also struggled with mounting debt caused by executives in Bain & Company who used Bain Capital's employee stock ownership plan as a source of cash against their equity. Romney was called upon to manage negotiations with partners and banks, and eventually reached an agreement that shifted control away from William Bain and early Bain & Company partners. They voluntarily returned about $130 million to Bain Capital, most of which had been borrowed from the employee stock ownership plan. When Bain & Company's business fell off following the financial crash of October 1987, Romney was asked to serve as chief executive of his old company and to get it out of its slump. He worked with creditors, cajoling in some cases but playing hardball in others, such as a $1 million bill from the company's landlord. He also got company founders to return $100 million, or about half of their payout. Romney visited what by then had grown into a worldwide company of one thousand employees, helped to create a new governing structure, and changed the firm's compensation structure. In the end, Bain & Company survived. All told, Romney's action in negotiation, recapitalization, and restructuring of Bain & Company offers one of his most important, but little known, acts in the field of private equity. By 1991, he had completed the transformation and returned to Bain Capital where he remained until 1999.[22]

Over its first fifteen years, Bain Capital evolved from a company with an orientation that "was by and large to acquire businesses that were out of favor and in some cases in trouble," which it hoped to build or fix with the needed capital it could supply, to one that "shifted toward the potentially more lucrative business of leveraged buyouts—acquiring control of businesses by using investors' money amplified by debt." Like Boston venture capital firms, Bain Capital had a number of very profitable successes that more than made up for any losses.[23]

TA Associates and the Rise of Advent International

TA Associates became one of the first venture capital firms not affiliated with family fortunes. From its founding in 1968 by Peter Brooke and over the next two decades, it was involved in several major IPOs of the era, including Biogen, Continental Cablevision, and Federal Express. Slowly TA Associates raised larger and larger funds, and from more diverse and global sources. The limited partners of its first fund, Advent I, came from wealthy New England families; three decades later, capital was raised from global and institutional funds. By 1980, Advent IV was capitalized at $60 million, and Advent V, three years later, drew $167 million. The rising size of the funds moved the firm to focus on later-stage investments in fast-growing businesses. As Kevin Landry, Brooke's successor later explained, "We wanted to manage more money, and we couldn't spend 75 percent of our time working with early-stage portfolio companies." Under Landry, TA Associates moved boldly into new and somewhat radical investments in new areas, such as financial services and financial technology, and was also an early investor in a number of hedge funds. In the 1990s, it had achieved great success in software, networking, and asset management areas, and was devoting more capital for money management, healthcare, and non-tech investments. By 2004, TA had set up twenty-one funds since its creation, none of which had lost money and nearly all of which had outperformed those of its private equity competitors.[24]

While TA Associates became a successful firm under Landry, things had been less certain in the difficult economic climate of the 1970s and early 1980s. At that time, Brooke had to find other sources of revenue to hold his small but growing company together. The path he took, as noted earlier, was to consult on developing private equity in Europe where the concept was barely known at the time. As a result, in 1972, Sofinnova, a name derived from a French word for venture capital, was founded in France through the combined efforts of the French Ministry of Industry, Crédit National, and TA Associates. Brooke continued to look for sources of capital in Europe and by 1980, TA Associates had opened up its first affiliated office in London. In the years that immediately followed, TA opened other offices throughout Europe and Asia. By 1985, when Brooke left TA Associates, he combined those affiliate offices, his international network intact, to form Advent International, which quickly added a focused, worldwide presence to Boston's role in the development of private equity.

The idea behind Advent had been slow to develop but provided much potential, and also forms a chapter in TA Associates' early history. Originally, the affiliate offices Brooke created in Europe and Asia were used to find investors and sources of investment funds for TA. But there was also an underlying assumption that their role could be enlarged and become a two-way street: finding promising companies for development in Europe whose technology might be useful in the United States, and finding U.S. companies that wanted to expand their own technological advancements to Europe. These goals would become more fully implemented when Brooke formed Advent International and secured his affiliates in Europe and Asia from TA Associates for a 15 percent interest in Brooke's new company.

Brooke's initial problem was that Europe in the 1970s was far behind the United States in understanding the role of entrepreneurship and how innovation was created. He had to overcome many cultural barriers and attitudes, but history soon helped to accommodate him. Europeans had long believed that innovation came from large, industrial bureaucracies rather than small, entrepreneurial companies. They also had no appreciation that small companies should actually be nurtured and developed. "Having all the right structures and incentives in place will do little to promote entrepreneurship," Brooke noted, "without a culture that encourages creativity, adaptability, and risk taking. Such a culture did not exist in Germany or anywhere else in Europe in the 1970s." As the technological gap between the United States and Japan in relation to Europe widened, Europeans began to question for the first time "whether collective research was really the only route to innovation—possibly the individual entrepreneur did have a role to play."

Brooke took his approach to Europe one country at a time. In 1977, Brooke started his efforts in Great Britain by forming a company with British partners called the Trans-Atlantic Business Growth Fund, to help channel British investment funds to TA Associates and bring TA's venture capital know-how to Britain.[25] After the Margaret Thatcher government came to power in 1979, it abolished exchange controls, which then allowed British pension and insurance companies to invest in U.S. venture capital. Soon other restrictions against limited partnerships were removed and taxes were reduced. The next step was to set up Advent Limited, the first venture capital firm in Europe built on the U.S. limited-partnership model, in 1981. Within a span of four years, Advent Ltd. had created three funds, and Brooke was turning his attention to the continent where he sensed "the economic and cultural tides of Europe were shifting in my favor," enabling him to "build the network of European venture capital firms of which I dreamed." Brooke had gained a foothold in France through Sofinnova more than a decade earlier, and now he was eager to return to the continent to begin the development of a global network of affiliates, first in Western Europe and then in Asia.[26]

Each of the Western European countries in which he set up affiliates presented its own set of problems, but the restrictive, post–World War II economic policies he had observed in France and Britain only a few years earlier were coming to an end throughout the region. Brooke's strategy for expansion was to find "a leading financial institution or corporation that was a national opinion leader" and search out likely investors to raise the investment fund. The second network member, Advent Belgium, was founded in 1982 through the help of Dutch and Belgium investment companies. Belgium was producing few technology companies, so Advent Belgium focused more on expansion capital or restructuring rather than technology or start-ups. The earlier success of European investors in TA's funds gradually led them to become more interested in investing locally. Still, it was a slow process to educate potential investors in each country, help them recognize the innovative capabilities of small companies, and raise funds of $20 to $60 million during the early to mid-1980s. And it would take even longer for investments in local enterprise to reshape the business landscape of Europe.

At the same time, Brooke was also becoming involved with Asia through the International Finance Corporation of the World Bank. Asia was even further behind Europe, except for the "East Asian Tigers" of Taiwan, Hong Kong, and South Korea. But enlightened leadership in places like Singapore sought to shift from labor-intensive, low-value production to more advanced, high-tech-oriented, science-based, and knowledge-driven work. Brooke made efforts to develop an investment group in Singapore but had no luck until almost the last moment in finding a local champion who could round up Singaporean and Malaysian investors. Brooke continued to use the business model he had developed in Europe as he worked in Asia, making Singapore his "base from which I spread my missionary message of venture capital to other regions in Asia." He next moved on to set up an affiliate in Japan but eventually expanded to other affiliate locations along the eastern Pacific.[27]

During the late 1980s, 1990s, and 2000s, Advent shifted from simply an affiliate network to setting up its own foreign offices, so that it could create a strong local presence. This began with one in California's Silicon Valley in 1988, but spread to offices in London (1989), Frankfurt and Milan (1991), Buenos Aires and Mexico City (1996), Paris and Sao Paulo (1997), Warsaw (1998), Bucharest (2000), Madrid (2002), Prague and Kiev (2007), Mumbai (2009), New York City and Istanbul (2010), and Bogota (2011). By 2012, the company employed over 170 investment professionals representing 29 nationalities.

Beginning with its first private equity fund of only $14 million in 1985 for a Nabisco corporate venture program, the size and scope of Advent's private equity funds have grown appreciably, and have included some of the first private equity regional funds in various places in the world as well as some of the largest regional and worldwide funds in several categories. The company has raised cumulative capital of $26 billion and invested in over six hundred companies in forty-one countries. Like many early venture capitalists, experiences overseas, particularly in Europe, persuaded Brooke to shift from early-stage investing to a private equity later stage and buyout strategy: "I had always understood that [we] would have to adapt . . . international strategies to the realities on the ground in local markets." Despite the company's growth, it has largely stayed on the sidelines in Asia, even though it has had some presence in the region over the last several decades.[28]

The Long and Short of It: The Growth of Hedge Funds as an Alternative Investment

Major alternative investment classes, as we have seen, are largely defined as private equity, commercial or private real estate, and hedge funds, but have expanded to include others over time like natural resource partnerships, emerging markets, venture capital, and commodities. In other words, alternative investments cover most investments outside of publicly traded debt, equity, and real estate. Fundamental to all of them is that they are generally illiquid and largely unregulated; as such, they are not subject to the Investment Company Act of 1940. Their illiquidity can present problems during economic difficulties, but they do not necessarily track the stock market or other market indices like traditional investments do. As a result, these so-called noncorrelated assets can become more valuable to investors during economic downturns or when more traditional investments provide little increase in value over time. In addition, they provide participants with a wide variety of financial markets and strategies not available to traditional investors.

Hedge funds are widely misunderstood, but they attract private pools of capital. The hedge fund managers leverage these assets to the hilt, borrowing on some securities and buying others on margin—the long and short sides—the so-called hedge. Managers of these funds usually receive about 20 percent of what the portfolio makes and are not subject to regulation by the Securities and Exchange Commission (SEC) because they are private partnerships. Indeed, regulation and public exposure of a hedge fund's assets and, inferentially, its investment strategy could be damaging competitively and dangerous for the fund itself, as rival funds might invest against it for their own prospective gain. Thus, hedge funds have remained relatively small, secretive, and reclusive. Like private equity, hedge funds rely on borrowed money (and buying on margin), compared to using high-yield debt to magnify private equity bets, so both are subject to rapid reversals of fortune depending on the timing. Turnover in hedge fund portfolios, particularly those securities on the short side, tends to be greater than in other investment pools.

In a hypothetical $10 million hedge fund, the manager leverages it 40 percent by buying some listed securities at 80 percent margin and borrowing money on some of its over-the-counter securities, making all the money work at 140 percent effectiveness. If the market is going up, the manager can keep 110 percent of the portfolio on the long side and the other 30 percent in securities sold short with the portfolio's exposure at only 80 percent (110 less 30 percent). The manager hedges a substantial portion of his or her long position to avoid any possible errors in reading the market outlook. Managers pick stocks that will rise more than average, and select stocks for shorting—a difficult, complex, and even treacherous process—that will perform worse, perhaps actually fall, than average stocks in a rising market. Depending on how the overall market is reacting, the manager can shift his or her position, even going net short when the market appears to be falling. By contrast, mutual funds have only one way to go—either up or down. The hedge fund manager, in effect, can bet on both extremes by readjusting the securities' positioning.

Although hedge funds appear to be a new alternative investment, they have been around for some time. *Institutional Investor* noted in 1968 that, "until recently there were only a handful of hedge funds." However, the article continued, "this year [1968] they have been sprouting like weeds in a damp summer." Where there had been previously only a handful, "there are now more than 100 hedge funds, and their combined assets may be approaching $2 billion." Even so, the earliest hedge funds first appeared almost two decades earlier.[29]

The first hedge fund was developed by Alfred Winslow Jones, a Harvard graduate with a Ph.D. in sociology. By the 1930s, Jones had become interested in finance and served briefly as a *Fortune* magazine editor. He then turned to freelance writing, preparing a 1949 article in *Fortune* on "Fashions in Forecasting," which discussed technical approaches to understanding the stock market. This assignment eventually led him to formulate the idea of the hedge fund. Jones used securities shorting not just as a cushion for market setbacks but also for making money in a falling market. He next convinced four friends to invest $100,000 total, and in 1949, he founded his firm, A. W. Jones and Company. He charged fees that would become standard in the industry and similar to those in private equity—about 2 percent as a management fee and a performance fee of about 20 percent for any investment gains generated. It would be almost two decades before the term *hedge fund* would be coined in another *Fortune* magazine article published in 1966.

Jones's company remained a largely closed affair, but information about its success slowly drifted out. Between the late 1950s and late 1960s, for instance, the company made gains in excess of 1,000 percent, and even in a bad market year, like 1962, it was able to make a small gain. By 1968, the company managed more than $100 million. This success led partners to bolt the firm and set up their own operations, as did brokers who sold his fund. The legacy of Jones's idea was that selling a portion of the portfolio short could offer protection for the investor. "The logic of the idea was very clear," he later noted. "It was a hedge against the vagaries of the market. You can buy more good stocks without taking as much risk as someone who merely *buys*." Later hedge funds did not always hue to Jones's blueprint, as many did not necessarily short, or hedge, but they did continue to employ other characteristics of the business. The term has since become so broad as to include almost any private investment made outside of SEC public disclosure rules that it is not publicly marketed. Hedge fund investors range from stock pickers and arbitrageurs (who look for mispriced assets relative to similar assets due to "market inefficiencies") to macro investors, who monitor economic trends like exchange rates, inflation, and growth, and quants, who sift through enormous amounts of data to spot significant opportunities before they execute their trades. Furthermore, these investors can employ more than two dozen different fund strategies, each of which has its own risk and return attributes.[30]

The early period for hedge funds may have crested about 1969, when the SEC estimated that there were two hundred hedge funds with accumulated assets of about $1.5 billion. During the 1970s, an era of poor financial performance throughout the investment management industry, hedge funds almost vanished. By 1977, hedge fund assets had declined to as little as $250 million, and many companies migrated over to managing pension funds where there was more predictable cash flow and a strong growth rate. Even Jones was quoted as saying, "I don't believe it is ever going to become a big part of the investment scene, as it was in the late 1960s. The hedge fund doesn't have a terrific future."[31]

By the 1980s, however, the hedge fund world began to blossom again. It matured in the following decade as new investors like Paul Tudor Jones (no relation to Alfred Winslow Jones), George Soros, and Julian Robertson entered the business. Hedge funds expanded beyond wealthy families to public and corporate pension funds; each of the latter two contributed about one-third to the investment pool of hedge funds while another quarter came from government-run sovereign wealth funds, such as Singapore's. By the mid-1990s, there was also increasing interest in hedge funds of funds, in which asset managers like banks placed investible funds among a number of hedge fund managers. The main motivation for investing in hedge funds was that it involved a strategy *uncorrelated* to equities, like investing in distressed securities and merger arbitrage.[32]

That decoupling of hedge funds from the traditional financial markets was observed in recessions following the stock market crash of 1987 and the dotcom bust of 2000. Between 1990 and 2007, hedge funds earned about 14 percent, but in 2008, they incurred large losses estimated at around 20 percent, the largest fall in their history. While many funds suffered or temporarily lost ground, their numbers and size continued to grow. By 2011, there were ten thousand hedge funds worldwide with about $2 trillion under management, or roughly where they had stood in 2007. Some see the next ten years as a period of regression in the hedge fund industry. As one well-known hedge fund manager has noted, "We are still in a deleveraging period [of selling assets rapidly to reduce debt]. We will be in a deleveraging period for ten years or more." Other observers like Sebastian Mallaby argue that "the future of finance lies in the history of hedge funds."[33]

Hedge Funds in Boston

The beginnings of hedge funds in Boston have more to do with the concept than the practice, as some of the early hedge fund strategies were developed in Boston. As noted earlier, Boston was important after World War II in the development and marketing of orange juice concentrate. Two decades later, that same commodity played a role in setting up one of the first commodities-based hedge funds. According to Amos Hostetter Jr., a Boston venture capitalist and cofounder of Continental Cablevision,

> One of my closest friends was a graduate student at MIT who was doing his Ph.D. thesis on econometric modeling of commodity prices. There had been a frost in Florida, and he called to tell me that the market hadn't reacted to what was clearly going to be a damaged citrus crop. "We should buy concentrated orange juice," he told me.
> "What are we going to do with it?" I asked.
> "We are just going to keep it," he said.
> So we went to Arthur [Snyder] and convinced him that he ought to loan us $10,000 to buy concentrated orange juice. It stayed in a food warehouse, and we never took delivery of it. Nine months later, we sold it back to the same wholesaler, Quincy Cold Storage, for twice our investment.[34]

Snyder was one of Boston's earliest venture capitalists, and would later help Hostetter and his partner, Irv Grosbeck, finance Continental Cablevision.

F. Helmut Weymar, Hostetter's close friend at MIT, went on in 1969 to found Commodities Corporation, one of the most widely influential and successful commodity trading companies, with Amos Hostetter Sr., the legendary trader of stocks and commodities at Hayden Stone, who became, according to Weymar, "our 70-year old guru." During his years at the company, Hostetter Sr. was a driving force, acting as the senior trader and documenting his trading systems for the company. Even though the company was located in Princeton, New Jersey, its founders included MIT economist Paul Samuelson, Weymar's thesis adviser, and Paul Cootner, an MIT professor of finance who wrote *The Random Character of Stock Market Prices* (1964). Commodities Corporation also gave a number of hedge fund managers their start, including Paul Tudor Jones, found of Tudor Investment Corporation, and Bruce Kovner, founder of Caxton Associates. A research-oriented company, Commodities Corporation employed eight Ph.D.'s by the early 1980s. They and a professional staff of forty searched through commodity data looking for trading opportunities. One of them developed a technical system known as *trend following,* which was soon developed into a technical computer system. The fund's trend-following strategies typified the approach taken by many hedge fund investors in the 1980s and early 1990s, an era epitomized by Amos Hostetter Sr.'s remark, "cut your losses and ride your winners."[35]

In Boston, hedge funds only became prominent in the 1990s and especially the 2000s. The earliest hedge funds in Boston were likely managed by the Essex Investment Management Company in the late 1970s, when founder Joseph C. McNay began managing three Swiss hedge funds—one, an overseas mutual fund, Global Asset Management or GAM, as well as two other pools of money owned by Swiss banks. At the time, Swiss investors seemed to be more sophisticated than U.S. investors in hedge funds, but soon endowments became actively involved and interested in that kind of investment. By the late 1980s and early 1990s, McNay handed over much of the responsibility for these funds to James J. Pallotta, who also helped to develop the Essex Preferable Fund. In 1993, following his work at Essex Investment Management, Pallotta moved on to start the Boston office of Paul Tudor Jones's Greenwich, Connecticut-based Tudor Investment Corporation, where he managed Tudor's equity investments, particularly the very successful Raptor Global Funds from 1993 until he left Tudor in May 2009. Over that period of time until 2007, the fund compounded at an annual rate of approximately 15 percent compared with the S&P 500's 6.5 percent. Pallotta's fund suffered badly in 2007 and 2008, declining precipitously from about $11 to $5 billion. In 2008, Pallotta left Tudor and started Raptor Capital Management through which he continued to manage the Raptor Fund. As one report noted, "Jones, a commodities and trend following expert, was never comfortable in the equities world, although he trusted Boston native Pallotta enough to let him work from an office at Rowes Wharf in Boston, about 150 miles from Tudor Investment's Greenwich, Connecticut offices," but in 2008, both decided to part ways.[36]

Another Boston pioneer was Seth Klarman, founder of the Baupost Group, who set up his company in 1983, the year after he graduated from Harvard Business School. Similar in some respects to early venture capital funds and multiple family offices, and different from most hedge funds, Baupost became the investment adviser for four families that had been close friends for many years. "Each of my colleagues," Klarman later wrote, "went out on a long, thin limb to bet on me and my abilities, not only to manage their own money but also that of their families and close friends, which was perhaps the greater act of faith." Over the years, other families (approximately forty in all, creating about seven hundred individual accounts) were added from friends of the original clients, and investments were carried out through several investment partnerships, including one invested in municipal bonds, a mutual fund for clients' smaller accounts, and some institutional managed accounts. Investments have been made in a wide variety of securities and asset classes, ranging from domestic and foreign stocks and bonds to distressed securities, performing and nonperforming bank loans, and other illiquid investments. In 1993, the company set up Baupost Realty Partners, a group of entities to invest in real estate partnerships, properties, and loans, and in the following year, it set up an offshore entity in Bermuda to make investments unavailable to U.S. investors on their own.

Between its founding, when Baupost had only $27 million in assets, and 2011, the company made a return, net of fees, of 19 percent a year. It had steady growth until 2008, the year most hedge funds sharply declined in value, when Baupost actually started doubling its assets to $22 billion over the next two years. This growth was the result of emphasizing risk management, focusing on absolute returns, and practicing value investing within a hedge fund format. As a value investor, Klarman focuses on protecting capital and tends not to invest at all if he cannot find opportunities. As a result, he keeps as much as 40–50 percent of his assets in cash on occasion. He has also stayed away from U.S. stocks for the last two decades, which account for less than 10 percent of his portfolio, because of over-speculation and inflated values. Conservative but unconventional in his investment strategies, Klarman has made unusual investments in unpopular (undervalued, often distressed) assets yet, at the same time, avoids leverage and, unlike typical hedge funds, places only a minimal amount in shorts, finding other ways to hedge. Baupost's investment philosophy was probably best summed up in a 1995 letter to shareholders when Klarman noted that "The Baupost Fund is managed with the intention of earning good absolute returns regardless of how any particular financial market performs. This philosophy is implemented with a bottom-up value investment strategy whereby we hold only those securities that are significantly undervalued, and hold cash when we cannot find alternatives."[37]

Klarman's investment philosophy was developed before he arrived at Harvard Business School. Previously, he worked with value investors Michael Price and Max Heine at the Mutual Shares Fund. Later, he noted that "my learning in two years working with Max and Mike probably eclipsed what I learned in the subsequent two years at Harvard Business School." In 1991, Klarman authored the highly influential *Margin of Safety: Risk-Averse Value Investing Strategies for the Thoughtful Investor,* a book that has become a value-investing classic. In its over two hundred pages, the author describes losing investment strategies and the pitfalls of most investors, and then focuses on his value-investment philosophy and the value-investment process. "Value investing, the strategy of investing in securities trading at an appreciable discount from underlying value, has a long history of delivering excellent investment results with very limited downside risk," he notes. Among the key concepts in his book is the importance of fundamental analysis, and how to determine the liquidation value of tangible assets below which they become attractive assets. "Ideally this will be considered, not a book about investing, but a book about thinking about investing."[38]

During the 1970s and 1980s, some Boston firms, like Wellington and Grantham, Mayo, Van Otterloo, gradually transitioned from mutual funds to pension funds and then from pension funds to hedge funds. By the 1990s and 2000s, as new Boston hedge fund companies emerged, they were quite often founded by former money managers like George Noble (Noble Partners, 1996), Jeffrey Vinik (Vinik Asset Management, 1996), and Paul S. Stuka (Osiris Partners, 2008), all from Fidelity; from other mutual funds like Richard A. Mayo (Mayo Capital Partners, 2002), formerly of Keystone Funds, Batterymarch Financial Management, and Grantham, Mayo, Van Otterloo & Company; or from longtime veterans of Harvard Management Company, such as Jonathon S. Jacobson of Highfields Capital Management (1998), Robert Atchinson and Phill Gross of Adage Capital Management (2001), and Jack Meyer of Convexity Capital Management (2006). As a result, Boston hedge funds have tended to be equity oriented, with investments based on analysis and research like mutual funds and other asset groups typically managed in the city, and different from Klarman's value-investing focus, or that of quant or macro hedge fund managers. And because so many Boston hedge funds have been established by such experienced asset managers, the city tends to have fewer out-of-the-blue start-up hedge funds or the high failure rate of such start-ups as in places like New York or London.[39]

Boston has become a major center for hedge funds in an industry that has tripled its assets from $470 billion to $1.4 trillion between 2000 and 2006. By 2008, there were eight thousand separate funds, but after surviving heavy losses that year, averaging almost 20 percent, the number of funds grew to nine thousand by 2011 with assets of some $2 trillion. While aggregate statistical information about Boston hedge funds is sketchy at best, one 2006 *Boston Globe* report noted that the Hub managed "more than $150 billion in hedge funds and other private investments, about 10 percent of the $1.5 trillion that the Securities and Exchange Commission estimates is held in private funds nationwide." As one lawyer in a major Boston hedge fund practice noted, "Boston has historically been one of the largest players in the hedge-fund industry, because the city has a tremendous pool of talented managers in the financial-services sector," while a Boston University finance professor described how "hedge funds are a natural step for a local financial-service sector that began with insurance companies, then progressed to mutual funds and money-management. The hedge-fund business is a natural outgrowth of the firms that are here, and their people who leave to set up their own firms."[40]

In its first annual postings of the world's largest hedge fund companies, *Institutional Investor* listed a number of Boston firms in its 2003 survey including Tudor Investment Company, half of whose assets came from the Boston-based Raptor Global Portfolio (ranked 11th), Highfields Capital Management (24), Wellington Management (31), Baupost (34), Brookside Capital (44), Numeric Investors (67), K Capital Partners (69), and Sirios Capital Management (96). Over the first two years of these rankings, Boston had five firms in the top 50 and ten in the top 100, or 10 percent of all the leading hedge fund firms worldwide. Using just the Raptor assets from Tudor, the top ten Boston firms had $32.9 billion in assets in 2003, while the top 100 firms had combined assets of $439 billion. As a result, Boston firms accounted for about 7 percent of all assets of the top 100 firms. The following year Boston increased that asset percentage to 7.8 percent.[41]

Another statistical source, Richard Wilson's influential "Hedge Fund Blogger," reported in 2007 that six of the top twenty-five hedge funds were located in Boston: Highfields Capital Management (ranked 3rd), Wellington Management Company (4), Adage Capital Management (11), Baupost Group (17), Brookside Capital Partners (Bain Capital) (18), and Grantham, Mayo, Van Otterloo & Company (25). Only New York City reported more companies in the list (11), with Greenwich, Connecticut, a distant third with three. Boston funds have continued to grow, with Baupost, for instance, tripling its assets to a little over $23 billion between 2007 and 2010.[42]

Data compiled in 2012 and collected by the SEC in the aftermath of the Dodd-Frank financial overhaul law and the financial crisis of 2008 provides some of the most recent information on Boston's hedge fund community. The largest hedge fund managers in Boston are Baupost Group, the fifth largest hedge fund in the United States; Adage Capital Management; Convexity Capital Management; Highfields Capital Management; Wellington Management Company; Grantham, Mayo, Van Otterloo & Company; Sankaty Advisors (Bain Capital); Vinik Asset Management; Brookside Capital (Bain Capital); and Abrams Capital Management. Globally, hedge funds controlled investment pools of at least $2 trillion. While hedge fund assets in Boston were more than $130 billion in total, New York firms held about $760 billion, or 57 percent of the $1.34 trillion managed in the Western Hemisphere. In the United States, Boston ranked behind only the New York–Greenwich, Connecticut, area, and California, two larger and more populous financial centers.[43]

The Wealth Explosion and the Growth of Family Offices

"Not since the late 19th century has America experienced such a flowering of new wealth," noted the lead-in to several articles on this subject in a 2007 periodical. "The surge of dot.com, whiz kids, handsomely paid CEOs, and lavishly rewarded entertainers is transforming everything from the market for private jets to the nature of philanthropy." The merely affluent were doing well, too, though at a somewhat lesser scale. "But while the money is flowing freely, most of it is flowing uphill. As fortunes large and small pile up, there is cause for celebration, and some healthy skepticism too." What had once been the industrial rich and the inherited rich had now become the "Sudden Wealth Syndrome" of "the incidentally rich, the accidentally rich, the golden-parachute rich, the buyout rich, and the lottery rich," and what had once been the luxury of the truly rich is now luxury for all.[44]

While this change has been largely observational, research has shown that income and wealth inequality, based on pretax wage and salary income of households, began to rise in the last quarter of the twentieth century and has returned to levels not seen since before World War I. By World War I, however, the income of the most wealthy started to decline relative to others, and, at the same time, that income was taxed punishingly at nearly 80 percent rates—a pattern that was strikingly reversed later in the century. The return to more inequality of wealth took place in the 1970s, the very time of tremendous economic and financial stress but also the beginnings of significant technological change. In 1973, for instance, the top 1 percent of U.S. households held only 8 percent of U.S. pretax wage and salary income, but this doubled to 16 percent by 2004. At the same time, the top 0.1 percent (annual incomes of about $5 million), or 130,000 households, increased their share of all income from 2 to 7 percent.

An important and singular difference between the two wealth eras was that the top 1 percent of households in the early twentieth century held 40 percent of the nation's private wealth. This was reduced to about 20 percent in the resurgence of wealth at the end of the twentieth century. But there was much that was alike. Each surge corresponded to significant changes in the economy. Likewise, "the [new] working rich have replaced the rentiers at the top of the income distribution." The earlier period represented a rise in industrialism and massive new manufacturing industries; the period closer to our own time reflects an era of technological and information change, the so-called high-tech boom of the 1980s and 1990s, globalization, and financial transformation.[45]

One of the results of the sudden rise of new fortunes was to bolster the creation of many new foundations for various charitable purposes, a topic familiar to the Rockefellers and Carnegies of a century ago, but also to create family investment companies or offices.[46] In addition to new money, there has already been a prodigious rise in generational wealth transfers, which is expected to grow to over $41 trillion during the first half of the twenty-first century. In the Boston metropolitan area, that figure might reach from $1.254 to $4.297 trillion, based on different estimation models.[47] All of these current or pending developments involving family wealth suggest that professional investment management will become even more important in the coming decades, and that the family office or small investment companies may be pivotal institutions in its management.

From a broad, worldwide perspective, the family office has already developed into a complex institution. By 2006, for instance, at least three progressively more intricate offices were recognized by researchers, based on the level of wealth, type of assets, size of the family, and objectives it was to serve. The first category is the administrative family office, for families with assets of $50 million to several hundred million dollars, which employs outside bookkeeping, tax, and administrative services (ranging in cost from $100,000 to $500,000 a year) on an often part-time basis. The hybrid family office, used by families with assets of from about $100 million to $1 billion, often employ family members to pursue strategic and investment functions if the family has expertise in those areas, while many of the administrative functions are handled by office employees or outside sources. Finally, the comprehensive family office, for families whose assets exceed $1 billion, employ in-house expertise on administrative, tax, legal, risk management, and core investment management, but more specialized investments in hedge funds, venture capital, private equity, and emerging market investments are likely outsourced. The overhead for each type of office rises substantially. Administrative offices have overhead of about $500,000, hybrid offices up to $2 million or more, while comprehensive offices might run as high as $10 million per year.[48]

While family offices may be relatively new in other parts of the country and the world, they have been around in Boston for more than a century, though perhaps not as elaborate or structured as those described above. Bostonians have had their own personal financial advisers ever since the early nineteenth century, when families used Boston trustees to handle their financial affairs. During the first half of the twentieth century, the private Boston trustee model began to change and expand in several directions. Some trustees remained private trustees; other men of wealth and experience in investing opened family offices, while a few became corporate trustees. This last kind of investment company could set up common trust funds (an investment pool) for their clients that private trustees could not. In Boston, these organizations ran and still run the gamut: some were and are more or less pure family offices for a single family, while others are much larger in size and service a number of clients and their needs, from legal work and estate planning to investment management. Family offices in Boston are "all so different," noted one family office partner. "We do have the same objectives here, and we don't hire nannies or buy symphony tickets, run the chauffeurs, or walk the dogs, or things like that." No matter what form they take, the purpose of these offices has been to conserve and appreciate family wealth.[49]

The complex history, organization, and role of family offices reveal how important they have been throughout modern Boston history. "Boston is a club, everyone knows everyone," one private trustee remarked, while a corporate trustee exclaimed that the area around 35 Congress Street "was a little bit of a dormitory for family offices." And although they are not familiar with each other's business, they are aware of their place and role in the Boston financial community. Family offices in Boston are a mix of organizations, with very different histories. "Each office is a little different." As a result, the Boston family office is more of a concept than a single kind of entity, because it actually reflects several different types of organizations. All of them, as one private trustee remarked, are unique creatures, and even the descriptions of them below do not give them full justice. They include at least three general or generic kinds of offices—the single family office, the private trustee, and the corporate trustee—with ascending numbers of clients, larger assets, and more staff and services. Despite their size, in most ways it is impossible to distinguish them from a small- to medium-sized investment company, and all are regulated by the SEC as investment companies. By most accounts, their numbers in Boston are growing, reflecting new wealth in the area from early postwar venture capital and the rise of local computer hardware companies in the 1970s, to more recent financial fortunes from other kinds of business enterprise.

Examples of the first type of organization, the single family office (which might also include collateral families) include Saltonstall & Company, whose wealth came from Peter Chardon Brooks's fortune in eighteenth- and nineteenth-century marine insurance, and later from Chicago real estate. The office has a managing and an administrative partner, and receives some investment advice from outside; it also has tax, legal, and estate work done on the outside. Some other old line offices include the Lee Family Office, from the Lee family of Lee, Higginson & Company, a Boston investment banking company established in 1849; and Cabot-Wellington, the family office of Thomas D. Cabot of Cabot Corporation, a Boston company that produces various performance materials and specialty chemicals for industry. Other offices set up for a single family include the Brandegee family office, primarily to manage the assets of the William F. Weld (1800–1881), a fortune he created as a trader, importer, western railroad entrepreneur, and ship owner (the largest one in the country at the time), and the Ayer family office, created by Frederick Ayer and his fortune in patent medicines and textiles. Some more recently created ones include the offices of Amos Hostetter Jr., a Boston venture capitalist, and Edward C. Johnson III of Fidelity Investments.

Some family offices are private trustee offices that serve more than one family. For instance, Nicholas & Pratt (1977) is a combination of former law firm trust clients and family money (Standard Oil), serving various needs for its clients including trusteeship, estate planning, law, and investing. Another private trustee is the Howland family office, which goes back to China trade fortunes but since 1967 has been known as Howland Capital Management and has an expanded clientele. Others include the Woodstock Corporation and Boston Financial Management, which manage assets of the Paine family acquired through ownership of Paine, Webber brokerage and underwriting firm, among other clients. J. M. Forbes & Company, another office, began as John Murray Forbes's trading and investment company in the 1830s when he was principally involved in the China trade. Forbes continued to invest broadly throughout the nineteenth century, in railroads, land, and minerals, and by the 1880s, he had established numerous trusts for family members, which were managed by the company. The company continues to actively invest, and functions as a family office but with an expanded clientele. Another multi-client Boston investment company, the North American Management Company, was originally established in 1928 as the Stone family office, which had ties to Hayden, Stone & Company, a Boston securities firm founded in 1892.

The third type of Boston family is the one run by corporate trustees. According to one account, this type of Boston fiduciary relationship began in the 1920s, when Robert Gardiner transformed his family office, which was started in the 1880s, into a corporate trust called Fiduciary Trust. Under the legislation of that era, Gardiner was able to set up what has come to be known as a limited purpose trust company, under which he could conduct his fiduciary business without having to accept deposits, make loans, or generally carry on a banking business. In a word, Massachusetts law "permitted the establishment of trust companies that did not have to offer loans, mortgages and savings accounts and all those kinds of things." This form of organization had certain advantages. One was that it could set up a common investment trust to manage the assets of many more (and also smaller) clients than a private trustee. It also allowed Fiduciary Trust and other trust companies like it to appoint successor trustees for accounts, and thus to carry on the same fiduciary relationship beyond a single generation. While very few trust company charters have been granted that do not require full banking responsibilities, several older companies have them, including Welch & Forbes and Loring, Wolcott & Coolidge, discussed in chapter 3.

Another aspect of family offices has been their expansion far beyond Boston. This had been increasingly true throughout the twentieth century, but more acutely evident by the twenty-first century. One trustee boasted that "I have more business from Ohio than I do from Massachusetts, because the fortunes were so much bigger." But as old offices expand nationally, newer offices, often called wealth managers, are being set up to handle the wealth created in Boston following the area's economic expansion over the last few decades, which have included fortunes made in high-tech, venture capital, private equity, financial services, and biotech, or in encouraging family wealth to come to Boston where there is an wide array of new family investment advisers.

Boston has also become an important center in modernizing the family office, such as CCC Alliance, a national consortium of family offices in Boston's Financial District. The organization, which started out as two family offices created from Standard Oil and Pittsburgh Plate Glass fortunes, helps share best practices among family offices and combines buying power for some ninety family offices around the world, each with over $100 million in assets. Another development has come from Boston law firms, long a source of Boston trustees. Firms like Choate, Hall & Stewart have created Choate Investment Advisors with a family office approach to wealth management rather than a lawyer-trustee model that seeks investment advice from the outside. For Choate, "multigenerational wealth is the key, because we are trying to provide a true family office experience for people" in the $5–100 million market. A trust administrator coordinates operations for each client and arranges for the services of a team of over fifty people, including lawyers, investment professionals, tax preparers, trust and estate administrators, and support staff, with no proprietary products or hidden fees. Choate oversees over $2 billion in assets of high-net-worth individuals and families, but they are not alone in developing this new wealth market.

Boston wealth managers, often called fee-only registered investment advisers or RIAs, generally rank highly nationwide, but such rankings use different measurements, making for little or no uniformity in those ratings. In a recent *Forbes* survey, for instance, six Boston firms were among the top fifty in terms of discretionary assets. Among them were SCS Capital Management (4), Calibre Advisory Services (13), Welch & Forbes (15), Athena Capital Advisors

(37), Silver Bridge (43), and Choate Investment Advisors (46). Most of *Forbes*'s list was widely scattered geographically, with New York having only two more than Boston. Companies that provided value-added service included other Boston firms like Shepherd Kaplan; Loring, Wolcott & Coolidge Fiduciary Advisors; Eaton Vance Investment Counsel; GW & Wade; and Ballentine Partners, again with New York City scoring a few more firms than Boston in the rankings. Other ranking sources, like Bloomberg's *Wealth Manager Magazine,* use average AUM per client and have included still more Boston firms like Federal Street Advisors, Reynders, McVeigh Capital Management, and RINET Company. While these ranking sources seem to indicate that there is a critical mass of these firms in Boston, they do not account for the concentration and numbers of them in the very small geographic area that makes up Boston. The large numbers of investment managers and organizations, as well as their concentration in Boston, has been and will continue to be an important aspect of this four-century-old story.[50]

CHAPTER 12

Thinking Long Term: Boston's Place in Investment Management

Looking back from a four-hundred-year perspective, investment management in Boston has not been an unbroken string of successes. There have been notable failures as well, and they tell us something about both Boston and the management of wealth in Boston. Earlier in this book, we saw how the brokerage business, which combined retail securities sales with securities underwriting and investment banking, became an important activity in Boston and had broad influence throughout the country. By the early twentieth century, however, that second part of the business had begun to decline as New York became the principal underwriting and investment banking center of the country. Boston's role in investment banking came to a virtual halt following the stock market crash of 1929 and the demise of one of Boston's most storied firms.

Another development in Boston, this time during the second half of the twentieth century, was the decline of the city's important role in commercial banking. While commercial (and savings and trust) banks were all affected by downturns in the economy in the 1980s and 1990s, which led to cycles of mergers and acquisitions (or "rollups") during the period, these consolidations allowed two small, Rhode Island banks to take over control of nearly all long-standing Boston banking institutions. There then emerged a further period of consolidation, primarily in the 2000s, which led to control of Boston banking by national banking concerns. Both of these stories merit some discussion.

Rise and Demise

During much of the twentieth century, a number of the city's local brokerage houses, many whose names were almost household words across the country fifty or even twenty-five years ago, moved their headquarters or principal operations to New York. In 1893, for instance, Boston directories listed various well-known local companies and their addresses, including Hayden, Stone & Company; Estabrook & Company; Tucker, Anthony & Company; R. L. Day & Company; Hornblower & Weeks; Lee, Higginson & Company; Jackson & Curtis; Moors & Cabot; Kidder, Peabody & Company; Paine, Webber & Company; F. S. Moseley & Company; and H. C. Wainwright & Company, located principally along State, Congress, and Devonshire Streets in the heart of Boston's financial district. Within about two decades, however, many of these companies were beginning to change, some through a readjustment of their business activities in Boston and others through migration to New York due to the rise of industrial stocks, the need to raise more capital, and the growing underwriting business in New York. A parallel development was the rise of the New York Stock Exchange and decline of Boston's exchange near the beginning of the twentieth century. While the Boston exchange predominated in the nineteenth century with its listings of manufacturing stocks, such as textile mill securities, New York rose in the new era of large-scale, national industrial expansion, with such companies as U.S. Steel, General Electric, and American Telephone & Telegraph, the latter two having previously been tied to Boston.[1]

Paine, Webber's history epitomizes this transition. A Boston firm founded in 1880, it was not until 1916 that the company opened its first office in New York to handle business that had previously been done over its private "wires" with a number of leading New York houses that acted as correspondents. As a prelude of things to come, "by January, 1916, the volume of this business had increased to the point at which it became evident that Paine, Webber & Company should open their own New York office in order to clear these transactions themselves." By 1930, the New York office had much larger quarters and employed 375 people who worked under the direction of four resident partners, one of whom was also a governor of the New York Stock Exchange. By comparison, the Boston office, though much expanded, had only 170 employees at the same time.[2]

Unlike a number of Boston brokerages, it was not until the 1920s that Paine, Webber entered the investment banking business. The company fared well until the Great Depression; in June 1942, it merged with another Boston brokerage firm, Jackson & Curtis, which had been started by Charles Cabot Jackson and

Laurence Curtis in July 1879. The merged firm, called Paine, Webber, Jackson & Curtis, had twenty-two branch offices around the country. Paine, Webber continued to keep a strong presence in Boston, with its offices on the tenth through twelfth floors of 24 Federal Street, but eventually it moved its headquarters to New York in 1963. Seven years later, it was incorporated as PaineWebber, and made its initial public offering in 1974. During the 1970s, it acquired a number of investment research and advisory firms and security companies, many in the wake of the "May Day" demise of the traditional fixed minimum brokerage fee structure in 1975. In effect, PaineWebber and other retail stockbrokers found, following the change in fee structure, that their revenue now depended on *selling advice* (and their own securities), rather than just *selling general securities* and providing free advice. By 1980, the company had 161 branch offices in 42 states and 6 Asian and European offices, and in the 1990s, it acquired Kidder, Peabody & Company from General Electric. In November 2000, it was merged into the United Bank of Switzerland (known as UBS), and in 2003, the name PaineWebber disappeared from the corporate rolls.[3]

Other Boston firms of "bankers and brokers" that did not migrate to New York were soon merged into larger financial conglomerates, a number of them from New York, following the consequences of May Day 1975. For instances, Hornblower & Weeks was acquired by Loeb, Rhoades & Company in 1977, while White Weld & Company was sold to Merrill Lynch in 1978. After several mergers in which it was the lead player, Hayden, Stone & Company, a major securities firm, finally fell in 1981 when it was acquired by Shearson American Express. Another widely respected Boston firm, Tucker Anthony & R. L. Day, became part of John Hancock Financial in 1982, was then spun off in 1996, and became part of the Royal Bank of Canada's RBC Dain Rauscher in 2001. As one young Boston PaineWebber employee of that period observed, stock brokerages just "started disappearing," never to be seen again.[4]

Of course, much of Boston's investment banking business was long gone before these events. Indeed, the denouement occurred following the crash when another Boston investment banking company, Lee, Higginson & Company, succumbed early in the early 1930s, a casualty of a poor and highly optimistic investment in the Swedish match monopoly. Since then, there has not been a strong investment banking presence in Boston. In 2007, for instance, a listing of the Boston area's largest investment banks showed that the top fourteen were predominantly branches of New York firms, with a few from Canada and London, and none from Boston. Local Boston firms did hold eight of the next eleven positions in the city's top twenty-five investment banking firms, but the value and number of their deals were miniscule and insignificant by comparison.[5]

While the decline of securities brokerage and investment banking was gradual and, after a time, predictable, the story of Boston's commercial banks was an entirely different matter. Boston banks grew, multiplied, and flourished during the nineteenth and early twentieth centuries because they were, unlike in other sections of the country, relatively conservative and stable institutions that withstood the frequent economic panics of that era. By the turn of the last century, Boston possessed more banks and twice the capital of New York banks. In the pre- and early post–World War II era, there were four major Boston Banks—First National, Merchants, National Shawmut, and State Street. First National's assets made it the country's fifth largest bank, with additional major foreign business in Latin America. What was different in Boston was not the major consolidation of local banks that took place from the 1970s onward, or even the loss of Boston headquarters for the national banks. Those developments occurred in most major U.S. cities as well.[6] Boston was exceptional in that those developments were preceded by the acquisition of the major Boston banks by two relatively small Rhode Island banks in the late twentieth century. This unique history may tell us more about Boston's place and growth in investment management than any other developments.

From about 1970s on, various natural forces led to the consolidation of smaller banks into larger ones, and to economic and legal events that forced the same process. From a national perspective, the 1980s was a period of deregulation, including the passage of the Depository Institutions Deregulation and Monetary Control Act of 1980. Among other things, the act swept away years of deposit rate controls, after which banks could compete with market rates and thereby keep up with the high interest rates money market funds offered to customers. The Garn–St. Germain Act of 1982, in turn, created new kinds of investment opportunities for thrift institutions. That same year, a bill was introduced in the U.S. Senate to create the first regional interstate banking compact in the country, and another to "harmonize the powers of state-chartered thrift and commercial banks." Full interstate banking had become a focal point of interest by the late 1980s.[7]

New England, however, was already ahead of this trend. By the early 1980s, New England states had set up under reciprocal laws the merger of banks of different New England states. The first of these mergers took place in 1984 between Boston's Bank of New England, the fourth largest bank in the region, and CBT Corporation, the holding company for Connecticut Bank and Trust Company, the third largest banking group in New England, with $6.1 billion in assets. Despite some legal tussles by other banks, the merger was completed in 1985. Not to be outdone, other banks like First National, renamed the Bank of Boston in 1982 (and then shortened again to BankBoston), soon acquired regional banks in Connecticut and Vermont.

This was a sharp contrast from only a couple of decades earlier, when Massachusetts banks had been prohibited from operating in more than a single county. That restriction was soon lifted to the extent a Massachusetts bank could operate branches within a 40-mile radius of the bank's main office, regardless of county lines. Interstate banking beyond New England and on a national scale would take another decade and a half until the end of the century before it was fully implemented. The interstate restrictions (and need for state permission) were repealed by the Riegle-Neal Interstate Banking and Branching Efficiency Act of 1994, which allowed full interstate banking throughout the country, subject to certain conditions and regardless of state law, while additional limitations were removed five years later in the Gramm-Leach-Bliley Act.[8]

As the law helped the process of consolidation, so did economic events. While the savings and loan scandal of the late 1980s and early 1990s, involving the over-extension of credit for mortgages, was focused on the U.S. South and West, the real estate collapse also affected Massachusetts banks, particularly the Bank of New England, which had only recently emerged as New England's first regional bank.[9] The New England banking crisis started in September 1988, and by the end of the following year, losses at the Bank of New England topped $1 billion. In the aftermath of aggressive growth and acquisition strategies that the bank undertook in the 1980s, which contributed to these losses, the bank was eventually seized by the Federal Deposit Insurance Corporation (FDIC) in 1991, with its assets distributed largely to Fleet National Bank of Providence, Rhode Island, which was looking for a beachhead into the Boston market. The sale had momentous consequences not seen at the time. Lawrence K. Fish, who ran the beleaguered bank for the FDIC, suggested almost twenty years later that "if it had been sold to the old First National Bank of Boston [i.e., BankBoston], which was one of its competitors, who knows . . . it might have created something that survived" as a national bank in Boston. During the 1990s, there was further consolidation in Boston: Harvard Trust and BayBanks became part of BankBoston, and National Shawmut Bank was merged into Fleet National Bank in December 1995—the latter seen as another lost opportunity for BankBoston to become a national bank and Boston a U.S. banking center. State Street, the only other strong local bank left following this fracas, had largely shed its commercial banking/branch office business by selling it to another outsider from Providence—Citizens Bank—as it took on the role of a global custody bank.[10]

Citizens Bank had started doing business in 1828 as the High Street Bank in Providence. In 1988, when it was acquired by the Royal Bank of Scotland, it was still a small savings bank. By 1992, it was being run by Lawrence K. Fish, who had worked for First National Bank of Boston for nearly twenty years in various international capacities and had previously presided over the breakup of the Bank of New England. His new position in an outside (of Boston) bank gave him "a platform and capital" just as other banks in the region were coming out of a banking depression. Citizens followed a much different strategy in its roll-up of New England banks than Fleet would. It made smaller, step-by-step transactions in the middle tier area of the regional banking industry, including many local savings and trust banks. Its bigger break came in 1999 when Fleet acquired BankBoston. This moved Citizens to first approach State Street Bank to acquire their commercial banking operations. Citizens also acquired U.S. Trust of Boston, a Boston bank that had previously acquired branches of BayBank when they were divested by BankBoston. As a result of all of these actions, Boston had only two large commercial banks by 2001, both of which operated in most of the New England states but were headquartered in Providence—not Boston. Providence had become what Boston should or at least might have been. After 2001, under strong local leadership and with foreign backing, Citizens expanded into the mid-Atlantic, buying Mellon Bank's commercial operations in Pennsylvania, and then going on into the Midwest. Even after the merger of Fleet with Bank of America in 2005, Citizens remained Boston's second largest banking institution with $153 billion in assets and 23,000 employees in twelve northeastern states.[11]

Fleet's arrival in Boston came under far different circumstances and was largely the work of Terrence ("Terry") Murray, the son of a Rhode Island factory worker. The younger Murray dropped out of school but later returned, worked the night shift at a textile mill, and then went on to Harvard. He started his banking career at Providence's Industrial National Bank, helping to transform it, first by renaming it Fleet, then by buying up other banks, beginning with Norstar Bancorp of Albany, New York, in 1988. As interstate banking took off in the early 1990s, New England banks were concerned about buyouts or roll-ups by New York banks, but were more sanguine about New England mergers, giving Murray open season on a growing number of potential acquisitions in the region. He was able to get a toehold in Boston with the demise of the Bank of New England. With the financial backing of Kohlberg Kravis Roberts, Murray was able to outbid BankBoston and Bank of America for the doomed bank's assets. The move made Fleet a player in future Boston bank mergers. A few years later, Murray stepped into merger negotiations between BankBoston and National Shawmut, Boston's remaining large commercial bank of the postwar era, and succeeded in acquiring Shawmut for Fleet. BankBoston's response was to acquire BayBanks, an up-and-coming, highly innovative retail Boston bank. But by 1999, BankBoston finally capitulated to the Rhode Island bank, after an investment banking acquisition BankBoston made became too expensive to justify, and its South American banking business, by then a century old, began to falter. BankBoston became the "451st stand-alone bank to be swallowed in the Fleet maw."[12]

By the time of the Great Recession of 2007–2009, Boston banking had been largely consolidated and reduced to a few major players from out of town—including the United Kingdom, Spain, and Canada.[13] The consolidation fell in line with a general nationwide trend over the last twenty years during which 17,345 federally insured banks and thrifts declined to 8,534. The only bright spot for the local Boston banking scene was that the head of Bank of America, now Boston's largest bank but headquartered in North Carolina, was Brian Moynihan, who had previous worked at FleetBoston. He became president with the help of Bostonians who served on the national bank's board, but Moynihan's rise was largely because of his work as a lawyer and the generalist skills he developed in mastering the complexities of modern banking, not taking on the role of a traditional banker. Perhaps the reason why Boston lacked a next generation of banking leadership in the late twentieth century was that young Bostonians—both home-grown and newly minted—headed to careers in venture capital, private equity, money management, and hedge funds instead, where the work was seen as more exciting and personally rewarding.[14]

The Ascent of Investment Management in Boston

Despite this lack of total symmetry in Boston's financial story, it has seen remarkable development over four centuries. Bringing with them a shared sense of fiduciary responsibilities from their medieval and English past, Bostonians and other New Englanders carefully guarded the assets of their churches, schools, and benevolent and mutual benefit societies in the seventeenth and eighteenth centuries. Before the industrial revolution, wealth in these institutions was modest, usually consisting of land, cash, and other valuables like silver, or money collected in the form of a premium. Fiduciaries, in turn, rented out land for a fee or money at interest. In a few instances, institutions might be given large grants of land in the New England hinterlands, a monopoly right like an exclusive privilege to ferry passengers across a river for which they could charge a fee, or a direct infusion of cash by the colony.

Even though Massachusetts was a predominantly agricultural society, wealth in the form of securities was not just limited to institutions. By the 1780s, for instance, decedents' wills and inventories outside Boston began to list shares of stock in bridges, turnpikes, banks, insurance companies, and other business enterprises, and soon thereafter state and federal government notes as well—a transformation that had become widespread by the 1830s. Even earlier, these rural Massachusetts inhabitants had loaned money at interest to others in complex sets of relationships that extended far beyond their own local communities. Wealth and its management were becoming important concerns for many, and especially in Boston, where personal fortunes grew, were becoming more concentrated and derived from new sources of income.

The revolution marked an important turning point, not only in moving from colony to nation but in providing additional kinds of assets, including state and federal government debt. The postrevolutionary period marked the beginning of state banks and, for a time, a national bank, whose shares provided an important source of income for a rising group of share owners. With the growth of industry, particularly in textile mills, stock shares and bonds became important sources of wealth and soon part of the investment portfolios of both institutions and individuals. The endowments of Harvard, Yale, and Dartmouth dramatically show this transition from assets in land and cash bequests to stocks and bonds in railroads and mining companies over the first two centuries following settlement.

Knowledgeable in how to gather and manage assets, Bostonians and New Englanders alike sought ways to increase wealth. From the late eighteenth to the late nineteenth century, enterprising Bostonians created new wealth through far-flung trade with China, India, and other remote destinations. This was followed by a slightly younger group of entrepreneurs who founded New England's woolen and cotton mills. Both groups contributed to a third wave of enterprise that invested in railroads and mineral wealth, both before and after the Civil War. As wealth increased, so did the need for outside financial management services. One of the first such service was the uniquely Boston institution, the so-called Boston trustee. The trustee's role was to manage this new wealth, often after the death of the wealth creator. Protected by Massachusetts's unique legal views on trusteeship, Boston trustees guarded the fortunes of families well into the twentieth century, when much of this work was taken over by corporate trustees or family offices that continued to approach trusts in ways unique to Boston and the commonwealth.

During the nineteenth and twentieth centuries, others also provided investment management services. Trust companies were first established after the Civil War and reached their zenith around the turn of the century, providing investment management to a broader group of wealthy Bostonians than those serviced by Boston trustees. Many of the leading brokerage and underwriting firms got started in Boston in the nineteenth century, and they too advised their clients on portfolios well into the late twentieth century. Boston's stable, conservative, and numerous banks helped their customers with their investments. As the number of securities grew in the early twentieth century, a new group of younger Bostonians created another service, investment counsel, which quickly became popular in other parts of the country as well.

While the trust or fiduciary relationship was important in many of these activities, the trust itself became an important organizing mechanism for raising capital. A product primarily of Massachusetts case law, the so-called Massachusetts business trust concept was used to form the Boston Personal Property Trust in 1893, and the first mutual fund, the Massachusetts Investors Trust, in 1924. While small in the 1920s, mutual funds survived the crash and depression, and dwarfed in size the closed-end investment trusts that had once held sway in the investment community. Boston became the center of the mutual fund industry throughout the twentieth century, combining an easy-to-understand investment concept with the perception that Boston invested conservatively and with "prudence."

At the same time that the mutual fund was becoming popular, the New England economy was decaying. Since the revolution, Boston had developed an economic system based on commerce and both small and large industry, but by the early twentieth century, much of this had dissipated and the region was in decline. At the turn of the twentieth century, newer local companies like General Electric and American Telephone & Telegraph were moving their operations to New York, and Boston's premier stock exchange was being surpassed by the one in New York. In addition, the vast textile mills of the countryside surrounding Boston were closing down or moving to the South. Having worried about decline or "declension" since the mid-seventeenth century, Bostonians and New Englanders alike sought ways to revive and rejuvenate the mid-twentieth-century local economy.

One of the earliest attempts to regenerate it was through venture capital—providing funds to help grow new companies. Long before there were investments in so-called high-tech companies, organizations like American Research & Development (AR&D) began investing in enterprises that were perceived to have a strong future but needed some financial aid, perhaps for many years. A number of leading Boston banks—some with a number of highly specialized lending groups—also used bank loans in the 1950s and 1960 to subsidize ventures around Boston. Venture capital hit its stride in 1968 when Digital Equipment Company in Maynard, Massachusetts, went public. AR&D made 550 times its original investment in the company that year, creating the first "grand slam" in venture capital investment, the Holy Grail that others sought in the years that followed. By that time, the term *venture capital* had also come to be associated with high-tech enterprises.

During the remaining decades of the last century, asset management (and investment and financial services generally) and high-tech (and information technology) were joined by higher education and healthcare, two sectors that grew during and after World War II due to massive infusions of federal money, to form the core segments of Boston's and the region's new economy. Each of these sectors played a key role in advancing the interests of the others. It is a cluster of activities that Professor Michael E. Porter of Harvard Business School has noted "would be the envy of most nations." In Boston's investment world, as this new local economy grew, venture capital and later-stage private equity rose in importance—first locally, then nationally, and now even globally. During the 1970s and early 1980s, many of Boston's investment counsel firms and its mutual fund companies began managing pension funds from all over the country; these funds have grown almost exponentially over the last few decades.[15]

Wealth created from Boston's high-tech industry, such as computer hardware in the 1970s and 1980s, has led to a new generation of family wealth in the area and the creation of family offices and similar investment management organizations to handle Boston's new wealth. That wealth has also been used to create new private equity and hedge funds in Boston.[16] Success in all of these enterprises has helped to attract wealth from outside Boston needing to be managed. So significant was the rise of this activity that by the mid-1990s, several leading surveys determined that Boston was one of the world leaders in investment management—behind only New York, London, and Tokyo.[17] In the United States, Boston has been ranked over time first or second in size in nearly every form of investment management, although New York outranks Boston in the sheer quantity of assets managed.[18]

Despite the ebb and flow of events and rankings, Boston and, when states are compared, Massachusetts are among the leaders in various investment management categories. For instance, one 2010 survey ranked Boston as one of three global financial service centers in the United States (along with New York and San Francisco) and among eight worldwide; it is home to three of the top ten retirement money managers, "making it the number one cluster of market leaders." In comparison with other states, Massachusetts is the third largest mutual fund center based on assets under management (21 percent), with New York and California just slightly ahead; it is third in the number of private equity firms behind only California and New York, and home to two of the top ten private equity firms based on total funds raised over the last ten years. It is also third in hedge funds (and funds of funds) assets under management, behind New York and Connecticut, with eighty-two firms that manage about $1 trillion in assets. It has the fourth largest number of venture capital firms (101), behind California, New York, and Texas, and is the country's leader in savings banks' total deposits. It has one of the top two custodial banks not just in the United States, but throughout the world. It even has a presence in the insurance industry. Investment management in Boston takes on even more significance when comparing the relatively small size of the city to its nearby archrival, New York City, or the country's most populous state, California. For its size, it is a concentration of activity unmatched by any place in the country.[19]

The Changing Economic Complexity of Boston
The growth of investment management employment in Boston and the Hub's relative size, which has only intensified the significance of this profession's importance, requires a closer statistical look at changes over the past half century. Although most statistical sources are far from complete—often too specific or not specific enough, and using different sets of data that do not correspond to one another—employment in Boston's financial services sector, which is a much broader category than investment management, as a whole grew significantly in the 1970s, 1980s, and 1990s. Statistics kept by the Commonwealth of Massachusetts help to show this progression. These figures provide a useful impression of employment growth but are not entirely accurate because the Standard Industrial Classification system (SIC), the then-prevalent system that categorized the work of employees, treats each of them according to the specific kind work they do rather than the business in which they work. Even a modest mutual fund company, for example, has a number of separate operations, ranging from portfolio management to fund administration work (like data processing) to selling fund shares. Trying to develop sound data on employment in Boston financial services became even more difficult in 1997 when the United States and the U.S. Census adopted NAICS, the North American Industry Classification System, a more detailed breakdown of employment classifications. Given such caveats, it is still possible to show, at least in broad terms, the growth of Boston's financial services industry over four decades as detailed in table 7.

Over this longer period, reflected in table 7, Boston financial services—as measured by employment in depository institutions, nondepository institutions, security and commodity brokers, and holding and other investment offices—more than doubled, as it did in Massachusetts as a whole. Even greater growth took place just outside of Boston—in Cambridge, Wellesley, Waltham, and other locations—as investment management in particular (areas like venture capital and some private equity) expanded beyond the geographical boundaries of Boston. A report compiled by the Boston Planning and Economic Development Office also states that by 1996, statewide financial

Table 7. Job Growth in the Financial Services Industry, 1967–1995, in Massachusetts

AREA	1967	1990	1995
Boston	22,854	40,540	47,054
Metropolitan Region	32,641	76,170	83,197
Massachusetts	46,625	103,069	102,255
Banking	38,218	76,887	67,050
Investment	8,407	26,182	35,205

Sources: *Investing in Jobs: A Report on the Financial Services Industry—Its Importance to Boston, the Metropolitan Region, and the State* (Boston: Boston Planning and Economic Development Office, 1996), 7, which is based on data in Massachusetts Department of Employment and Training, ES-202 (Employment Security 202 Series), passim.

services as a whole was a $7.5 billion industry. Boston claimed $3.45 billion of that figure and 46 percent of the jobs. Boston's 47,000 financial service jobs had a payroll of $3.2 billion, which contributed $155 million in state income taxes.[20]

Other data over specific periods of time provide insights into the growth of Boston's financial services. Some refined census data, entitled *County Business Patterns,* show significant growth took place from the mid-1960s to mid-1970s. Financial services in this data include banking, credit agencies other than banks, security and commodity brokers and services, and holding and other investment companies. Between 1964 and 1973, those groups grew from 38,068 to 47,697 workers, a rise of 125 percent, and from 9.4 to 10.6 percent of employment in Suffolk County; Boston's economy constituted about 95 percent of Suffolk County's economy.[21]

Another report for financial services (banking, insurance, and securities and brokers) between 1988 and 1994 notes that the sector lost 7,000 jobs in that period, but remained nearly constant at 119,000 from 1991 to 1993, and then rose to 125,000 in 1994. These overall figures, however, did not correspond with the securities industry (including investment companies), which grew every year between 1988 and 1994 from 18,827 to 28,358, an increase of nearly 51 percent.[22]

Employment statistics since 2000 are difficult to obtain because they have become even more complex since 1997 when NAICS was inaugurated. But using just one important NAICS subclassification, NAICS 5239, other financial investment activities, which covers some of the actual investment functions, employment under that category increased from 15,421 in Boston in 2001 to 19,539 in 2011, a jump of 27 percent, despite two financial crises at the beginning and end of the decade.[23] While figures are not available for the Boston Metropolitan Statistical Area during this period, employment in this subcategory increased throughout the state from 19,900 to 26,683 over that period, a rise of a little over 34 percent.[24]

The most recent study of the Massachusetts economy, which was published in 2010, discussed the state's financial sector and included insurance, banking, venture capital, hedge funds, private equity, mutual funds, and pension management. That sector was responsible for 170,000 jobs in the commonwealth, or 5.4 percent of the total state employment. Together these industries contributed $35.5 billion in gross state product (GSP), or 10 percent of the state's output. The sector also provided the "backbone" of Massachusetts's economy along with for-profit information technology (4.6 percent of state employment) and life sciences (2.1 percent) industries, as well as two not-for-profit industries, healthcare (16.4 percent) and education (10.8 percent). Finance also directly affected other industries, such as legal services and consulting services, all of which contributed another 5.4 percent of the state's employment. While the number of finance jobs fell by 2 percent from 2005 to 2009 in Massachusetts, they fell even further in states like New York (5 percent) and California (16 percent). Massachusetts's finance industry contributed over 30 percent of the taxes from businesses during those five years.[25]

While these figures collectively show trends in employment over the last five decades, perhaps a more definitive measure of importance is the *concentration* of investment management in Boston compared to its only U.S. rival, New York City. By the mid-1970s, New York City had a population sixteen times the size of Boston, but Boston managed fully one-third of the mutual fund capital in the country. As one contemporary account noted, "Few cities in the U.S., or indeed abroad, can match the concentration of people engaged in the vocation of professional investment management as those brought together by Boston's many insurance companies, bank trust departments, investment company complexes, universities and endowment funds, trust-oriented law firms and investment advisory and brokerage houses."[26] So when Boston ranks second to New York in, say, the number of leading U.S. money management companies, those Boston companies play a more significant role and have far more influence in the economic life of the Hub than do their counterparts in New York.

One final perspective on Boston's growth as an investment center has been the sheer increase in recent years of money, not just within Boston but also that has come to Boston to be invested. Indeed, one Boston trustee recently noted that he has more clients in one midwestern state than he does in Boston, while the head of an investment counsel and mutual fund company calculates that 80 percent of his firm's clients are from outside of Boston. Why is Boston such a major money management city? Why is it such a magnet for outside money? Why does any company that needs money managed "have to come to Boston"? "I suppose it's a tradition," money manager George Lewis explained. "Boston isn't a bad place to live, and did anybody expect Fidelity and Wellington and Putnam to grow as big as they did? ... I think the market expanded. There was a lot more money around, so where was it going to go? On one hand, they prospered where the banks and Scudders and other ones went the other way [i.e., to their demise], but maybe it's integrity or trust that Boston has been known . . . [for] . . . the Boston trustees. I don't know. Maybe we're riding on a tattered coattail." Maybe luck was an important element in Boston's growth, but in a typical Boston understated sentiment, luck may not last forever.[27]

Professional Life in the Hub

Boston is small enough and its investment management business so concentrated that it has created a unique culture in the Hub. In the 1970s and 1980s, for instance, Boston was viewed by investment managers as competitive but friendly, a place where perhaps the city's top money managers talked to one another to share information, though not on specific securities they bought and sold. As one investment manager noted, "Boston was small enough and independent enough to do this, and still does to some extent." "There was a common ground and a common history" made up of working in professional groups, following practices like the "prudent man" rule and the affirmation of other long-held beliefs. It was and is a culture framed by the buy side rather than the sell or transactional side of the investment business, and an open and inquiring attitude and intellectual curiosity about investment management as a profession. That attitude remains. One private equity manager recently commented, "I've always found people in the town very forthcoming. If you ask them questions about how they handle certain things, they'll share the sort of evolution of their thinking on these things. So I think it's great. I think the town has a lot to be proud of."[28]

Over the years, Boston's investment community established a number of social and professional groups. Around the turn of the twentieth century, Boston trustees often met at the Boston City Club on Ashburton Place. By the late 1950s, it was a "favorite meeting spot where prudent men gather for a quiet lunch and conversation about investments." Before its move in the early 1900s to its modern quarters, members could only enter the club at its older location "though the washroom." Another Boston club, the Downtown Club (not to be confused with the Harvard Downtown Club), flourished before and after the war, and had members from other financial institutions other than investment management, including banking and insurance. Even as late as the early 1970s, a *Boston Globe* columnist described the city's financial community as a homogeneous group: "They eat at the same clubs, sometimes creating small associations like The Long Table Syndicate, which meets several times a year at the Union Club, or for investment purposes like the Twenty Trust, where they pool their own money."

Nevertheless, the oldest lunch club in Boston was the Central Luncheon

Club, formed in 1875, which merged with the City Club Corporation fourteen years later. The "Lunch Club," as it was called, was located in an old house on Central Street in the middle of the Financial District until 1958, when it moved two blocks away to 4 Liberty Square on the seventh floor. While frequented by professionals of all stripes in the financial district, the club had an almost unique seating arrangement. According to one visitor, "the seating was at long tables and more or less by age, the oldest group at what could have been known . . . as the Mount Auburn table—their next move being to that famous cemetery." There were many other lunch clubs—Slagle's, for instance, established in 1933 and located in an alley (Spring Lane) between Washington and Devonshire Streets; the ever popular Bell in Hand, a tavern founded in the eighteenth century on Union Street; or Schroeder's Restaurant on High Street where Gerry Curtis's "downtown discussion group" of equity analysts met for lunch to discuss stock-picking.[29]

The most broadly based investment-related organization is the Boston Security Analysts Society. It was founded in 1946 as the second oldest group of its kind, and has sought to "advance the professional competence, integrity and fellowship of our members through events and educational programs, for the benefit of their clients and the broader investing public." When the society was founded, women were not allowed to become members. A few years later, it changed its policy and admitted its first female candidate, Natalie Bolton, a security analyst at Eaton & Howard. When the group met for luncheon at the Union Club in the 1940s and 1950s, Bolton, it was said, had to come into the building through a service entrance, but was recognized at the meetings when the speaker began his talk by acknowledging his audience as "Miss Bolton and Gentlemen." Meeting regularly over the years, the society's membership by 2011 had grown to 5,206 men and women, representing major Boston investment companies like Fidelity, Wellington Management, State Street Corporation, Eaton Vance, Cambridge Associates, GMO, Harvard Management Company, and many others. During the 2010–2011 season of events, for instance, the society sponsored thirty-seven luncheons, several seminars, networking events, career programs, and Chartered Financial Analyst (CFA) reviews; it supported fifteen society committees, ranging from career development, hedge funds, venture capital, and private wealth management to quantitative investing, socially responsible investing, and value investing. Another organization that meets on a regular basis to discuss common issues of Boston's financial community is the Boston Economic Club.[30]

Boston investment managers have been responsible for creating nationwide organizations, such as in the mutual fund industry and investment counsel profession. The Financial Analysts Federation, founded in 1947, was another such group. Prime movers in its founding were George Hansen of Keystone Custodian Funds and Kennard Woodworth of Eaton & Howard. By 1980, the federation had grown to fifty-one constituent societies in U.S. and Canadian financial centers. The federation arranges seminars and conferences for members to advance professional standards. Earlier, in 1959, the federation established the Chartered Financial Analysts (CFA) Institute, which conducts a testing program and sets out other requirements to credential investment and financial professionals. Another important group in Boston is the Boston Bar Association Securities Law Committee, a bar group that includes members from law firms, investment companies, government agencies, and educational institutions. There have been many other groups as well, including bond and money market professionals, who meet for dinners at the Union Club and elsewhere.[31]

Research has always played a large role in investment management in Boston. Boston trustees like Alfred Bowditch served on corporate boards and visited companies in the early 1900s to learn more about their businesses for investment purposes. The practice continued in the mutual fund business when Boston analysts would go out and visit companies, a practice Paul Cabot used to call "checking the trade." Boston investment managers knew the importance of research. During the 1920s, shortly after each firm was founded, Scudder, Stevens & Clark, Eaton & Howard, and State Street Research all founded research departments—a development that was not followed elsewhere until the 1930s. Research has been important in Boston primarily because Boston's investment managers are, by and large, active, not fashion- or trend-oriented, managers who have favored equities since at least the days of Judge Putnam and his "prudent man" rule. Surprisingly, Harvard Business School and other area business schools have not loomed large as a force in the Boston financial community, per se. An MBA is perhaps a useful union card to gain admission into a firm, but of little use on its own past that point.[32]

Another characteristic of Boston's investment management community is that it is small enough and far enough away from New York to be effective and productive. As a money manager with one foot in New York and the other in Boston once commented, "I've always thought that we've stood up very well to New York in terms of money management. Not so much in the private equity business, or leveraged funds and things like that, but they're driven more by investment banking and so forth. [We've] always claimed . . . in Boston to be a little bit away and that was a healthy thing." Another top Boston money manager viewed the Hub as an oasis for reflection: "It wasn't New York, . . . it wasn't running hot, and [it's] an easy city to hide away and do your thing." "You don't have to stay plugged in. [I'm] perfectly happy not to be New York.

Yet easy access to anyone you need to see. . . . [Boston has a] critical mass." Even forty years ago, Boston's exceptionalism was obvious to outsiders. "It's much better to be from Boston than New York," stated a Minnesota transplant who worked for one of Boston's money managers. "Divorced from Wall St. and the herd, we are thought to have an independent point of view. People think here's a group that can sit back and reflect." Finally, one founder of a Boston private equity company described competing with New York: "We love to go out to the Midwest and know that our competition is a New York firm. We're going to win that deal more often than not. If it's a beauty contest where the management has a significant say in it, we're going to win."[33]

The Need for Constant Reinvention

Despite Boston's rise as a global investment manager, there is periodic and disquieting news that it will not last. And much of that criticism is not just about the financial community but Boston's larger economy, which is also dependent on high-tech and information technology, healthcare and life sciences, and higher education. One local commentator even went so far as to state in 2007 that Boston is "becoming a place that has more and more to be modest about." Whatever future consequences await Boston's economy, an apocalyptic scenario or not, it will have an impact on the future of investment management in Boston as well.[34]

One of the strongest—and most perennial—concerns is that Boston is becoming less important to itself and to outsiders. It is, for instance, becoming a "branch office" city, with so many corporate headquarters leaving Boston and Massachusetts in recent years—from FleetBoston Financial's being sold to North Carolina's Bank of America in 2004 to the Gillette Company becoming part of Cincinnati's Procter & Gamble a few years later. Besides the perception of declining importance, the problem with this exodus is the expectation that less money will go to local charities and amenities like museums, and to local spending generally, which, in turn, will make Boston a less vibrant place to live or one that will be unable to attract a younger and creative population.[35]

Besides large corporate migrations, there are other occasional changes that have made Boston's investment community pause. One recent announcement was that Greylock Partners, Boston's oldest private venture capital firm, planned to move its headquarters to Menlo Park, California, although it would maintain a much smaller local office in Harvard Square. "The move reflects a recognition that the center of gravity for Greylock's investments in entrepreneurial start-ups—mainly in consumer Internet and enterprise technology—has shifted to Silicon Valley," noted a company spokesperson. Responding to the move, Tom Hopcroft, CEO of the Massachusetts Technology Leadership

Council, thought it "says more about who they're choosing to invest in than about the technology community here [in Boston]." While Greylock's move might be more symbolic, other changes are more palpable. Over recent years, for instance, Fidelity Investments has opened operations in Rhode Island, New Hampshire, Kentucky, North Carolina, New Mexico, and Texas as its workforce in Massachusetts shrunk from thirteen thousand to eight thousand.[36]

Some events in Boston's investment community have shaken public confidence. One, of course, was the financial scandal in Boston's mutual fund industry in the early 2000s, after which Massachusetts Financial Services and Putnam Investments lost $116.1 billion between 2001 and 2006 in customer withdrawals. There were concerns that Boston was no longer the dominant player in the industry. But other Boston mutual fund concerns—Fidelity Investments, State Street Global Advisors, GMO, John Hancock Funds, Eaton Vance, IXIS Asset Management, Evergreen Investments, and Columbia Management Group—had a combined net inflow of $181.2 in the same, troubling period. Furthermore, companies like Putnam made a comeback under new management and ownership. Even so, there have been published reports that employment in Massachusetts's securities and investment field declined from a high of 55,000 in 2001 to about 46,000 by 2006.[37]

On a broader scale, another concern has been that Boston's image as a high-tech city has become dated. The argument goes that the city needs a new image to attract new companies, which, in turn, would be financed by local venture capitalists. According to one account, investment and political leaders need to recognize that the old "Route 128 America's Technology Highway" moniker of "the glory days of the minicomputers, has grown stale." Others suggest a need to rebrand, or redefine, the New England "brand" in light of the demise of Digital Equipment Company and other hardware computer manufacturers, Tracerlab, and Polaroid, and the decline in military spending and its effect on companies like Raytheon. It is additionally argued by critics that Boston's technology has to become more consumer-, rather than business-, based, to compete with products and services created in California's Silicon Valley. But others cite Boston's predominance in biotech, healthcare, robotics, and educational technology, which plays to the city's present and future strengths, compared with Silicon Valley and New York. Even with these painful local adjustments in high-tech over the past few decades, Boston ranked third among the top twenty-five high-tech areas in North America in 2007, although it was down a peg from second in a 2003 survey.[38]

Despite such cautionary tales, the Boston economy still has much going for it and is improving in unanticipated ways. In recent years, scientific breakthroughs in the healthcare and life sciences industry in Boston were made as a result of people working collaboratively in small geographic pockets, particularly around Longwood Avenue, out past Copley Square and the Fenway. Density made collaboration possible and successful. There is already another such cluster in the Massachusetts General Hospital / MIT area, spanning Boston and Cambridge, and another is anticipated in the Harvard / Brighton-Allston area, again a Boston and Cambridge collaboration, once Harvard develops its property on the Boston side of the Charles River. Boston is now considered the center of the life science field in the United States and attracts a growing number of European firms, but these clusters in Boston and Boston-Cambridge are not limited to biotechnology.

Working in research clusters is now also becoming a reality for high-tech ventures housed in two innovation centers in Cambridge's Kendall Square and the Boston Seaport District near South Boston, which are both expected to become densely packed and collaborative entrepreneurial centers. Harvard University's fledging innovation lab in the Allston area of Boston is also meeting with early success. The already flourishing Cambridge Innovation Center is in a part of Cambridge that was torn down following an urban renewal project in the 1960s to accommodate a NASA space center planned under the Kennedy administration, but which ended up in Houston, Texas, after Lyndon Johnson became president. An eyesore for decades, the vacant Kendall Square area started growing in the 1990s into a dynamic high-tech center with modern buildings and facilities, and the growth of whole new industries like biotech. Another development affecting these centers has been "accelerator" programs, such as MassChallenge, in which those from local start-ups or those from other parts of the country and abroad come for three-month stints to get mentoring advice, some funding, and free office space.[39]

Clusters have long been a characteristic of Boston's financial industry, with most mutual funds in downtown Boston and some in Back Bay, family offices around the Post Office Square area, and private equity and hedge funds (the "alternative-asset crowd") in Back Bay, particularly in the new John Hancock Tower, which abuts Copley Square. The only exception was Boston's venture capital industry. For decades, more than a dozen of Boston's premier venture capital companies like Charles River Ventures, North Bridge Venture Partners, Matrix Partners, and Battery Ventures were located at "Mount Money," in a business office complex in Waltham, Massachusetts, near Route 128. Recent trends, however, show that the "new core of Boston venture capital has moved in closer to the city, toward Copley Square and Harvard Square." These include new companies like Flybridge Capital (Back Bay) Spark Capital (Back Bay), PureTech Ventures and Third Rock Ventures (Back Bay), and an office of Venrock (Cambridge), the longtime venture firm started by the

Rockefellers. Even Greylock Partners, which recently moved its headquarters to California, has opened an office in Harvard Square, while other established companies, like Highland Capital Partners and Battery Ventures, have or will move from Route 128 to Kendall Square. With only 2.3 percent of the country's population, Massachusetts and particularly these venture companies in and around Boston were receiving about 15 percent of venture capital dollars nationwide by 2011.[40]

The concentration of skills and financial backing exist in other forms as well. The Boston area is home to various academic research centers, such as the MIT Entrepreneurial Center, the Center for Venture Research at the University of New Hampshire in Durham, and, further afield, the Tuck Center for Private Equity and Entrepreneurship at Dartmouth, not to mention whole curricula on these subjects at nearby Bentley and Babson Colleges. The area has more than two dozen organized groups of angel investors—a significant number but one that could be improved upon. This concentration and dedication of purpose may have other consequences for the future as well. While insurance is a small sector of the Hub's financial community, particularly following the merger of New England Financial and John Hancock with outside companies a decade or more ago, Boston's Liberty Mutual Insurance Company remains an important player as the fifth largest U.S. property and casualty insurer. Considering the fact that Liberty Mutual could have gone anywhere rather than expand at their current site in Boston, it decided in 2011 not only to remain in the city but also to build a $300 million tower in Back Bay and increase the size of its workforce there. There is little doubt that the vibrancy of Boston's financial community, as well as its civic and cultural life, had something to do with that decision.[41]

Another significant feature of the New Boston has been the city's ability to attract young, highly educated twenty- to thirty-four-year-old young adults, who play an important part in driving entrepreneurial activity in the Boston area and are helping to reinvent the constantly changing investment management industry with the newest talents and skills. Boston's success in attracting these people is due in part to another cluster, a concentration of educational institutions in the area, with some thirty-six colleges and universities within the city's bounds, and several hundred more within a relatively short distance; some 500,000 college students live within a 25-mile radius of the city. The turning point for Boston in terms of this age group came in the 1970s. During that period, the number of twenty to thirty-four year olds jumped by over 32,000; this made them the largest age group in the city. That trend has, with minor demographic exceptions, continued to this day.

In addition to attracting this age cohort to Boston, the 2010 census ranks the Hub number one with the highest proportion of young adults among the top twenty-five major U.S. cities. Fully 35 percent (216,213) of the city's population is now in that age group, which is an 11 percent increase from the 2000 census when the Hub placed second in this category. In addition, the 2010 census reveals that 39.2 percent of that Boston age cohort holds bachelor's degrees, a higher percentage than any other metropolitan area in the country. As a result, Boston is home to a large knowledge-based workforce that is highly educated, entrepreneurial, and vital for Boston's financial sector. "Youth is a key to this business," exclaimed a retired partner at Wellington Management, whose workforce had an average age of thirty-four when he left. Boston has become a young person's town whose youth "rejuvenates us and is very beneficial to Boston businesses."[42]

Despite such positive trends, perhaps the greatest threat to Boston's future is not internal but external. According to a 2007 report that looks at the future of Boston in 2015, the state's financial services economy is at a "critical inflection point" with outside forces threatening "to relegate Massachusetts to second-tier status in financial services, even in the sub-sectors where the state has traditionally excelled: asset management, asset servicing, and insurance." This would put at risk 180,000 jobs and $38.5 billion in GSP. The report also cites the fact that the number of Fortune 500 companies in the state had declined from seventeen to nine during the previous decade, and many of the largest remaining companies were shipping out middle-income jobs to other states. In addition, there has been "a virtual revolution in technology and communications [that] has turned companies like Fidelity and State Street into information companies first and foremost; in many ways, these institutions have more in common today with IBM than with the asset managers or asset servicers of a few decades ago." The report's "Vision for 2015" sought for Boston to "become a globally recognized, top-tier financial services center known for the top talent, greatest innovation, and the best firms in asset management, asset servicing, and insurance." The report lists several goals: preserve and expand a diverse employment base (which includes strengthening higher education and attracting innovative financial services firms), become a global center for talent and innovation (including the establishment of a financial services–specific research center and finding ways for talent retention), make the area a more stable and competitive place to do business (especially from a regulatory perspective and a more predictable tax environment), and find more ways for the public, private, and academic sectors to collaborate.[43]

Another goal for Boston investment managers is to continue to think long term. They cannot afford to be like many Boston trustees of the first half of the twentieth century, particularly after the rise of the "spendthrift trust," who elected to invest conservatively in fixed assets or only property they could see out of their office windows rather than the innovative stocks acquired by previous generations of trustees for their clients. That lack of fiduciary accountability "strangles enterprise and perpetuates absentee ownership and trust control," noted one Boston writer more than half a century ago. As corporations have to cannibalize aging products and their core businesses to invent and distribute new products for a changing economy, Boston investment managers cannot fall in love with their own legacies because, by doing so, they will ultimately lose their grip on the investment market and investing public. Boston's tradition of prudent investing, and thinking about the future rather than the next day or month, will always be a good guide.

Still, Boston investment managers have much to think about. What will they do with an aging population, a demographic bulge that moves from investments to withdrawals? What about Boston's active management approach in a world of index funds, fewer investment management "stars," and the quant approach so favored in alternative investing? What might regulation do to private equity and hedge funds, and how might that affect Boston? What will happen to pension funds, how might they change, and will this require breaking into new and difficult markets in the future? How might the investment world change if it shifts away from institutions to a growing number of high-net-worth individuals? Will there be a retrenchment from alternative investments, or the reverse, in an effort to obtain above average returns? Or might there be a recasting of alternative investments "based on how they might perform under various economic circumstances like slow economic growth or high inflation"? There are a lot of questions to ask and answer as opportunities develop and the investment world continues to change.[44]

One of the great strengths of Boston's investment management community is how it has grown and developed, particularly during the last forty to fifty years. The mutual fund industry, and banking in an earlier generation, served as a *nursery* for the city's growing and expanding personnel needs in the investment management industry that was to come. While hard data is difficult to come by, the mutual fund analysts and portfolio managers interviewed for this book alone often later ended up in private equity, pension fund management, hedge funds, and even venture capital. Individuals like Arthur Snyder (Merchants Bank), Peter Brooke (First National Bank), Bill Egan (Merchants Bank), and Richard Burnes (National Shawmut Bank) all started out with banking backgrounds but ended up in venture capital and private equity. Nicholas Thorndike began at Fidelity but formed a firm that eventually became Wellington Management, one of Boston's and the world's largest money managers. The number of managers from Fidelity and Putnam alone who have gone on to form or serve in other companies in Boston is legend. Others, too, have found success. Jeremy Grantham was at Keystone and Batterymarch Financial, both mutual fund companies, before he founded Grantham, Mayo, Van Otterloo & Company, another internationally recognized Boston money management firm, with two partners with much the same experience. Again, it bears repeating that Boston's small, clustered, and concentrated environment has been an important incubator for the industry.

Boston's investment management industry was able to make the transition in the 1970s from what Walter Cabot has called "a client service trust selling business to a performance driven product business," as well as the transition from just managing the investment business to *growing* it. "There may be some of that assurance and prudence about Boston" that attracts investors to Boston, noted a Boston private equity partner, "but cities [like Boston] with expertise are sticky. Once you have a dominance of leadership, it's self-sustaining. Even with private equity and hedge funds, [there's] some residual."[45]

And although Boston seems to have made all of the important transitions as investment management has changed over time, and Bostonian investment managers continue to remain highly competitive among themselves, when it comes to management, they still tend to view money differently from their contemporaries elsewhere. As one Boston trustee modestly noted over eighty years ago, "We're not smart men, but we are prudent. If you want smart fellows, you'd better go to New York. And ask them how they did during the crash." The Boston asset manager is not concerned with the quickest or largest return, but with a steady, conservative return, one that can help to create for his or her client a comfortable but not ostentatious life. That modest attitude toward wealth was perhaps best summed up over a century ago when Samuel Eliot Morison, the historian, recalled the era in which he grew up. "There were no distinctions of wealth," he noted. "We were vaguely conscious our families were 'top drawer,' although there was not yet any Social Register to tell us so. Once you were 'in,' more or less wealth made no difference." It was not until he attended St. Paul's School with the millionaire sons of Pittsburgh and New York that "I encountered the notion that one's social rating depended on such externals as steam yachts, stables of race horses and Newport 'cottages.' It is true that Boston society was too simple to attract bloated 'gate-crashers'; nor did it breed multi-millionaires. People such as they stormed the social citadels of New York, Washington, Newport and London." Things of course have changed, but Boston attitudes toward investment management seem to endure.[46]

NOTES

Introduction

1. Charles Phillips Huse, *The Financial History of Boston: From May 1, 1822 to January 31, 1909* (Cambridge: Harvard University Press, 1916); William H. Wilson, *The City Beautiful Movement* (Baltimore: Johns Hopkins University Press, 1989).

2. See, for example, Alice Hanson Jones, *Wealth of a Nation to Be: The American Colonies on the Eve of the Revolution* (New York: Columbia University Press, 1980), 59, 75, 79, 140, 141, 184–85.

3. Leslie Poles Hartley, *The Go-Between* (1953; repr., New York: New York Review Books, 2002), 17; Frederick Simpich, "Boston through Midwest Eyes," *National Geographic Magazine,* July 1936, 37–82.

4. H. Lee Silberman, "50 Years of Trust: Massachusetts Investors Trust, 1924–1974," typescript, Massachusetts Financial Services, 1974, 20–21, in possession of the author; Daniel Golden and David Mehegan, "The Boston Potential: Changing the Heart of the City," *Boston Globe,* September 18, 1983.

5. One of Boston's well-known nicknames originated in the nineteenth century in Oliver Wendell Holmes Sr.'s 1858 book *The Autocrat of the Breakfast Table,* in which the Massachusetts State House on Beacon Hill was referred to as "the Hub of the Solar System." The expression was later expanded by locals to "the Hub of the Universe" and referred to the whole city.

6. Joseph F. Dinneen, "Now It Can Be Told: How and Why Boston Staged Big Jubilee," *Boston Globe,* May 22, 1950.

7. "In Investing, It's the Prudent Bostonian," *Business Week,* June 6, 1959, 56–57.

8. On the city's transition to the "New Boston," see Louis M. Lyons, "Boston: A Study in Inertia," in *Our Fair City,* ed. Robert S. Allen (New York: Vanguard Press, 1947), 16–36; "Is Boston Beginning to Boil?" *Fortune,* June 1957, 286–88; Walter McQuade, "Boston: What Can a Sick City Do?" *Fortune,* June 1964, 134–35; "Rebalancing Boston," *Newsweek,* April 26, 1965, 60–61; Thomas H. O'Connor, *Building a New Boston: Politics and Urban Renewal, 1950–1970* (Boston: Northeastern University Press, 1993); and essays in *The Good City: Writers Explore 21st Century Boston,* ed. Emily Hiestand and Ande Zellman (Boston: Beacon Press, 2004).

9. William Hall, "Boston," *Financial Times Survey,* March 6, 1984, https://archive.org; Golden and Mehegan, "The Boston Potential," which discusses the gradual transformation of the city, especially in the 1970s and early 1980s, and Boston's "downtown boom." For further details, see also James C. O'Connell's recent treatment, *The Hub's Metropolis: Greater Boston's Development from Railroad Suburbs to Smart Growth* (Cambridge: MIT Press, 2013), 181–200.

1. Investment Management in Early New England

1. W. K. Jordan, *Philanthropy in England 1480–1660: A Study of the Changing Pattern of English Social Aspirations* (London: George Allen and Unwin, 1959), 15–18; An Act for the Relief of the Poor, 43 Elizabeth, chap. 2 (1601). The institutions and mechanisms created by this legislation would also have an impact on the development of early colonial Massachusetts only a few decades later in the 1630s. See David Grayson Allen, *In English Ways: The Movement of Societies and the Transferal of English Local Law and Custom to Massachusetts Bay in the Seventeenth Century* (Chapel Hill: University of North Carolina Press, 1981), 68–69, 72–74, 136–38, 146–51, 151n, 187–90.

2. An Act for Charitable Uses, 43 Elizabeth I, chap. 4 (1601).

3. Jordan, *Philanthropy in England,* 18–20, 40–53.

4. In their simplest form, trusts were mechanisms whereby donors or benefactors gave real or personal property to a trustee or trustees who manage the assets for the benefit of a third party. The trustee is a fiduciary, and acts in a fiduciary capacity or in behalf of the beneficiary, and not for him- or herself.

5. For a more detailed account on these developments, particularly the growth of endowments, see Jordan, *Philanthropy in England,* 109–25, 240–53, 367–77, and the general source for his discussion on trusts, Austin W. Scott, *The Law of Trusts,* 5 vols. (Boston: Little, Brown, 1956). On the investment side of English endowments—using charitable endowments for loan funds—little work seems to have been done, except for Francis Godwin James, "Charity Endowments as Sources of Local Credit in Seventeenth- and Eighteenth-Century England," *Journal of Economic History* 8, no. 2 (1948): 153–70, in which the author finds that endowments were used in lieu of local and provincial banking facilities, which were scarce, if not nonexistent, at that time.

6. David D. Hall, personal communication, May 1, 2007; David D. Hall, "The Experience of Authority in Early New England," unpublished paper, and *The Faithful Shepherd: A History of the New England Ministry in the Seventeenth Century* (Chapel Hill: University of North Carolina Press, 1972), 190–94. See also Hall's *A Reforming People: Puritanism and the Transformation of Public Life in New England* (New York: Knopf, 2011), 164–65.

7. Patricia E. Kane, *Colonial Massachusetts Silversmiths and Jewelers: A Biographical Dictionary Based on the Notes of Francis Hill Bigelow and John Marshall Phillips* (New Haven: Yale University Art Gallery, 1997); Barbara McLean Ward, "'In a Feasting Posture': Communion Vessels and Community Values in Seventeenth- and Eighteenth-Century New England," *Winterthur Portfolio* 23, no. 1 (1988): 1–24; John R. Ellement, "Church to Savor Vintage of Its Long-Stored Silver," *Boston Globe,* January 14, 2009 (First Parish Church of Cohasset); Charles A. Radin, "Salem Church Sets Storied Silver Work on the Auction Block," ibid., December 16, 2006 (First Parish Church in Quincy, First Parish Church in Salem); David Filipov, "Old Church Pays in Silver for Repairs: Historical Collection in Beverly to Go up for Auction," ibid., December 25, 2009 (First Parish Church of Beverly); Meghan E. Irons, "Church Selling Silver, at a Cost," ibid., December 11, 2011 (First Parish in Dorchester).

8. *Records of Trinity Church, Boston, 1728–1830,* ed. Andrew Oliver and James Bishop Peabody (Boston: Colonial Society of Massachusetts, 1980), 32–135, and Appendix C, "Original Accounts and Records of the Greene Foundation, September 15, 1776 to December 12, 1814, 489–512.

9. Joseph Ballard, *Account of the Poor Fund and Other Charities Held in Trust by the Old South Society, City of Boston, with Copies of Original Papers Relative to the Charities*

and to the Late Trial before the Supreme Court of Massachusetts in 1867 (Boston: George C. Rand and Avery, 1868), esp. 11–25, 19, 20, 21–25, 30–31, 132, and Deacon's Book, Appendix 2, 157–233. For a discussion of Massachusetts's mediums of exchange in the colonial period to the revolution, and various changes noted above, see John J. McCusker, *Money and Exchange in Europe and America, 1600–1775: A Handbook* (Chapel Hill: University of North Carolina Press, 1978), esp. 131–33, 142.

10. This was an increase from approximately £366 in English pound sterling to about £3,874. On postrevolutionary British pound / U.S. dollar exchange rates, see note 34, below.

11. Second Church (Boston) Account Book, 1711–1714, vol. 1A; Account Book, 1721–1776, vol. 5A; Account Book, 1729–1813, vol. 5B, all MS N-2037, Massachusetts Historical Society. Some other early Boston churches may have similar financial records. See Harold Field Worthley, *An Inventory of the Records of the Particular (Congregational) Churches of Massachusetts Gathered 1620–1805* (Cambridge: Harvard University Press, 1970), 53–106.

12. The Boston Latin School, still an operating high school in Boston, was actually older, having been founded a year before Harvard in 1635. Although Boston Latin received funds from various sources in its early history—voluntary contributions and income from town lands, docks, ferries, and house rents, plus personal gifts and legacies of land and money—it was primarily tax-supported, whereas the Roxbury school shunned public funding even during periods of difficult financial circumstances. Pauline Holmes, *A Tercentenary History of the Boston Latin School, 1635–1935* (Cambridge: Harvard University Press, 1935), 27–53.

13. F. Washington Jarvis, *Schola Illustris: The Roxbury Latin School, 1645–1995* (Boston: David R. Godine, 1995), 103–8. See also Roxbury Latin School, Old School Book [1645–1780], MS Am 1488, Houghton Library, Harvard University, which records the meetings of the feoffees, who selected the schoolmasters to "Keep the School," and those of the donors who elected the feoffees.

14. Jarvis, *Schola Illustris*, 110–14, 119–25. In addition, the school did own land granted to it by the town of Roxbury, and land given to it as bequests (see, e.g., Old School Book, 48, 108), but it was apparently not as substantial or important as the Bell lands.

15. Jarvis, *Schola Illustris*, 126–30, 133–36.

16. During much of the twentieth century, the school was known as Governor Dummer Academy, but in 2006, its name was shortened to the Governor's Academy.

17. John W. Ragle, *Governor Dummer Academy History, 1763–1963* (South Byfield, Mass.: Governor Dummer Academy, 1963), 11, 13–14, 16, 28, 35–38.

18. Frederick S. Allis Jr., *Youth from Every Quarter: A Bicentennial History of Phillips Academy, Andover* (Hanover, N.H.: Phillips Academy, Andover, 1979), 53, 61, 78, 92–93. When originally incorporated in 1780, Phillips Andover could receive "by gift, grant, devise, bequest or otherwise" both real estate and personal property but was limited to an annual income from real estate of £500 and from personal property of £2,000.

A comparable endowment was created at Phillips Exeter Academy, founded in 1781, where John Phillips had given gifts and bequests totaling "at least $98,400 in currency of the day." Originally a preacher and then a teacher, Phillips went on to become successful in business in general merchandise, trade, real estate, and banking. By 1858, land, buildings, and invested funds at Exeter had grown to $135,000, and it was viewed as "altogether the best-endowed institution of its class in the State of New Hampshire, if not in the country." Myron R. Williams, *The Story of Phillips Exeter* (Exeter, N.H.: Phillips Exeter Academy, 1957), 19–20, 29, 49.19. Margery

Somers Foster, *"Out of Smalle Beginings . . .": An Economic History of Harvard College in the Puritan Period (1636 to 1712)* (Cambridge: Belknap Press of Harvard University Press, 1962), 106–15.

20. Ibid., 115–20.
21. Of this figure, £4,782 was committed to large outlays for capital purposes, such as plant or buildings, whereas the balance of about £5,300 became the college's endowment assets. Ibid., 121. Except for the ferry franchise from Cambridge to Boston, Harvard, unlike Yale, did not rely on the colonial legislature during its early years. See below.
22. Ibid., 123, 199.
23. Ibid., 45.
24. Ibid., 110, 112, 156–59. See also note 5, above.
25. Seymour E. Harris, *Economics of Harvard* (New York: McGraw-Hill, 1970), 293–94. Harris employs the Massachusetts "lawful money" figures that were used by Josiah Quincy in his history of Harvard (see note 26, below) rather than the "New England pounds" used by Foster for seventeenth-century Harvard income and endowment figures. Rather than conform all figures to a constant and likely controversial standard, I choose to emphasize here that Harvard's endowment grew *proportionately larger* within each time frame, no matter which system of measurement is used or how Harris calculates "lawful money" into U.S. dollars.
26. Josiah Quincy, *The History of Harvard University*, 2 vols. (Cambridge, Mass.: John Owen, 1840), 2:231n, 239, 411; Harris, *Economics of Harvard*, 363–66.
27. Quincy, *History of Harvard University*, 2:557–58, 353–69. Unlike other colleges, Harvard was rarely a recipient of government largess, at least to the point that it received much value for what it was given. Harvard had been given numerous land grants by the General Court in the seventeenth century, but nearly all failed to take effect through a conflict of ownership, while lands granted in the eighteenth century, principally in Maine, never appreciated in value, and thus were unsaleable before the new State of Maine (1820) gave the title to those lands to others. Harvard, or rather a few Harvard officials (the president and several professors), received direct annual grants of several hundred pounds, but none ended up in the endowment. Ibid., 1:39–43, 510–12; 2:224–30, 253.
28. Only four colleges were founded in New England before the revolution—Harvard (1636), Yale (1701), Brown (1764), and Dartmouth (1769)—while three other colleges were founded by 1800: Williams (1793), Bowdoin (1794), and Middlebury (1800). The schools selected covered the years of the early, middle, and late colonial periods, and offered some distinct differences in how and what kinds of wealth colleges collected over some two hundred years.
29. Brooks Mather Kelley, *Yale: A History* (New Haven: Yale University Press, 1974), 24–25, 30. Cotton Mather suggested that the school be named for Yale so that it might receive additional gifts from him. When Yale died a few years later, however, no benefaction was left in his will, although a new draft showed that he intended to leave £500 for "Connecticote College," a purpose that relatives subsequently blocked.
30. For the small, personal donations, see Yale Treasury Book, Series I: General Accounting Books, box 13, folder 56, RU 151, Records of the Treasurer, Manuscripts and Archives, Yale University Library (hereafter RU 151, Yale).
31. "An Acc't of All the Lands &c Belonging to Yale College 1747," Series V: Investments, box 426, folder 11, RU 151, Yale. In 1743, college representatives visited these "college farms" to evaluate and report on them. For the most part, they were superior land for

tillage, grassland, and hardwoods. "The Report of Messrs Anthony Stoddard & John Trumble, concerning ye Colledge Farms—1743," ibid., box 428, folder 32. By 1800, the Litchfield Country lands, consisting of five farms in Warren, six in Cornwall, four in Goshen, two in Norfolk, four in Canaan, and eight in Salisbury yielded an annual income, mostly in rents, of £728.55. "College Farms in the County of Litchfield," 1800, ibid., box 428, folder 33.

32. For a complete list of benefactors, see "The Benefactors of Yale College. Collected and Recorded July 5. 1784," Series IV: Benefactors, box 370, folder 2, RU 151, Yale. There were also many small donations—several pounds or less—in subscriptions for building a house for the professor of divinity and the college chapel, but no large benefactors except for the state. See other details in "Catalogue of the Principal Deceased Benefactors to the Academical Department of Yale College," ibid., box 370, folder 4, and "Memoranda Relative to Donations to Yale College (Derived from the Records of the College)," ibid., box 370, folder 4.

33. Donations from the State of Connecticut, ibid., box 370, folder 1, RU 151, Yale; George Wilson Pierson, *Yale Book of Numbers: Historical Statistics of the College and University, 1701–1976* (New Haven: Yale University Press, 1983), 515–40.

34. To provide a reference on the British pound / U.S. dollar exchange rate in this and subsequent paragraphs, the pound was worth $4.55 in 1791 and rose to $4.86 by 1832, with yearly fluctuations between $4.13 (1799) and $5.22 (1816) in between. Lawrence H. Officer, "Dollar-Pound Exchange Rate from 1791," Measuring Worth, 2013, www .measuringworth.com.

35. Edmund S. Morgan, *The Gentle Puritan: A Life of Ezra Stiles, 1727–1795* (New Haven: Yale University Press, 1962), 325–26. According to Quincy, *History of Harvard University,* 2:224–28, 247–50, and passim, there were no annual grants from the legislature to the college. Stiles was probably referring to annual grants given to the Harvard president and several professors, none of which went to the treasurer or into the endowment. Even if this amount were not counted, Harvard received about 4.5 times the amount of annual investment income as Yale.

36. Kelley, *Yale: A History,* 151, 110; Morgan, *The Gentle Puritan,* 325–26, 406. In 1791, Yale also bought seven shares of the new Bank of the United States at $25, and then sold them three months later for $175. This and the loan office investments were probably Yale's most successful early investments, but in 1791, Harvard's endowment was still more than twice as large as Yale's, being £2,745. Morgan, *The Gentle Puritan,* 406.

37. Kelley, *Yale: A History,* 150.

38. Yale University, Summary of Financial History, 1700–2000, Table M-15 (9/19/00), typescript, Yale University Office of Institutional Research, New Haven, Conn.; Kelley, *Yale: A History,* 150–56.

39. Halsey C. Edgerton, comp. and ed., *Dartmouth College: Terms of Gifts and Endowments and an Annotated Copy of the Charter of Trustees of Dartmouth College (Corporate Title of Dartmouth College)* (Hanover, N.H.: Dartmouth College, 1940), 175–77, 291–93, 200–201, 222–26, 47, 182, 51, 123–24, 6–8, 185–86, 40–47.

40. Fewer than a dozen charitable institutions operated in Boston before 1800. These included the Scots Charitable Society (founded 1657), Boston Episcopal Society (1724), Charitable Irish Society (1737), Boston Marine Society (1742), Massachusetts Charitable Society (1762), the Humane Society of Massachusetts (1785), Massachusetts Congregational Charitable Society (1786), Massachusetts Charitable Fire Society (1792), Roxbury Charitable Society (1794), Massachusetts Charitable Mechanics Society (1795), and the Boston Dispensary (1795). Katharine D. Hardwick, *As Long as*

Charity Shall Be a Virtue: Boston Private Charities from 1657 to 1800 (Boston: N.p., 1964).

41. Laws of the Society, Boston Episcopal Charitable Society, MS N-1886, Massachusetts Historical Society.

42. Ibid.; Tryal Ballence of Societys Books (April 18, 1786–April 20, 1835); Ledger, "B.E.C.S." (Account Book, December 3, 1807–April 1850), MS N-1886, Massachusetts Historical Society.

43. Charitable Irish Society, vol. 1, Records, 1737–1804, MS N-1474, Massachusetts Historical Society.

44. William A. Baker, *A History of the Boston Marine Society, 1742–1967* (Boston: Boston Marine Society, 1968), 6–9, 308–9.

45. The Massachusetts Charitable Society, another organization founded twenty years later in 1762, operated in a similar manner, protecting members and their families, and managing and investing quarterly payments. Rules of the Massachusetts Society, Massachusetts Charitable Society, Records, vol. 7, 1762–1796, MS N-450 Extra Tall; Treasurers Cashbook, 1762–1857, vol. 15, MS N-450, both Massachusetts Historical Society.

46. Act of Incorporation and By-Laws of the Massachusetts Congregational Charitable Society (Boston: I. R. Butts, 1853), Massachusetts Congregational Charitable Society Records, vol. 1, MS N-511, Massachusetts Historical Society; Conrad Edick Wright, *The Transformation of Charity in Postrevolutionary New England* (Boston: Northeastern University Press, 1992), 104–5.

47. Massachusetts Mutual Fire Insurance Company Records, vol. 1, 1798–1822, Act of Incorporation, Historical Collections, Baker Library, Harvard Business School, Boston.

48. Ibid.; see June 2, 1807, April 4, 1809, September 7, 1819, and July 2, 1822, as examples of entries declaring dividend payments.

49. Wright, *The Transformation of Charity in Postrevolutionary New England*, 160–62, 168. See chapter 4 for further discussion of the Massachusetts Hospital Insurance Company.

50. This transition was part of a "financial revolution," so called by financial historians who have noted that a modern financial system was created in a short period of time in the early 1790s following the creation of the federal government. See, for example, Richard Sylla, "U.S. Securities Markets and the Banking System, 1790–1840," *Federal Reserve Bank of St. Louis Review* 80, no. 3 (1998): 85–87, and "Hamilton and the Federalist Financial Revolution, 1789–1795," *New-York Journal of American History* 65, no. 3 (2004): 32–39.

2. The Creation of Wealth in Boston's Nineteenth-Century Commercial and Industrial Economy

1. Even mutual insurance companies were profit-making, but their dividends were paid to policyholders, not stockholders.

2. On the success of the Calumet & Hecla Mining Company, see Russell B. Adams Jr., *The Boston Money Tree* (New York: Thomas Y. Crowell, 1977), 165.

3. See David Grayson Allen, *In English Ways: The Movement of Societies and the Transferal of English Local Law and Custom to Massachusetts Bay in the Seventeenth Century* (Chapel Hill: University of North Carolina Press, 1981), 227–31 and *passim;* cf. Joan Thirsk, "Patterns of Agriculture in Seventeenth-Century England,"

in *Seventeenth-Century New England,* ed. David D. Hall and David Grayson Allen (Boston: Colonial Society of Massachusetts, 1984), 39–54. On the transition from a traditional to a market economy, see Winifred B. Rothenberg, "The Market and Massachusetts Farmers, 1750–1855," *Journal of Economic History* 41, no. 2 (1981): 283–314.

4. For two more recent articles on the controversy that review the literature and various points of view, see Joyce Oldham Appleby, "The Vexed Story of Capitalism Told by American Historians," *Journal of the Early Republic* 21, no. 1 (2001): 1–18, and especially Naomi R. Lamoreaux, "Rethinking the Transition to Capitalism in the Early American Northeast," *Journal of American History* 90, no. 2 (2003): 437–61.

5. Winifred B. Rothenberg, "The Emergence of a Capital Market in Rural Massachusetts, 1730–1838," *Journal of Economic History* 45, no. 4 (1985): 787–89, 792–95, 806 (emphasis added), and "The Invention of American Capitalism," in *Engines of Enterprise: An Economic History of New England,* ed. Peter Temin (Cambridge: Harvard University Press, 2000), esp 78–86. Stock ownership, of course, existed elsewhere, but it might have been limited (internal improvement securities) and transitory (a bust once dividends did not materialize), or had widespread popularity followed by waning interest (bank stocks) after the period's economic panics. See John Majewski, "Toward a Social History of the Corporation: Shareholding in Pennsylvania, 1800–1840," in *The Economy of Early America: Historical Perspectives & New Directions,* ed. Cathy Matson (Philadelphia: University of Pennsylvania Press, 2006), 294–316.

6. Hamilton Andrews Hill, "The Trade, Commerce, and Navigation of Boston, 1780–1880," in *Memorial History of Boston, Including Suffolk County, Massachusetts, 1630–1880,* ed. Justin Winsor, 4 vols. (Boston: James R. Osgood, 1882–1886), 4:195–210, 215–16; James R. Gibson, *Otter Skins, Boston Ships, and China Goods: The Maritime Fur Trade of the Northwest Coast, 1785–1841* (Seattle: University of Washington Press, 1992).

7. More than just the leader of Boston's merchants, Perkins was also the uncle of John Perkins Cushing and John Murray Forbes, and step-uncle of William Sturgis, all of whom would play significant roles in the China trade, and directly or indirectly as investors later on in western railroads. Kinship ties proved to be important in both enterprises. On Perkins, see Carl Seaburg and Stanley Paterson, *Merchant Prince of Boston: Colonel T. H. Perkins, 1764–1854* (Cambridge: Harvard University Press, 1971)

8. Hill, "Trade, Commerce, and Navigation of Boston, 1780–1880," 4:195–210, 215–16; John P. Cushing, "Memo: For Mr. Forbes Respecting Canton Affairs," *Business History Review* 40, no. 1 (1966): 98–107. Cushing spent a quarter-century in Canton as agent and factory supervisor for Perkins & Company, Thomas Handasyd Perkins's firm. By the late 1810s, the Perkins firm and Bryant & Sturgis, known at the time as the "Boston Concern," were also involved in the opium trade as that commodity became more popular and lucrative than ginseng and fur skins. Cotton textiles from Massachusetts mills and cash were also increasingly used for the trade with the Chinese.

9. Hill, "Trade, Commerce, and Navigation of Boston," 4:220–24, 229–30; Samuel Eliot Morison, "The India Ventures of Fisher Ames, 1794–1804," *American Antiquarian Society Proceedings,* new series, 37 (1927): 14–23. For a recent treatment of Tudor, see Carl Seaburg and Stanley Patterson, *The Ice King: Frederic Tudor and His Circle* (Boston: Massachusetts Historical Society, and Mystic, Conn.: Mystic Seaport, 2003).

10. Hill, "Trade, Commerce, and Navigation of Boston," 4:220–24, 229–30.

11. Jacqueline Barbara Carr, "'As Remarkable as the Revolution Itself': Boston's Demographics, 1780–1800," *New England Quarterly* 73, no. 4 (2000): 583–602.

12. Henry P. Kidder and Francis H. Peabody, "Finance in Boston," in Winsor, ed., *Memorial History of Boston*, 4:153–57.

13. Carroll D. Wright and Horace G. Wadlin, "The Industries of the Last Hundred Years," in Winsor, ed., *Memorial History of Boston*, 4:70, 78–80; Kidder and Peabody, "Finance in Boston," 4:153–57, 160; Samuel Eliot Morison, *The Maritime History of Massachusetts, 1783–1860* (Boston: Houghton Mifflin, 1923), 41.

14. Henrietta M. Larson, "A China Trader Turns Investor—A Biographical Chapter in American Business History," *Harvard Business Review* 7 (1934): 345–58.

15. Arthur M. Johnson and Barry E. Supple, *Boston Capitalists and Western Railroads: A Study in the Nineteenth-Century Railroad Investment Process* (Cambridge: Harvard University Press, 1967), 19. There are, of course, exceptions to all generalizations. Israel Thorndike, for instance, managed to move his fortune from maritime activities to manufacturing, then to some small local early railroads and land speculation. J. D. Forbes, *Israel Thorndike, Federalist Financier* (Beverly, Mass.: Beverly Historical Society, 1953).

16. Wright and Wadlin, "Industries of the Last Hundred Years," in Winsor, ed., *Memorial History of Boston*, 4:81–91.

17. Ibid., 92; Daniel Webster, Speech on the Tariff, Faneuil Hall, Boston, *Boston Daily Advertiser*, October 11, 1820, in *The Writings and Speeches of Daniel Webster*, ed. James W. McIntyre, 18 vols. (Boston: Little, Brown, 1903), 13:5–21.

18. Joseph G. Martin, *Seventy-Three Years' History of the Boston Stock Market, from January 1, 1798 to January 1, 1871* (Boston: J. G. Martin, 1871), 66; Robert F. Dalzell Jr., *Enterprising Elite: The Boston Associates and the World They Made* (Cambridge: Harvard University Press, 1987), 47–51.

19. Robert B. Zevin, "The Growth of Cotton Textile Production after 1815," in *The Reinterpretation of American Economic History*, ed. Robert W. Fogel and Stanley L. Engerman (New York: Harper and Row, 1971), 141; Dalzell, *Enterprising Elite*, 51–53, 56–57.

20. Ibid., 58; Lance Edwin Davis, "Stock Ownership in the Early New England Textile Industry," *Business History Review* 32, no. 2 (1958): 215–16, 218. Davis sampled eleven "Massachusetts type" cotton mills to analyze stock ownership. Although women and trustees owned a quarter of the shares, trustees were the second largest single group of stockholders behind only merchants and mercantile firms (excluding textile). Their relative position grew steadily in samples taken between 1844 and 1859. Ibid., 220.

21. Rothenberg, "The Invention of American Capitalism," 98; cf. Dalzell, *Enterprising Elite*, 79–80, 233–38.

22. William H. Bunting, comp. and annotator, *Portrait of a Port: Boston, 1852–1914* (Cambridge: Belknap Press of Harvard University Press, 1971), 3, 6, 8, 10, 17.

23. Walter Muir Whitehill, *Boston: A Topographical History*, 2nd edn. (Cambridge: Belknap Press of Harvard University Press, 1968), 73–74; William J. Sheehan, "Unique to Boston Are the Famous 'Boston Trustees,'" *Boston Evening Transcript*, July 28, 1934; *"Our First Men": A Calendar of Wealth, Fashion and Gentility, Containing a List of Those Persons Taxed in the City of Boston, Credibly Reported to Be Worth One Hundred Thousand Dollars; with Biographical Notices of the Principal Persons*, rev. edn. (Boston: All the Booksellers, 1846), 3, 8. The term "Boston Associates" was coined by Vera Shlakman in her depression-era study *Economic History of a Factory Town: A Study of Chicopee, Massachusetts* (Northampton, Mass.: Department of History, Smith College, 1935).

24. Although the first chartered turnpike company in the United States, the Philadelphia and Lancaster Turnpike, was begun in 1792 and completed three years later.

25. Charles Francis Adams Jr., "The Canal and Railroad Enterprise of Boston," in Winsor, ed., *Memorial History of Boston*, 4:116–19, 125–26, 130. See also Stephen Salsbury, *The State, the Investor, and the Railroad: The Boston & Albany, 1825–1867* (Cambridge: Harvard University Press, 1967).

26. Adams, "The Canal and Railroad Enterprise of Boston," 4:143. In a few instances, Massachusetts railroad building demonstrated a continuity of activity among different generations of investors. Elias Hasket Derby (1803–1880), the grandson of the man by the same name (1739–1799) who owned the first ship from Massachusetts to enter the China trade in 1785, was in England in 1843 buying iron for the Fitchburg Railroad. Derby, *Two Months Abroad; or, A Trip to England, France, Baden, Prussia, and Belgium in August and September, 1843* (Boston: Redding & Company, 1844).

27. Johnson and Supple, *Boston Capitalists and Western Railroads*, 47–56. On Boston's role in the financing of railroads outside of New England in the 1830s and 1840s, see also Alfred D. Chandler Jr., "Patterns of American Railroad Finance, 1830–1850," *Business History Review* 28, no. 3 (1954): 254–63.

28. State- and locally financed internal improvements—canals and some early railroads—had proven a disaster in Michigan, Ohio, Indiana, and Illinois due to bad timing (the Panic of 1837), poor planning and execution of projects, and other factors, which provided an opportunity for private investors to finance railroads in those states by the 1840s. Johnson and Supple, *Boston Capitalists and Western Railroads*, 74–78.

29. Adams, "The Canal and Railroad Enterprise of Boston," 4:144–46; Johnson and Supple, *Boston Capitalists and Western Railroads*, 88–99, 100–103, 109–15. This was followed in 1851 when Forbes and his group began work on a railroad connection (the Great Western of Canada) between Buffalo and Detroit via southern Canada, which was completed several years later and linked Boston with Chicago completely by rail. Ibid., 115–21.

30. Ibid., 135, 140–41, 158–62, 163–75, 223–25, 236.

31. Ibid., 195–96, 198–221, 241. Boston's influence on the line rose once again in 1884, when Charles Francis Adams Jr was named president of the Union Pacific and its headquarters were moved back to the Boston, to the eight floor of the Ames Building on Court Street. Unable to get help from the federal government for the railroad's rising debt and crippled by the effects of a stock market crash, however, Adams reluctantly had to hand over control to Jay Gould and his New York associates for a second time. Ibid., 242–63.

32. Ibid., 287; Clarence W. Barron et al., *The Boston Stock Exchange: With Brief Sketches of Prominent Brokers, Bankers, Banks, and Moneyed Institutions of Boston* (Boston: Hunt & Bell, 1893; repr., New York: Arno Press, 1975), unpaginated.

33. Johnson and Supple, *Boston Capitalists and Western Railroads*, 291–302, 322–30; Barron et al., *The Boston Stock Exchange*.

34. Johnson and Supple, *Boston Capitalists and Western Railroads*, 318, quoting the *Boston Herald*, November 16, 1880; Kidder and Peabody, "Finance in Boston," 4:166; [Parker B. Willis et al.], *History of Investment Banking in New England* (Boston: Federal Reserve Bank of Boston, 1973), 4.

35. On the Calumet and Hecla mines, see William B. Gates Jr., *Michigan Copper and Boston Dollars: An Economic History of the Michigan Copper Mining Industry* (New York: Russell and Russell, 1951), esp. 43–45, 195, 215, 230.

36. Martin, *Seventy-Three Years' History of the Boston Stock Market*, 7. Brokers were financial intermediaries who merely transferred securities from a buyer to a seller, whereas

dealers actually bought securities to create a modest inventory (by means of short-term bank loans) for direct sales to interested customers. By the mid-1780s, federal and state war debt—which was virtually the entire securities market at that time—amounted to about $50 million in principal and accrued interest, although the market value was substantially less, perhaps $10–15 million. Edwin J. Perkins, *American Public Finance and Financial Services, 1700–1815* (Columbus: Ohio State University Press, 1994), 312–13, also citing E. James Ferguson, *The Power of the Purse: A History of American Public Finance, 1776–1790* (Chapel Hill: University of North Carolina Press, 1961), 251, 258.

37. Joseph S. Davis, *Essays in the Earlier History of American Corporations*, 2 vols. (Cambridge: Harvard University Press, 1917), 1:197, 199. On speculation and security prices in Boston in the late 1780s and early 1790s, see ibid., 1:142, 181–82, 196, 306, 339–40, and on the "evils resulting from the multiplication of banks, and from speculations in public securities" in Massachusetts and elsewhere, see the contemporary pamphlet by former Massachusetts Governor James Sullivan, *The Path to Riches: An Inquiry into the Origin and Use of Money; and into the Principles of Stocks & Banks* (Boston: J. Belcher, 1809), preface, 10, and *passim*. Robert E. Wright even suggests that Boston "enjoyed a relatively active public securities market by the mid-1760s," and notes that Philadelphia brokers began operations after they had started in Boston. *The First Wall Street: Chestnut Street, Philadelphia, and the Birth of American Finance* (Chicago: University of Chicago Press, 2005), 26, 72–74.

38. Stuart Banner, "The Origin of the New York Stock Exchange, 1791–1860," *Journal of Legal Studies* 27, no. 1 (1998): 114–16; Philadelphia Stock Exchange Finding Aid, 1–4, Collection 3070, Historical Society of Pennsylvania. Stock exchanges, per se, were not that important until the arrival of industrial stocks in about the 1830s. Indeed, probably half of the securities (federal debt) were not traded in the exchanges at all but through personal broker-dealer relationships. Wright, *The First Wall Street*, 94; Robert E. Wright, *One Nation under Debt: Hamilton, Jefferson, and the History of What We Owe* (New York: McGraw Hill, 2008), 161–85, 349–52, 293.

39. John P. Caskey, "The Evolution of the Philadelphia Stock Exchange," *Federal Reserve Bank of Philadelphia Business Review* (2nd Quarter 2004): 18; Wright, *The First Wall Street*, 166–67; Banner, "Origin of the New York Stock Exchange," 117–18, 119; Walter Werner and Stephen T. Smith, *Wall Street* (New York: Columbia University Press, 1991), 162, 164, 184–89; *The Boston Stock Exchange: Its Inception, Early History, and the Important Contribution It Has Made to Developing New England as a Financial and Investment Centre* (Boston: N.p., 1930), 8–10; Domenic Vitiello with George E. Thomas, *The Philadelphia Stock Exchange and the City It Made* (Philadelphia: University of Pennsylvania Press, 2010), 1–75.

40. Gene Smiley, "The Expansion of the New York Securities Market at the Turn of the Century," *Business History Review* 55, no. 1 (1981): 75. On comparing the three cities, both Philadelphia and Boston developed substantial security markets in the early nineteenth century but not the speculative one that New York did. Because of that distinction, New York in time came to dominate as the primary U.S. market and eventually the top world market. Before 1850, however, New York was not the leading U.S. market for the raising of investment capital. Both Boston and Philadelphia financed railroads, yet when railroads became a more speculative enterprise, certainly by the Civil War and the decades thereafter, New York became the center for trading shares. In brief, Boston put its money in discrete activities—shipping, manufacturing, railroads, and mining—and dealt with its local clientele, whereas New York's orientation became national. In effect, the two employed a different use

of stocks and bonds, and the stock market itself; Boston was less interested in trading per se than it was in investing because it was a *buying*, not a *selling*, community.
Werner and Smith, *Wall Street*, 43–46.

41. *The Boston Stock Exchange*, 5, 7–8; Barron et al., *The Boston Stock Exchange*; Joseph G.
Martin, *Twenty-One Years in the Boston Stock Market, or Fluctuations Therein from
January 1, 1835, to January 1, 1856* (Boston: Redding and Company, 1856), 5.

42. Martin, *Seventy-Three Years' History of the Boston Stock Market*, 64, 75, 90; Martin,
Twenty-One Years, 19, 22; *The Boston Stock Exchange*, 8–9; Barron et al., *The Boston
Stock Exchange*.

43. *The Boston Stock Exchange*, 11, 13–15.

44. Barron et al., *The Boston Stock Exchange*.

45. *The Boston Stock Exchange*, 17, 19, 21–22. The Boston Stock Exchange remained an
important local institution well past the mid-twentieth century, but then faced a
period of decline as did nearly all other regional stock exchanges. It was eventually
sold to Nasdaq in 2007. Robert Galvin, "Lack of Volume Brings End to Financial
Chapter," *Boston Globe*, October 3, 2007.

46. For accounts of early Boston brokers, see Barron et al., *The Boston Stock Exchange*.

47. Vincent P. Carosso, *More than a Century of Investment Banking: The Kidder, Peabody
& Co. Story* (New York: McGraw-Hill, 1979), vii–viii, xii, 13–26.

48. *Paine, Webber & Company, 1880–1930: A National Institution* (Boston: Oxford-Print,
1930), 9–10.

49. Ibid., 11, 13.

50. Ibid., 65 and *passim*. Paine, Webber & Company was a "wire house" broker, a national
brokerage house with multiple branches in which branch brokers had access to proprietary investment products, research, and technology, i.e., a national company that
supplied its branches with the same level of access to information.

51. Kidder and Peabody, "Finance in Boston," 4:175–76.

52. Vincent P. Carosso, *Investment Banking in America: A History* (Cambridge: Harvard
University Press, 1971), 4, 13, 42, 44; Thomas R. Navin and Marian V. Sears, "The Rise
of a Market for Industrial Securities, 1887–1902," *Business History Review* 29, no. 2
(1955): 110.

53. [John P. Marquand], "Boston," *Fortune*, February 1933, 36, 98.

54. *The Boston Stock Exchange*, 22; Frederick D. McCarthy, "Boston: A Diversified
Financial Center," *Greater Boston Business*, May 1959, 34–35.

3. The Practice and Legacy of the Boston Trustee

1. *Harvard College and Massachusetts General Hospital* v. *Francis Amory*, 26 Mass. (9
Pickering) 446, at 458–60. For Judge Putnam's full decision in this 1830 case, see
appendix A at http://scholarworks.umass.edu/umpress/. It would appear that the trust
reflected the stockholdings of McLean's estate and were in similar proportions, as
the trust consisted of stocks, one-eighth of which were in banks, about three-eighths
in fire and marine insurance companies, and half in the Boston Manufacturing
Company and the Merrimack Manufacturing Company. Furthermore, the Amorys
were able to obtain good returns from the stocks: dividends received by the trustees
over the first five years was $20,493, or 8.2 percent, when the common rate of interest
for the period was 5 percent. These two circumstances, a combination of the trustees'
imitation of the testator's investment allocations and the success of that investment
strategy, may have gone some way in supporting the ultimate outcome of the case.

2. Ibid., 461, 465. On the history of *Harvard College* v. *Amory* in Massachusetts law, see also cases cited in note 6 of Stephen A. Bergquist, "The Prudent Man Rule in Massachusetts Today," *Trusts & Estates* 122 (1983): 44–50.

3. This would also apply to an institutional trusteeship like a charitable trust, which likewise required chancery jurisdiction.

4. *Prescott* v. *Tarbell*, 1 Mass. 208 (1804); *Bridgen* v. *Cheever*, 10 Mass. 453 (1813); Edwin H. Woodruff, "Chancery in Massachusetts," *Law Quarterly Review* 5 (1889): 379–80. See also *Parsons et ux.* v. *Winslow*, 6 Mass. 169 (1810). So engrained was the notion that there was no equity jurisdiction in Massachusetts courts that lawyers continued to make that point in cases involving a trust estate even after the law was changed. See *Vose* v. *Grant*, 15 Mass. 505, 517 (1819).

5. Woodruff, "Chancery in Massachusetts," 371–77.

6. Ibid. Chancery courts in Massachusetts also had a popular association with arbitrary rule, particularly by royal governors and the "king's prerogative, unsuitable for a democratic state." See William J. Curran, "The Struggle for Equity Jurisdiction in Massachusetts," *Boston University Law Review* 31, no. 3 (1951): 271–72.

7. *Massachusetts Acts & Resolves,* May 1815–February 1819 (Boston: Russell & Gardner, 1819), ch. 87, approved February 10, 1818. See also ch. 190, An Act to Regulate the Jurisdiction and Proceedings of Courts of Probate, *Massachusetts Acts & Resolves,* May 1815–February 1819, esp. 647–52. The whole development of equity law through statutes and case law in Massachusetts is described in detail by John Norton Pomeroy, *A Treatise on Equity Jurisprudence as Administered in the United States of America; Adapted for All the States, and to the Union of Legal and Equitable Remedies under the Reformed Procedure,* 3 vols. (San Francisco: A. L. Bancroft and Company, 1881–1883), 1:341–52.

8. Woodruff, "Chancery in Massachusetts," 377–83; Curran, "The Struggle for Equity Jurisdiction in Massachusetts," 274–75, 280, 287.

9. Oliver Wendell Holmes Sr., *The Autocrat of the Breakfast-Table* (Boston: Houghton Mifflin, 1894), 70. On general changes in testamentary trust law from the 1820s through the 1870s, see Peter Dobkin Hall, "What the Merchants Did with Their Money: Charitable and Testamentary Trusts in Massachusetts, 1780–1880," in *Entrepreneurs: The Boston Business Community, 1700–1850,* ed. Conrad Edick Wright and Katheryn P. Viens (Boston: Massachusetts Historical Society, 1997), 379–96.

10. Sheldon A. Jones, Laura M. Moret, and James M. Storey, "The Massachusetts Business Trust and Registered Investment Companies," *Delaware Journal of Corporate Law* 13, no. 2 (1988): 421–58; *Alvord* v. *Smith*, 5 Pickering, 22 Mass. 232 (1827). See also Oscar and Mary Flug Handlin, *Commonwealth: A Study of the Role of Government in the American Economy: Massachusetts, 1774–1861* (New York: New York University Press, 1947), 167–71. The origins of the mutual fund are discussed in chapters 5 and 6.

11. Donald Holbrook, *The Boston Trustee* (Boston: Marshall Jones, 1937), 10–11, 13–15. One of the interesting ironies of Boston asset management has been its general focus on the role of businessmen and management of equity assets, whereas lawyers, who until more recent times dominated trustee ranks, tended to invest far more conservatively in fixed assets, including local property.

12. Ibid., 8–9; Hall, "What the Merchants Did," 385–88; *Broadway Bank* v. *Adams*, 133 Mass. 170 (1882); *King* v. *Talbot*, 14 New York 76 (1869); Augustus Peabody Loring, *A Trustee's Handbook,* 4th edn. (Boston: Little, Brown, 1928), 132–40. By 1928, there were only a few scattered states that followed the "Massachusetts Rule" of independent investment judgment, and they included California, Kentucky ("substantially"),

Michigan, Mississippi, Missouri, North Carolina ("Massachusetts rule approved"), Ohio ("substantially"), Rhode Island, South Dakota, Vermont, and Washington state. Ibid., 143–52. Because they required a trustee to judge the funds created and managed by others, it took mutual funds even longer to become accepted by states for trustees to purchase for their clients under the "prudent man rule." In 1945, only seventeen states approved of mutual funds, but this increased to forty by 1962. David Grayson Allen, *Eaton Vance and the Growth of Investment Management in the United States* (Boston and Concord, Mass.: Eaton Vance and Allen Associates, 2007), 80.

For some useful further discussion on the difference between a "dynamic" and a "caretaker" trust, as epitomized in the Massachusetts and New York cases, see Lawrence M. Friedman, "The Dynastic Trust," *Yale Law Journal* 73, no. 4 (1964): 547–92.

13. James Freeman, "Character of the Hon. George Richards Minot, Esq . . . Extracted from an E[u]logy Delivered a Few Days after His Death," *Massachusetts Historical Collections,* 1st ser., 8 (n.d.): 86–109. Minot's few professional papers are found in the Sedgwick Family Papers, box 109, Ms. N-851, Massachusetts Historical Society.

14. William Minot (1783–1873) Papers, box 6 (loose papers), vol. 25, Account Book, 1843–47, and vols. 26 and 27, Benjamin & Minot Account Book, 1843–47, 1847–54, Ms. N-2244.1; William Minot, Jr., Papers, box 1, Ms. N-2244.2, both Massachusetts Historical Society. For further background on the two Franklin trust funds, see Bruce H. Yenawine, *Benjamin Franklin and the Invention of Microfinance,* ed. Michele R. Costello (London: Pickering and Chatto, 2010).

15. "Noteworthy Union of 'Boston Trustees,'" *Boston Evening Transcript,* January 5, 1935.

16. "Property Management Firms Merge into Minot, DeBlois & Maddison," *Boston Globe,* November 7, 1949; Anthony J. Yudis, "200-Year-Old Hub Realty Firm Purchased," *Boston Globe,* September 14, 1985.

17. Trustees were, of course, not restricted to just Boston, but they did live and work near families of wealth, which generally included Boston and surrounding towns, as well as rich North Shore communities like Salem. Still, by the late 1930s, Donald Holbrook, a Boston trustee himself, did see his profession tied to the city: "The Boston Trustee is an integral part of the rise to maturity of our city." *The Boston Trustee,* vii.

18. Lawrence Coolidge, interview, June 24, 2003. Little, for instance, exists in extant documents or secondary accounts about Nathaniel Bowditch's business career or work as a trustee. There are only short references to Bowditch's business in [Henry Ingersoll Bowditch], *Memoir of Nathaniel Bowditch* (Boston: James Munroe and Company, 1841), 92–93, 117–18, and nothing in the major collection of his papers. See *The Papers of Nathaniel Bowditch in the Boston Public Library Organized and Edited by James W. Montgomery, Jr., and Laura V. Monti* (Boston: Boston Public Library, 1983), and Margaret Munsterberg, "The Bowditch Collection in the Boston Public Library," *Isis* 34 (1942): 140–42. A great-grandson, August Peabody Loring Jr., later concluded that Nathaniel as well as later generations of Bowditch trustees destroyed "a great deal of material . . . when it apparently was useless for purposes of the business." In addition, the great-grandson wistfully noted, "every time the office was moved, masses of material were consigned to the furnace, which is a great shame." Augustus Peabody Loring Jr., *Nathaniel Bowditch (1773–1838) of Salem and Boston, Navigator, etc.* (New York: Newcomen Society, 1950), 9, 16.

19. Loring, *Nathaniel Bowditch,* 16–19. On December 27, 1816, Rev. William Bentley of Salem noted in his diary: "This day was buried Mr. Charles Henry Orne, aet. 28, son of the late W. Orne, a rich merchant of Salem. This young gentlemen has bestowed from the great wealth he inherited a rich legacy on the Cambridge Institution for

education of Candidates for the Ministry & several other valuable legacies of which I have not the correct history. He was educated at Cambridge, his wife is dead & he has no children. A Brother & Sister survive him who have an equal share in the wealth of the Father." *The Diary of William Bentley, D.D., Pastor of the East Church Salem, Massachusetts,* 4 vols. (Gloucester, Mass.: Peter Smith, 1962), 4:429. On the interconnectedness of Salem families, see Bernard Farber, *Guardians of Virtue: Salem Families in 1800* (New York: Basic Books, 1972), 93, 119, 118, 121.

20. Gerald T. White, *A History of the Massachusetts Hospital Life Insurance Company* (Cambridge: Harvard University Press, 1955); Loring, *Nathaniel Bowditch,* 19–20.

21. Ibid., 9–10; Peter Loring, interview, May 8, 2008; Lawrence Coolidge, interview. For the Bowditch-Loring family genealogy, see figure A at http://scholarworks.umass.edu/umpress/.

22. Loring's father, Augustus Peabody Loring, a lawyer, trustee, and briefly North Shore politician, was the author of *A Trustee's Handbook* (1898), a publication discussed later and still used today.

23. Alfred Bowditch Papers, 1907–1914, Ms. N-2284, Massachusetts Historical Society; Charles Henry Pope, comp., with Katharine Peabody Loring, *Loring Genealogy, Compiled from "The Chronicles or Ancestral Records" of James Speare Loring* (Cambridge, Mass.: Murray and Emery Company 1917), 263–64, 336–38; Samuel Eliot Morison, "Augustus Peabody Loring, Jr., 1885–1951," *Transactions of the Colonial Society of Massachusetts* 42 (1964): 13.

24. Pope, comp., *Loring Genealogy,* 263–64, 336–38; Morison, "Augustus Peabody Loring, Jr.," 13. Other trustees created different ways to handle both legal and financial aspects of the Boston trustee business. For instance, beginning in the late 1920s, Fiduciary Trust Company, which grew out of Robert H. Gardiner's Boston trustee practice begun in 1885, allied itself with Scudder, Stevens & Clark, which provided investment advice for the trusts that Fiduciary managed, a practice that continued on for many decades. "Firm to Work with Fiduciary Trust Co.," *Boston Herald,* June 5, 1929.

25. Loring, *Nathaniel Bowditch,* 9–10; Walter Muir Whitehill, *Augustus Peabody Loring, Jr. 1885–1951* (Salem, Mass.: Peabody Museum, 1952), 7–8; Lawrence Coolidge, interview; Peter Loring, interview.

26. E. Sohier Welch, Obituary, *Boston Herald,* June 28, 1948.

27. A Sketch of Charles A. Welch, 1815–1901, and Supporting Materials, Ms. S-827, Massachusetts Historical Society; Milton Lehman, "The Prudent Man's Last Stand," *Nation's Business,* March 1949, 82; [John P. Marquand], "Boston," *Fortune,* February 1933, 36. Apparently only Robert H. Gardiner and Philip Dexter might have amassed as much as Welch in their trustee work.

28. E. Sohier Welch, "The Professional Trustee: Responsiveness to Changing Investment Situations and Personal Requirements of Fiduciary Clients," excerpts reprinted from *Trust Companies* magazine (c. 1936), in A Sketch of Charles A. Welch, 1815–1901, and Supporting Materials, Ms. S-827, Massachusetts Historical Society.

29. E. Sohier Welch, *Twenty-Fifth Anniversary Report, 1909–1934 / Harvard College Class of 1909* (Cambridge: Harvard University Press, 1934), 656–58, 660, 661.

30. F. Murray Forbes Jr., videotape interview conducted by Welch & Forbes, c. 1994, Welch & Forbes, Boston.

31. Welch, Obituary; Welch, *Twenty-Fifth Anniversary Report,* 654. At the time of his death, Welch was deeply involved in many business and institutions. He was president and director of three wharf or storage warehouse companies, and trustee of ten real estate trusts, two charitable or nonprofit organizations, three railroad or

railway companies, five financial institutions, and four manufacturing companies, plus numerous professional and social organizations, all of which sought his business and investment advice.

32. Sketch of Charles A. Welch, and Supporting Materials; "In Investing, It's the Prudent Bostonian," *Business Week,* June 6, 1959, 68.

33. Albert Boyden, *Ropes-Gray 1865–1940* (Boston: N.p., 1942), 49, 86, 137, 147, 153–54, 157, 179, 191, 192. In addition to their trustee work, a number of Boston law firms, including Ropes & Gray and Storey, Thorndike, did work to certify the legal validity of municipal, county, and state bonds and notes (securities often acquired by trustees), a practice that increased in the late nineteenth and early twentieth centuries. Ibid., 98, 125. For Ropes & Gray's later trustee work, particularly in the post–World War II era, see Carl M. Brauer, *Ropes & Gray 1865–1990* (Boston: Ropes & Gray, 1991), 26–27, 83–85, 126–28. By 1989, the firm held $1.25 billion under custody or as trustee. Ibid., 154.

34. At the end of the nineteenth century, Harvard Law School professor Samuel Williston described the "practice at that time in Boston was more individual than it has since become. There were no large firms, and many of the most distinguished lawyers were practicing alone . . . , They had juniors in their offices, but did not form firms." *Life and Law: An Autobiography* (Boston: Little, Brown, 1940), 110–11.

35. Guido R. Perera, *Leaves from My Book of Life,* 3 vols. (Boston: N.p., 1974–1977), 1:61.

36. "How Many There Are and Some of Those Who Get the Big Fees," *Boston Record,* July 31, 1886; Lawrence T. Perera, "Hemenway & Barnes—The First Hundred Years, 1863–1963," typescript, esp. 13–21, in possession of the author; Christopher Rowland and Ross Kerber, "Dow Jones Family's Power Rests with Hub Law Firm," *Boston Globe,* May 3, 2007; Sacha Pfeiffer, "Murdock Bid Puts Light on Hub Lawyer: Discreet, Behind-the-Scenes Player to Mediate Dow Jones Family Talks," *Boston Globe,* July 20, 2007. Clarence Barron and the business information empire he built are discussed in chapter 5.

37. Beth Healy, "What Do These Two Have in Common? They Use Their Lawyers as Money Managers," *Boston Globe,* November 2, 2000; Kit Chellel, "Some Turning to Law Firms to Invest Funds," *Boston Globe,* July 15, 2010; Michael Puzo, interview, June 8, 2009.

38. Loring's papers and manuscripts, most of which are related to his work on the *Trustee's Handbook,* are in the special collections of the Harvard Law School.

39. Undated newspaper clippings in Augustus Peabody Loring Diary, 1903–1905, Augustus Peabody Loring Papers, Harvard Law School.

40. William J. Sheehan, "Unique to Boston Are the Famous 'Boston Trustees,'" *Boston Evening Transcript,* July 28, 1934.

41. John P. Marquand, *The Late George Apley: A Novel in the Form of a Memoir* (Boston: Little, Brown, 1937), esp. 18–19, 114–15, 148, 207–8, 305, 312–13; George Santayana, *The Last Puritan: A Memoir in the Form of a Novel* (New York: Charles Scribner's Sons, 1936), esp. 6–9, 35, 43, 112, 246, 326–27, 380, 424, 602.

42. Sheehan, "Unique to Boston Are the Famous 'Boston Trustees'"; Lehman, "The Prudent Man's Last Stand," 33. Phillip Dexter had a hard time trying to describe his life as a Boston trustee even to his Harvard classmates. "Some people have been good enough to want me to take care of their property, which has been during the past fifteen years sufficiently absorbing to preclude other occupations. . . . I have been sticking to that job, and although it interests me, I don't know how to tell about it in a way that will interest any one else. There is not much romantic excitement in other people's coupons." *Twenty-Fifth Anniversary Report, 1889–1914 / Harvard College Class of 1889* (Boston: Cockayne, 1914), 327.

43. [Marquand], "Boston," 36, 98.
44. Ibid., 98.
45. Ibid., 100, 102, 106; "In Investing, It's the Prudent Bostonian," 57. On Boston's decline in the early twentieth century, see Frederic Jesup Stimson, *My United States* (New York: Charles Scribner's Sons, 1931), 71–108. Boston's conservative nature was also pointed out by Boston trustee Donald Holbrook, who noted that "Boston has maintained a closer relationship to the English tradition than any other American city. This is true of finance, of society, and of its philosophy of living. Here one finds little evidence of frenzied pursuit of expansion and grandiose development. There is far more concentration upon the maintenance and perfection of what now exists. . . . Boston has an attending degree of stability more in keeping with its maturity, and gladly turns over the exuberance of pioneering to other sections of the country. To weigh in the balance what is and what is not worth while comes naturally to its inhabitants. Boston trustees rarely create great buildings, or monuments of industrial success, which they may leave as landmarks of their standing." *The Boston Trustee,* 21–22.
46. Welch, "The Professional Trustee"; Lehman, "The Prudent Man's Last Stand," 83; Holbrook, *The Boston Trustee,* 16–17, 28–29; John L. Thorndike, interview, December 12, 2007.
47. John L. Thorndike, interview; Lawrence Coolidge, interview. Much of this will be covered in chapter 11, below.

4. Financial Intermediaries in Boston through the Early Twentieth Century

1. By the late 1950s, "financial intermediaries" had grown as a group to encompass a variety of financial organizations, including "the banking system, personal trust departments, private and government insurance organizations, savings and loan associations, credit unions, sales and personal finance companies, land banks, investment companies, investment bankers, and government lending institutions." Raymond W. Goldsmith, *Financial Intermediaries in the American Economy since 1900: A Study by the National Bureau of Economic Research, New York* (Princeton: Princeton University Press, 1958), 3n. Except for insurance companies and banks, the variety and growth of these financial intermediaries only started to take off rapidly in the late nineteenth century; those institutions that had a marked presence in Boston are covered in later chapters. Ibid., 57–66.

Because of the number of different financial intermediaries, not all of them can be discussed in this or subsequent chapters. Savings and loan associations, for instance, also called building and loan associations, and known in Massachusetts as cooperative banks, were important institutions from 1852, when the Suffolk Mutual Loan and Accumulation Fund Association was incorporated, to the end of the twentieth century when many were rolled up (merged) into commercial banks. Their history is well covered in David L. Mason's *From Buildings and Loans to Bail-Outs: A History of the American Savings and Loan Industry, 1831–1995* (New York: Cambridge University Press, 2004), in which the author even includes a case history of one Massachusetts cooperative, the Medford Cooperative Bank (297–317). On the general history of Massachusetts cooperative banks and the movement as a whole, see also H. Morton Bodfish, ed., *History of Building and Loan in the United States* (Chicago: United States Building and Loan League, 1931), 79–84, 425–41.

2. John A. Bogardus Jr. and Robert H. Moore, *Spreading the Risks: Insuring the American Experience* (Chevy Chase, Md.: Posterity Press, 2003), 14–15.

3. Osborne Howes Jr., "The Rise and Progress of Insurance in Boston," in *Memorial History of Boston, Including Suffolk County, Massachusetts, 1630–1880*, ed. Justin Winsor, 4 vols. (Boston: James R. Osgood, 1882–1886), 4:179–80; Edwin J. Perkins, *American Public Finance and Financial Services, 1700–1815* (Columbus: Ohio State University Press, 1994), 282–92; Edward R. Hardy, *Reports of 1888–1900, with an Account of Early Insurance Offices in Massachusetts, from 1724 to 1801* (Boston: Frank Wood, 1901). See also Christopher Kingston, "Marine Insurance in Britain and America, 1720–1844," *Journal of Economic History* 67, no. 2 (2007): 379–409. Even after marine insurance became common, many ship owners continued the age-old practice of dividing up ownership of the ship and cargo into fractional shares, so that no one shareholder was exposed to severe risk. Marine insurance was to a large extent the formalization of this process.

4. William M. Fowler Jr., "Marine Insurance in Boston: The Early Years of the Boston Marine Insurance Company, 1799–1807," in *Entrepreneurs: The Boston Business Community, 1700–1850*, ed. Conrad Edick Wright and Katheryn P. Viens (Boston: Massachusetts Historical Society, 1997), 160–66, 167.

5. Bogardus and Moore, *Spreading the Risks*, 18–20, 22; Howes, "The Rise and Progress of Insurance in Boston," 182–85. The case was *Stetson v. Massachusetts Mutual*, 4 Mass. 300 (1808).

6. Howes, "The Rise and Progress of Insurance in Boston," 185–86; *Explanatory Remarks and Observations on the Subject of Fire Insurance* (Boston: James Loring, 1823).

7. Howes, "The Rise and Progress of Insurance in Boston," 190. The number of mutual fire insurance companies also grew outside of Boston during this period. In Salem alone, six companies were started between 1829 and 1847, while overall, fourteen mutual fire insurance companies were established in Massachusetts in a twelve-year period beginning in 1823. John J. Fox with Carl G. Ryant, *Insuring the Future: The Holyoke Mutual Insurance Company in Salem, 1843–1993* (Acton, Mass.: Tapestry Press, 1993), 3.

8. Howes, "The Rise and Progress of Insurance in Boston," 190–94.

9. Ibid., 187–89.

10. Gerald T. White, *A History of the Massachusetts Hospital Life Insurance Company* (Cambridge: Harvard University Press, 1955), 7–22, 27.

11. Ibid., 9 (emphasis added). Previously, the company's charter had limited its capital to "the funded debt of the United States, or of this Commonwealth, or in the stock of the bank of the United States, or of any of the banks incorporated within this Commonwealth, or in the purchase of ground rents, or mortgages on real estate." For Bowditch's trustee work, see chapter 3.

12. Ibid., 4, 27, 192.

13. Ibid., 34–38.

14. Ibid., 3, 5, 41–54, 195–96, citing the work of James G. Smith, *The Development of Trust Companies in the United States* (New York: H. Holt, 1928), 238–46; Tamara Plakins Thornton, "'A Great Machine' or a 'Beast of Prey': A Boston Corporation and Its Rural Debtors in an Age of Capitalist Transformation," *Journal of the Early Republic* 27, no. 4 (2007): 567–97.

15. Phillips's volumes, among others, include *A Treatise on the Law of Insurance*, 2 vols. (Boston: Wells and Lilly, 1823–1834); *Manual of Political Economy, with Particular Reference to the Institutions, Resources, and Conditions of the United States* (Boston:

Suffolk System was needed not only to control the stability of out-of-Boston banks but to deal with the overwhelming number of non-Boston notes. In about 1824, it was estimated that Boston had more than half of the banking capital in New England, but that its notes or currency represented only about 1/25 of bills in circulation. Ibid. On the Boston Clearing House, see Dudley P. Bailey, "Boston Clearing-House," in *Professional and Industrial History of Suffolk County*, 2:375–97. For a good summary on how well the New England banking system worked into the post–Civil War era, see Peter Temin, "The Industrialization of New England, 1830–1880," in *Engines of Enterprise: An Economic History of New England*, ed. Peter Temin (Cambridge: Harvard University Press, 2000), 149–51. For some other viewpoints on the Suffolk System, see J. Van Fenstermaker and John E. Filer, "Impact of the First and Second Banks of the US and the Suffolk System on New England Money, 1791-1837," *Journal of Money, Credit, and Banking* 18, no. 1 (1986): 28–40; Donald J. Mullineaux, "Competitive Monies and the Suffolk Banking System: A Contractual Perspective," *Southern Economic Journal* 53, no. 4 (1987): 884–98; and Bodenhorn, *State Banking in Early America*, 95–122.

30. Howes and Williams, "The Financial History of Suffolk County," 2:205–6. On the histories of each Boston bank in the nineteenth century, see ibid., 2:219–374; Knowles et al., *Shawmut*, 37.

31. Bailey, "Boston Clearing-House," 2:394; Edwin A. Stone, *A Century of Boston Banking* (Boston: Rockwell and Churchill, 1894), 25–30; Frederic H. Curtiss, "Fifty Years of Boston Finance, 1880–1930," in *Fifty Years of Boston: A Memorial Volume Issued in Commemoration of the Tercentenary of 1930*, ed. Elisabeth M. Herlihy (Boston: Subcommittee on Memorial History of the Boston Tercentenary Committee, 1932), 230–31, 235.

32. "Savings Banks," in *Professional and Industrial History of Suffolk County*, 2:398–99, 409–35; Frank P. Bennett Jr., *The Story of Mutual Savings Banks* (Boston: Frank P. Bennett and Company, 1924), 38–39, 45–47, 60–64, 91–92; Lance Edwin Davis and Peter Lester Payne, "From Benevolence to Business: The Story of Two Savings Banks," *Business History Review* 32, no. 4 (1958): 387. The class identification of savings banks was common at the time. Nathaniel Bowditch of the Massachusetts Hospital Life Insurance Company referred to the trust business at his institution as "a species of Savings Bank for the rich and middle class of Society." White, *Massachusetts Hospital Life Insurance Company*, 34. For a brief history of the Provident, see Walter Muir Whitehill, *The Provident Institution for Savings in the Town of Boston, 1816–1966* (Boston: Provident Institution for Savings, 1966).

33. Davis and Payne, "From Benevolence to Business," 388–89, 391–93.

34. Ibid., 395–405; Whitney, *The Suffolk Bank*, 41, 70–71, 74; "Savings Banks," 2:400. Dividends from Boston bank stocks varied from year to year but usually yielded somewhat less than the Suffolk Bank's performance. For semiannual bank stock returns from the 1780s to 1869, see Martin, *Seventy-Three Years' History of the Boston Stock Market*, 45–50.

35. "Trust Companies," in *Professional and Industrial History of Suffolk County*, 2:436–42; Larry Neal, "Trust Companies and Financial Innovation, 1897–1914," *Business History Review* 45, no. 1 (1971): 36–39; William W. Wolbach, *Boston Safe Deposit and Trust Company: The Story of New England's Largest Independent Trust Organization* (New York: Newcomen Society, 1962), 11, 14, 16–20; Ralph E. Winter, "'Prudent Man' Push: Bank Trust Sections Abandon Old Stuffiness to Fight for New Clients," *Wall Street Journal*, November 30, 1956. On U.S. trust companies generally, see Ernest

Heaton, *The Trust Company Idea and Its Development* (Buffalo, N.Y.: The White-Evans-Penfold Company, 1904), esp. 9–14.

36. Stone, *A Century of Boston Banking*, 44.

37. Curtiss, "Fifty Years of Boston Finance, 1880–1930," 230–34; Naomi R. Lamoreaux, "Bank Mergers in Late Nineteenth-Century New England: The Contingent Nature of Structural Change," *Journal of Economic History* 51, no. 4 (1991): 539, 540. Cf. Knowles et al., *Shawmut*, 64–68, 69–71.

38. Marian V. Sears, "The National Shawmut Bank Consolidation of 1898," *Business History Review* 39, no. 3 (1965): 369–72, 374, 375–84, 386; Knowles et al., *Shawmut*, 58–59, 79–83; Richard P. Chapman, *One Hundred Twenty-Five Years on State Street: "Merchants National of Boston" (1831–1956)* (Princeton, N.J.: Newcomen Society, 1956), 16.

39. Lamoreaux, "Bank Mergers," 547–48.

40. Lamoreaux, *Insider Lending*, 123, 154–56; Knowles et al., *Shawmut*, 90–92; Ben Ames Williams Jr., *Bank of Boston 200: A History of New England's Leading Bank, 1784–1984* (Boston: Houghton Mifflin, 1984), 66–67, 68–84, 85–89. Gras described Wing as "a westerner. Not knowing the traditions of Boston, he did not suffer from the limitations of those who did. His eyes looked out from Boston to the West, to New York City, to Europe, South America, and the Orient." *Massachusetts First National Bank of Boston*, 159.

41. Curtiss, "Fifty Years of Boston Finance, 1880–1930," 242–43; Knowles et al., *Shawmut*, 106–7; Williams, *Bank of Boston 200*, 247. On The First's rise to "primacy," see Gras, *Massachusetts First National Bank of Boston*, 158–73, 201.

42. Curtiss, "Fifty Years of Boston Finance, 1880–1930," 242–43; Knowles et al. *Shawmut*, 41, 69, 84–86, 106–7, 108–9, 111–12, 127–37, 148–56; Gras, *Massachusetts First National Bank of Boston*, 182–84.

43. Williams, *Bank of Boston 200*, 161.

44. Edward Weeks, *Men, Money and Responsibility: A History of Lee Higginson Corporation, 1848–1962* (Boston: N.p., 1962), 8–10; Vincent P. Carosso, *Investment Banking in America: A History* (Cambridge: Harvard University Press, 1970), 11.

45. Weeks, *Men, Money and Responsibility*, 11–13; Carosso, *Investment Banking in America*, 26, 30, 44, 69, 95, 140–41.

46. Eighty-five percent of the company's stockholders were Massachusetts residents even as late as 1894. Parker B. Willis et al., *History of Investment Banking in New England* (Boston: Federal Reserve Bank of Boston, 1973), 35.

47. Weeks, *Men, Money and Responsibility* 14, 18, 20–22; Carosso, *Investment Banking in America*, 102–3, 43, 93–94; Henry Greenleaf Pearson, *Son of New England: James Jackson Storrow, 1864–1926* (Boston: Thomas Todd Company, 1932), 99–103, 123–27, 135–38. In addition to his work for Lee, Higginson and General Motors, where he also served briefly as president, Storrow conceived of the idea of creating the Boston Esplanade, which required the damming of the Charles River, creation of the Charles River Basin, and improvement of the riverbanks for use as public parks—and indirectly the problems of tidal pollution and low-tide smells. Later a highway on the Boston side called Storrow Drive was named after him. Ibid., 33–42.

48. Weeks, *Men, Money and Responsibility*, 25–29; Carosso, *Investment Banking in America*, 317–19. For a recent treatment on Kreuger and his businesses, see Frank Partnoy, *The Match King: Ivar Kreuger, the Financial Genius behind a Century of Wall Street Scandals* (New York: Public Affairs, 2009). For the reactions of a Boston Lee, Higginson partner to the company's decline, see Mark I. Gelfand, *Trustee for a City: Ralph Lowell of Boston* (Boston: Northeastern University Press, 1998), 81–87.

49. Louis M. Lyons, "Boston: Study in Inertia," *Our Fair City,* ed. Robert S. Allen (New York: Vanguard Press, 1947), 29.

50. Besides information in chapter 2 on Kidder, Peabody, see also Carosso, *Investment Banking in America,* 34–37, 90, 309–11, and his more lengthy treatment in *More Than a Century of Investment Banking: The Kidder, Peabody & Co. Story* (New York: McGraw-Hill, 1979), 30–33, 40–42, 47–54, 58–61, 66–69.

51. S. Melvin Rines, *Al Gordon of Kidder, Peabody* (Weston, Mass.: Southport Press, 1999), 25–26, 41–59, 68, 70, 74–75, 80; Carosso, *Investment Banking in America,* 309–17. On the effects of the crash and the reorganization that followed, see ibid., 311–18, and *More Than a Century of Investment Banking,* 71–99, 105.

52. Willis et al., *History of Investment Banking in New England,* 40, 43, 45–46, 48–49, 52–55, 61, 64, 78–79, 84–87, 147. By 1934–1938, Boston ranked third in the number of corporate underwritings larger than $1 million (33) compared to Chicago (75) and New York (524). Ibid., 92. Not only did this municipal bond business become important in Boston, remaining after large industrial underwritings went to New York, but it also spawned a large municipal bond practice in Boston law firms, including Storey Thorndike Palmer & Dodge, which continued throughout much of the twentieth century. *Palmer Dodge Gardner & Bradford—Storey Thorndike Palmer & Dodge, Seventy-Fifth Anniversary 1887–1962* (Boston: Palmer Dodge Gardner & Bradford, 1962), 32–34.

5. Developing New Investment Ideas, Information, and Services in Boston

1. On early Massachusetts statutory law affecting corporations, see E. Merrick Dodd Jr., "Statutory Developments in Business Corporation Law," in *Harvard Legal Essays Written in Honor of and Presented to Joseph Henry Beale and Samuel Williston,* ed. Morton Carlisle Campbell et al. (Cambridge: Harvard University Press, 1934), 65–132; E. Merrick Dodd Jr., *American Business Corporation until 1860 with Special Reference to Massachusetts* (Cambridge: Harvard University Press, 1954), esp. 123–363. The legislature developed general statutory models for incorporation of certain entities, like banks and manufacturing companies, and passed general acts on regulations that applied to various kinds of corporations, creating by the 1840s a "mixed system" through which corporations were covered under both general and special acts. This did not, however, reduce the number of entities that wished to be incorporated, and special acts continued on after 1851. William C. Kessler, "Incorporation in New England: A Statistical Study, 1800–1875," *Journal of Economic History* 8, no. 1 (1948): 43, 44, 48–50; Pauline Maier, "The Debate over Incorporations: Massachusetts in the Early Republic," in *Massachusetts and the New Nation,* ed. Conrad Edick Wright (Boston: Massachusetts Historical Society, 1992), 112–13.

2. Maier, "Debate over Incorporations," 74–78, 79–81, 91; *Trustees of Dartmouth College v. Woodward,* 17 U.S. (4 Wheaton) 518 (1819); Oscar Handlin and Mary F. Handlin, "Origins of the American Business Corporation," *Journal of Economic History* 5, no. 1 (1945): 1, 7, 10, 14, 18–22.

3. Naomi R. Lamoreaux, "The Partnership Form of Organization: Its Popularity in Early-Nineteenth-Century Boston," in *Entrepreneurs: The Boston Business Community, 1700–1850,* ed. Conrad Edick Wright and Katheryn P. Viens (Boston: Massachusetts Historical Society, 1997), 278–85.

4. Early on, these were sometimes called copartnerships, even when more than two individuals were involved.

5. Lamoreaux, "The Partnership Form of Organization," 293–94. Of course, partnerships had important nonlegal attributes over sole proprietorships in allowing its members the advantages of complementary skills, division of labor, and emotional benefits, among others.

6. Massachusetts statute law allowed corporations to own and deal with real estate in 1912, but by that time, it was too late to make much of an impact on Massachusetts practice.

7. *Alvord* v. *Smith*, 22 Mass (5 Pickering) 232 (1827). For the development of the Massachusetts business trust, see Sheldon A. Jones, Laura M. Moret, and James M. Storey, "The Massachusetts Business Trust and Registered Investment Companies," *Delaware Journal of Corporate Law* 13, no. 2 (1988): 421–58, esp. 421–28, and William D. T. Trefry, *Report of the Massachusetts Tax Commissioner on Voluntary Associations*, Massachusetts House Report no. 1646 (Boston: Wright & Potter, 1912), hereafter referred to as the 1912 Report.

8. *Tyrell* v. *Washburn*, 6 Allen 466 (1863) at 474. See also *Tappan* v. *Bailey*, 4 Metcalf 529 (1864).

9. *Ricker* v. *American Loan & Trust Company*, 140 Mass. 346, 5 N.E. 284 (1885), at 348–49. The decision mirrored previous cases, such as *Hoadley* v. *County Commissioners of Essex*, 105 Mass. 519 (1870), another tax case that also noted that an association is not a corporation, which "can only be created and exist by sanction of the legislature. This is a voluntary association of individuals, and its articles of agreement, although they adopt some of the forms of managing the business usual in corporations, constitute a partnership." Ibid., 526. Again in *Gleason* v. *McKay*, 134 Mass. 419 (1883), the court made the same stark distinction between corporations and partnerships, and no form of organization in between: "The defendant in this case is not a corporation. It is merely a partnership, with all the incidents and responsibilities of a partnership." Ibid., 425. The same was true in *Whitman* v. *Porter*, 107 Mass. 522 (1871), where "the association between the proprietors of the ferry boat was in substance a partnership" and not a corporation. Ibid., 524. In 1878, the Massachusetts legislature passed a law, chapter 275, that placed associations on the same footing as corporations for tax purposes, but in *Gleason* v. *McKay*, the court declared the statute unconstitutional. Ibid., 426.

   In Oliver Wendell Holmes Jr.'s opinion for the court in *Phillips* v. *Blatchford*, 137 Mass. 570 (1884), he noted that "it is too late to contend that partnerships with transferable shares are illegal in this Commonwealth. They have been recognized as lawful by the court, from *Alvord* v. *Smith*, 5 Pick. 232, to *Gleason* v. *McKay*, 134 Mass. 419. Even if the question were a new one, we should come to the same result. The grounds upon which they were formerly said to be illegal in England, apart from statute, have been abandoned in modern times." Ibid., 512.

10. *Mayo* v. *Moritz*, 151 Mass. 481, 24 N.E. 1083 (1890) at 484 (1083).

11. The Massachusetts business trust seems not to have evolved from its most logical and direct path, the development of the trust type of organization itself. There was at least one relevant case, *Attorney General* v. *Proprietors of the Federal Street Meeting-house in Boston*, 3 Gray 1 (1854), in which the court referred to companies "formed without incorporation, consisting of numerous members, for the purchase of wild lands, with a view to resale or other like purposes" in which "the grant is made to trustees in trust for several members designated, and a certificate of such right to an aliquot [fractional]

part of the beneficial interest is usually issued by the trustees to the several parties, indicating what aliquot part each holds in such trust property or beneficial interest." Ibid., 46. The case is not even referenced in *Mayo* or the 1913 *Williams* case, discussed below, probably because of the tax issues those Massachusetts business trusts posed.

12. "Boston's Biggest Taxpayers: Twelve Per Cent. of the Levy Paid by Thirty-four Persons and Corporations," *New York Times,* January 20, 1894 (reprinted from the *Boston Herald*). The Boston Personal Property Trust, a somewhat elusive document to undercover, was reprinted in John Harold Sears, *Trust Estates as Business Companies,* 2nd edn. (Kansas City, Mo.: Vernon Law Book, 1921), 418–32. For the complete document, see appendix B at http://scholarworks.umass.edu/umpress/.

13. Boston Personal Property Trust, *passim.* The document was later amended to omit "scrip" and create certificates in amounts of $100 rather than $1,000; see appendix B at http://scholarworks.umass.edu/umpress/.

14. William Howard Steiner, *Investment Trusts: American Experience* (New York: Adelphi, 1929), 43–44.

15. Roger W. Babson, *Actions and Reactions: An Autobiography of Roger W. Babson* (New York: Harper and Brothers, 1935), 90–91. Many large organizations, particularly utilities, used the Massachusetts business trust. See James Abbott Vaughan, "The Massachusetts Business Trust," M.B.A. thesis, College of Business Administration, Boston University, 1939, 44–45.

16. 1912 Report, 1–3, 25–26. On legislative efforts to change the law on associations between the abortive attempt in 1878 and 1912, see ibid., 10–12.

17. Ibid., 26–27.

18. *Williams* v. *Inhabitants of Milton* [and other combined cases], 215 Mass. 1 (1913) at 5, 6.

19. Ibid., 8.

20. The case was *Smith* v. *Anderson,* 15 Ch. D [Court of Appeal, Chancery Division], 247 (1880); *Williams* v. *Inhabitants of Milton,* 13.

21. *Eliot* v. *Freeman,* 220 U.S. 178 (1911) at 178; *Harvard College* v. *Amory,* 26 Mass. (9 Pickering) 446. Later federal revenue acts and subsequent Supreme Court decisions kept the issue of whether Massachusetts business trusts were taxable under federal corporate tax law in flux and somewhat unclear, but in the 1936 Revenue Act, open end investment company mutual funds as a kind of Massachusetts business trust were not required to pay taxes due to the so-called conduit theory discussed in chapter 6. Jones et al., "The Massachusetts Business Trust," 447–49. For some further case law after *Williams,* see Sears, *Trusts Estates as Business Companies,* 142–50.

22. Austin W. Scott, "The Progress of the Law, 1918–1919: Trusts," *Harvard Law Review* 33, no. 5 (1920): 704, as cited in Sears, *Trusts Estates as Business Companies,* v–vi, vi–viii. Sears notes that statutes relating to trust estates as business companies were passed in 1909, 1913, 1914, and 1916, making Massachusetts business trusts a fairly well-known organizational device by the 1910s in Massachusetts. Ibid., 409–11. Books and articles written on the Massachusetts business trust during this period include Sydney Russell Wrightington, *The Law of Unincorporated Associations and Similar Relations* (Boston: Little, Brown, 1916), and his *The Law of Unincorporated Associations and Business Trusts* (Boston: Little, Brown, 1923); Sears, *Trust Estates as Business Companies;* Alfred D. Chandler, *Express Trusts under the Common Law* (Boston: Little, Brown, 1912); H. L. Wilgus, "Corporations and Express Trusts as Business Organizations," *Michigan Law Review* 13, no. 2 (1914): 71–99, and no. 3 (1915): 205–38; and Guy A. Thompson, *Business Trusts as Substitutes for Business Corporations* (St. Louis: Thomas Law, 1920), which cites these sources, 14.

23. Ibid., 17, 31–34, 35–40, 42–46, 47–54 (Boston Bar member Felix Rackemann's trust declaration form).
24. Vaughan, "The Massachusetts Business Trust," 4, 29–33.
25. Both kinds of trusts, the closed-end trust first developed in Europe and the open end trust based on the Massachusetts business trust, were called trusts until about the end of the 1930s when they all became known as investment companies in federal legislation.
26. On the Dutch experience, see K. Geert Rouwenhorst, "The Origin of Mutual Funds," in *Origins of Value: The Financial Innovations That Created Modern Capital Markets,* ed. William N. Goetzmann and K. Geert Rouwenhorst (New York: Oxford University Press, 2005), 249–69. See also Hugh Bullock, *The Story of Investment Companies* (New York: Columbia University Press, 1959), 1–13, and David Grayson Allen and Kathleen McDermott, *Accounting for Success: A History of Price Waterhouse in America, 1890–1990* (Boston: Harvard Business School Press, 1993), 9–12.
27. Steve Bailey, "Downtown: 'The Bribe Memo' and Collapse of Stone & Webster," *Boston Globe,* March 15, 2006; David Neal Keller, *Stone & Webster, 1889–1989: A Century of Integrity and Service* (New York: Stone & Webster, 1989), 23–25, 34, 38, 119, 139, 146. Edwin S. Webster, one of Stone & Webster's two founders, and his son Edwin S. Webster later played an important role in keeping the Boston stock brokerage and investment banking firm of Kidder, Peabody afloat following the stock market crash of 1929. Earlier on, Edwin Sr.'s father, Frank G. Webster, had been a senior partner at Kidder. See chapter 4.
28. One interesting investment fund created in Philadelphia during this period was the W. Wallace Alexander Fund (1907). Like later mutual funds, Alexander allowed investors to make withdrawals based on the value of their investment on the day of the sale, but the fund was more of an informal collective investment than a pooled investment, as Alexander personally invested the clients' money and provided receipts. The fund issued two series of shares annually in $100 units of participation and with a 6 percent return. The fund was not a trust since shareholders elected the board of overseers and Alexander could be forced to sell securities if shareholders did not like them through the approval of the overseers. The fund was small and remained so, valued at only $1.5 million in the mid-1920s. Bullock, *The Story of Investment Companies,* 16–17. On other pre-1920 proto-investment trust companies, see ibid., 17–18, and Steiner, *Investment Trusts,* 44–46, which includes the Overseas Securities Corporation, set up in April 1920 but devoted exclusively to foreign securities.
29. Theodore J. Grayson, *Investment Trusts: Their Origin, Development, and Operation* (New York: John Wiley and Sons, 1928), 131–38.
30. Steiner, *Investment Trusts,* 51–63; Marshall H. Williams, *Investment Trusts in America* (New York: Macmillan, 1928), esp. 19–26, 55–69; Bullock, *The Story of Investment Companies,* 18–19. Bullock noted that "The Founders' group, above all others, was the hallmark of the Roaring Twenties. Organized in 1921, the first actual capital of $500 was contributed the following year. By 1929 it had developed into a pyramided system of investor trusts and investment holding companies with paid in capital of over $686 million, some $503 being contributed by the public and some $182 million being subscribed by various companies within the group. No other investment trust or group had ever raised this amount of capital. Nor, in retrospect, was all of it soundly raised." Ibid., 35.
31. Steiner, *Investment Trusts,* 55–59; Bullock, *The Story of Investment Companies,* 19–20.
32. Ibid., 28–29; John Francis Fowler Jr., *American Investment Trusts* (New York: Harper

and Brothers, 1928). Fowler methodically analyzes trusts by type, organization, and other categories. For a critique on investment trusts in Great Britain and the United States just before the stock market crash, see Paul C. Cabot, "The Investment Trust," *Atlantic Monthly,* March 1929, 401–8. See also Grayson, *Investment Trusts,* 131–213.

For a more expansive discussion of the investment trust and the trust movement in the 1920s, and the broad range of companies engaged in some form of investing prior to 1929, all from a post–stock market crash perspective, see "The Origin, Scope and Conduct of the Study, Nature and Classification of Investment Trusts and Investment Companies, and the Origin of the Investment Trust and Investment Company Movement in the United States," in Securities and Exchange Commission (SEC), *Investment Trusts and Investment Companies* (Washington, D.C.: Government Printing Office, 1939), part 1.

33. Edward E. Scharff, *Worldly Power: The Making of the Wall Street Journal* (New York: Beaufort Books, 1986), 10–21, 89–90; Lloyd Wendt, *The Wall Street Journal: The Story of Dow Jones & the Nation's Business Newspaper* (Chicago: Rand McNally, 1982), 37–38, 40, 79–90, 101–9, 297–99; Jerry M. Rosenberg, *Inside the Wall Street Journal: The History and Power of Dow Jones & Company and America's Most Influential Newspaper* (New York: Macmillan, 1982), 21–24, 34, 39–40, 42–44. Regrettably, there is no biography of Barron, and few of his business papers are extant.

34. Babson, *Actions and Reactions,* 134–35.

35. Babson's life and career was much broader than can be discussed here, including a brief stint in politics when he ran as the nominee for the Prohibition Party in the 1940 presidential election. For more on Babson, see the Babson College website, www.babson.edu, which includes an annotated bibliography of his works (http://digitalknowledge.babson.edu). See also Babson, *Actions and Reaction,* esp. 90–95, 114–15, 133–44, 147–57, 213–23, 276–85, and Earl L. Smith, *Yankee Genius: A Biography of Roger W. Babson, Pioneer in Investment Counseling and Business Forecasting Who Capitalized on Investment Patience* (New York: Harper and Brothers, 1954), esp. 7–16, 79n, which largely reformats the thoughts and ideas already in Babson's autobiography.

36. For an account of the beginnings of this change in security offerings, see Thomas R. Navin and Marian V. Sears, "The Rise of a Market for Industrial Securities," *Business History Review* 29, no. 2 (1955): 105–38.

37. Theodore Townsend Scudder, Biographical Accounts, one three-page document signed, one six-page document unsigned, n.d., copies in possession of the author; David Grayson Allen, *The History of Scudder, Stevens & Clark* (Boston: Scudder, Stevens & Clark, 1994), 6–7; Allen and McDermott, *Accounting for Success,* esp. 50, 54–55, 61–73. The Scudder biographical accounts were published in part in Roland I. Robinson et al., *Financial Institutions* (Homewood, Ill.: Richard D. Irwin, 1960), and in earlier and later editions of this work. On the history of "evolving standards and lagging practice" in the field of financial reporting, see David F. Hawkins, "The Development of Modern Financial Reporting Practices among American Manufacturing Corporations," *Business History Review* 37, no. 3 (1963): 135–68.

38. Edgar Lawrence Smith, *Common Stocks as Long Term Investments* (New York: Macmillan, 1924), esp. 18–67. The result of these cumulative tests was that they tended "to show that well diversified lists of common stocks selected on simple and broad principles of diversification respond to some underlying factor which gives them a margin of advantage over high grade bonds for long term investment." Smith also advocated a form of investment management similar to the one Scudder was developing in his Boston company. Ibid., 68, 114–18.

39. Allen, *Scudder, Stevens & Clark,* 7–8; David Grayson Allen, *Eaton Vance and the Growth of Investment Management in the United States* (Boston and Concord, Massachusetts: Eaton Vance and Allen Associates, 2007), 12; *Historical Statistics of the United States: Colonial Times to 1970* (Washington, D.C.: Bureau of the Census, U.S. Department of Commerce, 1975), part 1, 224. In addition, before the 1920s, small investors had few opportunities to make investments. Theodore J. Grayson noted that by 1928, "it is well known that until recently there have been very few avenues of first class legitimate investment open to the many of small means, because the smallest investment unit has ordinarily been the $500 bond, and in the majority of instances nothing less than a $1,000 piece has been offered." *Investment Trusts,* 3. See also SEC, *Investment Trusts and Investment Companies,* part 1, 57–62. Other studies have focused on the growing influence of brokerage houses, corporations, financial companies, and even the New York Stock Exchange itself, or of technology in developing middle-class participation in stock investing. See Edwin J. Perkins, "Growth Stocks for Middle-Class Investors: Merrill Lynch & Co., 1914–41," in *Coping with Crisis: International Financial Institutions in the Interwar Period,* ed. Makoto Kasuya (New York: Oxford University Press, 2003), 178–99; Julia C. Ott, *When Wall Street Met Main Street: The Quest for an Investors' Democracy* (Cambridge: Harvard University Press, 2011); and David Hochfelder, "'Where the Common People Could Speculate': The Ticker, Bucket Shops, and the Origins of Popular Participation in Financial Markets, 1880–1920," *Journal of American History* 93, no. 2 (2006): 335–58.

40. Allen, *Scudder, Stevens & Clark,* 10–11. The Curtiss quotations come from his 1965 interview, which was conducted by Scudder long-time employee James N. White. A slightly different version of this story appears in Dwight Rogers, *A Brief History of the Investment Counsel Association of America* (New York: Investment Counsel Association of America, 1982), 6–7.

41. Allen, *Scudder, Stevens & Clark,* 10–11; Scudder, Biographical Accounts.

42. Transcript of talk given by F. Haven Clark in Boston, July 15, 1930, Scudder, Stevens & Clark General Information Memorandum #50-1, October 1, 1976, in possession of the author; Allen, *Scudder, Stevens & Clark,* 11, 12–14.

43. Allen, *Scudder, Stevens & Clark,* 16–18, 59; transcript of F. Haven Clark talk, 1930, 2. A few years later in 1926, Shaw founded his own firm, Shaw, Loomis & Sayles, which became a Boston rival of Scudder's and Clark's firm.

    Over the years, various individuals have stated that they invented investment counsel, and since it took Scudder some time to lay down a clear definition of what the business was, beyond a fee for investment advice, it is easy to understand why others might make such claims. "Counsel" as opposed to "advice" meant several things in the 1920s. One of them was there could be no direct financial stake in the outcome of a client's investments, a distinction Scudder arrived at following a few years of experimentation. Scudder's understanding culminated with the 1927 publication of the firm's "A Professional Charge for Investment Counsel" and a firm policy that its fee would not be based on the buying and selling of securities, but rather an annual fee of one-half of one percent of the client's principal. Another significant distinction was the role of research to provide a more objective guide to investing. By 1924, the firm had "enough assured income" to establish its own research department, probably the earliest research department in any asset management organization. Allen, *Scudder, Stevens & Clark,* 27–29, 50–53.

    The firm's only rivals as the first investment counsel organization were Harlan T. Pierpoint, a solo practitioner in Worcester, Massachusetts, who claimed to have begun the practice in 1912 but did not use the term until the late 1920s, and A. M. Clifford of Los Angeles, another solo practitioner who built an investment counsel business in Southern California in the 1930s. Clifford stated that he began investment counsel work as early as 1916 and practiced it exclusively from August 1921 onward. Scudder, of course, began as early as 1914 (based on outside evidence) and had his own firm as early as 1919, which, through various publications and accounts, defined and named the profession during the 1920s. One such publication was Scudder's "Fundamental Problems of the Investor and Their Solution," which appeared on August 1, 1921. Clifford's first public statement that he provided investment counsel services, though not called by that name, appeared in an advertisement in the *Los Angeles Times* twenty-one days later. Memorandum: David Allen to Tom Joseph, Scudder, Stevens & Clark, March 18, 1994, re: "First" Investment Counsel, in possession of the author; Rogers, *A Brief History of the Investment Counsel Association of America*, 6–9.

44. Allen, *Scudder, Stevens & Clark*, 31–36.
45. Allen, *Eaton Vance*, 32–35, 37.
46. Charles F. Eaton Jr., "Growth of Investment Fund: Successful Money Management Needs Many Skills," *Christian Science Monitor*, May 2, 1956.
47. Allen, *Eaton Vance*, 39; Allen, *Scudder, Stevens & Clark*, 24–25.
48. Compiled from *Who's Who in Investment Counsel 1940* (New York: Bishop's Service, 1940). While the statistics gleaned from this source may not be entirely accurate or complete, they provide a good indication as to how the profession grew at this time. Other Boston investment counsel firms of this era included Loomis, Sayles & Shaw (later Loomis, Sayles & Company); Standish & Company (later Standish, Racy & McKay, and then Standish, Ayer & McKay); Cambridge Associates, Inc. (not the current consulting firm by the same name); Nathan D. Bugbee; Franklin Management Corporation; The Holbrook Company, Inc.; John Babcock Howard & Company; Meyer & Company; Chester F. Pero; Kimball Russell & Company (later Russell, Berg & Company); and Ward, Osgood & Park.
49. Rogers, *A Brief History of the Investment Counsel Association of America*, 37.
50. Ibid., 37–39; Allen, *Scudder, Stevens & Clark*, 78–81.
51. H. Bradlee Perry, interview, October 15, 2007; David L. Babson & Company, Memorandum: H. Bradlee Perry to Staff, re: Dave Babson, December 17, 1998, which includes Babson's February 15, 1968, Weekly Staff Letter entitled "What's Wrong with 'Investment Performance,'" in possession of the author. In that Staff Letter, Babson discussed his role as a pioneer in growth stock investing, but by 1968, he believed that, "with everybody jumping on the bandwagon, the trend is toward highly speculative issues of fledgling companies with very limited marketability. With many of these stocks selling at 50–100 times earnings and 10–15 times sales, 'performance' may already be running out its string." My thanks to H. Bradlee Perry for much of this information.
52. Ibid.; Rogers, *A Brief History of the Investment Counsel Association of America*, 51–54. Another significant change in shrinking the importance of "investment counsel" is that it has become merely a subset of the more generalized term *independent registered investment adviser*. This dilution was completed in 2005, when the Investment Counsel Association of America (ICAA), founded in 1937, was renamed the Investment Adviser Association, losing its distinctiveness in the sea of individuals and organizations now involved in the financial planning industry. Since the mid-1970s, other organizations (some of whom are rivals) have appeared, including the Financial Planning Association (FPA) in 1975, the National Association of Personal Financial Advisors (NAPFA) in

1983, the Investment Management Consults Association (IMCA) in 1985, and two boards, the Certified Financial Planner Board of Standards (CFP Board) in 1989, and the Financial Planning Standards Board (FPSB) in 2003. This expansion of financial planning for middle- and upper-middle-class Americans was largely due to an under-performing 1970s and a broadening of investment markets for them by the 1980s. On some of these changes, see *The Age of Independent Advice: The Remarkable History of the Independent Registered Investment Adviser Industry* (San Francisco: Charles Schwab, 2007), and Cerulli Associates, *The Cerulli Report: Retail Registered Investment Advisers in Transition* (Boston: Cerulli Associates, 2004).

53. Natalie R. Grow, "The 'Boston-Type Open-End Fund'—Development of a National Financial Institution: 1924–1940," Ph.D. diss., Harvard University, 1977, 47–53; Allen, *Eaton Vance*, 14–15, 25–26. Gipp L. Ludcke, another Swedish American graduate of St. Paul College, knew Leffler in Boston and credits him with the invention of the mutual fund. Ludcke's brief account, however, contains so many serious errors or omissions that it is far from convincing. According to Ludcke, Leffler worked for the International Securities Trust of America in Boston, but Leffler never mentioned such a connection before Congress more than a decade later. We are told that Leffler studied European trusts and the "Massachusetts trustee practice," neither of which was important in developing M.I.T., yet Ludcke fails to mention the Massachusetts business trust, which was central to its formation. Ludcke gives *some* credit to Learoyd and Foster as his "employers" who "put up the money to start his [Leffler's] new company," but the cost to capitalize M.I.T. would hardly have been an insignificant investment for them, and not the kind of risk one takes on to please a new employee. Ludcke also quotes Merrill Griswold, who became an M.I.T. trustee in 1925, as one of the Boston attorneys who viewed the mutual fund redemption practice as "bad business and bad law," and fails to note that despite Leffler's strong advocacy for a shareholder redemption privilege, the original deed of trust contains no such provision. G. L. Ludcke, "Who Really 'Invented' the Mutual Fund?" *Investment Dealers Digest*, July 4, 1966, 47.

54. Allen, *Eaton Vance*, 15. For the text of the deed of trust of the Massachusetts Investors Trust, see appendix C at http://scholarworks.umass.edu/umpress/.

55. Allen, *Eaton Vance*, 23–24.

56. Ibid., 63, 67, 69, 78.

57. "Business & Finance: Boston Trusts," *Time*, October 5, 1936. The article started out by noting that the SEC had come to Boston as part of their investigation of investment companies. After spending a week in the Hub, "it unearthed not one whiff of scandal, [and] received for a change an instructive lesson in safe money management."

6. The "Boston Type" Investment Trust

1. For a more detailed account of early Boston mutual funds, see Natalie R. Grow, "The 'Boston-Type Open-End Fund'—Development of a National Financial Institution: 1924–1940," Ph.D. diss., Harvard University, 1977. An excellent study, my only basic criticism with Grow, as well as with others who have written on the Boston's mutual fund industry, is the view that it was established and developed by "old 'Brahmin' families" (ibid., 1, 4, 47, and *passim*), when many major early participants were actually Boston outsiders, including a number of so-called swamp Yankees. Grow's view seems largely shaped by a single interviewee, a contemporary of and participant in events, William A. Parker.

2. It was not until the 1960s, when share sales declined while management fees remained relatively steady, that the more profitable end of the business—fund management rather than fund distribution—changed. Leffler proved to be unique among the three M.I.T. founders in that he spent some portion of his career in all three of the earliest mutual fund companies, working to create a national distribution system for fund shares.

3. David Grayson Allen, *Eaton Vance and the Growth of Investment Management in the United States* (Boston and Concord, Mass.: Eaton Vance and Allen Associates, 2007), 29, 63–65. Besides direct sales to the public, which did not become significant until the 1970s, fund shares were occasionally distributed through the fund organization itself or its investment counsel business, usually without charging a sales commission or "load" but requiring the payment of a periodic management fee. Arthur Weisenberger reported in 1946 that only three companies did not use a broker-dealer distribution system, and as late as 1970, according to the ICI, broker-dealers dominated the sales end (73%). Thereafter, the percentage of firms using this system began to fall, so that the broker-dealer community accounted for 65 percent of all fund sales in 1973. Arthur Wiesenberger, *Investment Companies 1946 Edition* (New York: Arthur Wiesenberger & Company, 1946), 232; H. Lee Silberman, 50 Years of Trust: Massachusetts Investors Trust, 1924–1974, typescript, Massachusetts Financial Services, 1974, 41, in possession of the author; Matthew P. Fink, *The Rise of Mutual Funds: An Insider's View* (New York: Oxford University Press, 2008), 74.

4. Allen, *Eaton Vance*, 65–66; R. J. Tosiello, interview of Paul C. Cabot, ca. 1972, p. 2, Historical Collections, Baker Library, Harvard Business School, Boston. On the State Street Investment Corporation and one of its founders, see Michael R. Yogg's biography, *Passion for Reality: Paul Cabot and the Boston Mutual Fund* (Philadelphia: Xlibris, 2006).

5. Amory Parker, *Twenty Crucial Years: The Story of Incorporated Investors, a Pioneer Investment Company, 1925–1945* (Boston: The Parker Corporation, [1946?]), 13, 22–26, 56A and B; Allen, *Eaton Vance*, 66.

6. By the 1930s and owing to changes in the stock market, some funds were set up with just bonds, i.e., bond funds, or were modified with bonds (and perhaps preferred stock and cash) to create "balanced" funds, but the idea of ordinary rather than exotic securities for the fund's portfolio remained the model. Furthermore, closed-end funds with their more complex portfolios remained fixed, whereas open end funds were constantly buying new securities as their funds grew, or were buying and selling securities to enhance the value of the fund.

7. This debate continues to this day, but usually for different reasons. Some claim that if a particular fund gets too large, it loses its performance edge. More recently, investment companies have closed funds to new shareholders because they want to cool down hot funds that have shown very large increases in size and performance. Once the rush has quieted down, the general public has been allowed to buy shares again.

8. Investment in well-known common stocks, which could expedite liquidity, if necessary, and relatively more open disclosure, including the names and quantities of the fund's assets, were other features that separated open end from closed-end funds. The broader, public use of the term "mutual" to refer to this kind of investment seems to have originated in an M.I.T. advertisement carried in Boston newspapers in early November 1927, when it described the trust as "a mutual investment association—one class of shares" (see fig. 7 on p. 143). The term became more common following the passage of the Revenue Act of 1936, when "mutual investment companies" were given preferential tax treatment. Allen, *Eaton Vance*, 29; Hugh Bullock, *The Story of Investment Companies* (New York: Columbia University Press, 1959), 73.

9. Allen, *Eaton Vance*, 63–65, 67–68, 73; Grow, "The 'Boston-Type Open-End Fund,'" 90–101.

10. Allen, *Eaton Vance*, 72–75; Grow, "The 'Boston-Type Open-End Fund,'" 238, 342, 409–10; Securities and Exchange Commission (SEC), *Investment Trusts and Investment Companies* (Washington, D.C.: Government Printing Office, 1939–1942), part 2, ch. 2, 27, 56, 58–61; Bullock, *The Story of Investment Companies*, 98, 99. Fink, *Rise of Mutual Funds*, 18, 263, states that the "now accepted figure" for mutual fund assets in 1940 was $450 million, but even though less than noted above, those assets rose from just 5 to 36 percent of all AUM in investment companies between 1929 and 1940.

11. SEC, *Investment Trusts and Investment Companies*, is divided into five parts: Part 1: The Origin, Scope and Conduct of the Study, Nature and Classification of Investment Trusts and Investment Companies, and the Origin of the Investment Trust and Investment Company Movement in the United States; Part 2: The Statistical Survey of Investment Trusts and Investment Companies; Part 3: Abuses and Deficiencies in the Organization and Operation of Investment Trusts and Investment Companies; Parts 4–5: Control and Influence over Industry and Economic Significance of Investment Companies. The documents generated by the SEC and the U.S. House and Senate on this issue were enormous. For a rundown on relevant governmental documentation, see Bullock, *The Story of Investment Companies*, 189–90.

12. Tosiello, interview of Paul Cabot, 8–10.

13. Silberman, 50 Years of Trust, 14–16; Tosiello, interview of Paul Cabot, 8–10.

14. Silberman, 50 Years of Trust, 16; Tosiello, interview of Paul Cabot, 6. For further detail, see Yogg, *Passion for Reality*, 85–95, and Grow, "The 'Boston-Type Open-End Fund,'" 451–72. Walsh's provision gave tax relief to "mutual investment companies" under certain conditions, which included that they permitted redemption of their shares at NAV. Another important outcome of the "conduit" tax was that mutual fund companies, anxious to keep shareholder dividends, began reinvestment programs so that shareholders could directly invest those dividends for new shares, usually incurring no load or sales charges. The issuance of fractional shares, a necessary development for dividend reinvestment plans, also followed, often after shareholders approved changes in basic investment company documents, like declarations of trust, and became more universal by about 1970, when fractional shares could be comfortably handled by company mainframe computers. Fink, *Rise of Mutual Funds*, 26, regards the Revenue Act of 1936 as "the most important event in mutual fund history."

15. Silberman, 50 Years of Trust, 16–17; Tosiello, interview of Paul Cabot, 12; Bullock, *The Story of Investment Companies*, 76–78. For more detailed treatments of events leading up to the passage of the Investment Company Act of 1940, see Grow, "The 'Boston-Type Open-End Fund,'" 506–53, and Yogg, *Passion for Reality*, 95–114.

16. Parker, *Twenty Crucial Years*, 84–86.

17. Boston's presence at the hearings was so noticeable that one congressman asked, "Why is it that all of the open-end companies apparently come from Boston: is there something peculiar about that section of the country that accounts for that?" Investment Trusts and Investment Companies, Hearings before the House Committee on Interstate and Foreign Commerce, on 76 H.R. 10065, U.S. House, 76th Congress, 3rd sess., June 13–14, 1940 (Washington, D.C.: Government Printing Office, 1940), 77 and *passim*.

18. Hearings before a Subcommittee of the Committee on Banking and Currency on S. 3580. U.S. Senate, 76th Congress, 3rd sess., part 2, April 12–26, 1940 (Washington, D.C.: Government Printing Office, 1940). Jerome N. Frank, chairman of the SEC,

wrote to Roosevelt shortly before final passage of the bill to suggest that the president invite all government and industry parties to the White House for a signing ceremony. Among the eleven specifically mentioned were three from Boston—Cabot, Gardiner, and Motley. Confidential Memorandum, Frank to the President, August 12, 1940, Franklin Delano Roosevelt Presidential Library, Hyde Park, New York.

19. Interview of James H. Orr, n.d., in papers given to the author by James H. Orr Jr. On the specific distinctions between the SEC bill and the final act, see Fink, *Rise of Mutual Funds*, 38–43.

20. SEC, *Protecting Investors: A Half-Century of Investment Company Regulation*, Report 1504, extra edition, May 29, 1992 (Chicago: Commerce Clearing House, 1992), xx, xviii, which also provides a summary on the growth and development of the act. For a contemporary analysis of the law by one of the participants, see Alfred Jaretzki Jr., "The Investment Company Act of 1940," *Washington University Law Quarterly* 26, no. 3 (1941): 303–47, and see also Bullock, *The Story of Investment Companies*, 79–96. The Act of '40 recast "investment trusts" as "investment companies," the term used to this day. Following the act and into the 1940s, investment companies started to use the terms "open end" and "closed-end," a distinction the SEC had made between those two entities. Ibid., 73. For further details on the legislative process leading up to passage, see Yogg, *Passion for Reality*, 95–99, 104–14, and Grow, "The 'Boston-Type Open-End Fund,'" 472–553.

21. SEC, *Investment Trusts and Investment Companies*, part 1, ch. 1, 4; ibid., part 2, 27; SEC, *Protecting Investors*, xviii–xx.

22. SEC, *Protecting Investors*, xx. For more specific detail on these changes, see also Fink, *Rise of Mutual Funds*, 66–74.

23. As an example, Incorporated Investors continued on into the 1960s, rising in the mid-1950s to assets of $258 million and 13 million shares. In 1968, however, it merged into Putnam Investments, some thirty-one years after Putnam's founder, George Putnam, had been squeezed out of the company. William A. Parker, "Incorporated Investors Geared to Stockholders," *Christian Science Monitor*, May 22, 1956.

24. In 1934, M.I.T. acquired the two-year-old Supervised Shares, a small fund, from Brown Brothers Harriman & Company, a New York banking and brokerage concern, which was forced to sell because of the Glass-Steagall Act (the Banking Act of 1933). Among other banking reforms, the act separated investment banking from commercial banking activities and from security selling affiliates. As a result, Brown Brothers sold to M.I.T. Supervised Shares and its distributing company (which became part of M.I.T.'s distributing company), and some fixed trusts, which were later merged into that fund. The fund was renamed the Massachusetts Investors Second Fund until 1952, when it became the Massachusetts Investors Growth Stock Fund.

25. Tosiello, interview of Paul Cabot, 13.

26. On Keystone, see Weisenberger, *Investment Companies*, 282; S. L. Sholley, "Mutual Fund Tills Market in Bid for Varied Harvest," "Mutual Fund Offers Choice," and "Capital Analysis Featured by Keystone," *Christian Science Monitor*, May 11, 12, 14, 1956; Evan Schulman, interview, September 9, 2003. Keystone was merged with First Union's Evergreen Funds in 1996, and two years later became part of the Wachovia Corporation, which was then merged into Wells Fargo in 2008.

27. Weisenberger, *Investment Companies*, 258; Allen, *Eaton Vance*, 79; Vincent C. Johnson, "Mutual Fund Diversifies Its Investments in 'Growth Industries': Century Shares Trust Exploits Rising Stocks," *Christian Science Monitor*, June 2, 1959; Philip Carret, *Classic Carret: Common Sense from an Uncommon Man* (Boston: Pioneer Group, 1998).

28. Edwin Webster, O. Kelly Anderson, Edward Marshall, Roger Amory, and Donald Douglas started the fund, and named their investment company Wamad Associates by taking the first letter of each of their last names.

29. On the Boston Fund's early history and development, see "Men Who Make Decisions: Managing for 30,000 Investors," *Business Week*, May 24, 1958, 52–54, 56, 58, 61–62.

30. Weisenberger, *Investment Companies*, 304; Grow, "The 'Boston-Type Open-End Fund,'" 419–20; George Putnam Jr., Personal Recollections of the Putnam Funds and Their Associated Putnam Companies: An Informal History, 1951–2001, typescript, ca. 2001, 10, 11, 16–17, Massachusetts Historical Society.

31. Weisenberger, *Investment Companies*, 267; Mahlon E. Traylor, U.S. Senate, Committee on Banking and Currency, Investment Trusts and Investment Companies, Hearings before a Subcommittee of the Committee on Banking and Currency, April–May, June 1940, 76th Congress, 3rd sess. (Washington, D.C.: Government Printing Office, 1940), 459–61; Bullock, *The Story of Investment Companies*, 156–59. Data on Fidelity assets are courtesy of the Fidelity Archives, Boston.

32. Stone & Webster's important role in sponsoring and managing securities companies is described in chapter 5.

33. James H. Orr, "Diversification Keys Mutual Fund," and "Launched in Boston 1905," *Christian Science Monitor*, April 16, 17, 1957; Colonial Management Associates and fund information is all courtesy of James H. Orr Jr., interview, February 6, 2008.

34. Weisenberger, *Investment Companies*, 272, 273, 302; Henry E. Kingman, "Quarter Century of Service: New England Fund Adjusts for Growth," and "New England Fund Trustees Guide Flexible Investment Policy: Programs Designed About Risk Reduction," *Christian Science Monitor*, November 19, 20, 1956; Grow, "The 'Boston-Type Open-End Fund,'" 316.

35. Ibid., 249.

36. David Grayson Allen, *The History of Scudder, Stevens & Clark* (Boston: N.p., 1994), 39–40; James N. White, "Counseling Firm Relates Gains: Fee 'Pool' Aids Investors," *Christian Science Monitor*, May 19, 1956.

37. Allen, *Eaton Vance*, 40–44; Charles F. Eaton Jr., "Money Management: Investment Funds Serve Many Purposes," *Christian Science Monitor*, May 3, 1956; Weisenberger, *Investment Companies*, 289.

38. Bullock, *The Story of Investment Companies*, 103–4, Allen, *Eaton Vance*, 56–57.

39. Grow, "The 'Boston-Type Open-End Fund,'" 421. Figures for Boston's predominance in open end funds in 1945 were compiled from data in Weisenberger, *Investment Companies*, 247–313. Company assets are as of December 31, 1945. Hugh Bullock noted in the late 1950s that "1932 can be marked as the year during and after which almost all newly organized investment companies for the next quarter of a century took the form of a mutual fund." *The Story of Investment Companies*, 72.

40. To be sure, investment companies created a few new types of funds, such as the Canadian funds, which became popular for a few years in the 1950s because Canada had no capital gains tax. At its height of activity in 1954, three Boston companies (Scudder, Canada General, and Keystone) had assets of $172 million in their Canadian funds, which numbered about eight at that time. Bullock, *The Story of Investment Companies*, 110, 127–30.

41. On the problems of state "blue sky" restrictions, see Natalie R. Grow, The Putnam History, 1937–1992, vol. 1, 1937–1981, typescript, ca. 1992, 33–47, Massachusetts Historical Society. The term *blue sky* was coined in Kansas in 1911, when a state legislator complained of fraudulent schemes that would exploit local farmers by capitalizing everything, including the "blue skies."

42. Bullock, *The Story of Investment Companies,* 113. See also chapter 3, note 12, above.

43. Grow, The Putnam History, 1937–1992, 145–57; "Big Money in Boston," *Fortune,* June 1949, 116–21, 189–90, 194, 196; "Wall Street: The Prudent Man," *Time,* June 1, 1959, 74–78, 80. "Big Money in Boston" also provides a good midcentury perspective on Boston's leading mutual fund of the era, M.I.T, as it grew from about $123 million in assets in 1940 to about $1.4 billion by 1958.

44. Putnam, Personal Recollections, 39; Grow, "The 'Boston-Type Open-End Fund,'" 554–58; Allen, *Eaton Vance,* 55.

45. George B. Bookman, "How Good Are Mutual Funds?" *Fortune,* June 1960, 195. Besides the rise in mutual fund sales, there was also renewed middle-class interest in stocks in the 1950s, often through employee stock ownership plans, which had been absent since the depression. See Janice M. Traflet, *A Nation of Small Shareholders: Marketing Wall Street after World War II* (Baltimore: Johns Hopkins University Press, 2013).

46. Memorandum to San Francisco Office, February 26, 1959, in San Francisco Office Papers; Eaton & Howard Board of Directors and Shareholders Minutes (interleaved in 1959 materials), Eaton Vance Corporate Archives, Boston.

47. Putnam, Personal Recollections, 25, 26–27, 37–38, 46, 68–71. For a detailed treatment of Putnam during these years, see Grow, The Putnam History, 1937–1992, 6, 9–10, 32, 211–28, 242–45, 292–94, 418–38, 443.

48. John Brooks, *The Go-Go Years* (New York: Weybright and Talley, 1973), 139. Boston fund managers as a whole seemed to view growth stocks, at least at first, as "this latest binge by the public," "a fad . . . one with inherent dangers." One Fidelity shareholder queried, "Growth is wonderful, but when do you mature?" Paul R. Mosher, "Investment Companies: Fund Managers' Concern Mounting over Public's Growth Stock Binge," *New York Herald Tribune,* April 12, 1961.

49. Brooks, *The Go-Go Years,* 127–40, 145–49; Joseph Nocera, *A Piece of the Action: How the Middle Class Joined the Money Class* (New York: Simon and Schuster, 1994), 47–52, 72–74; Diana B. Henriques, *Fidelity's World: The Secret Life and Public Power of the Mutual Fund Giant* (New York: Scribner, 1995), 127–41, 151–57. Fidelity fund statistics were provided by the Fidelity Archives.

50. Allen, *Eaton Vance,* 101; Grow, The Putnam History, 442. The reporting period for Putnam was slightly different and a year longer, from 1972 to 1979.

51. Allen, *Eaton Vance,* 110–11, 138–39; Grow, The Putnam History, 274–90.

52. Allen, *Eaton Vance,* 81, 115–19, 123–27, 138–39; George Bissell (MFS), interview, December 2, 2003.

53. Frederick D. McCarthy, "With Over $3 Billion in Assets: Greater Boston Investment Companies Offer Diversity Plus a History of Shrewd Money Management," *Greater Boston Business* 45, no. 5 (1956): 14.

54. Bullock, *The Story of Investment Companies,* 159–60; Silberman, 50 Years of Trust, 23. Bullock also states that in 1958, New York had 89 percent of all closed-end assets. By the 1970s, according to some sources, there were indications that New York mutual funds actually outperformed those from Boston. Ron Scherer, "Boston Mutual Funds vs. N.Y. Mutual Funds: What's the Latest Score?" *Christian Science Monitor,* January 20, 1978.

55. Fink, *Rise of Mutual Funds,* 74. Here, as elsewhere, Fink relies on statistical findings of ICI's research department. In 1958, some two decades earlier, Hugh Bullock reported that the five largest mutual fund companies were M.I.T., Wellington, Fundamental Investors, Affiliated Fund, and Investors Mutual, while the five largest mutual fund complexes were M.I.T. and related funds, Wellington, Hugh W. Long,

IDS, and Waddell & Reed. *The Story of Investment Companies,* 156–59. During that time, Fidelity had surpassed M.I.T. as Boston's largest open end investment company.

56. Richard Phalon, "Ned Johnson of FMR: Watch your Flank, Merrill Lynch," *Forbes,* October 26, 1981, 158–61.

57. On the growth of insurance companies in the mutual fund business, see Fink, *Rise of Mutual Funds,* 59–63. By 1970, insurance companies had a 15 percent share of mutual fund assets. Ibid., 74.

58. In some cases, the marriages did not last long. Members of Colonial's former management actually reacquired their business from State Mutual (renamed Allmerica Financial Corporation, and, later, the Hanover Insurance Group) in 1982, and Travelers soon sold its interests too. During most of the 1970s, sales of mutual fund investment companies was due to declining fund assets. These sales crested near the mid-decade as brokerage houses, insurance companies, and other financial institutions looked for ways to dispose of them. In 1973, for instance, there were twenty such mergers and acquisitions, a record that was surpassed twofold the following year. David R. Francis, "Mergers Sweeping Mutual-Fund Industry," *Christian Science Monitor,* December 31, 1975. The pattern of life insurance acquisitions of Boston mutual fund companies continued in the early 1980s, beginning with Travelers in 1979, and followed by Sun Life's purchase of Massachusetts Financial Services in 1982, and Metropolitan Life's merger with State Street Research and Management Company in 1983.

59. Allen, *Eaton Vance,* 101–2.

60. Putnam, Personal Recollections, 81.

61. Ibid., 88.

7. The Rise of Venture Capital in Postwar Boston

1. The term *venture capital* may have first been used in a public forum by Jean Witter in his presidential address to the Investment Bankers Association of America convention in 1939 (Martha Louise Reiner, "The Transformation of Venture Capital: A History of the Venture Capital Organizations in the United States," Ph.D. diss., University of California, Berkeley, 1989, 1), although there was a slightly earlier usage by Lammot du Pont, chairman of the DuPont Chemical Corporation, in the company's 1938 annual report. The New Products Committee of the New England Council used the term in 1939 when it concluded that "New England is not hindered by the lack of venture capital; the need rather is for organization and technique to appraise opportunities for specific enterprises." David H. Hsu and Martin Kenney, "Organizing Venture Capital: The Rise and Demise of American Research & Development, 1946–1973," *Industrial and Corporate Change* 14, no. 4 (2005): 585, 587n. All three sources of this term, however, looked at venture capital not as a specialized area of asset management but as a rather traditional component in the portfolios of wealthy individuals, such as the Rockefellers, Whitneys, and Mellons.

2. Most financial writers today regard venture capital as a form of private equity along with buyouts and special situations funding, and there is no disagreement with that in this account. Until the 1960s, most venture capital was tied to wealthy families, government-financed investment companies, and AR&D. It was only after the rise of private venture capital companies that the distinction between venture capital and private equity, at least in the Boston area, tended to disappear.

3. For a discussion of the New England "capital gap" in the 1970s, see the New England

Regional Commission, "Report of the New England Regional Commission Task Force on Capital and Labor Markets," Task Force on Capital and Labor Markets, Findings and Recommendations to the New England Governors and the New England Regional Commission (Boston: New England Symposium, November 12, 1975). A year later, this report was supplemented by Peter Brooke and TA Associates in a report entitled "New England Business: Verification of Capital Gaps in New England," which was published by the New England Regional Commission on September 30, 1976. Peter Brooke, interview, January 7, 2008.

4. For accounts of the venture capital start-up process, from venture criteria in the business evaluation to stages of funding and eventual liquidation, see Amar V. Bhide, *The Origin and Evolution of New Businesses* (New York: Oxford University Press, 2000), 141–65, or William D. Bygrave and Jeffrey A. Timmons, *Venture Capital at the Crossroads* (Boston: Harvard Business School Press, 1992), 10–16. For a more delineated discussion, see Paul A. Gompers and Josh Lerner, *The Venture Capital Cycle* (Cambridge: MIT Press, 1999), esp. 1–17.

5. Unlike modern venture capitalists, however, Hubbard and Sanders focused on creating profits through dividends rather than concentrating on growth, and they eventually lost control of Bell to New York financial interests. See Thomas M. Doerflinger and Jack L. Rivkin, *Risk and Reward: Venture Capital and the Making of America's Great Industries* (New York: Random House, 1987), 115–46. There were, of course, many other individual examples throughout U.S. history—the McCormick reaper, Henry Ford's automobile, and Pan American Airways, all financed by individuals or a group of individuals, but none of this was in the formal and disciplined way that later venture capitalists would employ. John W. Wilson, *The New Venturers: Inside the High-Stakes World of Venture Capital* (Reading, Mass.: Addison-Wesley, 1985), 15.

6. Nathan Cohn, "Elihu Thomson: Citizen of Swampscott," *IEEE Power Engineering Review* 7, no. 6 (1987): 19–21.

7. On Bush and his science/entrepreneurial activities, see G. Pascal Zachary, *Endless Frontier: Vannevar Bush, Engineer of the American Century* (New York: The Free Press, 1997), esp. 33–35, 39–46, 50–52, 57, 73–83, 256–58, and Otto J. Scott, *The Creative Ordeal: The Story of Raytheon* (New York: Athenaeum, 1974). The broad history of U.S. industrial research has been covered well in David A. Hounshell, "The Evolution of Industrial Research in the United States," in *Engines of Innovation: U.S. Industrial Research at the End of an Era,* ed. Richard S. Rosenbloom and William J. Spencer (Boston: Harvard Business School Press, 1996), 13–85. On the development of MIT's "Big Science" and its applications in the post–World War II era, see Stuart W. Leslie, *The Cold War and American Science: The Military-Industrial-Academic Complex at MIT and Stanford* (New York: Columbia University Press, 1993), esp. 11–43, 76–101, 132–59, 188–211. See also Roger L. Geiger, "Science, Universities, and National Defense, 1945–1970," *Osiris,* 2nd ser., 7 (1992): 26–48, for a broader perspective.

8. "Venture Capital," *Fortune,* February 1949, 84–85. Little information about New Enterprises exists, but see Henry Etzkowitz, *MIT and the Rise of Entrepreneurial Science* (New York: Routledge, 2002), 90, 159n.

9. Courtland D. Perkins, "Richard Stetson Morse, 1911–1988," in *Memorial Tributes: National Academy of Engineering,* vol. 5 (Washington, D.C.: National Academies Press, 1992), 205–8; Wolfgang Saxon, Obituary of Richard S. Morse, *New York Times,* July 4, 1988. Minute Man was brought to market through an investment of J. H. Whitney & Company, a New York family venture fund.

10. William L. Stoddard, "Small Business Wants Capital," *Harvard Business Review* 18,

no. 3 (1940): 268; Rudolph L. Weissman, *Small Business and Venture Capital: An Economic Program* (New York: Harper and Brothers, 1945), 50.

11. Hsu and Kenny, "Organizing Venture Capital," 581, 582–83.

12. Compton's and especially MIT's strong role in the rise of a science-based regional economic development model that helped to create venture capital is strongly argued in Etzkowitz, *MIT and the Rise of Entrepreneurial Science,* 78–88.

13. Ralph E. Flanders, *Senator from Vermont* (Boston: Little, Brown, 1961), esp. 186–89. See also "Flanders of New England," *Fortune,* August 1945, 135–36, 264–72, esp. 135, 267, 272.

14. Flanders, *Senator from Vermont,* 188–89. On the sluggishness of trust fund capital in the era, see Louis M. Lyons, "Boston: A Study in Inertia," in *Our Fair City,* ed. Robert S. Allen (New York: Vanguard Press, 1947), 29–30. Flanders would continue to express his belief that venture capital was a necessary process that had to be undertaken continuously. "We cannot float along indefinitely on the enterprise and vision of preceding generations. To be confident that we are in an expanding, instead of a static or frozen economy, we must have a reasonably high birth rate of new undertakings." In a 1949 issue of *Fortune* he went on to say, "The postwar prosperity of America depends in a large measure on finding financial support for that comparatively small percentage of new ideas and developments which give promise of expanded production and employment, and an increased standard of living for the American people." J. Richard Elliott Jr., "Something Ventured: American Research and Development Corporation Shows What Capitalism Can Do," *Barron's National and Financial Weekly,* March 6, 1967; "Venture Capital," *Fortune,* 84. Flanders repeated his major thesis on the need to invest fiduciary funds and create new businesses with them many times. See also his "The Problem of Development Capital" (November 29, 1945) as quoted in *Venture Capital Journal,* January 1980, 13. Note: *Venture Capital* became *Venture Capital Journal* later in 1980, but is usually identified in libraries by the latter name, which is used here and throughout.

15. For further details about the Whitneys, Rockefellers, and Mellons, see Reiner, "The Transformation of Venture Capital," 138–61. Unlike other family venture firms, John Hay Whitney set up his organization as a partnership, which became the prevalent structure of venture capital firms after the early 1960s.

16. "Venture Capital," *Fortune,* 85–86. It should be mentioned here that there has been another investor group, rising in increasing numbers in the last half of the twentieth century, which has provided start-up financing for projects. Generally known as "angels," these individuals, usually wealthy businessmen or professionals, numbered about 250,000 by the mid-1980s and invested between $20–30 billion annually. William E. Wetzel Jr., "The Informal Venture Capital Market: Aspects of Scale and Efficiency," *Journal of Business Venturing* 2, no. 4 (1987): 299–313.

17. The best overall history of AR&D is Patrick Liles, *Sustaining the Venture Capital Firm* (Cambridge, Mass.: Management Analysis Center, 1977), which has been used in this account of the company.

18. For example, in order for investment companies to become investors in its stock, AR&D needed the SEC to grant an exemption to §12(e) of the Investment Company Act of 1940, which provided an exception for firms "engaged in the business of underwriting, furnishing capital to industry, financing promotion enterprises, and purchasing securities of issuers for which no ready market is in existence." Furthermore, AR&D needed an exception for itself so that it could own more than 3 percent of the stock in its portfolio companies. Hsu and Kenney, "Organizing Venture Capital,"

590. On the difficulties of getting AR&D started, particularly some of the regulatory hurdles it had to overcome, see Reiner, "The Transformation of Venture Capital," 171–76, and Spencer E. Ante, *Creative Capital: Georges Doriot and the Birth of Venture Capital* (Boston: Harvard Business School Press, 2008), 110.

19. Udayan Gupta, ed., *Done Deals: Venture Capitalists Tell Their Stories* (Boston: Harvard Business School Press, 2000), 223–24. For a fuller account of Doriot's life and work, see Ante, *Creative Capital,* Doriot's new and only major biography.

20. Gene Bylinsky, "General Doriot's Dream Factory," *Fortune,* August 1967, 104. Doriot was married but childless.

21. So important did "active management" of the portfolio company become to the concept of venture capital that Waite has since defined venture capital, even though that term has become murky over time, as "involved investment at whatever stage it might be in." Charles M. Waite, interview, June 26, 2008.

22. Although MIT played an important role in creating AR&D, it changed its policy of support by the early 1950s, though not its role in developing entrepreneurial enterprise in the Boston area. See Edward B. Roberts, *Entrepreneurs in High Technology: Lessons from MIT and Beyond* (New York: Oxford University Press, 1991), esp. 3–46. Harvard Business School also developed its own self-directed course of action. MIT did play a larger role in venture capital and private equity investing starting in the 1970s through its treasurer's office, which invested the school's pension and endowment funds in those activities. David W. Scudder, interview, December 4, 2007. Likewise, the Harvard Management Company invested in those activities also beginning in the 1970s. See chapter 9.

23. *High-tech* is, of course, a loaded term that means different things to different people. A cable television company may mean high-tech to some, but others see it as simply a highly capital intensive service company. For a summary of AR&D's investment priorities, see graph A, Changes in AR&D Portfolio Base, 1946–1973, at http://schol-arworks.umass.edu/umpress/.

24. Hsu and Kenney, "Organizing Venture Capital," 592, 594–95, 597, 598–99.

25. "Venture Capital," *Fortune,* 84–85.

26. Francis Bello, "The Prudent Boston Gamble," *Fortune,* November 1952, 124, 208.

27. Ibid., 213, 214.

28. Christopher G. Hartman, *Advance Man: The Life and Times of Harry Hoagland, Together with a History and Genealogy of the Hooglandt Family by Rebecca Rector* (Boston: Newbury Street Press, 2005), 73.

29. Hartman, *Advance Man,* 71–76.

30. Bylinsky, "General Doriot's Dream Factory," 103–7, 130, 132, 134, 136. Unfortunately, none of the accounts about AR&D's success with DEC stock are based on a full analysis of AR&D's investments and what it received when it sold the stock, which would provide a better idea of DEC's impact. This will require a more thorough analysis of AR&D's annual reports, books, and regulatory information than is currently available.

31. Much of the account in this section is based on Ante, *Creative Capital,* and AR&D annual reports from 1946 through 1973, which are available at the Stanley E. Pratt Library, MIT Entrepreneurship Center, Massachusetts Institute of Technology, Cambridge, Massachusetts. The Pratt Library contains over 1,500 items of primary and secondary source materials (books, reference sources, correspondence, statements, and reports) on the venture capital industry, and consists of three personal collections, which include those of Georges F. Doriot, Daniel Holland, and Stanley

E. Pratt. Pratt was the founding general partner of Abbott Capital Management, and also the former publisher and editor of *Venture Capital Journal* and *Pratt's Guide to Venture Capital Sources.*

32. Hartman, *Advance Man,* 67–68, 69–70.

33. Ante, *Creative Capital,* 192–98.

34. Ibid., 200–201; Waite, interview.

35. Gupta, ed., *Done Deals,* 224. On AR&D's ultimate demise as a publicly traded venture capital firm, see Ante, *Creative Capital,* 221–56.

36. Gupta, ed., *Done Deals,* 246.

37. Brooke, interview.

38. Bill Egan, interview, June 16, 2008; Brooke, interview; Arthur F. F. Snyder, interview, June 28, 2007. "Shattuck on trusts" was probably Mayo Adams Shattuck, *An Estate Planner's Handbook* (Boston: Little, Brown, 1948), or Augustus Peabody Loring, *A Trustee's Handbook,* rev. edn. by Mayo Adams Shattuck (Boston: Little, Brown, 1940).

39. Snyder and Egan, interviews; Roberts, *Entrepreneurs in High Technology,* 37. A great lender, Snyder was not without his eccentricities. He did not like to lend to people who had beards or people who were both president and treasurer of their company ("P and T disease" he would call it). He was also reticent about husband-and-wife businesses.

40. Arthur F. F. Snyder, *Generalizations of a Banker* (N.p.: N.p., 2008), 176–81; Snyder, interview.

8. The Growth of Venture Capital and Emergence of Private Equity

1. Public Law 85-699 (August 21, 1958), 72 Stat. 689, Sections 102, 307, 308. For details on the act and its implementation, see William John Martin Jr., and Ralph J. Moore Jr., "The Small Business Investment Act of 1958," *California Law Review* 47, no. 1 (1959): 144–70; Edward N. Gadsby, "S.E.C. Aspects of the Small Business Investment Act of 1958," speech before the Federal Bar Association of New York, New Jersey, and Connecticut, and the City Club of New York, New York City, February 17, 1959; and Manuel F. Cohen, "The Small Business Investment Act of 1958 and the SEC," speech before the Federal Bar Association and Bureau of National Affairs, Chicago, February 19, 1959, SEC Papers, www.sechistorical.org. On the legislative history of the act, see Charles M. Noone and Stanley M. Rubel, *SBICs: Pioneers in Organized Venture Capital* (Chicago: Capital Publishing Company, 1970), 26–30.

2. Raymond Frost, "The Macmillan Gap 1931–53," *Oxford Economic Papers,* new series, 6, no. 2 (1954): 181–82, 197–98. See also Lord William Piercy, "The MacMillan Gap and the Shortage of Risk Capital," *Journal of the Royal Statistical Society,* series A (General), 118 (1955): part 1, 1–7, and Richard Coopey, "The First Venture Capitalist: Financing Development in Britain after 1945, The Case of ICFC/3i," *Business and Economic History* 23, no. 1 (1994): 262–71.

3. During the 1960s, a number of businesses moved into venture investing, although just like commercial banks, the stakes were not high, and in most cases, were a source for funding. They included insurance companies and some large industrial firms— Ford, American Can, General Mills, Monsanto, Scott Paper—either through creating a division or forming an SBIC. Martha Louise Reiner, "The Transformation of Venture Capital: A History of the Venture Capital Organizations in the United States," Ph.D. diss., University of California, Berkeley, 1989, 330.

4. Noone and Rubel, *SBICs,* 30–34, 90. In general, on the SBICs of commercial banks,

see Reiner, "The Transformation of Venture Capital," 306, 307, 317, 320. A total of fourteen banks started up affiliated SBICs before 1965 for venture investing, and from 1966 to 1970, the number was increased by eleven banks, eight of which created SBICs and three other types of venture capital affiliates.

5. Obituary, *Boston Globe*, February 2, 1993; *Princeton Alumni Weekly*, December 2, 1960; *Princeton Alumni Weekly*, November 28, 1972; Vin Ryan, interview, June 12, 2008.

6. "Boston to Hollywood," *Time*, May 21, 1956, www.time.com.

7. Richard Farrell, interview, June 4, 2008; Ben Ames Williams Jr., *Bank of Boston 200: A History of New England's Leading Bank, 1784–1984* (Boston: Houghton Mifflin, 1984), 262–78.

8. Farrell, interview.

9. Rick Burnes, interview, April 7, 2008; Udayan, Gupta, ed., *Done Deals: Venture Capitalists Tell Their Stories* (Boston: Harvard Business School Press, 2000), 238; John W. Wilson, *The New Venturers: Inside the High-Stakes World of Venture Capital* (Reading, Mass.: Addison-Wesley, 1985), 98.

10. Noone and Rubel, *SBICs*, 90.

11. Compiled from data in Leroy W. Sinclair, *Venture Capital 1971* (New York: Technimetrics, 1971).

12. William D. Bygrave and Jeffrey A. Timmons, *Venture Capital at the Crossroads* (Boston: Harvard Business School Press, 1992), 21–22, 23.

13. Reiner, "The Transformation of Venture Capital," 281–82. See also Small Business and Venture Capital Associates, *Encouraging Venture Capital for Small Business* (New York: Associated Educational Services Corporation, 1967), 8, 57, and Stanley M. Rubel, "What Venture Capital Financing Has Done for Small Business," *The Business Lawyer* 24, no. 3 (1969): 955–59.

14. Cynthia A. Beltz, ed., *Financing Entrepreneurs* (Washington, D.C.: AEI Press, 1994), 9–10. Despite some occasional upticks in SBIC numbers, their influence declined from the mid-1960s onward. While they accounted for 75 percent of all venture capital financing in 1963, by 1978 that figure had declined to just 7 percent. Reiner, "The Transformation of Venture Capital," 425.

15. Bygrave and Timmons, *Venture Capital at the Crossroads*, 23. Between 1969 and 1977, the pool of venture capital fluctuated between $2.5 and 3.5 billion. Robert Premus, *Venture Capital and Innovation: A Study Prepared for the Use of the Joint Economic Committee, Congress of the United States* (Washington, D.C.: Government Printing Office, 1985), 6.

16. While the "prudent man rule" goes back to the 1830 *Harvard College* v. *Amory* case described in chapter 3, the term became more generalized by the twentieth century and usually refers to any investment beyond a "legal list" of acceptable investments or, later, an investment in which there are some or substantial risks beyond standard or typical investments in stocks and bonds.

17. "The Labor Department proposed this policy in January 1978 in a position paper that stated, 'Clearly, we believe the stocks of smaller companies have a place in investment portfolios, . . . when prudently selected to include adequate diversification, these stocks can offer above average potential and will significantly add to the overall diversification and return on pension assets.'" "ERISA Council Recognizes Need for Pension Investment in Smaller Businesses," *Venture Capital Journal*, March 1978, 4.

18. Wilson, *The New Venturers*, 24; Paul A. Gompers, "The Rise and Fall of Venture Capital," *Business and Economic History* 23, no. 2 (1994): 10, 12–14. As Gompers and

many of the interviewees noted, the tax changes in 1978 were less important than the introduction of pension funds (and endowments, trusts, and foreign companies) into venture capital, since most of that new capital was tax exempt anyway.

19. Bygrave and Timmons, *Venture Capital at the Crossroads,* 23–25.

20. Paul A. Gompers and Josh Lerner, *The Venture Capital Cycle* (Cambridge: MIT Press, 1999), 6, 8, 10.

21. Figure B at http://scholarworks.umass.edu/umpress/ provides a general schematic of how major Boston area venture capital firms developed from about the mid-1960s to the mid-1980s.

22. "Special Report: Venture Capital in Boston," *Venture Capital Journal,* January 1979, 10–20; February 1979, 10–20 and *passim.* As *Venture Capital Journal* and other venture sources make clear, the industry made little distinction between private venture capital firms and SBICs during the 1970s and into the 1980s, even though SBICs had become an increasingly insignificant part of this risk capital business. "Special Report: SBICs after 20 Years: The Unsung Heroes of Business Development," *Venture Capital Journal,* October 1978, 13–22. The article notes, "From a peak of 722 SBICs in 1964, the number of licensees dropped to 272 by the end of 1976" (13).

23. Elfers had graduated from Princeton and then from Harvard Business School in 1943. Because of Doriot's wartime commitments in Washington, Elfers was one of a few individuals at AR&D who had never had the General for his teacher. On Greylock, see Elfers's book *Greylock: An Adventure Capital Story* (Boston: Greylock Management Corporation, 1995), which covers the firm's history during its first three decades. Elfers started what has become a tradition among venture capitalist firms by naming his company for the street he lived on in Wellesley Hills.

24. Elfers, *Greylock,* 4–15, 18, 44; Charles Waite, interview, June 26, 2008.

25. Elfers, *Greylock,* 20–43; Waite, interview. As Charlie Waite noted, "At Greylock in the early days, we weren't oriented to start-ups." Elfers liked more information to go on. And because "we weren't doing start-ups, . . . we didn't have the huge wins." Gupta, ed., *Done Deals,* 227, 233.

26. Investors in Greylock's partnerships remained remarkably stable over the years. As Waite noted in the late 1990s, "We've now raised nine partnerships, and not one of the original investors or of the other investors we've added along the way has ever dropped out. Where people have died, their sons or daughters or trusts are writing the checks today. That's part of the same culture and we're very proud of it. The last time we made a major change in our investor format was in 1978, when Harvard University, in the person of Walter Cabot, came to us and asked to invest in Greylock." The family investors resisted Harvard's desire to participate, but eventually they relented. This was Harvard's first venture capital investment. Dartmouth, where Walter Burke was an alumnus and Charlie Waite had close connections, which included being a guest speaker and teacher on entrepreneurship at the Tuck School for over twenty years, followed suit. Gupta, ed., *Done Deals,* 234; Waite, interview.

27. Elfers, *Greylock,* 48–60, 70–73.

28. Much of this account comes from Peter Brooke, interview, January 7, 2008, and Gupta, ed., *Done Deals,* 245–57.

29. Peter Brooke, interview; C. Kevin Landry, interview, May 23, 2008.

30. TA Associates tends to view company investment stages as start-up, developmental, revenue, and profitable, the last coming before the better-known "late" stage. By focusing on this profitable stage, the company has come to define its focus as a mid-market growth private equity firm. Later, studies convinced TA Associates

that at least until 1997, investments in later-stage companies were not only less risky and only slightly more expensive but also provided superior returns compared with longer, higher-risk venture capital investments.

31. Gupta, ed., *Done Deals*, 259–68; C. Kevin Landry, interview; C. Kevin Landry, "Observations on 40 Years in Private Equity," Speech to Pantheon Private Equity, November 7, 2007; William Egan, interview, June 16, 2008.

32. Another candidate for a (quite) pure Boston venture capital company is Battery Ventures, a Waltham (now Boston), Massachusetts, firm founded in 1983.

33. About the same time that Charles River Partners was set up, Carter was also an adviser-founder of the West Coast Mayfield Fund, which had close connections with Stanford University as well as Charles River Partners.

34. Gupta, ed., *Done Deals*, 237–43; Burnes, interview. Later CRP funds grew exponentially. CRP X (1998) was $500 million, while CRP XI (2001) was $1.25 billion. Ibid.

35. Christopher G. Hartman, *Advance Man: The Life and Times of Harry Hoagland; Together with a History and Genealogy of the Hooglandt Family by Rebecca Rector* (Boston: Newbury Street Press, 2005), 68–69; Galen Moore, "Fidelity's Venture Capital Arm Breaks Off," *Boston Business Journal,* January 11, 2010.

36. Hartman, *Advance Man,* 68–69, 97–105.

37. Perhaps the best general discussion of where venture capital stood near the end of the 1970s—focusing on capital gaps and just before changes in capital gains taxes and reinterpretation of the "prudent man rule" in ERISA—is Stanley Pratt's two-part "Special Study" called "Gaps in Capital Distribution: The Crisis for Business Development Financing," *Venture Capital Journal,* February 1978, 19–30, and March 1978, 19–29. During the last half of the twentieth century, Boston venture capital went through several major cycles, each one larger than the last. The first (symbolized by minicomputers) peaked in the late 1960s and early 1970s, while the next centered on microcomputers in the late 1970s and early 1980s. Software was the focus of the cycle in the 1980s, followed by the internet and connectivity development in the 1990s.

38. Stanley M. Rubel, "The Venture Capital Industry—Shedding Some Light on this Somewhat Mysterious Financial Community," speech during the country's first seminar on venture capital, New York City, January 19–20, 1970; "A Special Report—The Evolution of an Industry: Venture Capital Redefined for the 1980s," *Venture Capital Journal,* January 1980, 14–15; Stanley E. Pratt, "The Role of Venture Capital in Economic Revitalization," 1989, Pratt Papers, Pratt Library at the MIT Entrepreneurship Center, Massachusetts Institute of Technology; *Venture Capital Journal,* July 1990, 14; Stanley E. Pratt, "A Historical Timeline of the Venture Capital Industry 1961 to the Present, October 24, 1990," Pratt Papers; Gompers, "The Rise and Fall of Venture Capital," 19; Gompers and Lerner, *The Venture Capital Cycle,* 8; *Venture Capital Journal,* April 1987, 9; ibid., March 1989, 9.

39. Rubel, "The Venture Capital Industry." Rubel's publications tended to emphasize the SBIC part of the industry long after its importance in developing venture capital had vanished. Another industry group, predominantly along the East Coast though with little visibility, was the Small Business and Venture Capital Center of the Committee for Economic Development, formed in 1964, though little is known about it. Reiner, "The Transformation of Venture Capital," 336–37.

40. See graph B at http://scholarworks.umass.edu/umpress/.

41. Beltz, ed., *Financing Entrepreneurs,* 13–14, 21; Gompers and Lerner, *The Venture Capital Cycle,* 8; Elfers, *Greylock,* 84. By 2002, the composition of venture pools had shifted again. Pension funds contributed 42% of all venture funds, financial and insurance 26%, endow-

ments and foundations 21%, individuals and families only 9%, and corporations 2%. Edwin A. Goodman, "Venturing Forth," *Investment Advisor* 24, no. 2 (2004): 62–64, 66.

42. Blaine Huntsman and James P. Hoban Jr., "Investment in New Enterprise: Some Empirical Observations on Risk, Return, and Market Structure," *Financial Management* 9, no. 2 (1980): 44–51.

43. General Accounting Office, *Report to Senator Lloyd Bentsen, Joint Economic Committee, Government-Industry Cooperation Can Enhance the Venture Capital Process,* GAO/AFMD-82-35, August 12, 1982, 1–2. For later efforts by Congress to return to higher capital gains taxes, see Statement of Stanley E. Pratt, Chairman, Venture Economics, Inc. before the Senate Small Business Committee, June 4, 1986, and his "Economic Impact and Capitalization of Venture Capital-Backed Companies," Venture Economics, June 1986, Pratt Papers.

44. For West Coast venture capital developments, see John Wilson's dated but thorough treatment in *The New Venturers,* which tends to focus on developments in California.

45. The Boston area and Silicon Valley have been the two largest and most important areas of venture capital activity. By some measures, the shift from Boston to Silicon Valley began early. According to Gompers and Lerner, and based on tabulations of unpublished *Venture Economics* databases, California had 65 to Massachusetts's 45 venture capital investments in the period 1965–1969; by the 1990–1996 period, the number was 3,380 to 1,028 investments, respectively. During the same two periods, disbursements were $247 compared with $69 million in 1965–1969, and $15,436 compared with $3,842 million in 1990–1996. This data, of course, does not measure all important aspects of venture capital activity, and underappreciates the size and population of California versus the area and population of eastern Massachusetts. Gompers and Lerner, *The Venture Capital Cycle,* 14. In addition, those authors note that "information on venture capital investments is difficult to gather from public sources. Unlike mutual funds, venture capitalists are typically exempt from the Investment Company Act of 1940 and do need not reveal their investments or organizational details in public filings." Ibid., 329.

46. Brooke, interview; Gompers, "The Rise and Fall of Venture Capital," 8, 10, 12–14.

47. Henry Etzkowitz, *MIT and the Rise of Entrepreneurial Science* (New York: Routledge, 2002), 103, 104; Brooke, interview. On the inherent dangers of close relationships between Stanford University and Silicon Valley technology companies, see Ken Auletta, "Get Rich U.," *New Yorker,* April 30, 2012, 38–47.

48. AnnaLee Saxenian, *Regional Advantage: Cultural and Competition in Silicon Valley and Route 128* (Cambridge: Harvard University Press, 1994); Scott Kirsner, "Will You Ever Catch Up?" *Boston Globe,* July 22, 2007; D. C. Denison, "Manufacturing's Fast Lane," ibid., May 13, 2012. Some see Route 128 as the Product Lifecycle Management or "PLM Highway," focused on business applications.

49. This view of a staid, conservative postwar Boston financial community was perhaps most eloquently described by Russell B. Adams Jr. in 1977, when he wrote, "Boston remained Boston, its prevailing spirit formed and jelled—not to say solidified—over many generations. The upper reaches of the city's financial establishment had opened of necessity to talented and ambitious men from other parts of the country, but the old traditions had been little disturbed. Prudence and integrity, qualities frequently honored elsewhere in their breach, were still scrupulously maintained in Boston, and if the city's investment community was sometimes chided for an excess of caution, it was never charged with stinting on rectitude—or with losing sight of its past." *The Boston Money Tree* (New York: Thomas Y. Crowell, 1977), 300.

50. This shift was not just true in Boston but many other regions as well. See "What Is Venture Capital? Something Old, Something New," *Venture Capital Journal,* March 1987, 10–11, and Gompers, "The Rise and Fall of Venture Capital," 16–19, which suggests that there was rising pressure on short-term investment performance.

51. Stanley E. Pratt, "Venture Capital Investing: The Art, the Craft, and the Science: A Seminar for Japanese Venture Capitalists," January 11, 1999, Pratt Papers.

9. Rising Assets to Manage

1. For a detailed description of these developments, see Steven A. Sass, *The Promise of Private Pensions: The First Hundred Years* (Cambridge: Harvard University Press, 1997), 4–87.

2. Ibid., 113–24.

3. For an account of bank management of pensions at this time, see Longstreet Hinton, "The Birth of a Trust Department," in *Classics II: Another Investor's Anthology,* ed. Charles D. Ellis with James R. Vertin (Homewood, Ill.: Business One Irwin, 1991), 7–8, and Sass, *Promise of Private Pensions,* 152–68. Part of the problem with the performance of insurance companies at this time was that they were not allowed to hold more than "trivial amounts of equities." Ibid., 154.

4. Ibid., 168–69.

5. "I think the 401(k) has become America's retirement system," noted Robert L. Reynolds, chief executive of Putnam Investments, in May 2011. "It covers half of working Americans." "On the Hot Seat: Reynolds Is Outspoken Advocate for Overhaul of US Retirement System," *Boston Sunday Globe,* May 15, 2011; Ken McDonnell, "Facts from EBRI [Employee Benefit Research Institute]: The U.S. Retirement Income System," *EBRI Notes* 26, no. 4 (2005): 6.

6. The 1978 act restricted 401(k) contributions to workers' cash bonuses, but an enterprising employee-benefits consultant, R. Theodore Benna, thought the wording vague enough to include regular income as well and launched the first 401(k) plan. In 1981, the IRS gave its official legal approval to Benna's idea. John Cassidy, "Striking It Rich," *New Yorker,* January 14, 2002, 63–64. The history of ERISA is covered in detail by Sass, *Promise of Private Pensions,* 179–226. Participation in 401(k) plans expanded rapidly. By 1995, 75% of all eligible employees participated in them, up from 62% in 1986. *401(k) Plans: How Plan Sponsors See the Marketplace,* Investment Company Institute, Research Report, Winter 1995, 5.

7. *Fundamentals of Employee Benefit Programs* (Washington, D.C.: Employee Benefit Research Institute, 2009), 3; Steven A. Sass, *Reforming the U.S. Retirement Income System: The Growing Role of Work* (Boston: Center for Retirement Research, Boston College, 2003).

8. "The Markets: Pursuing Pension Money: Mutual Fund Industry Hopes Employee Benefit Plans Will Help It Crack a Market Previously Dominated by Banks," *Business Week,* October 25, 1969, 30–31.

9. "Performance: The New Name of the Game," *Institutional Investor* 1 (April 1967), 10–17, in which the rising importance (and meaning) of investment performance is discussed. This publication, begun only a month earlier, was established to assist the emerging professional *institutional* money managers and their increasingly complex responsibilities. Gilbert Kaplan, "A Necessary Venture," *Institutional Investor* 1 (March 1967): 13.

10. Sass, *Promise of Private Pensions,* 179, and sources noted in table 7. In addition, as examples, see "The Pension Market: 1990," *Fundamentals,* Mutual Fund Research

in Brief, ICI Research Department, March 1992, 1–2, and "Households with IRAs," *Fundamentals,* May/June 1995, 1–2. Tentative figures from the 2000s (2000 to 2009) suggest that the rate of growth for that decade was possibly not even 150%, and was likely due to the absence of growth in equity assets, a decline in pension contributions, some cashing out, and an inability to sustain a high growth rate as pension fund assets reach a certain size. Federal Reserve Flow of Funds Accounts, tables L.118 (private companies), L.119 (state and local governments), L.225i (Individual Retirement Accounts), www.federalreserve.gov.

11. *Bernstein Research: The Future of the Money Management Industry, Strategic Analysis/Financial Forecast* (New York: Sanford C. Bernstein & Company, 1990).

12. Chris Welles, *The Last Days of the Club* (New York: E. P. Dutton, 1975), ix–xi, 3–16, 25–40, 436, and 335–427 *passim.*

13. "Bank Trust Assets II," *Institutional Investor* 2 (December 1968): 86–87. The terms *employee benefits* and *employee benefit fund management* meant at the time both pension and profit-sharing plans. The latter, however, declined in significance in the decades that followed.

14. Compiled from "Who Are the Largest Pension Managers?" (1977 and 1978) *Institutional Investor* 11 (August 1977): 102; 12 (August 1978): 97, and "The Largest Pension Managers" (1979 and 1980), *Institutional Investor* 13 (August 1979): 97; 14 (August 1980): 115.

15. "Boston's Money Managers," *Boston Globe,* July 30, 31, August 1–3, 1972.

16. Robert Porterfield, "The Money Managers: Boston Companies Control Billions of Dollars Worth of Other People's Assets. It's a Good Business," *Boston Globe,* April 29, 1980. The article contains a list of all major money management companies in New England, and notes that Boston firms had $123.935 billion, Massachusetts (outside Boston) $13.064 billion, Connecticut $79.362 billion, Rhode Island $4.673 billion, Vermont $1.691 billion, and Maine $1.927 billion for a total of $224.652 billion.

17. Julie Rohrer, "Money Management Powerhouses," *Institutional Investor* 24 (January 1990): 44–46. *Institutional Investor* kept track of the nation's largest pension fund managers (and changes in the assets they managed) shortly after the journal started in the late 1960s, but began to rank the largest "money managers" (originally trust departments, insurance companies, management companies, and investment counselors) in 1975 as the "*Institutional Investor* 300," a feature that continues to this day. By August 1981, the publication had discontinued the pension fund manager list and only wrote on "Ranking America's Top Money Managers," a sign that money management had taken on a broader, more encompassing role, which included endowment, nonprofit, and foundation funds, and perhaps other asset management activities as well.

There are two markets for mutual funds: the *retail* market for individuals or their pension funds, which is the primary story in chapters 6 and 10, and the *institutional* market for the types of organizations discussed in this chapter. Institutional mutual funds are similar to the retail funds in terms of investment objectives and the securities that are used, but an institutional asset manager might offer only index funds (few actively managed ones) or one certain type of investment approach such as value or growth. Company pension managers then shop around to provide the mix of funds for their company's pension program, usually using third-party "consultants" for advice in choosing them.

18. Edward H. Ladd, interview, November 25, 2003.

19. David Grayson Allen, *The History of Scudder, Stevens & Clark* (Boston: Scudder, Stevens & Clark, 1994), 132.

20. State Street Research & Management, which was acquired by Metropolitan Life in 1983 and by BlackRock in 2004, has no relationship with State Street Bank & Trust, now called State Street Corporation, or its major subsidiary, State Street Global Advisors (SSgA). In this chapter, these two companies will be referred to as State Street Research and State Street Corp., or just State Street, respectively.

21. Charles Flather, interview, June 24, 2003.

22. George Bennett, interview, July 15, 2003; Robert Lawrence, interview, June 28, 2003; Robert Beck, interview, September 17, 2003.

23. Bennett and Flather, interviews. According to Bennett, one of the reasons that they sold the company to MetLife in 1983 was that "we were missing the boat by not getting into the mutual fund business marketing end of things actively, because we had the management and we had the reputation. We weren't capitalizing on it as far as the mutual funds were concerned." Bennett, interview. Flather recalled that the firm had $12 billion in AUM at the time of the sale, with $8 billion in the pension business, $2 billion in mutual funds, and presumably another $2 billion in endowment funds. Flather, interview.

24. Ibid.

25. Peter Vermilye, interview, June 21, 2007; Beck and Flather, interviews. After his stint at State Street Research, Vermilye became chairman and president of Alliance Capital Management in Boston until 1977, when he then commuted to New York to serve as global chief investment officer at Citicorp until 1984. Upon his return to Boston, Vermilye kept close to pension and endowment investing, joining Baring America Asset Management as chairman until 1990, and as senior adviser and portfolio manager from 1986 to 1995. Baring had previously acquired Endowment Research & Management, a Boston endowment advisory company. Vermilye also served as a trustee at Boston University and chairman of its investment committee for thirty-five years during which the school's endowment rose from $28 million to more than $1 billion in 2006. Peter Vermilye, obituary, *Boston Globe,* March 16, 2009. On Vermilye's reputation and career, see Anise Wallace, "Citibank's Investment Comeback," *Institutional Investor* 15 (July 1982): 84–86, 89, 90.

26. Beck and Flather, interviews.

27. Some interviewees believed the figure was more like $100,000, but all involved saw it as essentially "charity work." Flather, interview.

28. Barry Rehfeld, "Walter Morgan: The Last of the Mutual Fund Pioneers," *Institutional Investor* 31 (October 1998): 17.

29. On Thorndike, Doran, Paine & Lewis's early years, see Robert W. Doran, "You DO Have a Chinaman's Chance!" Harvard Business School *Bulletin* 39, no. 3 (1963); W. Nicholas Thorndike, interview, July 8, 2003; George Lewis, interview, June 9, 2011. Much of Wellington's early history is also covered in some detail in a Harvard Business School case study: Robert J. Boehlke and Audrey T. Sproat, Wellington Management Company, #9-371-525, September 1971.

30. Thorndike, interview.

31. Unlike most colleges and universities, which used Teachers Insurance and Annuity Association and College Retirement Equities Fund, better known as TIAA-CREF, to manage employee retirement funds, MIT handled its own pension business.

32. Robert Lenzner, "MIT Mulls New Manager for $626m," *Boston Globe,* September 21, 1977; Lenzner, "MIT's Funds Swap—A Mystery," *Boston Globe,* October 9, 1977; Thorndike, interview; David W. Scudder, interview, December 4, 2007; Wellington Management Company, LLP, Brief Timeline, in possession of the author.

33. Robert Lenzner, "Wellington's New Status May Prove Boon for Partners," *Boston Globe,* October 30, 1979; Paul Braverman, interview, July 12, 2011.
34. Ibid. For some additional background, see Rich Blake, "Going Its Own Way: Wellington Is the Rare Money Manager Increasing Assets in a Tough Market," *Institutional Investor* 36 (July 2002): 35–40.
35. Cary Reich, "The LeBaron Phenomenon," *Institutional Investor* 19 (August 1985): 107–8, 112, 114; Stephen E. Clark, "They Call Him the Red LeBaron," *Institutional Investor* 25 (December 1991): 11–12; David Warsh, "Lakeside Guru," *Boston Globe,* August 8, 1999; Evan Schulman, interview, September 9, 2003; Jeremy Grantham, interview, August 2, 2011.
36. Laurie Meisler, "Can the New Investment Boutiques Make It Big?" *Institutional Investor* 12 (November 1978): 39–43, 55.
37. Grantham, interview; Andrew Capon, "The Messenger Shoots Back," *Institutional Investor* 37 (August 2003): 19.
38. On the Boston Company's transition, see Beth McGoldrick, "The Boston Co.'s New Lease on Life," *Institutional Investor* 21 (July 1987): 129–30, 133–34, and Alyssa A. Lappen, "The Puzzle Called Mellon," *Institutional Investor* 31 (September 1997): 55–58.
39. "Travelers, Mass. Co. Plan Merger," *Boston Globe,* January 10, 1969; "2 Funds Managers Merge in Boston," *Boston Globe,* June 8, 1979; "Travelers to Sell Unit to Keystone Managers," *Boston Globe,* September 28, 1989; "PNC to Acquire an Old Massachusetts Banking Concern," *New York Times,* February 24, 1993.
40. On some of these changes, see David Wessel, "Changing Times along State Street," *Boston Globe,* October 17, 1982; Steven Syre, "Mellon's Ties to Hub," *Boston Globe,* October 17, 2006.
41. Flather, interview.
42. Walter Muir Whitehill, "Allan Forbes," Massachusetts Historical Society *Proceedings,* 3rd series, 71 (October 1953–May 1957): 418, 419. A portion of Forbes's collection is described and pictured in *The Log of the State Street Trust Company* (Boston: State Street Trust Company, 1926). See also George F. W. Telfer, "Mergers Building 'Ship-Model' Bank," and "Boston Bank Builds on Trust," *Christian Science Monitor,* March 26, 27, 1962.
43. Whitehill, "Allan Forbes," 417, 421; John Appleton, interview, March 15, 2010.
44. Thomas P. Beal, *The Second National Bank of Boston* (Boston: Rand Press, n.d. [ca. 1955]); Appleton, interview. The merged bank was called Second Bank–State Street Trust Company until the 1960s, when it was renamed State Street Bank & Trust. Another bank, the Rockland-Atlas National Bank, was merged into State Street in 1961, which increased its business in the commercial and consumer banking areas.
45. Ibid.; Gary Pisano and Maryam Golnaraghi, State Street Bank and Trust Company: New Product Development, Harvard Business School case study, #9-696-087, April 12, 1996.
46. Susan Trausch, "The Professorial Banker," *Boston Globe Magazine,* August 28, 1977, 8–12, 14; William S. Edgerly, interview, May 22, 29, 2008.
47. Robert Teitelman, "Inside the State Street Machine," *Institutional Investor* 28 (June 1994): 59–64, 67; Edgerly, interview; Marshall N. Carter, interview, April 17, 2008; Piasno and Golnaraghi, "State Street Bank and Trust Company"; Kelley A. Porter, State Street Corporation: Leading with Information Technology (B), Harvard Business School case study, #9-799-034, January 7, 1999; Carol Power, "State St. Wins Recognition as Technological Leader," *American Banker,* October 23, 1998. For Carter's strategy, see also Erich Joachimsthaler, *Hidden in Plain Sight: How to Find*

and Execute Your Company's Next Big Growth Strategy (Boston: Harvard Business School Press, 2007), 127–36.

48. Jeffrey Kutler, "Joseph Antonellis of State Street Corp: The Joys of Specialization: The Boston Bank's Concentration on Investment Services Differentiates It from Other Custodians," *Institutional Investor* 38 (December 2004): 75–77. *Institutional Investor's* first annual ranking of global custodian banks appeared in the August 1992 issue and was followed by annual updates through 2010. For current data, I have used Assets under Custody, Worldwide, updated to June 14, 2011, www.globalcustody.net, as part of the publication *Global Custodian*. For changes in the years in between, see also "The World's Largest Global Custodians," *Institutional Investor* 34 (September 2000): 217–18; Tom Groenfeldt, "Money Isn't Everything: The Leading Global Custody Players Are All Huge," *Institutional Investor* 38 (September 2004): 209–10; Cliff Asness, "The Global Custody Conquest," *Institutional Investor* 41 (January 2007): 7, 14; and Julie Segal, "Global Custody—The Global in Global Custody," *Institutional Investor* 41 (September 2007): 189.

49. "America's Top 300 Money Managers," *Institutional Investor* 28 (July 1994): 113–17, 120, 123, 126, 129–30, 133–34, 137–38, 141–42, 144–46, 148, 150; 29 (July 1995): 73–77, 80, 83–86, 88–89, 91–92, 95, 98–102; 31 (July 1997): 77–82, 84, 88, 91–92, 95–96, 99–100, 102–6, 108, 110; "When All Assets Are Included," *Institutional Investor* 32 (July 1998): 112.

50. Charles Stein, "Money Magnet: Mutual Funds Rocket Boston near Top of World's Financial Centers," *Boston Globe*, November 10, 1996. For another similar assessment, see Ben Phillips, "The Asset Chase: Beantown Closes on New York," *Institutional Investor* 31 (August 1997): 143, noting that, "while Boston's stock portfolios tripled between 1992 and 1996, New York's stock portfolios failed to double."

51. "America's Top 300 Money Managers," *Institutional Investor* 32 (July 1998): 87–96, 99–100, 102, 104, 106, 108, 110, 112–14; "America's Top 300 Money Managers," *Institutional Investor* 33 (July 1999): 75–83, 86, 88, 90, 92, 94, 96–98, 100, 102–3; "America's Top 300 Money Managers," *Institutional Investor* 34 (June 2000): 95–100, 102, 104, 106, 108, 110, 112, 114, 116–22.

52. "America's Top 300 Money Managers," *Institutional Investor* 35 (July 2001): 57–58, 60–62, 64–66, 68–70, 72–76, 78–79; 36 (July 2002): 43–44, 46, 48–52, 54, 56, 58–60, 62, 64; 37 (July 2003): 45–46, 48, 50, 52–62; Michael Carroll, "Size Matters," *Institutional Investor* 38 (July 2004): 9. For rankings in 2007, see Michael Shari, "America's Top 300 Money Managers," *Institutional Investor* 41 (July 2007): 53–67, and for 2010, Julie Segal, "The II 300: America's Top Money Managers," *Institutional Investor* 44 (July-August 2010): 55–66. In addition to consolidation, SSgA fared badly in the 2008 great contraction because more than 90% of its $1.7 trillion in assets were in passive index strategies that fell in the stock market tumble. Ibid.

53. Scudder, interview; Robert Lenzner, "Boston's Money Managers," *Boston Globe*, July 30, 1972.

54. These figures have been compiled from several sources, including Daniel A. Wingerd et al., *The Growth of College Endowments, 1960–1990* (Westport, Conn.: CommonFund, 1993), 1-1–1-4; National Association of College and University Business Officers (NACUBO), *2007 Endowment Study* (Washington, D.C.: NACUBO, 2008); Talk: List of U.S. Colleges and Universities by Endowment, http://en.wikipedia.org; *NACUBO-CommonFund Study of Endowments* (Washington, D.C.: NACUBO-CommonFund, 2011).

55. "What We Need Is More Mileage from Endowments," *Institutional Investor* 6 (August 1972): 46–49.

56. Beck, interview; Advisory Committee on Endowment Management, *Managing Educational Endowments: Report to the Ford Foundation* (New York: Ford Foundation, 1969), esp. 37–47. See also William L. Cary, *The Law and the Lore of Endowment Funds: Report to the Ford Foundation (The Educational Endowment Series)* (New York: Ford Foundation, 1969), produced that same year, which examined the law governing endowment funds to help colleges and universities determine sound investment policies.

57. Daniel J. Coolidge, "William Henry Claflin, Jr.," *Massachusetts Historical Society Proceedings*, 3rd series, 94 (1982): 85–87; Morton and Phyllis Keller, *Making Harvard Modern: The Rise of America's University* (New York: Oxford University Press, 2001), 19–20, 144–45, 183–84; Angela Stent, "Harvard and Yale and Their Money," *Change* 5, no. 9 (1973): 9–12. On some other aspects of Harvard's twentieth-century endowment, see Seymour E. Harris, *Economics of Harvard* (New York: McGraw-Hill, 1970), 335–39, 357–60, 369–72, 383.

58. Letter to Harvard President Derek Bok, reprinted in Ellis with Vertin, eds., *Classics II*, 593–95. Cabot did note that Yale's investment policy was a factor, as it was. As part of Yale's investment plan, conceived in the early 1940s, it turned away from a rising market in stocks to one of falling bonds, which helped produce significant consequences to the growth of the endowment. Ibid., 282.

59. Keller and Keller, *Making Harvard Modern*, 184–85. For a fuller account of Cabot as Harvard treasurer, see Michael R. Yogg, *Passion for Reality: Paul Cabot and the Boston Mutual Fund* (Philadelphia: Xlibris, 2006), 141–54, 163–65.

60. "Annual Report of the Harvard Management Company," in *Harvard University Financial Reports for 1983–1984*, 35. Harvard University annual financial reports are available from 1830/1831 through 1992/1993 online at http://hul.harvard.edu.

61. Ibid., 366–68; George Putnam, Personal Recollections of the Putnam Funds and Their Associated Putnam Companies: An Informal History, 1951–2001, typescript, 102–6, Massachusetts Historical Society; Walter Cabot, interview, October 11, 2007. For a somewhat dated but outside account of Walter Cabot and the Harvard Management Company, see Carl A. Vigeland, *Great Good Fortune: How Harvard Makes Its Money* (Boston: Houghton Mifflin, 1986), 149–82.

62. "Yale's New Partners: Grimm, Ingraham and McNay," *Institutional Investor* 11 (March 1977): 88.

63. Bruce Davidson, "Boston Headquarters for New Yale Fund," *Boston Globe*, September 25, 1967; Stent, "Harvard and Yale and Their Money," 10. For other details, see Harvey D. Shapiro, "The Harvard-Yale Game," *Institutional Investor* 6 (September 1972): 46–49.

64. David Swensen, *Pioneering Portfolio Management: An Unconventional Approach to Institutional Investment* (New York: Free Press, 2000); Daniel Golden, "Cash Me If You Can," *Conde Nast Portfolio*, April 2009, 80–85, 98–100.

65. George Putnam Jr., interview, January 29, 2008; Scudder interview.

66. Jason Zweig, "The Intelligent Investor: Smart Money Takes a Dive on Alternative Assets," *Wall Street Journal*, January 17–18, 2009. Another study suggests that alternative investing moved from 23 to 42% of endowment portfolios between 2000 and 2007. Golden, "Cash Me If You Can," 83.

67. There was also a corresponding growth of "consultants" in the pension investment business, but these firms are spread widely around the country and play no direct role in the Boston story.

68. Putnam, interview; James Bailey, interview, April 10, 2008.

69. Ibid.

10. The Transformation of the "Boston" Open End Mutual Fund since 1970

1. Peter Fortune, "Mutual Funds, Part I: Reshaping the American Financial System," *New England Economic Review,* July–August 1997, 45–72; "Mutual Funds, Part II: Fund Flows and Security Returns," *New England Economic Review* 1 (January–February 1998): 1, 3–22.

2. Arthur Levitt, chairman, U.S. Securities and Exchange Commission, Testimony Concerning Appropriations for Fiscal Year 1999 before the Subcommittee on Commerce, Justice, State and Judiciary of the Senate Committee on Appropriations, March 19, 1998, www.sec.gov. From a broader perspective than just mutual funds, Joseph Nocera has written about "the astonishing transformation" of middle-class financial habits in the postwar United States, particularly from the 1970s to the 1990s, when it became "nothing less than a money revolution." "The financial markets were once the province of the wealthy, and they're not anymore; they belong to all of us." *A Piece of the Action: How the Middle Class Joined the Money Class* (New York: Simon and Schuster, 1995), 10–11.

3. 1965 Boston and industry figures (which reflect end of year 1964) were compiled from data in Arthur Wiesenberger, *Investment Companies: Mutual Funds and Other Types, 1965 Edition* (New York: Arthur Wiesenberger & Company, 1965). Regrettably, Wiesenberger is the only authoritative source for specific fund/company information until the 1980s, and it is arranged by fund rather than investment company or complex, making it difficult to track the information noted in the text here until the Investment Company Institute (ICI) took up this data collection task in about 1985.

   In 1965, there were seventeen Boston investment companies/complexes (and in one case an insurance company) noted in Wiesenberger: M.I.T.; Fidelity; Keystone; Putnam; Eaton & Howard; Incorporated Investors; Boston Fund; State Street Investment; Scudder, Stevens & Clark; Colonial; Century Shares Trust; Loomis Sayles; Massachusetts Life; Investment Trust of Boston; Pioneer Fund; Canadian General; and Income Fund of Boston.

4. The statistics are from George Putnam, Personal Recollections of the Putnam Funds and Their Associated Putnam Companies: An Informal History, 1951–2001, typescript, 93, Massachusetts Historical Society, Boston.

5. The Reserve Fund, which rose to become a $62 billion fund, collapsed in the fall of 2008, when its assets fell below $1 a share (a situation called "breaking the buck") due to $785 million in holdings in Lehman Brothers, which went out of business during the financial crisis of that year. Daisey Maxey, "Trial Is Sought in Reserve Fraud Case," *Wall Street Journal,* March 12, 2010. For a fuller account of the effective demise of Regulation Q, see Nocera, *A Piece of the Action,* 74–84, 207–12, 215–18, 221–28.

6. C. Bruce Johnstone, interview, June 22, 2009; William Byrnes, interview, October 9, 2007; Margaret Pantridge, "Semper Fidelity," *Boston Magazine,* March 1992, 92. See also Michael Vermeulen, "The Son Also Rises," *Institutional Investor* 20 (February 1986): 136–40, 143–44.

7. Peter Lynch with John Rothchild, *One Up on Wall Street: How to Use What You Already Know to Make Money in the Market* (New York: Simon and Schuster, 1989), 55; Nocera, *A Piece of the Action,* 86–88. Putnam Investments, a load company, saw money market funds as a "'storm shelter' into which existing shareholders could switch with no sales charge when they feared a market uncertainty or decline, rather than as a product that could be sold . . . in large quantities on its own." Despite the shift of some companies

to move from broker-dealer to no-load, direct-selling status, no-load funds rose from only 6 to 20% of industry assets from 1970 to 1980. Putnam, Personal Recollections, 114, 124; Natalie R. Grow, The Putnam History, 1937–1992, typescript MS in 2 volumes, Massachusetts Historical Society, 1:498–99. Over the course of about twenty years, the number of money market funds grew geometrically, from 40 in 1978 to 450 in 1982, and by mid-1989, there were over 570 of them with total assets of $325 billion.

8. Richard Phalon, "Ned Johnson of FMR: Watch Your Flank, Merrill Lynch," *Forbes,* October 26, 1981, 158, 160. Cash Reserves Fund and Daily Income Trust figures have been provided by Elena Demetriades, senior archivist of the Fidelity Archives, Boston.

9. Depository Institutions Deregulation and Monetary Control Act, PL 96–221, 94 Stat 132. NOW accounts were actually invented by a Worcester, Massachusetts, S&L executive named Ronald Haselton in 1970, and these interest-bearing transactional accounts were first offered in Massachusetts in 1974 by mutual savings banks to compete with larger commercial banks. Nocera, *A Piece of the Action,* 126–27.

10. Johnson's improvement of the money market fund with Fidelity's check-writing feature was typical of innovation in the mutual fund business. While being the "first" to create a certain kind of fund may be helpful, it is often the company that improves the basic idea that wins out in the long run. Money market funds did not grow without tremendous opposition by banks and savings and loan companies (S&Ls), and many state legislatures supporting them, but in the end, money fund products prevailed. See Matthew P. Fink, *The Rise of Mutual Funds: An Insider's View* (New York: Oxford University Press, 2008), 84–94.

11. Fidelity did not totally abandon broker-dealers or financial advisers. By the 1980s, it had created a number of broker-dealer funds that it could sell to clients. Nevertheless, most of its new business came directly from the public. Furthermore, on so-called premium funds like Magellan, Fidelity charged a "low load fund" of 2% before it raised it to 3%. Many specialty or sector funds also had loads, often continuing them until the 2000s. The only difference between these and more traditional loads was that Fidelity's charge went directly to Fidelity, not to an outside distributor.

12. Putnam, Personal Recollections, 112–13.

13. This was soon changed under the Tax Reform Act of 1976. See below.

14. Johnstone, interview.

15. Ibid.; Peter G. Gosselin, "Musical Chairs in the Back Office: Competition Forces Changes in Processing Mutual Funds," *Boston Globe,* October 29, 1985. On Johnson's "quirky love of gadgets and gimmicks," and his influence in bringing customer service technology to Fidelity, see Diana B. Henriques, *Fidelity's World: The Secret Life and Public Power of the Mutual Fund Giant* (New York: Scribner, 1995), 208–11, 269. On the gradual transition of Fidelity from load to no-load, see ibid., 214–15.

16. Data supplied by Fidelity Archives; Kris Frieswick, "Low Fidelity: Fidelity Investments Turns 60 This Year. But Its Customers May Not Be in a Celebrating Mood," *Boston Globe,* February 19, 2006. On Fidelity's need for office space in Boston and beyond, see Richard Kindleberger, "Bursting out of Boston: Fidelity Investments Seeks Suburban Space as a Backup to Boston Offices," *Boston Sunday Globe,* April 10, 1994. By 1994, Fidelity even had plans to build an office tower on the Devonshire Street office block it owned. Ibid.

17. Byrnes, interview.

18. Nocera, *A Piece of the Action,* 234. On Johnson's marketing skills, see also Vermeulen, "The Son Also Rises," 137–40, 143–44.

19. It is important to note that the 1970s were not entirely dismal for non–money market funds, and that following the nadir in 1974, even equity funds improved. As the *Wall Street Journal* observed, funds as a whole were 80% higher in value in mid-1980 than they were in mid-1975. During the first three-quarters of 1980 alone, equity fund investments grew by 23%; this came at a time when money market funds were declining because payouts were falling from as high as 20 down to only 9%. Despite these changes, it was not until a turnaround in the stock market in the summer of 1982 that a fundamental shift took place. Jill Bettner, "Your Money Matters: With the Money Market Now Less Rewarding Consider a Switch to the Equity Mutual Funds," *Wall Street Journal,* September 15, 1980.

20. On the revival and its aftermath, see John Cassidy, "Striking It Rich," *New Yorker,* January 14, 2002, 63–73, and Maggie Mahar, *Bull! A History of the Boom, 1982–1999: What Drove the Breakneck Market—and What Every Investor Needs to Know about Financial Cycles* (New York: HarperBusiness, 2003). See also Eric N. Berg, "Return of the Mutual Funds," *Wall Street Journal,* July 14, 1983.

21. Byrnes, interview. Despite Magellan's performance under Lynch, averaging about 29% annually, the fund's best annual return (116%) occurred in 1968, and it had a three-year record of 68% just before (1965–1967)—all under Johnson's management of the fund.

22. Lynch with Rothchild, *One Up on Wall Street,* 13, 36; Peter Lynch with John Rothchild, *Beating the Street* (New York: Simon and Schuster, 1993).

23. Lynch with Rothchild, *One Up on Wall Street,* 14–15. Fidelity, in particular, tended to create "star" fund managers and to develop a culture of win or fail. As Richard Teitelbaum noted years later, "in Fidelity's freewheeling, free-spending culture, portfolio managers get ample freedom and oodles of research, trading, and technological backup. They also get blamed when things go wrong," as they did in 1996 when "the company shuffled the managers of 27 funds in a restructuring." "Where to Invest Your Nest Egg: Big Fund Companies Want Your Money. Here's What You Should Know," *Fortune,* August 19, 1996, 156. On Magellan's less glorious later life, see Steven Syre, "Boston Capital: The Time Is Right," *Boston Globe,* January 15, 2008.

24. Compiled from figures supplied by Elena Demetriades, senior archivist, Fidelity Archives.

25. Johnstone, interview; Henriques, *Fidelity's World,* 232, 236. Despite gains in the institutional market, Fidelity's culture focused, according to Byrnes, "more on middle-class retail trade" that "serve[d] the masses rather than the classes," and offered a contrast with Putnam that went the other way during this period. See below.

26. Under then-current law, municipal bond mutual funds could only be created as a California partnership. This barrier was soon changed with the Tax Reform Act of 1976, which allowed tax-exempt interest in a mutual fund to pass through to a fund shareholder. As income became the focus of new funds in the late 1970s and early 1980s, Fidelity and other companies created and marketed a wide range of state municipal bond ("muni" bond) funds.

27. Johnstone, interview. Marketing is, Johnstone noted, "the underlying premise of our company . . . [and] nobody made the kind of marketing impact that Ned did." Ibid.

28. H. Lee Silberman, 50 Years of Trust: Massachusetts Investors Trust, 1924–1974, typescript, Massachusetts Financial Services, 1974, 11; MFS Performance Results: MFS Family of Funds, brochure, Massachusetts Financial Services, August 31, 1991, both items in possession of the author.

29. The information on Fidelity fund changes comes from Elena Demetriades, senior

archivist, Fidelity Archives. As the number of mutual funds increased, from a mere 1,038 in January 1984 to 6,235 by December 1996, the Investment Company Institute (ICI) categorized twenty-two groups of open end mutual funds under four major and two minor groups: Equity Funds (aggressive growth, growth, growth and income, equity-international, equity-global); Bond and Equity Funds (equity-income, flexible portfolio, balanced, income-mixed); Bond Funds (national municipal, state municipal, income-bond, government, GNMA [Government National Mortgage Association or Ginnie Mae], global bond, corporate bond, high-yield bond), Money Market Funds (tax-exempt national, tax-exempt state, taxable); Precious Metals Funds; and Option-Income Funds. Changes in asset allocation among the four main types of mutual funds over this period are presented in graph C at http://scholarworks.umass.edu/umpress/.

30. Fink, *The Rise of Mutual Funds*, 82.

31. Investment Company Institute, *2009 Investment Company Fact Book*, 112, www.ici .org. See graph C at http://scholarworks.umass.edu/umpress/.

32. For a brief summary of Fidelity history, see Fidelity Investments, *Our First Sixty Years: Fidelity Investments* (Boston: Fidelity Investments, ca. 2005).

33. Nocera, *A Piece of the Action*, 289–93.

34. Ibid., 404; Phalon, "Ned Johnson of FMR," 158, 160, 162; Fortune, "Mutual Funds, Part I," 60; Kenneth B. Noble, "Merrill Lynch's C.M.A. [Cash Management Account] Boom," *New York Times*, May 18, 1981.

35. Barbara Rudolph, "The Funds: Old Prints Are Not Enough: Asleep at the Switch—or, How a Venerable Boston Financial Institution Came to Be Owned by a Canadian Insurance Company," *Forbes*, November 21, 1983, 134–39; Putnam, Personal Recollections, 213.

36. Peter G. Gosselin, "Musical Chairs in the Back Office: Competition Forces Changes in Processing Mutual Funds," *Boston Globe*, October 29, 1985; Phalon, "Ned Johnson of FMR," 160.

37. Margaret Pantridge, "Fund City," *Boston Magazine*, June 1992, 71.

38. Fink, *The Rise of Mutual Funds*, 100–105, 109–10.

39. On the background of municipal bond funds, see ibid., 95–98.

40. Probably the most important intellectual underpinning for index funds came from Princeton professor Burton G. Maikiel and his *A Random Walk down Wall Street* (New York: Norton, 1973), which argued that active management of portfolios was inefficient and, over time, provided no value in fund performance. He was also a longtime director of Vanguard Funds.

41. Mahar, *Bull!*, 209.

42. Fink, *The Rise of Mutual Funds*, 105–9, 179–81; Putnam, Personal Recollections, 185–86; Mutual Funds with 12b-1 Plans, ICI Research Department, Fundamentals: Mutual Fund Research in Brief, March 1994, 1–2.

43. Fink, *The Rise of Mutual Funds*, 143; Nocera, *A Piece of the Action*, 404.

44. The IRA had anything but a consistent career. With the Tax Reform Act of 1986, tax benefits were restricted, while another act in 1997 actually expanded the provisions.

45. Lee L. Gremillion, *A Purely American Invention: The U.S. Open-End Mutual Fund Industry* ([Wellesley Hills, Mass.?]: National Investment Company Service Association, 2001), 17–25.

46. Kimberly Blanton, "High Fidelity: How Fidelity Investments Became the Largest Mutual-Fund Company in the World," *Boston Globe Magazine*, July 23, 1995, 14–16, 21–22, 25–30; Blanton, "Fidelity's New Frontier: From Its Perch Atop the US Market, Funds Colossus Makes an Assault on Europe," *Boston Globe*, November 20, 1994.

47. Securities and Exchange Commission (SEC), *Protecting Investors: A Half Century of Investment Company Regulation,* SEC Staff Report, Division of Investment Management, Report 1504, May 29, 1992 (Chicago: Commerce Clearing House, Inc., 1992), xx; Teitelbaum, "Where to Invest Your Nest Egg," 156. On Putnam's rise and use of marketing, see also David Whitford, "How Putnam Devoured America," *Boston Business,* June/July 1989, 26–31, 78–82.

48. Putnam, Personal Recollections, 96–100, appendix G, 202–3.

49. For more details on the transformation of pension funds and the role of Boston asset managers in that change, see chapter 9.

50. Putnam, Personal Recollections, 117–18, 126–29; Larry Lasser, interview, February 9, 2010. Deeply involved in the creation and sale of new Putnam fund products in the 1980s and 1990s, Lasser believed that the proliferation was due to a number of reasons, including the fact that new products sold better, Morningstar and other rating services encouraged the segmentation of fund offerings, allocation became a very important investment strategy, "families of funds" caught the attention of brokers and the institutional market, and some financial vehicles, particularly in the fixed-income area, lent themselves to becoming mutual fund products. Ibid.

51. Putnam, Personal Recollections, 181, 185–87, 198, 209; Grow, Putnam History, 2:617, 621.

52. Putnam, Personal Recollections, 191–92.

53. Teitelbaum, "Where to Invest Your Nest Egg," 156.

54. Grow, Putnam History, 2:634, 674–81, 695–98. On Putnam's growth in the 1980s and 1990s, see Kimberly Blanton, "Profile: Lawrence Lasser: Tough Team Leader at Putnam," *Boston Globe,* November 19, 1995.

55. Marsh & McLennan let Putnam run virtually on its own. "It is hard for me to state how uninvolved Marsh McLennan was involved in Putnam's history. . . . They had almost nothing to do with our business. . . . Putnam didn't even manage their pension fund. . . . [They] never tried to learn about the investment business." Lasser, interview; Blanton, "Profile: Lawrence Lasser."

56. Lasser, interview.

57. Putnam, Personal Recollections, 148–49, 188, 209; Grow, Putnam History, 2:618; Lasser, interview.

58. The others included T. Rowe Price, Vanguard, Franklin, Twentieth Century, Dean Witter, Merrill Lynch, IDS, and American. Teitelbaum, "Where to Invest Your Nest Egg," 156–160, provided no AUM figures for any of the companies, only the fact that all were among the top ten in size. Putnam came out as the fourth largest complex in this ranking, and may have been helped somewhat because short-term investments, i.e., money market funds, which Putnam did not have, were not counted.

59. See table A, Partial List of Mutual Fund Families in 1995 with Assets over $20 Billion, at http://scholarworks.umass.edu/umpress/.

60. David Whitford, Joseph Nocera, and Nelson D. Schwartz, "Has Fidelity Lost It? Performance Is Down, Fund Managers Are Bailing. Should the Millions of Americans Who Have Entrusted Their Money to Fidelity Be Reassured by Chairman Ned Johnson's Response," *Fortune,* June 9, 1997, 58–66; Fink, *The Rise of Mutual Funds,* 215–16. See also Roben Farzad, "Fidelity's Divided Loyalties," *BusinessWeek,* October 16, 2006, 60.

61. Data supplied by Fidelity Archives; David Grayson Allen, *Eaton Vance and the Growth of Investment Management in the United States* (Boston and Concord, Mass.: Eaton Vance and Allen Associates, 2007), 213. The Sarbanes-Oxley Act of 2002 (Pub. L. 107–204, 116 Stat 745) affected the board of U.S. public companies, company man-

agement, and public accounting firms by requiring more oversight by the boards, more accurate company financial information by management, and greater independence of outside auditors who reviewed that information. The act also made penalties for fraudulent activity more severe.

62. Fink, *The Rise of Mutual Funds,* 217; Andrew Caffrey, Beth Healy, and Ross Kerber, "In the Eye of Putnam's Storm: Charges Raise Questions on Lasser's Reign," *Boston Globe,* October 30, 2003; Steven Syre, "Lasser's Side of the Story," *Boston Globe,* November 2, 2006. Putnam's success was matched by Marsh & McLennan's salutary neglect, which virtually allowed Putnam to run on its own for over twenty years until the scandal broke.

63. Faith Arner with Lauren Young, "Can This Man Save Putnam?" *BusinessWeek,* April 19, 2004, 100–105; Syre, "Lasser's Side." The actual fines, penalties, and restitution for both companies rose over time. See Andrew Caffrey, "Putnam to Pay $40m to Settle SEC Probe," *Boston Globe,* November 10, 2004; Caffrey, "Putnam to Pay $193m in Scandal," *Boston Globe,* March 5, 2005; Steve Bailey, "Downtown: Putnam's Lessons," *Boston Globe,* February 2, 2005; and Steven Syre, "Boston Capital: For MFS, Cloudy Future," *Boston Globe,* August 31, 2006. See also Sam Mamudi, "Wealth Creators vs. Wealth Destroyers: Looking at Firms' Stumbles Since 2000," *Wall Street Journal,* March 3, 2010.

 For an overview of this scandal and the political reaction, including industry changes in practices, see Fink, *The Rise of Mutual Funds,* 231–32. A third Boston company involved was State Street Research, but far less regulatory action was taken. "NASD [the National Association of Security Dealers] fined State Street for not being aggressive enough in blocking timers, rather than for cutting deals with timers." Ibid., 239.

64. "Barron's Special Report: Best Mutual-Fund Families," *Barron's,* February 1, 2010; Daisy Maxey, "Putnam Is Launching a 'Total World' Fund," *Wall Street Journal,* April 20, 2010; "Businesses of the Decade: The Top Ten," *Boston Business Journal,* January 14, 2010.

65. Ross Kerber, "Cashing in on the Flow," *Boston Globe,* October 1, 2006; Charles Stein, "Decade Dims Hub's Luster as Mutual Fund Leader," *Boston Globe,* February 4, 2010. Changes in investment style also seem to have made a difference in the first decade of the 2000s, following the bear markets of 2000–2002 and 2007–2009. During this period, there was a shift away from the Boston tradition of active managers like the legendary Peter Lynch to index funds, an area in which Boston funds are not strong. As a result, the Pennsylvania-based Vanguard Group with its low-cost index funds, and Pacific Investment Management Company (PIMCO) in California with its highly successful $202 billion PIMCO Total Return Fund, became more important players in the industry. While this has led to a profound shift in the short term, it, like all investment styles, may be only temporary and fleeting. As a case in point, by the first quarter of 2012, Boston's actively managed growth stock equity funds, "the lifeblood of the city's leading fund managers," have again rebounded, with performance unequalled since 1998. Steven Syre, "Fidelity's Time to Shine," *Boston Globe,* April 3, 2012.

66. "The top ten, twenty, first fifty are in constant flux. Some of the once largest and best-known groups, such as Calvin Bullock, Citigroup, Hugh W. Long, Merrill Lynch, and Scudder, Stevens & Clark are no longer in the mutual fund business or in business at all." Fink, *The Rise of Mutual Funds,* 257–58. It should also be noted that calculations of size have raised many problems and may distort the larger reality. For instance, by one method, Fidelity was reduced to second place by Vanguard in 2002, and to third place

by American Funds in 2005, but the method of calculation did not take into account money market funds, which account for a significant share of Fidelity's assets, nor did it take into account, assuming that it should, the income or value from its other nonfund businesses, such as discount brokerage and real estate. Steven Syre, "Boston Capital: We're Number 3," *Boston Globe,* March 31, 2005. Note also that the percentages in table 6 are only based on the Boston companies that are in the top 50, not all of the Boston companies in the 300 to 400 or so top U.S. companies that existed during each period.

67. Todd Wallack, "Bulls Bolster Boston: The Investor Has Returned to the Stock and Bond Markets, and Mutual Funds Rejoice," *Boston Globe,* May 2, 2010. See also "Area's Largest Mutual Fund Managers," *Boston Business Journal,* April 18, 2009.

68. The only outright removal of a Boston family of mutual funds seems to be those of Scudder, Stevens & Clark, which was acquired by Zurich Financial in the late 1990s and then merged with Kemper. Scudder was later sold to Deutsche Bank before it disappeared entirely. Beth Healy, "The Demise of Scudder Was Long, Painful," *Boston Globe,* May 1, 2002.

69. Beth Healy, "Changes Dismantling State Street Research," *Boston Globe,* December 2004; Todd Wallack, "Bank of America Sells Mutual Fund Unit," *Boston Globe,* October 1, 2009; Sam Mamudi, "Fund Track: Wells Fargo Fund Unit Sees 'Advantage,'" *Wall Street Journal,* October 12, 2009.

While much remains the same, employment in the Massachusetts investment industry, which includes more than Boston, has dropped from 55,000 to 46,000 between 2001 to 2010, according to one local economist, and some companies have shrunk their presence in Boston. For instance, 64 percent of Fidelity's workforce was employed in Boston in 1990, but by 2006, it was only 23 percent. Stein, "Decade Dims Hub's Luster"; Frieswick, "Low Fidelity."

70. Pantridge, "Fund City," 70; Robert Gavin, "New England Niche: Boston Discovers Life after Banking Exists, in Asset Management," *Boston Globe,* November 9, 2003.

71. Putnam, Personal Recollections, 200. The names and number of veterans from Boston's fund industry who have moved on are incalculable but have included people like Norton H. Reamer (Putnam), who founded in 1980 United Asset Management Corporation; John ("Jack") F. O'Brien (Fidelity), who headed Allmerica Financial; and Jerry Jordan, Martin Hale, Steve Butters, Mike Hewett, and Brenda Gordon (all Putnam), who founded or joined the asset management firm of Hellman, Jordan. Some others include John Parker, who developed Putnam's institutional business in the late 1960s but left to start his own pension management company with his brother and several Putnam associates in the early 1980s; Walter Oschsle (Putnam), who started his own international investing business in the mid-1980s with about ten handpicked associates from Putnam; Jeff Vinik, who left Fidelity in the mid-1990s to found his own asset management firm; and even Fidelity big shots like Robert Posen and Robert Reynolds, who, in recent years, have taken over the helms at MFS and Putnam, respectively. The list of individuals and their unique influences in shaping Boston's asset management industry could go on indefinitely.

11. The Expansion of Investment Management Services in the Late Twentieth Century

1. Peter A. Brooke, *A Vision for Venture Capital: Realizing the Promise of Global Venture Capital and Private Equity* (Boston and Hanover, N.H.: New Ventures Press and University Press of New England, 2009), xvii–xviii.

2. The terms *buyout, leveraged buyout,* and *management buyout* are used interchangeably in this account.

3. C. Kevin Landry, interview, May 23, 2008; Will Thorndike, interview, January 4, 2008. Part of the problem with definitions for venture capital and private equity is, as the above experiences suggest, venture capital was historically recognized first, while private equity came later. From a conceptual point of view, however, venture capital is really only a subset of private equity, which is broadly defined as private money taking equity positions in private companies. While I want to keep this definition of private equity simple and understandable for discussion in this chapter, it is a very heterogeneous asset class with many subsectors. Private equity uses at least a half-dozen different investment strategies depending on circumstances, which include leveraged buyouts, venture capital, mezzanine debt, distressed investing, special situations investing, and growth capital.

4. Thorndike, interview; Valentine V. Craig, "Merchant Banking: Past and Present," *FDIC Banking Review* 14, no. 1 (2001): 29–32. The latter source defines the private equity market as both venture capital and LBO investments, but notes that before the mid-1980s, two-thirds of it was used to finance venture capital investments and that by 1999, only about 30% was used for that purpose. For another take on the distinctions between and similarities of venture capital and private equity, see David Carey and John E. Morris, *King of Capital: The Remarkable Rise, Fall, and Rise Again of Steve Schwarzman and Blackstone* (New York: Crown Business, 2010), 150–51. See also Harry Cendrowski et al., *Private Equity: History, Governance and Operations* (Hoboken, N.J.: John Wiley, 2008), 4–6, 21–24, 42–48.

5. The mid-1960s also marked the beginning of broader interest in mergers and acquisitions (an activity that later became part of many private equity firms), including a publication by the same name. See Jerry Abejo, "M&A's First Scribe," *Mergers & Acquisitions,* December 2007, 75.

6. Carey and Morris, *King of Capital,* 13–14, 32–33. Little has been written about the history of private equity firms except for the Carey and Morris book and two important accounts of KKR: Allen Kaufman and Ernest J. Englander, "Kohlberg Kravis Roberts & Co. and the Restructuring of American Capitalism," *Business History Review* 67, no. 1 (1993): 52–97, esp. 66–68, and George P. Baker and George David Smith, *The New Financial Capitalists: Kohlberg Kravis Roberts and the Creation of Corporate Value* (New York: Cambridge University Press, 1998), which carries KKR's history up to the early 1990s.

7. Andrei Shleifer and Robert W. Vishny, "The Takeover Wave of the 1980s," *Science,* new ser., 249, no. 4970 (1990): 745–49; David Grayson Allen, "The Foggy World of Antitrust," in "The American Century," paper prepared for Unilever PLC, London, England, January 1990. In addition, the work of business school professors Michael Jensen and William Meckling helped to provide an intellectual foundation on the value of buyouts. See their "Theory of the Firm: Managerial Behavior, Agency Costs and Ownership Structures," *Journal of Financial Economics* 3, no. 4 (1976): 305–60.

While some commentators have noted the alleged bad effects of takeovers, including unemployment, decreasing competition, increasing prices, and the reduction of physical capital and R&D, most studies suggest this is and was an exaggeration. See Shleifer and Vishny, "The Takeover Wave," 246–49. Cf. Sami M. Abbasi, Kenneth W. Hollman, and Joe H. Murray Jr., "Merger Mania: Human and Economic Effects," *Review of Business* 13, nos. 1–2 (1991): 30 and *passim,* although a lot of the criticism seems to be directed toward a minority of corporate raiders, noted later in the text. For a discussion of some other issues and developments in the 1980s affecting the rise of buyouts, see Bronwyn H. Hall, "Corporate Restructuring and Investment Horizons in the United States, 1976–1987," *Business History Review* 68, no. 1 (1994): 110–43, and Steven N. Kaplan and Jeremy C. Stein, "The Evolution of Buyout Pricing and Financial Structure in the 1980s," *Quarterly Journal of Economics* 108, no. 2 (1993): 313–57.

8. Carey and Morris, *King of Capital*, 15–16, 31–44, 62–63, 100–104. The RJR Nabisco buyout by KKR became the subject of a contemporary popular book, *Barbarians at the Gate: The Fall of RJR Nabisco*, by Bryan Burrough and John Helyar (New York: Harper & Row, 1990), while the impact of junk bond financing was the focus of Connie Bruck's *The Predators' Ball: The Junk-Bond Raiders and the Man Who Staked Them* (New York: Simon and Schuster, 1988). Still, the caricature of private equity as strip-and-flip firms is not supported by a growing body of academic research. See Carey and Morris, *King of Capital*, 8, 303–6, 371n–373n; Baker and Smith, *The New Financial Capitalists*, 37–40; and U.S. Government General Accountability Office (GAO), *Private Equity: Recent Growth in Leveraged Buyouts Exposed Risks that Warrant Continued Attention*, GAO-08-885, September 2008, 2, 4, and *passim*. In the end, the number of hostile takeovers in this era was small, but their size relative to the value of all buyouts was large. This situation was sufficient to create widespread press coverage, public discussion, and concern. LBOs were, by and large, seen as relatively benign. A study of over 21,000 of them from 1970 to 2007 concluded that "most LBO activity consists of acquisitions of private rather than public firms and LBOs provide a net positive flow of firms to public markets over the long run." Per Stromberg, "The New Demography of Private Equity," in *The Globalization of Alternative Investments Working Papers*, vol. 1, *The Global Economic Impact of Private Equity Report 2008* (New York: World Economic Forum, 2008), 3.

9. Carey and Morris, *King of Capital*, 78–79, 90–91, 96–100, 106–8, 115–17; Debra Sparks, "Return of the LBO," *BusinessWeek Online*, October 16, 2000; Thorndike, interview. Most small- and medium-sized private equity companies are not so reliant on debt markets as the larger private equity companies.

10. Carey and Morris, *King of Capital*, 93–94, 105, 134, 136–39, 148–57. For a summary of the last two decades of the century, see also Bengt Holmstrom and Steven N. Kaplan, "Corporate Governance and Merger Activity in the United States: Making Sense of the 1980s and 1990s," *Journal of Economic Perspectives* 15, no. 2 (2001): 121–44.

11. Felix Barber and Michael Goold, "The Strategic Secret of Private Equity," *Harvard Business Review* 85, no. 9 (2007): 53–61; Carey and Morris, *King of Capital*, 165–69, 208–10, 212–17, 225–29, 235–38.

12. Ibid., 218–23, 230; James B. Stewart, "The Birthday Party," *New Yorker*, February 11–18, 2008, 100, 111–13.

13. Carey and Morris, *King of Capital*, 279–300, 321–26, see also 3–6, 8–9, 10–11; Steven Syre, "Life after LBOs," *Boston Globe*, April 11, 2008; Peter Lattman, "RJR's Ghost Haunts Buyout Business," *Wall Street Journal*, December 2, 2008; Heidi N. Moore, "Private-Equity Forecast? Pain," *Wall Street Journal*, December 22, 2008; Steven Syre, "Big Funds, Big Problems," *Boston Globe*, March 17, 2009; Stephen Taub, "Hedge Funds Trounce Private Equity in Battle of Alternatives," *Institutional Investor*, April 8, 2010, www.institutionalinvestor.com; Gregory Zuckerman, "Private-Equity Firms Forced to Evolve," *Wall Street Journal*, January 6, 2012; Michael Corkery, "Pensions Increasing their Ties," *Wall Street Journal*, January 26, 2012.

14. *Private Equity International* has published two rankings of the fifty largest interna-

tional private equity firms, one in 2007, reflecting how much firms had raised since 2002 (www.prnewswire.co.uk; no longer available), and the other in 2011, based on what they had raised during the previous five years (www.privateequityinternational. com). For the other survey, see Mass Insight Global Partnerships, *The Massachusetts Financial Services Sector: A Complete Portfolio—Partners in Managing Assets and Fostering Innovation*, fall 2010, www.massinsight.com.

15. Berkshire Partners, "Private Equity: History, Strategy and Performance," management presentation, Spring 2012, 12–13, in possession of the author.

16. J. Christopher Clifford, interview, April 4, 2012.

17. Sparks, "Return of the LBO"; Brooke, *A Vision for Venture Capital*, 230; Clifford, interview.

18. Randall Smith and Jenny Strasburg, "Buyout Titan Weighs Hedge-Fund Revamp," *Wall Street Journal*, December 4, 2008; Clifford, interview; Thomas H. Lee Partners website, www.thl.com; Thomas H. Lee Company website, www.fundinguniverse. com.

19. www.baincapital.com; Robert Gavin and Sacha Pfeiffer, "The Making of Mitt Romney, Part 3: The Businessman," *Boston Globe*, June 26, 2007.

20. Ibid.; Michael Kranish and Beth Healy, "Mitt and the Junk Bond King," *Boston Globe*, June 24, 2012.

21. Gavin and Pfeiffer, "The Making of Mitt Romney, Part 3"; Steven Syre, "Little Is Clear about This Offer," *Boston Globe*, February 21, 2008. On job loss/creation, see also Robert Gavin, "As Bain Slashed Jobs, Romney Stayed to Side," *Boston Globe*, January 28, 2008; and on an example of one of Bain Capital's buyouts, see Beth Healy, "Domino's Delivered," *Boston Globe*, January 29, 2012.

22. Gavin and Pfeiffer, "The Making of Mitt Romney, Part 3"; Steven Syre, "Romney's Challenge," *Boston Globe*, January 17, 2012.

23. Mark Maremont, "Romney at Bain: Big Gains, Some Busts," *Wall Street Journal*, January 9, 2012.

24. Steven Brull, "Financing Finance," *Institutional Investor* 38 (June 2004): 125–28, 130; C. Kevin Landry, interview, May 23, 2008; Landry, "Observations on 40 Years in Private Equity," speech, November 7, 2007, in possession of the author.

25. As noted at the beginning of this chapter, Brooke and many Bostonians at this time regarded "venture capital" as simply investment in small companies—either start-ups or in later-stage development—with growth potential, the latter of which would be regarded as private equity investments today.

26. Peter A. Brooke, interview, January 7, 2008; Brooke, *A Vision for Venture Capital*, 50, 52–57, 74–80.

27. Ibid., 60–64, 68–72.

28. Ibid., 115–17, 144–45; www.adventinternational.com.

29. Peter Landau, "The Mystique of the Hedge Funds," *Institutional Investor* 2 (August 1968): 23, 25.

30. Ibid., 25–27, 29, 62–64. See also Peter Landau's "Alfred Winslow Jones: The Long and Short of the Founding Father," *Institutional Investor* 2 (August 1968): 49–50, 54, 57, 74–75; emphasis in original. Jones's earliest investors were friends deeply involved in social, artistic, and humanitarian causes whom he hoped would benefit from his enterprise. Jones himself hoped that if his company was successful, it would allow him to return to funding social causes. On the evolution of investment/ analysis/management styles of hedge funds, see Stephen J. Brown and William N. Goetzmann, "Hedge Funds with Style," Working Paper 8173, National Bureau of Economic Research, March 2001, www.nber.org.

31. Securities and Exchange Commission, Implications of the Growth of Hedge Funds, staff report, September 2003, appendix A, 1, www.sec.gov; John Thackray, "Whatever Happened to the Hedge Funds?" *Institutional Investor* 11 (May 1977): 71–72, 74.

32. Jack Willoughby, "Saving the World with Paul Tudor Jones," *Institutional Investor* 31 (July 1997): 60–66, 69–70; Alyssa A. Lappen, "The Hedge Fund as Equity Alternative?" *Institutional Investor* 31 (August 1997): 144.

33. John Cassidy, "Mastering the Machine: How Ray Dalio Built the World's Richest and Strangest Hedge Fund," *New Yorker,* July 25, 2011, 65; Sebastian Mallaby, "Learning to Love Hedge Funds," *Wall Street Journal,* June 12–13, 2010. See also www.hedge-fundresearch.com. A broad, though decidedly Wall Street–centric, history of hedge funds—investment theories, personalities, and developments—has been vividly captured in Mallaby's *More Money Than God: Hedge Funds and the Making of a New Elite* (New York: Penguin Press, 2010).

34. Arthur F. F. Snyder, *Generalizations of a Banker* (N.p.: N.p., 2008), 176–77.

35. On the early history of Commodities Corporation, see Shawn Tully, "Princeton's Rich Commodity Scholars," *Fortune,* February 1981, 94–98.

36. James J. Pallotta, interview, April 18, 2012; Jenny Strasburg, "Tudor's Hedge Split Was Planned," *Wall Street Journal,* August 8, 2008; Strasburg, "A New Era for Hedge Funds," *Wall Street Journal,* April 18, 2011; Beth Healy, "Pallotta Shutting His Hedge Funds," *Boston Globe,* June 3, 2009; Healy, "Pallotta Remaking Raptor," *Boston Globe,* September 18, 2010.

37. Seth A. Klarman, *Margin of Safety: Risk-Adverse Value Investing Strategies for the Thoughtful Investor* (New York: HarperBusiness, 1991), ix; "Tracking Seth Klarman's Baupost Group Holdings," Seeking Alpha website, http://seekingalpha.com; Alex Bossert, "Seth Klarman Comments on Money Management and Baupost's Approach," http://seekingalpha.com; Klarman, "MIT Remarks [on recent financial market events], October 20, 2007," www.1-kickout.typepad.com; Charles Stein, "The Financial Life: Seth Klarman," *Bloomberg Businessweek,* June 17, 2010; Roger Thompson, "Seth Klarman," *Harvard Business School Alumni Bulletin,* December 2008, www.alumni.hbs.edu; Mebane Fabr, "How to Ride Seth Klarman's Coattails," *Forbes,* February 25, 2010, www.forbes.com.

38. Klarman, *Margin of Safety,* xiii–xv. Klarman's book was soon out of print and currently sells on Amazon and eBay for up to $2,000 a copy when it is available. His other major writing on value investing appeared as the preface, "The Timeless Wisdom of Graham and Dodd," in the 6th edition (2009) of Benjamin Graham and David L. Dodd, *Security Analysis: Principles and Techniques* (New York: McGraw-Hill, 1934).

39. Robert G. Scott, interview, April 18, 2012; Pallotta, interview.

40. Jenny Strasburg and Steve Eder, "Hedge Funds Bounce Back," *Wall Street Journal,* April 18, 2011; Ross Kerber, "SEC Filings Show Boston Is a Leader in Hedge Funds," *Boston Globe,* April 21, 2006; Stewart, "The Birthday Party," 108–9.

41. "The Hedge Fund 100," *Institutional Investor* 38 (May 2004): 73–76; 39 (June 2005): 61–64.

42. http://richard-wilson.blogspot.com.

43. Beth Healy, "New Rule Provides a Peek Inside Workings of Hedge Fund Industry," *Boston Globe,* April 22, 2012. Even before the new financial rules, the SEC published on its website the 13-F quarterly filings on financial information of hedge funds overseeing more than $100 million.

44. "The Wealth Explosion," *Wilson Quarterly* 31, no. 1 (2007): 33; James B. Twitchell, "Lux Populi: If Rich Old King Croesus Were Living in America Today, He'd Be Hard-Pressed to Keep Up with the Joneses," *Wilson Quarterly* 31, no. 1 (2007): 37.

The "explosion" was noted almost twenty years earlier as the "new entrepreneurial elite" started demanding performance from their private bankers. See Claire Makin, "Banking: Cultivating the New Rich," *Institutional Investor* 23 (April 1989): 130–32, 135, 137, 139, and Harvey D. Shapiro, "The Coming Inheritance Bonanza," *Institutional Investor* 28 (June 1994): 143–46, 148. On the growth in number of family offices, see Everett Mattlin, "Rich Pickings," *Institutional Investor* 27 (June 1993): 55–64, 67.

45. Steven Lagerfeld, "The New Yacht Club," *Wilson Quarterly* 31, no. 1 (2007): 38, 40, 41, 43. Much of the empirical research on rising inequality, beginning in the late twentieth century and carrying it up to the present, has been done by University of California economist Emmanuel Saez. See Thomas Piketty and Emmanuel Saez, "Income Inequality in the United States, 1913–1998," *Quarterly Journal of Economics* 118, no. 1 (2003): 1–39, and Saez's tables and figures, updated to July 2010, as well as his "Striking It Richer: The Evolution of Top Incomes in the United States," at http://eml.berkeley.edu.

46. Leslie Lenkowsky, "Big Philanthropy: The Survey of New Wealth in America Is Creating a Bumper Crop of Large Foundations. History Suggests That They Can Accomplish a Great Deal. But It's Not Always Easy to Do Good," *Wilson Quarterly* 31, no. 1 (2007): 47–48.

47. John J. Havens and Paul G. Schervish, "Millionaires and the Millennium: New Estimates of the Forthcoming Wealth Transfer and the Prospects for a Golden Age of Philanthropy," report, October 19, 1999, Social Welfare Research Institute, Boston College, 2; Havens and Schervish, "Wealth Transfer Estimates: 2001 to 2055, Boston Metropolitan Area," reported, November 7, 2005, Boston College Center on Wealth and Philanthropy (formerly the Social Welfare Research Institute), 15.

48. Stephen Martiros and Todd Millay, "A Framework for Understanding Family Office Trends," 2006, www.cccalliance.com. Not only have family offices become more complex; they have now spread far beyond Boston and the United States to nearly every corner of the world. On the growth and character of this development, see, Raphael Amit et al., *Single Family Offices: Private Wealth Management in the Family Context*, Wharton Global Family Alliance Paper, May 2008, www.wgfa.wharton.upenn.edu.

49. This section is a composite picture of family offices derived from a number of interviews, including Lawrence Coolidge, June 24, 2003; John Thorndike, July 8, 2003, December 2, 2007; Joseph Patton, January 30, 2008; Harold I. Pratt, May 22, 2011; David S. Lee, June 5, 2011; Nelson Darling, March 4, 2008, May 27, 2008; Todd Millay, June 14, 2011; and George Lewis, June 9, 2011. For additional information, see also William F. Weld, obituary, *Boston Herald*, December 8, 1881; Francis Storrs, "A Stranger in the House of Ayer," *Boston Magazine*, December 2007, 128–31, 148, 153–59, 161.

50. "Top 50 Fee-Only Advisors," *Forbes*, March, 29, 2010, www.forbes.com; "Value-Added Services: Top 50 Wealth Manager RIAs," *Registered Representative Magazine*, July 1, 2011, www.wealthmanagement.com; Bloomberg Wealth Manager Magazine "2010 Top Wealth Managers," www.thinkadvisor.com.

12. Thinking Long Term: Boston's Place in Investment Management

1. Clarence W. Barron et al., *The Boston Stock Exchange: With Brief Sketches of Prominent Brokers, Bankers, Banks, and Moneyed Institutions of Boston* (Boston: Hunt & Bell, 1893; repr., New York: Arno Press, 1975), 26–32.

2. *Paine, Webber & Company, 1880–1930: A National Institution* (Boston: Oxford-Print, 1930), 19, 21.

3. Nelson Darling, interview, March 4, 2008, May 27, 2008. Despite relocation, Boston influence in these brokerage firms remained for a long time as they were controlled by "principal capital partners" in Boston for decades. That influence was largely dissipated after these firms moved from partnership organizations to corporations during the latter third of the twentieth century, but even then, Bostonians remained in important firm positions such as chairman for years after the reorganization. Ibid.

4. Isaac Baker, "Canadian Bank to Acquire Tucker Anthony," *Boston Globe*, August 2, 2001; Joseph Patton, interview, January 30, 2008.

5. "Area's Largest Investment Banks," *Boston Business Journal*, November 16–22, 2007, 36.

6. For a summary of these changes, including important recent mergers, see Dan Fitzpatrick, "Two Cities Lose 'Hometown' Banks Today," *Wall Street Journal*, December 23, 2008. Even though Boston possessed no national bank, it still held a considerable amount of bank assets, probably mostly in the wealth management category. Cities (and major banks) with the largest assets included: New York (J. P. Morgan Chase, Citigroup, and others) had $4,569.1 billion in bank assets, followed by Charlotte, North Carolina (Bank of America and Wells Fargo–Wachovia), with $2,707 billion; San Francisco (Wells Fargo–Wachovia) with $1,399.8 billion followed by Pittsburgh (PNC) $290.6 billion and Boston with $285.6 billion. Ibid.

7. "Remembering the '80s: Thumbnail History of a Turbulent Decade for Banks and Banking," *Massachusetts Banker* 4 (January 1990): 3–4.

8. Paul Taylor, "Radial Changes Now Under Way," *Financial Times Survey*, March 6, 1984, http://archive.org. The Bank Holding Company Act of 1956 did not allow out-of-state bank holding companies to own banks in another state, except a few that had been grandfathered, but in 1966, the so-called Douglas amendment to that act allowed the practice provided the individual states permitted it, which was what both Connecticut and Massachusetts did in allowing the first modern interstate bank merger.

9. For an overview of the crisis, see several Federal Deposit Insurance Corporation (FDIC) publications and symposia published in the late 1990s: *Managing the Crisis: The FDIC and RTC Experience*, vol. 1, *History* (Washington, D.C.: FDIC, 1998), esp. 635–51, www.fdic.gov, and *History of the Eighties—Lessons for the Future*, vol. 1, *An Examination of the Banking Crises of the 1980s and Early 1990s* (Washington, D.C.: FDIC, 1997), esp. 337–77, www.fdic.gov. See also Lynne E. Browne and Eric S. Rosengren, "Real Estate and the Credit Crunch: An Overview," 1–17, and Lynne E. Brown and Karl E. Case, "How the Commercial Real Estate Boom Undid the Banks," 57–113, both in *Real Estate and the Credit Crunch*, ed. Lynne E. Brown and Eric S. Rosengren, conference series 36, September 1992 (Boston: Federal Reserve Bank of Boston, 1992).

10. Lawrence K. Fish, interview, June 16, 2008. In his interview, Fish explained that 50% of New England's banking market (and economy) is within Interstate 495 (i.e., the greater metropolitan Boston), and he noted that under this scenario, that unless BankBoston, the last large local survivor, made a major acquisition of another major bank servicing the same area, it would not dominate in Boston. Instead, it would be compelled to compete with everyone else, and eventually lose out to national banks. On the New England banks affected, see Doug Bailey, "Banking Meltdown Déjà Vu," *Boston Globe*, September 20, 2008.

11. Fish, interview. On Citizens Financial, see Beth Healy, "Citizens Financial Hangs in the Balance," *Boston Globe*, November 9, 2009.

12. On Murray, see Ada Focer, "Terrence Murray: Businessperson of the Year," *New England Business*, January 1992, 15–19, and David Nyhan, "The Admiral of the Fleet Fleet," *Boston Globe*, November 24, 1991. On Fleet, see Steven Syre and Charles Stein, "Opposites Join in Uncertain Union with Corporate Cultures Miles Apart, Banks May Prove Hard to Blend," *Boston Globe*, March 15, 1999; Steve Bailey, "Make Fleet Compete," *Boston Globe*, April 23, 1999; David Nyhan, "Favorable Winds for the Fleet-BankBoston Merger," *Boston Globe*, July 7, 1999; and Steve Bailey, "Agent of Change," *Boston Globe*, December 28, 2001.

13. On the Great Recession, which lasted longer than any postwar recession, and what it means, see David Wessel, "A Big, Bad . . . 'Great' Recession?" *Wall Street Journal*, April 8, 2010, and Sara Murray, "Slump Over, Pain Persists," *Wall Street Journal*, September 21, 2010.

14. Robin Sidel and Damian Paletta, "Industry Is Remade in a Wave of Mergers," *Wall Street Journal*, September 30, 2008; Todd Wallack, "A Star's Rise to the Top at Bank of America," *Boston Globe*, December 27, 2009; Steven Syre, "For Gifford, a Clear Choice," *Boston Globe*, December 18, 2009; Syre, "North vs. South," *Boston Globe*, October 6, 2009.

15. Charles Stein, "Taking a Look Back for an Economic Fix," *Boston Globe*, December 8, 2002, citing Michael Porter, *The Competitive Advantage of Massachusetts* (Cambridge, Mass: Monitor Company, 1991).

16. In one recent accounting of Boston wealth, nearly half of the fifty wealthiest Bostonians were either in investment (12) or high-tech fields (12). An additional seventeen were in miscellaneous businesses (with some involved in new kinds of business or investment), followed by eight in real estate, and a lone individual, a professional in education, who had inherited her wealth. Francis Storrs, "The 50 Wealthiest Bostonians," *Boston Magazine*, March 2006, 111–17, 141–42, 14, 151–52, 154–55.

17. Charles Stein, "Money Magnet: Mutual Funds Rocket Boston near Top of World's Financial Centers," *Boston Globe*, November 10, 1996. How much money Boston manages, a question of infinite curiosity, is likely one that cannot be answered with any certainty because the information is not readily available. For instance, about 35 percent of Pennsylvania-based Vanguard's mutual fund stock portfolio was managed by Boston companies in 2006, and Boston serves as the subadviser of many other mutual fund companies, but it is not always apparent—or necessarily counted. Ross Kerber, "Investing by the Numbers, Hub Style," *Boston Globe*, April 2, 2006.

18. New York also focuses on the "sell side" of the business, rather than "buy side" as Boston uniquely does.

19. Mass Insight Global Partnerships, *The Massachusetts Financial Services Sector: A Complete Portfolio—Partners in Managing Assets and Fostering Innovation*, Fall 2010, www.massinsight.com.

20. Boston Planning and Economic Development Office, *Investing in Jobs: A Report on the Financial Services Industry—Its Importance to Boston, the Metropolitan Region, and the State* (Boston: Boston Planning and Economic Development Office, 1996), 1–2.

21. U.S. Department of Commerce, Bureau of the Census, *County Business Patterns*, Massachusetts, 1964, 1968, 1973.

22. Greater Boston Chamber of Commerce, Financial Services Leading Industries Committee, Financial Services Report, January 1995, draft copy, December 1, 1994, 2, in possession of the author, copy provided by Gregory W. Perkins, Boston Redevelopment Authority.

23. This category includes portfolio management, investment advice, and trust, fiduciary, and custody activities.

24. Massachusetts employment and wages information for all occupations (ES-202) is available from the website of the Executive Office of Labor and Workforce Development, www.mass.gov/lmi, for the period since 2001.

25. Mass Insight Global Partnerships, *The Massachusetts Financial Services Sector.*

26. Joseph F. Dinneen, "Now It Can Be Told: How and Why Boston Staged Big Jubilee," *Boston Globe,* May 22, 1950; H. Lee Silberman, 50 Years of Trust: Massachusetts Investors Trust, 1924–1974, typescript, Massachusetts Financial Services, 1974, 25–26, in possession of the author.

27. George Lewis, interview, June 9, 2011; Louis M. Lyons, "Boston: A Study in Inertia," in *Our Fair City,* ed. Robert S. Allen (New York: Vanguard Press, 1947), 16; Lawrence Coolidge, interview, 24 June 2003; H. Bradlee Perry, interview, 15 October 2007; Patton, interview.

28. Walter Cabot, interview, October 10, 2007; J. Christopher Clifford, interview, April 3, 2012.

29. "In Investing, It's the Prudent Bostonian," *Business Week,* June 6, 1959, 66, 68; Robert Lenzner, "Boston's Money Managers," *Boston Globe,* July 30, 1972; Alexander W. Williams, *A Social History of The Greater Boston Clubs* (Barre, Mass.: Barre Publishers, 1970), 50–51; Andrew L. Andrews, "Downtown: Eatery Closes after 53 Years," *Boston Globe,* December 24, 1986.

30. Boston Security Analysts Society, *2011 Annual Report,* www.bsas.org.

31. Sherwood E. Bain, "The Money Managers: Their Integrity Built-In," *Boston Globe,* May 18, 1980; Edward H. Ladd, interview, November 4, 2003.

32. Charles Flather, interview, June 24, 2004. A truer statement might be: Boston area colleges and universities attract talent to Boston, while Boston businesses, in turn, train Boston-educated people for the job.

33. Daniel Pierce, interview, July 11, 2003; Jeremy Grantham, interview, August 2, 2011; Lenzner, "Boston's Money Managers"; Clifford, interview. These comments are not far distant from those written by Russell B. Adams Jr. some thirty-five years ago, when he said that, "in isolated Boston, far from the frenzied hustle and bustle . . . of New York, solid sober experienced men could exercise what they were wont to call their instinctive feel for quality, their nose for investment with staying power. State Street was no Wall Street, but that very difference was part of its allure." *The Boston Money Tree* (New York: Thomas Y. Crowell, 1977), 290.

34. Alex Beam, "Boston: The Receptor City on a Hill," *Boston Globe,* December 10, 2007.

35. Steve Bailey, "Move Will Maintain a N.E. Influence," *Boston Globe,* March 15, 1999; Jerry Ackerman, "Company Mergers May Take Civic Toll with Fewer Home Offices in Boston; Charities and City Interests Could Suffer," *Boston Globe,* July 3, 1995.

36. Robert Weisman, "Greylock Moving Base out of Boston," *Boston Globe,* May 20, 2009; Todd Wallack, "Fidelity Move Pays Big Dividend in Texas," *Boston Globe,* November 1, 2011.

37. Ross Kerber, "Cashing in on the Flow," *Boston Globe,* October 1, 2006; J. R. Brandstrader, "Leading a Putnam Turnaround," *Wall Street Journal,* July 6, 1911; Todd Wallack, "Putnam's Progress," *Boston Globe,* May 15, 2011; Charles Stein, "In Chase for New Money, Boston No Longer Dominates," *Boston Globe,* April 25, 2004; Steven Syre, "Slightly Less Important," *Boston Globe,* March 10, 2005.

38. Scott Kirsner, "Let's Redefine New England's Brand Image," *Boston Globe,* December 28, 2008; Robert Weisman, "Wanted: A New Identity," *Boston Globe,* February 19,

2009; Scott Kirsner, "The Tech Bust: 10 Years After," *Boston Globe*, February 20, 2011.

39. Carolyn Y. Johnson, "Collaboration: The Mother of Invention," *Boston Globe*, May 8, 2011; Paul McMorrow, "The Tech Cluster Glut," *Boston Globe*, July 9, 2011; Scott Kirsner, "Why Waltham Doesn't Matter," Innovation Economy Blog, boston.com, August 24, 2009; Kirsner, "The Cultural Revolution: Which Side Are You On," Innovation Economy Blog, boston.com, August 31, 2009; Kirsner, "'Accelerator' Programs Can Help Start-Ups Take off Faster," *Boston Globe*, April 22, 2012; Steven Syre, "Mass. Biotechs Glitter in New Golden Age," *Boston Globe*, December 11, 2012; Michael B. Farrell, "Hatching Innovation," *Boston Globe*, September 26, 2012. On the transformation of Cambridge, see Megan Woolhouse, "Making of a High-Tech Mecca," *Boston Globe*, June 26, 2011.

40. Scott Kirsner, "Innovation Economy," *Boston Globe*, August 31, 2009; Paul McMorrow, "The Tech Cluster Glut," *Boston Globe*, July 9, 2011; Kirsner, "Why Waltham Doesn't Matter"; Kirsner, "The Cultural Revolution"; Steven Syre, "The Tales a Tower Tells," *Boston Globe*, May 23 2008; Michael B. Farrell, "Shifting Center: Battery Ventures Is the Latest Venture Capital Firm Moving to the Hub as the Region's Start-up Culture Changes," *Boston Globe*, December 21, 2012.

41. Scott Kirsner, "Hungry for Cash, Start-ups Seek Better Angles for their Ventures," *Boston Globe*, May 23, 2010; Casey Ross, "Liberty Mutual Sets Hub Expansion," *Boston Globe*, February 12, 2010; Michael Stone, "Bring in the Angels," *Boston Globe*, February 19, 2012; Michael B. Farrell, "Start-ups See More Angels Willing to Invest: Survey Says Boston Lags behind N.Y., Calif.," *Boston Globe*, October 11, 2012; "Instagram Deal Highlights Need to Bolster Tech Startups in Mass.," *Boston Globe*, April 13, 2012; Scott Kirsner, "Mass. IPOs May Mint Millionaires, but They Don't Seem to Create Many Angels," *Boston Globe*, May 13, 2012.

42. Boston Redevelopment Authority, *Boston's Dynamic Workforce: Attract, Attain, Absorb; The City of Boston's 20–34 Year Old Initiative* (Boston: Boston Redevelopment Authority, 2011); G. Scott Thomas, "Boston Leads the U.S. in Education Levels for Young Adults," *The Business Journals*, May 7, 2012; Paul Braverman, interview, July 11, 2011. Besides its importance with these age- and education-specific demographics, Boston, according to a recent survey combining the results of several other surveys, appears as the eleventh most important global city. Richard Florida, "What Is the World's Most Economically Powerful City?" *The Atlantic*, May 11, 2012, www.theatlantic.com.

43. Greater Boston Chamber of Commerce and Mass Insight Corporation, *Securing Massachusetts's Leadership Position in Financial Services* (Boston: Greater Boston Chamber of Commerce and Mass Insight Corporation, ca. 2007), 1 2, www.bostonchamber.com.

44. Frederic Jesup Stimson, *My United States* (New York: Charles Scribner's Sons, 1931), esp. 71–82; Lyons, "Boston," 29; Steven Syre, "Can Hub Get Mojo Back?" *Boston Globe*, January 1, 2010; Gina Chon, "An Alternative to 'Alternative' Assets," *Wall Street Journal*, March 10, 2010.

45. Cabot, interview; Will Thorndike, interview, January 4, 2008.

46. William J. Sheehan, "Unique to Boston Are the Famous 'Boston Trustees,'" *Boston Evening Transcript*, July 28, 1934; Samuel Eliot Morison, *One Boy's Boston* (Boston: Houghton Mifflin, 1962), 62–63.

INDEX

Page numbers in italics refer to illustrations.

DAVID GRAYSON ALLEN received a PhD in American legal and constitutional history (with training in law) from the University of Wisconsin, Madison. He has been a Research Fellow at Linacre College, Oxford, and a Charles Warren Fellow at Harvard University. He has also won other fellowships, including those from the American Bar Foundation, the University of Wisconsin, and the National Endowment for the Humanities.

His first book, *In English Ways: The Movement of Societies and the Transferal of English Local Law and Custom to Massachusetts Bay in the Seventeen Century*, won the Jamestown Prize of the Institute of Omohundro Early American History and Culture, Williamsburg, Virginia, and was considered for the Pulitzer Prize, while his *History of Scudder, Stevens & Clark* won the Gold Award in the Mercury Awards Competition and the Gold Quill Award of the International Association of Business Communicators (IABC). His *Eaton Vance and the Rise of Investment Management in the United States* received Best in Category for a professional illustrated book in the 2009 New England Book Show.

Mr. Allen served as an editor of the Papers of Daniel Webster (Dartmouth College) and the Adams Papers (Massachusetts Historical Society). He then became cofounder of Winthrop Group, Inc., a historical consulting firm, and was executive director of the Center for Applied History, both in Cambridge, Massachusetts, before he later left to form his own firm, Allen Associates, in Concord, Massachusetts, where he is a principal. Over the course of his historical consulting career, Mr. Allen has worked with a variety of clients, ranging from international firms like Unilever PLC and Price Waterhouse, to local and national financial services and law firms, various not-for-profit organizations, and government agencies, including some major technology and finance-related projects for the Department of Defense.